D1569536

Rickover and the Nuclear Navy

Rickover
and the Nuclear Navy

THE DISCIPLINE OF TECHNOLOGY

by
Francis Duncan

Naval Institute Press
Annapolis, Maryland

Published 1990 by the United States Naval Institute
Annapolis, Maryland

Copyright © 1990 on the foreword

Prepared by the Department of Energy; work made for hire.

Library of Congress Cataloging-in-Publication Data

Duncan, Francis, 1922–
    Rickover and the nuclear navy : the discipline of technology / by
    Francis Duncan.
        p.   cm.
    Includes bibliographical references.
    ISBN 0-87021-236-2
    1. Rickover, Hyman George.   2. Nuclear submarines—United States—
History.   3. Admirals—United States—Biography.   4. United States.
Navy—Biography.   I. Title.
V63.R54D86   1989
359.3'2574'0973—dc20   89-39097
                                                                      CIP
Printed in the United States of America

9   8   7   6   5   4   3   2   1

Contents

Foreword

No one in 1918, surveying that year's entering class at the U.S. Naval Academy in Annapolis, would have picked the diminutive Hyman George Rickover as the only one in that group of aspiring youths who would achieve the rank of full admiral (four stars), remain on active duty the longest (nearly 64 years), and attain international fame on an unprecedented scale. All this would happen through his development of an entirely new discipline not yet thought of by man. He would never participate in combat, the navy's ostensible mission, and yet he would be in some sort of battle all his life, accomplishing everything through a species of infighting never before seen in navy annals.

Those facts are almost mundane alongside all the other superlatives with which young Rickover's career was to be studded. Truth to tell, however, other than details such as the year he graduated from Annapolis (1922), his final retirement from the navy (1982), and the date of his death (1986), nearly everything else about the man has been surrounded by controversy. Even his birth date, officially January of 1900, is not fixed with certainty to everyone's satisfaction. He created, and remained in charge of, the most significant naval engineering program of all time, and yet even this tremendous advance in our navy's capabilities was, at least initially, accomplished against opposition from the U.S. Navy and virtually all other authorities in the land as well. He gained success because his machinery worked superlatively well, with extraordinary dependability, and because Congress and the press would not accept the notion that the navy bureaucracy, geared as it was to rotation for the sake of combat effectiveness (and its own sake as well), could maintain the engineering drive he was demonstrating.

In short, the navy was (and is) automatically opposed to the creation of any "empires" within its arena of concern, no matter how good the result. Thus, Rickover's methods were (and are still, and rightly so) anathema to it. But Congress did not care about this. It had faith in him and his brand of leadership where his peers and superiors in the navy did not. And his immediate subordinates, the relatively few in his inner circle, served him with a rare fanaticism. The press loved him, because his continual challenge to "the establishment" (much of it fully justified) was unfailing good copy. And he was adept at bringing forward, for the delectation of the media, the numerous instances of his unfair treatment at the hands of the navy hierarchy.

On the other hand, civilian industry felt his difficult iconoclastic personality and domineering methods more than any other segment of the nation, and here as in the navy, with but few exceptions, he was feared and to a large degree hated by those who had to deal with him. Feared because he personally controlled huge sums of money in the shape of contracts for nuclear research, engineering, or construction, and through this he wielded tremendous power, destructively as well as constructively, upon individuals and institutions alike. Hated because his form of leadership, undeniably successful, was demeaning in the extreme to his subordinates, often forcing them to servility to help their company or themselves. To the membership of Congress, however, the real source of his power, he showed an entirely different side of his personality. To say he was obsequious might be too strong, but he was invariably deferential in ways the navy and industry never saw.

He professed to delight in professional discussions based on intimate knowledge of fact or procedure, but there was only one ultimate authority, and anyone who did not quickly find this out was likely to find himself out of a job—as both naval officers and industry executives discovered.

From the beginning he pictured himself as the butt of mean-spirited slights in the naval officer fraternity. He was not above hinting at anti-Semitism: true in some instances, but since there were some popular Jewish officers in the navy, there must have been other factors operating as well. But whatever the slights, Rickover had a way of turning them to his benefit, usually by making them widely known, as he did, for example, with the story of the ladies' room. For a time the space assigned to him, in the old Main Navy building on Constitution Avenue in Washington, D.C., was a former ladies' room, complete with tile walls and marks where the fixtures had been. I visited him there a number of times. Once, obeying a summons from him, I dashed down the wrong hall and three feet into a real ladies' room, with real ladies in it—but after that I was more careful. Had this temporary office been assigned to anyone else, no one would have noticed except, perhaps, with good-natured humor. When Rickover "happened" to be put there it was probably deliberate, and the chuckles were not good-natured; but as usual he reveled in this "proof" of persecution.

A far more serious slight, which he handled in a far more direct way, occurred when his peers in the navy's engineer branch thought to get rid of him through failure of promotion above captain. This would entail automatic retirement at the thirty-year mark. But someone made the case to the U.S. Senate, charged by the Constitution with formal confirmation of military promotions. In that year, 1953, two years before the *Nautilus* first went to sea, the Senate failed to give its usual perfunctory approval of the navy admiral promotion list, and the press was outraged because Rickover's name was not on it. The situation was at an impasse. Without Senate approval nobody could be promoted. Ultimately an enlightened secretary of the navy, Robert B. Anderson, ordered a special selection board to sit. With some shuffling of feet it did what it had been ordered to do, and neither Congress nor the press cared that the navy's carefully created promotion system had been violated. Ninety-five percent of navy captains *must* retire regardless of how highly qualified because there are only vacancies for 5 percent of them to become admirals, and although vindictiveness has sometimes played a part in determining who shall fail of selection for promotion (thus also violating the system), never before or since have pressures from outside the navy overturned this form of career-termination.

Rickover personally interviewed every officer candidate for nuclear power training, and those interviews, numbering in the thousands, are legendary for their invective, unfairness, and personal destructiveness. He was one of the most senior officers in the navy, as much as sixty years older than some of the interviewees, who were usually midshipmen, ensigns, or junior grade lieutenants, all of them literally quaking at the thought of the career-determining confrontation ahead.

Tales of these interviews are legion in the U.S. Navy. Some have been retold by the press, but in no other situation, except perhaps in court circles of the middle ages, has it been customary to condone, even to praise, such offensive performances by the autocrat in charge. In no other instance has the press of this country invariably portrayed an arrogant, overbearing superior (especially in one of the military services) as acting disinterestedly, with only the best interests of the country at heart, whereas the anxious applicant is depicted as supercilious, shallow, even arrogant. Portrayed as the admiral's means of personally ensuring selection of the best candidates for nuclear power training, these interviews have long been known in the navy as his method of asserting personal dominance from the beginning. That they were intended for this purpose alone is obvious from their capricious context. Seldom, if ever, was anything related to nuclear engineering discussed or even mentioned. As usual, the navy surrendered, for there was no other choice. Only good candidates, already vetted by preliminary staff interview and benefited by a rather considerable degree of surreptitious coaching, were sent to the admiral for final interrogation. Those accepted were top caliber, as were those he rejected.

Having lost every battle with this redoubtable old man, the navy resigned itself to waiting him out. Ultimately he would retire or die, and the navy would survive, though many understood that it would not be unchanged. That it would be changed was also Rickover's outlook, and he had long since determined that he would never retire. He, who with reason felt himself disliked and ostracized by his peers in the navy, would change the navy more than any other individual before or since. Furthermore, he would have the mold broken after him; there would be no one like him to follow in his footsteps, a potential successor waiting in the wings. He saw to it, therefore, that there would be no such "heir apparent." Each was eliminated upon identification. In his later years he wanted and expected to remain in control of naval nuclear power, thus in a tangible sense in control of the navy itself, for the remainder of his life—and this was a goal he nearly achieved. For an unprecedented thirty-six years he was czar of nuclear power in the U.S. Navy, a law unto himself, becoming more irascible and unpredictable every year. Like other tyrants, he took no account of his own gradually failing powers; his displacement, at age eighty-two, came at the hands of a secretary of the navy half his age, and he died at eighty-six.

Hyman Rickover was also the creator of the *Nautilus*, unquestionably the greatest engineering advance ever experienced by warships. From the point of view of the "old guard" that wants always to maintain things as they were, what Rickover accomplished may not have been unilaterally to their benefit, or that of the U.S. Navy. For that matter, who indeed can say whether the coming of the nuclear submarine improved the world? But no one can deny that Rickover made the U.S. Navy the front-runner in the race for a totally new sort of warship, thus bringing about changes in the nature of sea warfare that will not be fully evaluated for a generation.

Our navy is, in short, indebted to Admiral Rickover in ways it still does not fully understand. Scientific progress, after all, drives itself; it cannot be responsible for the detritus left in its wake. Attempts to prevent it because the past was better, perhaps less fearful, are doomed to fail. America's Manhattan Project produced the atom bomb, and we used that awful weapon to terminate the most dreadful war ever fought by man. Our only choice, despite the terrible increase in destructiveness, was to make it. Hitler's scientists were also working on the atom, and it takes little imagination to visualize the result had they come in ahead of us. By analogous argument, without Rickover we would certainly today have nuclear-powered submarines to reckon with, but there is no assurance the United States would be leading the field.

Had Admiral Gorshkov, the enduring, far-sighted leader of the Soviet Navy, scented a possibility of establishing worldwide hegemony in nuclear submarines, there is little question that he would have put every effort into being first to develop such a vessel. Gorshkov might well have got his own *Nautilus* into operation before the United States and thus reversed today's balance of sea power. This may have been a goad to Rickover as he pushed the United States to be first with this ship of extraordinary, unprecedented military effectiveness. To accomplish this, he pushed American industry to the limit of technical capability. He did it against strong opposition, too, in and out of the navy, because not everyone in authority saw the tremendous potential inherent in such vessels, and others, even shorter of sight, saw nuclear propulsion principally as Rickover's avenue to personal power.

My own connection with Rickover goes back to his early days in the nuclear business. He had been sent to Oak Ridge with a nucleus of top-flight young naval engineering officers, their mission to learn all they could about nuclear engineering from the Manhattan Project people, and report back to the (then) Navy Bureau of Ships. (This group served as the nucleus of the larger group that designed and supervised the nearly simultaneous construction of the *Nautilus* prototype in the Idaho desert near Arco and the ship herself at the Electric Boat shipyard at Groton, Connecticut.) My assignment at this juncture was in the "Atomic Defense" section of "OPNAV," the Chief of Naval Operation's portion of the Navy Department, and in that capacity I was invited to go to Oak Ridge for a week to familiarize myself with the group's work. In a sense I was one of "Rickover's boys" from then on, though never, until ordered to the nuclear submarine *Triton,* under his direct command. In effect, I "moon-lighted" for him, and of course he used me, as he did everyone else he could. Having made twelve war patrols in diesel submarines in the Pacific and experienced all their limitations, including being virtually stationary during depth-charge attack, to me the prospect of a nuclear engine that could drive a submerged submarine fast enough and long enough to overtake, or escape from, any surface ship then in existence was breath-taking. What could we not have done with such a submarine during the war! I was a devotee from that moment. The nuclear-powered submarine, needing no air for its main engines, would need no electric propulsion motors and could run surfaced or submerged on the same main engines, at full speed, until its fuel ran out.

But there were problems. My OPNAV superiors were interested in maintaining the navy's participation in nuclear weaponry, not in developing nuclear engines. They rather clearly told me, for example, that excessive interest in Rickover would be contrary to my own best career interests. At this time (1947), the navy was revving up to counter the air force claim that only long-range bombers could deliver "strategic" (i.e., nuclear) weapons. In spite of the navy's important contributions to the development and delivery of the first atom bombs, there was a very real danger that it would be divested of all "strategic" weaponry, and with that, all strategic missions. The concern pervaded everything the navy did, causing it to concentrate the great preponderance of its research and development into putting a nuclear weapon capability into its aircraft carriers. A nuclear submarine was very much of a secondary objective.

This was the challenge Rickover faced at the beginning, not from the entire navy, definitely not from its submariners, but from a big part of it. His unpopular personality, already well known in the older (pre-war) submarine service and after that in the engineering-duty-only fraternity to which he had transferred a few years before the war, figured only in a peripheral way. He overcame the problem by getting a supporting directive from none other than Admiral Nimitz, fresh from the triumph of the war and now chief of naval operations. I'm proud to say I helped in spite of the implicit disapproval of my immediate bosses. Unfortunately, to do this Captain Rickover had to go over the heads of some of his immediate superiors, thus beginning—or maybe continuing—a habit of operating that produced good results on the one hand and brought much obloquy upon him on the other.

Throughout the early history of "the project," as he called it, Rickover first fought inertia, and then as he sought support outside the navy and his methods became more abrasive, he had to fight the type of personal opposition he had evidently encountered in much of his career to date. He realized, of course, that no failure on his part or by his immediate subordinates, no matter how insignificant, would be condoned. More important, long before it began to be clear to the general public and the press, he understood that there were new and unusual hazards in the use of nuclear energy. Were even a small accident to occur, of the type that had happened literally countless times in all industries and all professions—coal mining, oil wells, steam engineering, medicine, aviation, architecture, to name only some—the penalty would be twofold and severe.

For him personally, it would be the end, the excuse to get rid of him. Iconoclasts of his stripe as a general rule do not do well in the navy or anywhere else, and the coercive methods he used in furtherance of nuclear submarines, nuclear propulsion for surface ships, nuclear energy in civilian power plants, and nuclear power in general, had earned him more dislike in his new pursuit than he had experienced in any of the older disciplines in which he had worked. The big difference was, of course, that in nuclear power he was the unquestioned boss, but everyone knew, he more than anyone, that he could expect little mercy if anything important went wrong. On a larger scale, any serious accident would spell great delay in the project, and he had already begun to feel, long before anyone else thought this way, that being first and staying ahead in nuclear energy were important to the nation's safety.

He was equal to the challenge. His methods he would not change; they were ingrained in his nature, had been built into his system, and they worked. He led through example (no one worked harder than he, or longer hours); through punishment (most of which amounted to multiple unpaid overtime to make good any deficiency); through constant inspection (much of this he did himself, and woe betide anyone who did not have *all* the answers when asked); by demanding continual reports (he had his own representatives in shipyards and manufacturing firms who were required to write reports on a weekly basis for his eyes only, for which they earned the sobriquet of "Rickover's spies"); and by applying implacable responsibility arbitrarily to naval or industrial personnel with equal ruthlessness.

The final result of it all, aptly used as the title of this book, is a totally new discipline of technology, with "discipline" the operative word. Medical operating rooms are no longer the only immaculate work spaces: so are the Rickover-mandated "clean rooms" in which reactor work is done. Zero defects are not only an advertising gimmick: in Rickover's world anything less was cause for dismissal of the individual or individuals responsible. Utter devotion to the job at hand, to the exclusion of all else, twenty-four hours a day and even while sleeping, was only normal. Ironhanded employment of any and every way to get "the job" done better, on time, at less cost, was routine, to be expected. Certainly it was not considered exceptional. Contrasted to this, however, was his willingness to spend whatever time, trouble, and funds that might be necessary to get things right. This extended to ripping out and replacing already completed installations on the mere suspicion that all might not be as it should be. From the very beginning there was a severely enforced system of rigid review and deep inspection, extending to a meticulous X-ray of large sections of pipes or machinery. If, on top of this, there was even a suggestion that somewhere under all the expensive piping, control surfaces, radiation barriers, and heavy steel partitions, there might exist something not according to specifications, there was literally Hell to pay. This was many times demonstrated, especially in the early days before people learned how intolerant he was of slipshod or careless work, and what he would do when he discovered any.

Rickover could be kind, even humorous on occasion. When in the mood he could be pleasant company, given always that he would invariably control the conversation in directions of his own interest. But in business he had no kindness in him. He would use all the psychological weapons at his command, all of them coercive, to ensure that things would continue to proceed as he wished them to. The results are classic, and will remain so. Precise production, exactly in accordance with the most careful specifications, was his watchword. On this he never let up, for as he often said, to do so for even a moment was to court disaster. He believed this implicitly and followed it to the letter, all the time. No one else could have done so well.

The U.S. Navy cannot stand many men like Rickover in a single generation, but once in a great while, in a situation of transcendent importance, such a person is needed. Even Rickover's faults, great as they actually were, were useful to his objectives. No personal, financial, or extracurricular excess of any kind for him! None of the capital's social life—certainly no "wine, women and song"—but as for his work, excess was the norm. Increasingly better machinery for nuclear energy was his one obsession, begun with the submarine but later extending to surface ships and power plants on shore. Personal dominance, power, invective, and fear were his tools, and he used them exclusively to further nuclear power. Nothing else mattered. It would be equally correct to say that he used them also in a self-serving way, but he and nuclear power were indissolubly intertwined.

It has been said somewhere that "you always have to take the whole man. You can't take only part of him. He comes as he is, with all his faults and warts." In Rickover's case, even his warts, like them or not, somehow contributed to the extraordinary success of what he accomplished.

In a sense, Francis Duncan is Rickover's officially accepted biographer. The first book about Rickover in which he was directly involved, *Nuclear Navy 1946–1962* (written in collaboration with Richard G. Hewlett), was an Atomic Energy Commission project: Hewlett was the commission's chief historian, Duncan the assistant historian. Duncan is the sole author of the present book, *Rickover and the Nuclear Navy,* also an officially authorized document under the Atomic Energy Commission. Technically speaking, the book is not a biography of Rickover the man; by joint decision of the commission historians and Admiral Rickover himself, this would not be its thrust. On the contrary, as for *Nuclear Navy,* it is the documentation of a grand achievement, beginning essentially where the first book left off but with some overlap for the sake of readability and continuity. Between the lines the reader will gain appreciation of what sort of man the project leader was, and what were the pressures on him and his co-workers, bearing in mind that, being an officially sponsored book written with exclusive access to his most sequestered files, it has a special point of view. Among its interesting facets are the background of the Shippingport shore-power reactor that has replicated itself world-wide, and a careful, defensive analysis of the *Thresher* disaster.

Rickover never saw the manuscript. It was stipulated that he would not see it until it was ready for review, and in fact he never did. During his final days he received some of the chapters for Mrs. Rickover to read to him aloud.

Whatever else is said, it is worth repeating that this book is the history of a technology, not the biography of a man. Thus the focus of the book is not on Admiral Rickover the man, but on his work: on the development of the machinery, the decisions made, the techniques employed, what was built and for what purpose. The limitations of national security have forced intentional omissions in some areas, deficiencies that will be welcomed in circles loyal to the nation's best interests, but in the main it is packed with detail. To sum up, the book is the authoritative summation of an extraordinary man's achievements, written from files in his office that have never before been opened to historians.

Admiral Rickover had a keen sense of history and the way it judges individuals and their accomplishments. He knew no man would live forever (contrary to the impression he occasionally gave), but he knew also that the things one created during one's life just possibly might. Like the Egyptian pharaoh Cheops, he has built himself a monument for all time, in and out of the United States Navy (the *Nautilus* is his pyramid), and he was not so unassuming not to have thought of the comparison. If so, he may also have thought of how he could go Cheops one better, for here is the record of what he did, and according to his lights, why.

Edward L. Beach, Captain, USN
(Retired)

Preface

"Your job is to show what it takes to get a job done." The speaker was Admiral Hyman G. Rickover; the place a corner office in the third floor of National Center 2, one of a number of drab multistory buildings near National Airport in Arlington, Virginia; the time an overcast Saturday afternoon in the fall of 1974. For about three decades he had led the navy's nuclear propulsion program, a joint effort of the Navy Department and the Atomic Energy Commission. In that time he had served five presidents of the United States, a dozen secretaries of defense, fifteen secretaries of the navy, eleven chiefs of naval operations, and seven commission chairmen. To many of these men he had been an unruly subordinate. To the public he was the "father of the nuclear navy," an engineering genius who had developed atomic energy for ship propulsion and for electric power stations. He was notorious for his caustic comments on the military-industrial complex and for his vigorous criticism of American education. Before congressional committees and from lecture podiums he—to use his own words—"took on" all professions that he believed were failing to live up to the standards they professed. Shifting a massive pile of papers from his lap to his desk, he leaned back in his battered rocking chair and continued, "I can't tell you how you should do your job."

If he could not tell me how I should do my job he was determined to show me how he did his. I was to see him debate technical issues with his project officers and engineers; consider budget matters with his financial personnel; read, annotate, and route reports and correspondence; hold telephone conversations with his representatives at the laboratories and shipyards; interview midshipmen who wished to serve in the nuclear fleet; lecture prospective commanding officers before they left for their ships, prepare testimony and testify before congressional committees; attend contractor meetings; and conduct initial sea trials of nuclear-powered submarines and surface ships.

He did not confine my education to his official duties. Sometimes we would talk in the evenings in his office, sometimes he would telephone me at home on Sundays or late at night. I could never be sure what it was he wanted to discuss. It might be society and the disappearance of respect for hard work; education and its failure to inculcate a love of learning; television and its numbing effect on the mind; the decline of ethics in the legal profession; some incident in a biography or history he was reading; the inflated importance awarded to sports—the list of subjects was endless. He was determined that I understand how he thought.

He ruled out certain things. Operational matters were none of my business, nor were recent advances in nuclear propulsion or other areas of naval technology. He sometimes referred to disputes he was having with a chief of naval operations, secretary of the navy, secretary of defense, or a major contractor, but he warned me he could not go into detail.

In countless conversations he hammered at two main points. In the first he stressed over and over again that one cause of waste and inefficiency was that the professional civilian and military managers—no matter how well meaning—had to rely upon management precepts because they did not know the industry or project they were trying to run. In the second he emphasized that the future of mankind depended upon its control of technology. Although he recognized that the idea was hardly original, he thought that how he ran an important, complex technical program—one having civilian as well as military application—might contribute to the safety of a world increasingly dominated by technology.

As he well knew, I had never managed any project. Perhaps he thought this was a good thing. In any event I was a familiar figure to him. I had first met Admiral Rickover in 1969 when Dr. Richard G. Hewlett, chief historian of the Atomic Energy Commission, and I were completing the manuscript for *Atomic Shield*, vol. 2 of a *History of the United States Atomic Energy Commission*, published by the Pennsylvania State University Press in 1969. The admiral asked the commissioners to make our next assignment a study of the naval nuclear propulsion program. Engaged in seeing *Atomic Shield* through the final stages of publication and unable to take up the new task immediately, Dr. Hewlett asked me to move into the office that Admiral Rickover made available and to undertake some preliminary research and to survey records. Occasionally the admiral dropped in to talk, a practice he continued and expanded when Dr. Hewlett, freed of other responsibilities, joined me.

At that time Admiral Rickover and that small group he led—collectively and colloquially known as "Naval Reactors" or "NR"—were located in "N" building, a temporary structure run up to meet the demands of World War II. N Building was located just behind Main Navy, a huge sprawling temporary structure fronting on Constitution Avenue and hurriedly erected to meet the exigencies of World War I. Main Navy was fascinating, for it had seen a great deal of history, but to me its main attraction was that it housed the library of the Bureau of Ships with its technical journals and reports and the Navy Library with its superb collection of general works. For some time I had weighed the possibility of writing about the technical revolution that had transformed the navy between 1898 and 1917: from the return of Admiral William T. Sampson's squadron fresh from victory over the Spanish to the departure of Commander Joseph K. Taussig's destroyer flotilla for Europe and World War I. These two libraries held the major secondary sources I needed. Almost every night I stuffed my brief case with books. As it turned out, my official job made it impossible for me to realize my ambition. However, the reading and study gave me some familiarity with naval history and a background against which to assess the impact of nuclear propulsion upon the navy. More important, Admiral Rickover discovered my interest: increasingly our talks centered on navies, technology and history.

In *Nuclear Navy 1946–1962*, published by the University of Chicago in 1974, Dr. Hewlett and I traced the origins of the effort, the establishment of his organization, which reported to the navy's Bureau of Ships and the Commission's Division of Reactor Development, and the creation of the Bettis and Knolls Atomic Power Laboratories. We endeavored to explain how Admiral Rickover shaped his engineers in Washington, the laboratories, the shipyards, and industrial contractors into a lean and responsible instrument that in a remarkably short time overcame immense technical obstacles to develop reactors for submarines, surface ships, and a civilian power plant. *Nuclear Navy* is an account of a highly successful technological innovation.

Although closely linked to *Nuclear Navy*, the new book would be different. It could not be a biography; Admiral Rickover, Dr. Hewlett, and I agreed from the outset that such an approach would be inappropriate and unacceptable for an official undertaking. If it could not be about technological innovation (for that subject had been covered), it could be about technological application, about how standards of excellence were maintained against the erosion of familiarity. Obviously the new book would have to cover events occurring after 1962: among these the loss of the *Thresher*, the struggle over the application of nuclear propulsion to the surface fleet, the development of new submarine propulsion reactors, and the use of the Shippingport atomic power plant to demonstrate the feasibility of a light-water breeder reactor. In these and in other areas, new information could be made available to the public and the scholarly community.

Because Dr. Hewlett had other commitments, I was to work alone, except for a research assistant who I would choose, but Admiral Rickover would provide. In other respects the ground rules remained the same as they had been for *Nuclear Navy*. I was to have complete access to documents and staff, and the admiral was not to see the manuscript until it was completed. As it turned out, he died before he could see the finished manuscript. Although I was to work in his office, I was to remain a member of the historian's office of the Atomic Energy Commission.

Organizing the book was extraordinarily difficult. The information had to be placed in some context or else it would be little more than a series of aphorisms. Reluctantly and with some hesitation, I turned to the historical approach. I had to recognize several limitations and restrictions. The closer I came to the present, the harder it would be to maintain historical perspective. The information would be less available and less usable because of security classification. Many men and women, still active in professional careers, would be reluctant to talk of events and issues that they had not had time to consider and analyze. Some people would not want to be interviewed by a government historian attached to Admiral Rickover's office. Even under these constraints I believed it would be possible to illustrate the often troubled environment in which the program lived.

Choosing a chronological point of departure is a question that plagues all historians. After much thought and discussion with colleagues, I chose the end of 1957. It was possible to argue that at that point the technology developed in the naval nuclear propulsion program had reached maturity. By that statement I meant a period of development was being succeeded by one of application. The technology was competing against other forms of propulsion for submarines, had begun to produce electric power for civilian use, and was being installed in a surface ship. Research and development were vigorous and flourishing, but the basic technical principles were not in doubt. They were being pursued to reach new goals and extend the range of application. A completely chronological approach was impossible, but in the three areas of application I could sketch some of the history.

The result is a series of essays. Chapter one sets forth some background on pressurized-water reactor technology, Naval Reactors, Admiral Rickover, and the government framework in which the naval nuclear propulsion program functioned. Chapters two and three deal with the application of the technology to submarines, and chapters four, five, and six to naval surface ships. Chapter seven is about a proposal to use nuclear propulsion as a diplomatic pawn. Chapter eight is about the application of pressurized-water reactor technology at the Shippingport Atomic Power Station, the world's first full-scale civilian nuclear power plant, and about the light-water breeder effort.

In chapters nine, ten, and eleven the focus changes sharply, and is upon "the discipline of technology," a phrase Admiral Rickover frequently used to describe his own approach to technological innovation and operation. Chapter nine describes the organization of the program in the later years of his leadership, chapter ten how Naval Reactors maintained standards of excellence, and chapter eleven summarizes Admiral Rickover's philosophy of technology.

The frequent conversations with Admiral Rickover revealed a very complex man, far more complicated than the demanding, ruthless, and dictatorial individual portrayed by popular anecdote. At times he took a perverse pleasure in his notoriety and even found it useful. He often sent into my office articles he had annotated, documents he wanted me to see, and occasionally brief observations he had just dictated. One of the latter read: "People say I am like Captain Bligh. I am disappointed. I considered myself more like Attila the Hun." He could be rough and abrasive. He could shout and scream. To his own people he could be harsh. One engineer, incensed at a tirade, took the in-box from the admiral's desk and dashed it on the floor. Significantly, the man continued in Naval Reactors and kept the admiral's regard and respect.

Such incidents were the result of his concept of responsibility. He believed he was responsible to the nation for his work. That meant he was responsible to the executive, legislative, and even judicial branches of the government for doing the best he and the program—his Washington office, his field representatives, laboratories, contractors—knew how. His personal acceptance of responsibility made him a difficult person to work with, but it also accounted for the support that he got, not only from Congress but also from many men and women on his staff, in other parts of the government and from the public. Not every encounter was bruising and not every telephone conversation was stormy. He declared that if he were the man portrayed in *Rickover: Controversy and Genius—A Biography* by Norman Polmar and Thomas B. Allen and published by Simon and Schuster in 1982, he would never have accomplished what he did. Popular legend of "the real Rickover" could not account for the success of the program or the quality of the people he had around him. He asserted you can neither command technology nor hard work, dedication, or loyalty.

He could be persuasive and charming. He loved good writing and had a tenacious memory, enabling him to recite long passages of poetry learned during his youth. He could join a very young daughter of one of his representatives in gathering dandelions and giving them to her mother for a centerpiece at dinner. Irony lightened many moments and so did humor.

He was seldom at a loss for words. Rear Admiral William A. Brockett remembered one incident vividly. In 1963 he became chief of the Bureau of Ships. As a young ensign fresh from the Academy he had been assigned to the battleship *New Mexico* and for some months had served under Lieutenant H. G. Rickover, assistant engineer. The young ensign worked hard and learned a great deal. As chief of the Bureau of Ships he was now Admiral Rickover's superior officer. It was not always an easy relationship. Once over the telephone the two men got into a violent argument, broken off as each slammed the receiver down. A few minutes later Admiral Brockett walked into Admiral Rickover's office.

"Rick. That was a bad scene and I don't want to leave things that way. Maybe if we have a cup of coffee. . . ."

Admiral Rickover nodded and shouted to his outer office, "Admiral Brockett wants a cup of coffee." He paused: "Hold the hemlock."

Admiral Rickover drew a sharp line between his professional and his private life. Some of these aspects he allowed me to see because he was convinced that a technologist, no matter how skilled, could not be a successful leader of a technical program unless he had a greater horizon than that bounded by his job. The admiral was convinced that reading was by far the best way to place one's self and work in history and society and thereby recognize the meaning of responsibility.

His main interests, as I discerned them, were history and biography, particularly politics, diplomacy, and military affairs. He considered the German general staff under the Empire the epitome of military professionalism. He was widely read in naval biography, comparing his own career with that of Admiral William S. Sims, Admiral Benjamin F. Isherwood, Lord Fisher of Kilverstone, Sir Percival Scott, and others. Fictional and literary figures rarely attracted him. He avidly read book reviews—preferring those from English publications—believing they often contained more literate and judicious assessments than those in American periodicals and journals. From these and other sources he drew ideas he wanted to discuss.

The relation between history and historians intrigued him. Most historians, he observed, cannot live the experience they attempt to study—that was why he was giving me an opportunity to observe his work, talk to his people, and visit his installations. How did historians know the real world? How were they trained? He asked me who in the profession had personally influenced me the most. I replied one who had been wounded at Belleau Wood in World War I and another who had seized an opportunity to roam the interior of China during World War II. He declared I proved his point. These men had faced reality and from that glimpse could never escape. That was not the case with most historians: their lives were too thin. It took an exceptional individual, he concluded, to rise above a career spent in the cloisters of college, graduate school, lecture halls, seminar rooms, and government service.

Once he remarked that he was teaching me a great deal of history, but I was not teaching him much; he meant he could discuss history with me, but I could not discuss engineering with him. His commitment to history was apparent in his frequent references to it in congressional testimony, his request that Dr. Hewlett and I undertake the studies of the nuclear propulsion program; and his authorship of *Eminent Americans* and *How the Battleship* Maine *Was Destroyed*. From the latter venture in particular, he learned a great deal of the historian's craft and the pleasures and pitfalls of history. He believed historians had a mission, and it disconcerted him to learn that they were just like anybody else—good, bad, and indifferent.

Long before my assignment came to an end, I concluded that he was far more than a brilliant engineer: he was a great man. My assessment did not come only, or even primarily, from hours of conversation or watching him at work. It came from talking to contractor personnel, some in paneled offices, others on the shop floor. It came from watching officers and men training at the prototypes and later observing them on sea trials. It stemmed also from the caliber of the men and women in the program and their achievements. But above all it came from the propulsion plants themselves, whose record throughout the history of the naval nuclear propulsion program has been outstanding.

My relations with the staff evolved slowly. Admiral Rickover encouraged me to talk to people in the program, and without access to them my task would have been impossible. He asked them to make their files available to me and to give me information, but that alone was not enough. Seldom can files, no matter how extensive, nor documents, no matter how well-written, provide all the information required. I needed the background of decisions and procedures. To obtain these insights, certain rules, never discussed or written down, were nonetheless clearly understood. My questions had to be in the context of my work: confidences offered had to be respected. Sensitive issues currently being debated had to be excluded. By accepting this code I more than once received information I would never have gotten otherwise.

On 21 May 1985, three years after Admiral Rickover left the program, John Lehman, secretary of the navy, censured him for accepting gratuities, mostly from the General Dynamics Corporation. Its subsidiary, the Electric Boat Division, was the nation's principal builder of attack and missile submarines. Admiral Rickover acknowledged he had accepted some gratuities. A few were personal items; by far the greatest in number and value were for travel and lodging associated with business, and for small gifts he distributed widely, some to individuals in high places whom he wished to have a memento of the program, or perhaps of an event they had helped bring about. Providing personal mementos was and is a widespread practice at ship launchings and commissionings, although the perception of what is an acceptable gift has changed. Mr. Lehman observed that although the admiral had been wrong in accepting the gratuities, there was no evidence that they had in any way influenced him to lower the high standards he demanded from all his program contractors. Patrick Tyler's *Running Critical: The Silent War, Rickover and General Dynamics* published by Harper & Row in 1986 reached the same conclusion. Based on my own observations I never sensed he pulled his punches, but was uncompromising in protecting government money and holding contractors accountable.

On 14 July 1986 Admiral James D. Watkins, former chief of naval operations, spoke at the memorial service for Admiral Rickover held at the National Cathedral, Washington, D.C. A nuclear-trained officer, Admiral Watkins had a depth of understanding of the naval nuclear program that could only come from being a part of it for many years and observing it in operation. In his words:

> While others looked for short cuts, Admiral Rickover always insisted upon establishing rigorous standards of performance that matched technology to human potential. Sure, this required more effort, checks and balances, concern for quality, and extra care, but these are now the hallmarks of not only our Navy's nuclear power program but of our entire Navy's combat readiness as well.

The qualities Admiral Watkins described do not belong to the navy alone; they are also the legacy that Admiral Rickover left to us all. Excellence, responsibility, and hard work are inseparable.

Acknowledgments

During the years of research and writing this book, many people gave generously of their time and shared with me their thoughts on Admiral Rickover and the naval nuclear propulsion program. President Richard Nixon recalled that he had chosen the admiral to accompany him to the Soviet Union in 1959 because he exemplified the promise of America that those from humble backgrounds could rise high by their own efforts. President Jimmy Carter remembered his days in the early nuclear propulsion program, the lessons he learned, and his appreciation of Admiral Rickover as technologist, historian, and man. Former secretaries of the navy—Fred Korth, Paul R. Ignatius, and J. William Middendorf II—were most helpful in giving their assessments of the effort and its leader and some of the political problems the naval propulsion program faced. Admiral George W. Anderson, Jr., Admiral David L. McDonald, Admiral Thomas H. Moorer, Admiral Elmo R. Zumwalt, Jr., and Admiral James L. Holloway III—all former chiefs of naval operations—offered very perceptive and occasionally very frank comments on the effort and its leader. Two chairmen of the Atomic Energy Commission—John A. McCone and Glenn T. Seaborg—explained how the commission viewed its relations with the navy. Representatives Charles E. Bennett, Chet M. Holifield, Craig Hosmer, and Melvin Price gave valuable insights on reasons why they and other legislators supported the program.

The very existence of the book is due to Admiral Rickover, who gave me my assignment, and Admiral Kinnaird R. McKee, who gave unstinting support and encouragement. Many members of Naval Reactors suggested avenues to explore, discussed policy matters, and later read and commented upon the manuscript. Most are named elsewhere but a few went so far beyond what I had any right to expect that they should be included here: Carl H. Schmitt, deputy director for Naval Reactors, and his predecessors James W. Vaughan, Jr., and William Wegner; and David T. Leighton, former associate director for Surface Ships and Light-Water Breeder. Thomas L. Foster, director, Fiscal, Acquisition, and Logistics Management not only read the manuscript, but offered sage advice that more than once proved crucial to the fate of the project. Richard A. Guida gave invaluable assistance in making sure the manuscript met the requirements of classification review.

Jeffrey B. Cole and Mark H. Neblett gave unflagging help during the final stages of review. Beth J. Granger assisted in so many ways to help me obtain quick decisions to administrative problems. Sharon Custer, Vicki Lubonski, and Shirley S. Jessup with unfailing patience guided me to records in the Naval Reactors library and archives.

Within the Department of Energy my work received the support of William S. Heffelfinger, director of administration, his successor, Harry L. Peebles, and William V. Vitale, director, office of the executive secretariat. Dr. Richard G. Hewlett, chief historian, worked with Admiral Rickover to establish guidelines for the project. Dr. Hewlett's successor, Dr. Jack M. Holl, assisted the effort and made available the help of the history division. With great pleasure I acknowledge the very great debt I owe two colleagues in the division. Roger M. Anders and Dr. David K. Allison offered stimulating comments on conceptual approaches and furnished penetrating criticism. Alice L. Buck gave generously of her editorial skill and with Hazel E. Whitaker, formerly of the Office of Public Affairs, provided needed advice on photographic selection.

Two of the division's administrative officers were a constant source of help. During the early stages Travis C. Hulsey straightened out many difficulties with unfailing tact and diplomacy. In the final stages of manuscript preparation, Sheila C. Convis somehow always managed to solve complex scheduling problems with a dexterity and cheerfulness that filled me with admiration. Marian Scroger also assisted in making revisions in the final stages of manuscript preparation, and Pauline Robarge congenially scheduled and facilitated our meetings and consultations.

No one could have had more helpful research assistants. Edwina Smith laid the groundwork in searching out records and organizing files. Dana M. Wegner, an able student of naval history, undertook much of the research for the first part of the volume and contributed especially to the chapter on the loss of the *Thresher.* Annette D. Barnes did much of the research on the second part of the book and wrote special background papers on Operation Sea Orbit and the Shippingport Atomic Power Station. She also exercised her superb editorial skill. Their help, leavened with wit, humor, and friendship, means more to me than I can ever say.

The history program of the Department of Energy was established in

1957 by the Atomic Energy Commission to provide the public and the scholarly community with the history of a major government venture that has had, and continues to have, an important role in the economy and security of the nation. From its inception, the program has depended upon outstanding individuals in various fields for perspective and advice upon works in progress. In the present instance, Dr. Holl and I wish to thank Admiral James L. Holloway III, chief of naval operations 1974–1978, Dr. Richard W. Leopold, William Smith Mason Professor of American History Emeritus, Northwestern University; Mr. George Norris, counsel for the Joint Committee on Atomic Energy of Congress, 1953–1958, and counsel for the Armed Services Committee of the House of Representatives, 1965–1979; and Dr. Glenn T. Seaborg, chairman of the Atomic Energy Commission, 1961–1971. For their encouragement and penetrating comments we are deeply grateful.

Technology is a fascinating and challenging field of study, and never more so than when the area under scrutiny is modern, with military and civilian application, and with significance for today. If this book has stimulated interest in how Admiral Rickover exercised his concept of responsibility, it has served its purpose.

Rickover and the Nuclear Navy

At the end of 1957 the pressurized-water reactor technology developed by Admiral Rickover and the organization he created was being applied to submarines, surface ships, and civilian power. Nuclear propulsion was revolutionizing undersea operations, but how it would affect surface operations and civilian life, where its

CHAPTER ONE
Common Denominators

application was slower, remained to be seen. Admiral Rickover, who had led the effort from its beginning, continued to exercise vigorous and personal leadership. In the struggle to extend the application of the new technology, he was often on the national stage, dealing with senior military officers and officials of the defense establishment as well as congressional leaders. This chapter summarizes his background, surveys the program he led as it moved into its era of maturity, and describes the political framework in which both he and his program operated.

Even if the morning sky was bright and the breeze only strong enough to ripple the bunting decorating the speakers' stand, it was cold. More than two thousand people, most of them shipyard workers, cheerfully disregarded the low temperature and joked among themselves as they watched the individuals on the platform. Some of the dignitaries were company officials, others were state and local political leaders, and a few were prominent Washington figures. Several officers in uniform enlivened the scene; most of them clustered around Admiral Jerauld Wright, commander in chief, United States Atlantic Fleet. An eight-ton, sixty-foot-long steel keel plate rested in a cleared space where all could see. At the high point of the ceremony Admiral Wright and Raymond C. Kealer, mayor of Long Beach, California, came down from the stands to chalk their initials on two pieces of copper attached to the keel plate. A pair of welders stepped forward and inscribed the letters. At a signal from Wright, a crane lifted the plate and swung it into position on the dry dock floor. The keel of the cruiser *Long Beach*, the navy's first nuclear-powered surface ship, had been laid at the Fore River Yard of the Bethlehem Steel Company at Quincy, Massachusetts. The time was 11:48 A.M.; the date was 2 December 1957.

Earlier that morning a different scene had taken place some 500 miles to the south and west of Quincy. Since March 1955, the world's first full-scale atomic electric power plant had been under construction at Shippingport, Pennsylvania, a small town on the Ohio River about twenty-five miles northwest of Pittsburgh. In the early morning hours the control room was crowded with people—among them Rear Admiral Hyman G. Rickover, who was responsible for the design and construction of the reactor plant, and many of his key personnel. Also present were several individuals from Westinghouse Electric Corporation, which had designed, fabricated, assembled, and tested the reactor; personnel from the Duquesne Light Company, which would operate the plant and distribute its power; as well as representatives from other groups. All watched the reactor control panel intently. At 4:30 A.M. instruments showed that the reactor had reached criticality, a term that meant that it had achieved a self-sustained nuclear chain reaction.

Tension snapped. The meticulous preparation and testing that had gone into the project had paid off. The careful calculations that predicted the nuclear characteristics of the reactor had proved accurate and showed every probability that the atomic power plant would operate as it had been designed. One after another, the witnesses of the event, now in a relaxed and cheerful mood, posed for photographs and signed a graph that traced the rise to criticality. No power had yet been produced. Not until 23 December, after a series of carefully planned operations, would the Shippingport Atomic Power Station reach its capacity of 60,000 net electrical kilowatts, and then a long period of testing would follow during which substantial amounts of power would be delivered to the network of the Duquesne Light Company.[1]

The press at Quincy and Pittsburgh caught the significance of the date. At Chicago fifteen years earlier to the day, the Italian-born Nobel laureate Enrico Fermi had achieved the world's first self-sustained chain reaction, an event that had won acceptance as the beginning of the atomic age. Fermi and his small team of associates had achieved their goal by using a simple assembly of graphite, uranium metal, uranium oxide, and wood.[2] In contrast, the nuclear reactor at Shippingport and those under development for the *Long Beach* were highly complicated pieces of machinery, generating large amounts of heat, requiring elaborate cooling systems, depending upon metals that fifteen years earlier had been laboratory curiosities, and relying upon sophisticated components that did not exist when Fermi conducted his experiment.

In Washington Lewis L. Strauss, chairman of the Atomic Energy Commission, reported both events to President Dwight D. Eisenhower. The Shippingport plant, Strauss wrote, would be the first full-scale nuclear power plant in the world, so far as was known, designed *exclusively* for *civilian* power. He underlined both words. As for the *Long Beach*, Strauss expected the cruiser would be the world's first nuclear-powered surface ship.[3] Strauss had reason for emphasizing both points. On 4 October and again on 3 November 1957, the Russians had launched the first man-made satellites. The tiny motes of light that swept across the sky against the background of old and familiar constellations had shattered the complacency of Americans in their technological superiority.

On this fifteenth anniversary of the Fermi experiment, the world's first nuclear-powered ship, the submarine *Nautilus,* was quietly moored at Pier C in the yard of the Electric Boat Division at Groton, Connecticut. That summer the ship had seen arduous service. Under Commander William R. Anderson, the *Nautilus* had probed far beneath the Arctic ice. Although the exercise was part of the navy's growing interest in Arctic operations, Anderson had interpreted his orders broadly enough to make a dash for the Pole. Three things thwarted him from fulfilling an ancient quest of mankind: an accident to a periscope, a faulty gyrocompass, and a tight schedule that demanded that his ship take part in maneuvers with the British. Nonetheless, he had come within 200 miles of his goal.[4] Anderson was convinced that a voyage to the Pole was feasible. Operating beneath the ice and over unknown ocean floors, far from any possible assistance, would be dangerous, but a nuclear submarine was the ship for the job.

Common Denominators

Three common denominators united the cruiser, power plant, and sub-marine. Reactors for the three projects were the pressurized-water type. They and the pressurized-water reactor technology had been developed in the naval nuclear propulsion program, a joint effort of the navy and the Atomic Energy Commission. From its beginning the program had been under the direction of Rickover.[5]

A power reactor based on the fission of uranium needed materials with three properties. One was a coolant to control the temperature of the reaction. The second was a moderator to slow down the neutrons emitted during the fission so that the process could continue. The third was a heat-transfer agent to carry the heat from the core to a heat exchanger where it could be transformed into useful energy to generate electric power or drive machinery. With proper design, water efficiently performed all functions.

Pressurized-water reactors took their name from the heat-transfer medium. Water was contained in two separate loops or systems. In the primary system, pumps circulated water through the reactor core to a steam generator and back again. In the steam generator, the primary system gave off its heat to the secondary system where the water was converted to steam to drive a turbine. The water in the primary system was kept under pressure to prevent boiling. Because the coolant became radioactive when passing through the core, two independent loops were necessary. As a theoretical concept, the approach was not original with Rickover; what he and the joint navy/commission organization had done was to take the idea and make it practical, an effort involving the solution of extremely difficult problems in design, development, and fabrication.[6]

The Atomic Energy Acts of 1946 and 1954 forced close cooperation between the commission and the navy, although to a layman the division of functions was not always easy to follow. The legislation gave the commission responsibility for the design, development, and safe operation of the reactors. The navy, however, designed, built, and operated its ships. Only by working closely together could the two proceed concurrently with reactor and ship design, making sure that each effort was integrated with the other. The commission was responsible for the design and development of all naval reactors, although the navy contributed development funds for naval features required for a shipboard plant. The commission built the land prototypes, although here too the navy provided supplemental funds for some features. The navy paid for all shipboard plants except for those of the *Nautilus* and *Seawolf*. For these ships, the first nuclear-powered submarines authorized, the commission provided the funds for the plants. And it was the navy that maintained the nuclear ships of the fleet, while the commission exercised technical oversight for safety.[7]

The fundamental difference in responsibilities was to prove more enduring than the agencies. The commission was abolished in 1974, and most of its functions, including those pertaining to nuclear power, were absorbed by the new Energy Research and Development Administration. A few years later—in 1977—another reorganization replaced that administration with the Department of Energy. The structure of the navy also changed drastically, the functions of the dissolved Bureau of Ships passing in 1966 to the Naval Ship Systems Command and in 1974 to the Naval Sea Systems Command.[8] Through all of these changes the division of responsibility remained constant: the civilian agency for the design and development of the reactor, and the navy for safe operation and for keeping the civilian agency informed of operational experience and data, including safety standards.

Shippingport fell into a different category from the propulsion plants, for it was solely a commission project to demonstrate the feasibility of producing electric power for civilian application from a large-scale reactor.

The ownership and use of program facilities was additional evidence of the close relationship between the two parent organizations. The commission owned the two laboratories in which design and development of naval reactor plants took place: the Bettis Atomic Power Laboratory, operated by the Westinghouse Electric Corporation outside Pittsburgh; and the Knolls Atomic Power Laboratory, operated by the General Electric Company at Schenectady, New York. Success in the development effort had caused Rickover to set up in 1956 a new organization near Pittsburgh—the Plant Apparatus Department or "PAD"—to handle procurement for reactor plant components already developed. In 1959 he would set up the Machinery Apparatus Operation or "MAO" in Schenectady for the same purpose. These organizations, however, were financed by the navy.

Training was another area that illustrated the close ties between the navy and the commission. Officers and men who would operate the shipboard plants first received six months of classroom work at a nuclear power school owned and operated by the navy and six months of practical training at a land prototype. Because the prototypes were also used in reactor development, they were owned by the commission. At the end of 1957 the program had one land prototype in operation at the commission's National Reactor Testing Station in Idaho and another under construction at that site. At West Milton, New York, the commission was replacing one prototype with another and adding one more. Another at Windsor, Connecticut, was also being built.[9]

Work at the laboratories, PAD, MAO, and at the prototypes was directed toward the production of nuclear-powered ships. At the end of 1957 seven shipyards were in the program: the privately owned yards of the Electric Boat Division of General Dynamics Corporation; the Newport News Shipbuilding & Dry Dock Company at Newport News, Virginia; the Ingalls Shipbuilding Corporation at Pascagoula, Mississippi; the Bethlehem Steel Company at Quincy, Massachusetts; the New York Shipbuilding Corporation at Camden, New Jersey; and the navy yards at Portsmouth, New Hampshire, and Mare Island, California.

At the private yards Rickover had representatives who checked the contractor's work on the installation of the nuclear propulsion plants; at the navy yards the nuclear power superintendent was responsible for all work relating to the nuclear propulsion plant and for this purpose had his own shops and work force. Although trained by Rickover, who followed his activities closely, the nuclear power superintendent reported to the shipyard commander. With the growth of the nuclear fleet, that arrangement became inadequate; Rickover installed his own representative in the navy yards, and the arrangement closely paralleled that in the private yards.

The heart of the naval nuclear propulsion program was an organization that called itself "Naval Reactors" or more simply "NR." It consisted primarily of officer and civilian engineers, all carefully chosen and trained by Rickover, along with a few people who carried out supporting functions. Including engineers, officers on temporary assignment, and others, the total in the Washington office in late 1957 came to 126.[10] It was not readily apparent, nor did it matter, which were civilians and which were military, nor who was paid by the commission or who was paid by the navy, for everyone worked for the program. The absence of badges of rank or marks of hierarchy was a deliberate effort on Rickover's part to make sure that competence and hard work established an individual's position. Partly for security reasons and partly for peace and quiet, he blocked off the corridors of his part of the building so there were no knots of people gossiping or individuals rambling from one office to another. Naval Reactors did not coordinate, administer, or manage: it decided and directed. The atmosphere was sometimes tense but always conducive to hard work.

In 1957 Naval Reactors had some highly trained and experienced personnel. On technical matters Rickover relied upon I. Harry Mandil for the development of new reactor systems, Robert Panoff for submarine propulsion plants, Theodore Rockwell for general technical advice, and Milton Shaw for surface-ship propulsion. Mandil and Panoff had worked for Rickover during the war, while Rockwell had been at the commission's Oak Ridge laboratory in Tennessee when Rickover recruited him in 1949. Shaw came from Oak Ridge the following year. For officer assignments and liaison with the navy, Rickover looked to Captain James M. Dunford, a Naval Academy graduate. Both Rickover and Dunford had been part of that first small group of officers the bureau had sent to Oak Ridge after the war to learn reactor technology. Some men were to remain in the program for decades, among them Jack C. Grigg who worked on reactor controls and electrical systems, Alvin Radkowsky, chief physicist, and Howard K. Marks who, among other assignments, handled submarine fluid systems. Commander John W. Crawford, Jr., and Commander Edwin E. Kintner, both Naval Academy graduates, served in headquarters and in the field. Crawford was Rickover's representative at the Newport News Shipbuilding & Dry Dock Company, while Kintner was nuclear-power superintendent at the Mare Island Naval Shipyard.

Rickover also had some new and very promising personnel upon whom he would come to rely over the next decades. Lieutenant Commander David T. Leighton and Lieutenant William Wegner were from the Naval Academy. Leighton was project officer for the two-reactor submarine plant for the *Triton* and its prototype as well as the two-reactor plant for the frigate *Bainbridge*. In December 1957, Wegner was in the first few months of serving as the field representative at the Ingalls Shipbuilding

Corporation, Pascagoula, Mississippi. In later years Wegner and Leighton, along with Thomas L. Foster, a graduate of the Naval Reserve Officers Training Corps who entered the naval nuclear propulsion program in 1963, were the three individuals upon whom Rickover leaned most heavily for advice on policy.

Under Rickover's hard-bitten leadership the Naval Reactors organization had been hammered into an effective team, but that did not mean that they saw things from the same perspective. They argued with Rickover and with each other. Their length of service in Naval Reactors and the technical knowledge they had acquired combined to produce a strength and competence that their counterparts in the navy and the commission often lacked, because turnover in personnel in these organizations was higher and the technical objective was not so tightly focused. The two laboratories also contained individuals who had won Rickover's respect and confidence.

The two titles that Rickover held reflected the dual nature of Naval Reactors. In the commission he was chief of the Naval Reactors Branch, one of six technical branches in the Division of Reactor Development. The director of the division reported to the general manager, the chief executive officer of the five-man commission. In the navy, Rickover was assistant chief of the Bureau of Ships for Nuclear Propulsion and reported to the chief of the bureau. The bureau was that part of the navy responsible for the design, construction, and procurement of the navy's ships and for their maintenance and repair. The chief of the bureau reported to the secretary of the navy, but strong forces were already at work aimed at abolishing the organization and erecting over its functions a more complicated hierarchy. To fulfill his obligations to see that the navy operated its nuclear ships safely, Rickover had unusual authority: he reported directly to the secretary of the navy and on nuclear propulsion could deal with anyone in the navy.[11]

Rickover

Rickover arrived at his office about 8:00 o'clock each morning except Sunday, carrying an old leather briefcase filled with papers and books. He sat in a battered swivel chair behind a worn desk piled high with documents and reports, pads of paper, jars of pencils, and two telephones. A table—partly covered by newspapers, magazines, and books—and a few chairs completed the roster of furniture, except for the bookcases. These lined every available wall space and were crammed with books—mostly biographical but with a comfortable smattering on philosophy, government, engineering, and education, as well as a few classics of English literature.

No one doubted that Rickover ran the nuclear propulsion program.

Throughout the day and into the evening he worked. His telephones were often busy with calls between him and his field representatives, contractors, officials in the commission, the navy, the Department of Defense, and congressional leaders and their staffs. Across his desk flowed a torrent of papers and reports that he scanned, noted, and marked for attention. Frequently he called for members of his staff, or often they came to his office to report and seek guidance or a decision. At times the sessions were calm, but occasionally they became violent shouting matches, the sounds of which would carry down the corridors. Rickover had his office soundproofed. While it kept noise out and noise in, usually he worked with the door open.

In an outer office four women struggled—sometimes desperately—to cope with the constant telephone calls and flow of papers. Here, too, was an aura of simplicity in the desks that had seen better days, old safes, wooden cabinets—and more bookcases. Occasionally Rickover emerged from his own room to joke, tell a story, or play a raucous prank. From his own office staff he insisted upon and got loyalty, discretion, and long hours of work. Beneath a surface of informality flowed a strong current of discipline.

Rickover brought an unusual background to his work. Born 27 January 1900 in Makow, Poland, then under Russian rule, he entered the United States six years later with his mother and sister to join his father. The family moved to Chicago's West Side after a few years in New York. The neighborhood was poor but not a slum. Unlike most of his grade school classmates he continued his formal education. By working afternoons and weekends as a Western Union messenger boy, he was able to help support his family and still attend high school. American entry into the First World War, the expansion of the navy, and the political influence of an uncle combined to give him a chance to enter the Naval Academy in June 1918.

He barely passed the entrance examination. Aware of his weak background, he studied every possible moment. By deliberately avoiding any activity that would call attention to himself, he was not harassed as much as some other Jews. Each year his class standing improved: at his graduation in 1922 he stood 107 out of a class of 540.

His first sea duty was on the West Coast in the *La Vallette*, a destroyer commissioned after World War I. By working hard, he became the youngest engineer officer in the squadron only a year after leaving the academy. He liked navy life, finding none of the annoyances and irritations that had marked Annapolis. In January 1925 he reported on board the battleship *Nevada,* where he served first in the division that controlled the firing of the guns and then as electrical officer in charge of all the ship's electrical equipment. In June 1925 he was promoted to lieutenant, junior grade. Already he had established the characteristics that were to mark his career: intense interest and energy in doing his work and in achieving results, and an almost contemptuous disregard for the niceties of naval protocol.

He left the *Nevada* in 1927 to spend the next two years studying electrical engineering at the postgraduate school at Annapolis and Columbia University. Columbia greatly influenced him. Heretofore he had largely depended on memorization—emphasized at Annapolis—and practical experience for results. At the university he discovered and learned the importance and fascination of engineering analysis.

In 1929, after receiving his master's degree in electrical engineering, he requested submarine duty. Eager to get ahead, he thought that part of the navy offered the best chance for early command. From the New London submarine school he was assigned to the *S 48*. The years were not pleasant, although he became executive officer and qualified to command submarines. It was not the crowded and cramped quarters, the constant dampness from the sweating bulkheads, or the lack of privacy that bothered him; it was his inability to fit in. A senior lieutenant in June 1928, he was slightly older and more senior than most officers entering the submarine service. In addition he was, after Columbia University, intellectually lonely. When the *S 48* took part in a scientific survey of terrestrial gravity, he thoroughly enjoyed his contact with the two scientists, becoming almost a different man. But his service in the S-boats taught him a great deal, particularly about the sensitivity of those ships to the forces of nature. Even the movement of one man from a forward to an after compartment required adjusting the trim of the ship.

Beginning in mid-1933 he spent two years assigned to the office of the inspector of naval material. Stationed at Philadelphia, Pennsylvania, his job was to make sure that the material manufactured for the navy met specifications and schedules. In addition he drew upon his work at Columbia and his experience in the *Nevada* and *S 48* to revise the Bureau of Engineering manual chapter on storage batteries. As a labor of personal interest he translated *Das Unterseeboot*, a study on submarine warfare by Admiral Hermann Bauer, chief of staff, 1st Submarine Flotilla before World War I and commander, submarine flotillas until the summer of 1917, Imperial German Navy. Rickover's purpose was threefold: to gain a reputation, to learn German, and to make available to the United States Navy the thoughts of its defeated enemy on a most important professional subject.[12]

During the next two years he was assistant engineer officer of the battleship *New Mexico*. The chief engineer was content to leave Rickover in charge. In a period of intense engineering competition throughout the fleet, the standing of the *New Mexico* shot upward from sixth to first place among the battleships and held that position for two consecutive years. Rickover reduced fuel-oil consumption in every conceivable way—a key factor in achieving the standing. Not only did the main propulsion plant operate at peak efficiency, but he drastically cut down the expenditure of fuel oil for such purposes as distilling fresh water, providing heat, and generating electricity. The New Mexico was cold (once officers wore over-coats in the wardroom) and dark, but its engineering force, enthusiastic and zealous in competition, continued to seek more faucets and shower-heads to turn off and more light bulbs to unscrew.[13] Rickover trained his officers thoroughly, insisting that they know every part of the machinery spaces, calmly accepting mistakes and errors when honestly acknowl-edged, and giving each man as much responsibility as he could handle. Three of the young ensigns who served under him in the New Mexico made flag rank.

Promoted to lieutenant commander on 1 July 1937, he was sent to China for his first and only command, the minesweeper Finch. He was disheartened when he saw her—she was dirty and in poor shape. To improve her condition he worked himself and his crew hard. The men spent long hours chipping away rust and covering the scraped areas with anticorrosive paint—a bright orange—which had to dry thoroughly before it could be covered with navy gray. On the China station where so many foreign ships were gathered because of the Japanese-Chinese conflict, appearances were considered important. In this respect the Finch failed to measure up.

Increasingly aware that his progress along the normal course of ad-vancement might be difficult, in October 1937 he took a step that changed his entire career. In 1916 Congress had enacted legislation authorizing a few officers to specialize in engineering. Designated as "engineering duty only" and usually known as "EDOs," these men could never become eligible for command afloat; instead they worked on the engineering aspects of the design, construction, and maintenance of ships. Several factors had prompted Rickover to apply. Only a few officers bore that designation and they were an elite group. Fleet engineer officers who had witnessed his achievements on the New Mexico urged him to apply and promised their support. Finally, retirement as a commander was virtually assured. This was not the case for seagoing officers; at higher ranks the navy had more officers than it could promote, and those not selected were forced to retire. The most important reason was his growing love of the kind of engineering he had experienced on the La Vallette, Nevada, and New Mexico, and at Columbia.[14]

Detached from the Finch in October 1937, he became assistant pro-duction officer at the Cavite Navy Yard, located just southwest of Manila, Philippine Islands. As in previous jobs, he brought to his work an energy and industry that contrasted strikingly with the somnolent atmosphere. Years later an officer assigned to a destroyer that was overhauled at the yard credited Rickover by name with the excellence of his work, which enabled the ship to meet the brutal demands of the early years of World War II. Aware that he was living in a time and in an area undergoing great change, Rickover traveled widely, visiting in particular the Dutch East Indies and Indochina, often going third class from one point to another to better observe local life. In May 1939 he left Cavite, traveling across India and Europe to report to Washington to the electrical section in the Bureau of Ships.[15]

Rickover reported to the bureau at a time when the outlook for peace, in his own mind and that of many officers, was bleak. Already the president and Congress had provided funds for expanding the navy. Several types of ships, from battleships and carriers down to fleet auxiliaries, were under design or on the building ways. The electrical section had the bureau's responsibility for the maintenance and installation of electrical equipment. Beyond these broad terms were such diverse activities ranging from electrical propulsion to searchlights. Rickover expanded the section rapidly, adding new subsections—among them degaussing, minesweeping, equipment design, and procurement.[16]

He had been in charge of the electrical section for about one year when the Japanese attacked Pearl Harbor. By plans he worked out, the electric propulsion plants for the badly damaged *California* and *West Virginia* were reconditioned. The two battleships were able to return to the United States earlier than expected under their own power for rebuilding, modernization, and eventual return to action. While most sections of the bureau delegated design functions to field offices and confined themselves to administering contracts, the electrical section kept control of its technical work and took on additional areas such as infrared signaling and mine locating. The section and its contractors developed cable which, as it ran from one ship compartment to another, would not leak water from a flooded to a dry space. They devised a casualty power system consisting of portable cables and fittings so that the crew of a damaged ship could supply electric power to fire pumps, antiaircraft guns, steering gear, and other vital light and power circuits. They designed and developed improved circuit breakers and higher temperature-resisting insulation for wiring. Finding some components fabricated from a material that gave off a poisonous gas when burning, the section developed a new material that soon became standard for shipboard electrical equipment.[17]

Rickover studied every damage report and visited every ship he could that had suffered battle damage. He discovered that the effects of shock on equipment—especially electrical equipment— was far greater than had been expected. New and more powerful mines introduced since the beginning of the war might cause limited damage to the hull but render auxiliary machinery and the electrical equipment useless. Rickover fought vigorously and successfully for a major shock-test program.[18]

The growth of personnel reflected the pressure and increase in responsibilities. In 1938 the section had 23 people; when Germany surrendered in May 1945 the total had reached 343. Not all were officers or civil servants, for Rickover had persuaded and cajoled major contractors to loan him some of their brightest young engineers. Some of the best he later prevailed upon to become part of Naval Reactors or a major contractor organization. The administrative techniques he derived for the electrical section were to form the basis for those that he was to use to run Naval Reactors and the naval nuclear propulsion program.[19]

With every sign pointing toward victory in the war, the challenge of his duty in Washington lessened. Promoted to commander on 1 January 1942 and captain on 26 June 1943, he believed he could increase his chance of attaining flag rank by service overseas. He received a first-rate assignment—command of the industrial base being built at Okinawa to repair ships damaged in the final assault on Japan. After visiting other installations in the Pacific, he arrived at Okinawa on 20 July 1945. Less than a month later two atomic bombs brought the war to an end. In November he closed the base and returned to the United States.

A Career in Atomic Energy

At the end of the war, with the navy shrinking drastically as it converted to a peacetime routine, Rickover faced an uncertain future. On the headquarters staff of the Nineteenth Fleet from December 1945 to May 1946, he advised and inspected the officers and men who were inactivating ships. In Washington the Bureau of Ships was selecting a handful of officers and civilians to go to Oak Ridge, Tennessee, one of the major installations of the Manhattan Engineer District, which had built the atomic bomb. There Rickover and the others would join engineers from industry in learning the rudiments of reactor technology. No one knew when—or whether—it would be possible to build a nuclear-powered ship, but the navy had to have its own personnel familiar with the technology.

Arriving at the Tennessee site in June 1946, he placed himself in charge of a small group of naval officers. With him taking full part, they studied, attended lectures, and wrote reports. In many ways the next years were confusing and frustrating. The newly formed Atomic Energy Commission was inexperienced and overwhelmed with the magnitude of its responsibilities, among which naval propulsion did not stand high. For its part the navy was uncertain who it would place in charge of its share of the effort. The lack of direction allowed Rickover to take important steps at Oak Ridge and at Schenectady to lay the groundwork for naval propulsion projects. By hard work and skillful maneuvering, Rickover came to head the joint effort.[20]

He was an experienced and mature officer. Most of his sea duty had been spent in practical engineering, down in the engine-room compartments, where through the din and roar he learned to catch the sound of machinery slightly out of adjustment and to feel from the vibration of the outer casing that some hidden component was not running true. He was aware of the stresses upon machinery from the motion of a ship in a heavy sea. As head of the electrical section, he had run a major program, becoming thoroughly familiar with procurement and production problems and knowing firsthand the facilities and officials of some of the nation's largest industries. In his career he had taken every opportunity to learn and to assume responsibility.

He set a hard pace for himself, as well as for the few but growing number of engineers who became members of Naval Reactors, and for the contractors. He laid down two principles: engineering—not science—must dominate the program, and he and his engineers—not contractors—would make the technical decisions. So much had to be done. Metals and materials had to be tested for their behavior under prolonged irradiation, the reactor had to be designed to operate safely and reliably, and components had to be developed and fabricated to unprecedented standards. Initially, Naval Reactors developed two types of reactors for naval propulsion. One was the pressurized-water type for the *Nautilus;* the other was the sodium-cooled reactor type for the *Seawolf.* In both approaches Rickover followed the same strategy: a land prototype to contain an actual reactor propulsion plant arranged as if it were in a submarine. By developing the prototype and the ship reactor concurrently, he saved time and kept his objectives clear. Construction of the prototype for the *Nautilus* began in 1950, and the ship was laid down in 1952. Construction of the prototype for the *Seawolf* began in 1952, and her keel was laid in the next year.[21] In operation the pressurized-water reactor was to prove superior for naval ship propulsion.

During the first years of the decade he was in trouble. In July 1951 and July 1952 the navy passed him over for promotion to rear admiral. Under regulations he would be forced to retire in 1953. To an outsider the situation was puzzling. *Life, Time,* and the *New York Times Magazine* had featured stories on naval nuclear propulsion and its leader, and from every indication the navy through Rickover was successfully carrying out a most difficult technical project. To retire the man in charge did not make sense. The navy explained that other captains were better suited for promotion to the very few openings for rear admirals and that it had a number of captains well qualified to assume leadership of the program.

Without doubt, Rickover had created enemies during his career. Often scathing in his comments about the shortcomings of others and contemptuous of social niceties required in official life, he could be cutting and abrasive, leaving behind him resentment for remarks that were burned into memory. The promotion struggle reached the press and Congress. To prevent the lawmakers from overturning the promotion system and because a good many officers believed Rickover deserved promotion, the navy gave in. On 1 July 1953, Rickover was selected for rear admiral.[22]

From that time on, ties between Rickover and Congress were very close. As one nuclear ship after another—beginning with the *Nautilus* in January 1955—went to sea, Rickover won a reputation with Congress of a man who got things done, and the naval nuclear propulsion program was recognized as one of the most efficient enterprises in the government.

The Machinery of Government

Getting a nuclear-powered ship into the navy's annual construction program involved a number of laborious steps. Although details of the procedures changed over the years, the parts played by the executive branch, Congress, and the major departments remained much the same. The steps described below summarize the procedures of a later period— that during which Robert S. McNamara was secretary of defense. During those years Rickover and Naval Reactors fought some of their most bitter battles.

The navy had first to convince itself that it needed the particular ship in question. Because there were never enough funds for all that should be done, the navy had to choose what it required most. Upon this subject strong and able officers, along with civilian officials, could differ sharply. At some point the chief of naval operations, the highest-ranking military officer in the navy, and the secretary of the navy, the chief civilian, had to decide.

The shipbuilding program they proposed had to be reviewed and approved in the office of the secretary of defense. Three officials were critically important. They were the assistant secretary of defense (systems analysis), director of defense research and engineering, and the secretary of defense. The position of assistant secretary of defense (systems analysis) was established in 1965, although the function had been carried out since Secretary of Defense Robert S. McNamara took office in 1961. The assistant secretary provided quantitative estimates of requirements and performed cost-effectiveness studies to determine which among several possibilities for achieving a given purpose would cost less. His advice was important on the numbers of existing types of ships in a proposed construction program as well as on the first of a new type. The director of defense research and engineering, a position established in 1958, supervised all research and engineering in the Department of Defense.

He had to be convinced that the navy was justified in requesting funds to develop, for example, an advanced nuclear propulsion plant. The final decision belonged to the secretary of defense, one of the most important figures in the government and the president's principal advisor on defense issues. It was the secretary's responsibility to recommend to the president what the defense budget should contain.

Early in each calendar year the president submitted his budget (first scrutinized by his own budget office, which frequently held its own hearings) to Congress. Within the legislative halls and office buildings, congressional committees, each charged with a certain area of responsibility, held hearings. For the navy, the House and Senate Armed Services Committees examined the proposed budget, heard witnesses, and in time proposed legislation authorizing the expenditure of funds. The House and Senate Appropriations Committees, also holding hearings, drew up legislation appropriating funds. The armed services committees settled their differences on authorization bills in conference, and the appropriations committees also resolved their disagreements on appropriation legislation in conference. Each house accepted the conference compromise, passed the legislation, and sent it to the president for his signature.[23]

For a ship to be propelled by a new type of reactor, the situation became even more complicated. The Department of Defense identified a requirement for a new reactor. The Atomic Energy Commission included the development item in its own budget, won approval from the president, and defended it before the Joint Committee on Atomic Energy. Because the new plant would drive a navy ship, the two armed services committees and the two appropriations committees were also interested.[24]

The process did not lend itself to neat textbook progression. What the executive branch placed in its budget the legislative branch could delete, and what the executive branch omitted the legislative branch could add. Moreover, with what one house decided the other could disagree. Every phase offered opportunity for the fine art of politics. In this context the great strength of the naval nuclear propulsion program was its product: the propulsion plants were superb.

Technology At Maturity

At the end of 1957 it was possible to see the naval nuclear propulsion program moving into a new age. With the submarine, the power plant, and the cruiser, the technology developed by the effort was being applied to three different areas. To a certain extent the date is arbitrary, for not all were at the same stage. The *Nautilus* had completed its famous initial sea trials in January 1955. Since that time the ship had broken record after record for lengthy submerged voyages at high sustained speeds, and the navy had already begun to build its fleet of nuclear-powered submarines. The Shippingport Atomic Power Station would begin to deliver significant amounts of power in early 1958, but the *Long Beach* would not undergo initial sea trials until July 1961. Nonetheless, 2 December 1957 has a certain convenience for historical and analytical purposes.

The date marks a stage in which pressurized-water reactor technology had gained momentum and was challenging other technologies already in use. Individuals charged with maintaining the defense of the nation could choose between nuclear or diesel-electric submarines and between nuclear and oil-fired surface ships. For utility executives the issue was nowhere near as clear-cut, but by demonstrating the feasibility of civilian nuclear power, Shippingport was hastening the day when they, too, could consider whether a nuclear or an oil- or coal-fired power plant best met their needs. Although the *Nautilus* was demonstrating over and over again that a nuclear-powered submarine could revolutionize naval operations, significant consequences followed, among them the type and location of support facilities, the training of adequate personnel, the number of ships needed, and the timing of introducing new developments into the fleet. Construction of nuclear-powered surface ships raised many of the same questions. Whether surface ships or submarines, decisions had to be made against an ominous background of a growing Russian naval strength. For civilian power the problems differed, but stripped to their essentials, they bore a strong resemblance. The existence of such disputes is nothing new in the introduction of a technology and is in itself a strong argument that pressurized-water reactor technology had reached maturity.

Controversy over nuclear propulsion for the navy was virulent. One major factor was cost. The initial cost of nuclear-powered ships was higher than their conventionally powered counterparts. That fact alone forced hard decisions and painful compromises upon those officials and officers who had to match resources against worldwide national commitments. But in addition there was Rickover. Chiefs of naval operations, secretaries of the navy, secretaries of defense, and presidents served their terms and departed, but Rickover remained. Only in Congress were there individuals who continued in office for comparable lengths of time. Strong ties developed between Rickover and key legislators on defense and atomic energy, enabling him to exert unusual and unparalleled influence in the introduction of nuclear propulsion into the fleet. He never forgot it was a relationship based on his record for producing excellent propulsion plants and their superb record for safe operation.

How he strove to maintain standards of technical excellence is the subject of the following chapters.

In the late 1950s, the Naval Reactors program developed a reactor plant called the S5W. As versatile as it was reliable, it powered a large number of attack submarines and all the Polaris ballistic-missile submarines. Inevitably, as naval technology advanced, the S5W would have to be replaced by a new reactor plant. The

CHAPTER TWO
Submarines

characteristics of those that would follow, the effects they had on ship design, and the timing of their introduction into the fleet, were subjects of vigorous and often acrimonious debates throughout the executive and legislative branches of the government.

This chapter traces the involvement of Admiral Rickover and Naval Reactors in the introduction of new propulsion plants and classes of submarines. It covers the years between the S5W of the Skipjack *and* Thresher-Sturgeon *attack submarines and Polaris submarines on the one hand, and the S6G for the* Los Angeles *class of fast attack submarines and the S8G for the Trident missile submarines on the other. It also follows the story of the research vessel NR-1, which although out of the mainstream, occupied much time and attention of Naval Reactors during this period.*

The surfaced submarine drove steadily through the calm waters of Long Island Sound. Her bow raised a wave that crested and, breaking into foam at the conning tower, tumbled over the rounded hull to join the turbulent wake scarring the following sea. If her appearance was sinister, it was also beautiful. Every line spoke of grace, power, and speed. If a criterion of art is singleness of purpose and exclusion of all that is extraneous, the ship was a masterpiece. Even the conning tower, with the diving planes extending like fins from both sides, had been thinned down so much as to be called a sail. Passing between channel buoys, the submarine proceeded up the Thames River to the yard of the Electric Boat Division of the General Dynamics Corporation at Groton, Connecticut. On the morning of 10 March 1959, the *Skipjack* (SSN 585), under Commander William W. Behrens, Jr., was returning from two days of sea trials. Although the highest attained submerged speed could not be known until after the calibration of instruments and analysis of their reading, no one in the ship doubted they had set a new record.

Within the submarine, officers, men, and representatives of several contractors were elated. Grinning broadly, Behrens remarked, "Give her a Simoniz job and I'll buy her." Rickover spent the last few hours at sea going over the test results, consulting with his engineers, and as was his practice, signing letters announcing the successful completion of the trials to senior officials in the Atomic Energy Commission and the navy, congressional leaders, and those individuals in the propulsion program who in their work had ignored hours of the day and days of the week. "I want you to know that I appreciate all that you have done in helping to create this revolutionary submarine." At 10:30 tugs nudged the *Skipjack* into her berth. A crane swung a gangplank between the dock and the submarine, and tired but enthusiastic men began going ashore.[1]

The S5W reactor—the first of its kind—had operated faultlessly.* Because a vendor could not meet the standards for the main coolant pumps, the trials had been delayed almost a year, but those furnished by Westinghouse worked perfectly. Electric Boat had carefully prepared the ship, painting and smoothing the hull so that it was almost impossible to see a weld and, shortly before the submarine left the yard, putting her in dry dock for a final inspection and cleaning. For the first time, nuclear propulsion and a streamlined hull had been combined in a submarine.[2] Beneath the surface the *Skipjack* had behaved like an airplane, banking and rolling as she maneuvered at high speed.

For Rickover, his engineers, and the Bettis Atomic Power Laboratory operated by Westinghouse, the trials were the culmination of an effort that went back a surprisingly few years. In September 1955 Rickover had authorized the laboratory to begin work on the S5W, and that October the Department of Defense had officially asked the commission to develop the plant. Based upon the experience of the S2W for the *Nautilus* (SSN 571), Naval Reactors and the laboratory had found a land prototype unnecessary. Even before the trials of the *Skipjack,* the navy was heavily committed to the plant. Already five yards had laid down six attack and five Polaris submarines the S5W would drive. It was a mature and sophisticated organization, including Naval Reactors, the laboratories, and the shipyards, which had produced a reactor that was to become the mainstay of the underwater fleet and which would eventually propel six

---

*Reactor plants are designated by two letters and an intervening number. The first letter stands for the type of ship and the second for the designer. The number is the model of that type of plant by that designer. Hence the S5W was the fifth model of a submarine reactor designed by Westinghouse. See Appendix IV—Reactor Plant Designations, Prototypes, and Shipboard Plants (August 1985).

*Skipjack*s, fifty-one *Threshers* (including various subclasses), the turbine-electric-drive submarine *Glenard P. Lipscomb*, (SSN 685), and forty-one Polaris missile submarines.[3] With these ships—especially the *Thresher* class—the navy had an unchallenged superiority over any rival.

At some time the superiority would end; at some point the ships would become obsolete. When that occurred would not necessarily be determined by age and hard use but also by other factors, perhaps a striking advance in one or more of the technologies basic to the ship, or the need to meet an increasing threat to national defense.

An example of the rapid shift from one class to another for technological reasons could be seen by comparing the *Skipjack* and the *Thresher* (SSN 593). The first was laid down on 29 May 1956; the second, one day short of two years later. The *Thresher* submarines, although somewhat slower, could dive deeper, had better-placed sonar, and were quieter.[4] Variations occurred even within a class, for incorporating more equipment in later ships added to their weight and decreased their speed.

Never absent from the minds of those who designed the ships, planned the building programs, and voted the funds was the threat of a potential enemy. They found the rapid growth of the Russian submarine fleet alarming. In diesel-electric submarines the Soviet Union had an undersea force far greater than the Germans possessed at their greatest strength during World War II. The same energy poured into the construction of nuclear-powered submarines could lead to numbers the United States could not match. For that reason maintaining technological superiority was essential.

No one had an easy answer to the question of when the strength and capability of a potential enemy warranted bringing a new class to the fleet. No one could give a definitive response to the question of when innovations in one technical field were of sufficient magnitude to begin the design of a new class. No one had a firm reply to the question of whether it was best to introduce a new class by several ships at once and gain an important advantage over a rival, or to build one ship to assess the advances against the test of operational experience that might prevent costly changes to others of the class. Whatever the grounds of the decision, it was most unlikely that the United States would lay down any non-nuclear combat submarines.

Design and development of new reactor plants was the domain of Rickover, Naval Reactors, and the Atomic Energy Commission. The organization he had created—his headquarters, the laboratories, the shipyards, and the contractors—had a magnificent record of success and was anxious to exploit the new technology, sometimes at a rate that conflicted with the positions of the Navy Department and the office of the secretary of defense. The prestige of the program and its chief stood high among the members of Congress who authorized and appropriated funds for the navy. They listened to Rickover, not only on developing nuclear propulsion plants but upon other subjects, among them the strength of a possible aggressor and the size of the undersea fleet needed to counter it.

Philosophy of Conservatism

Rickover was conservative, and his engineering philosophy drew fire from some elements in the Bureau of Ships, some officers in the navy as well as the Department of Defense, and in private companies. They were convinced that it had to be possible to develop reactors that were more compact and weighed less and did not cost as much as the pressurized-water type. From this perspective, pressurized-water reactor technology, even with its striking success, was only a stage in the development of nuclear propulsion, roughly analogous to the position of aircraft-engine technology before the introduction of the jet. The argument ran that if Rickover could not proceed beyond pressurized-water reactors, perhaps others could.

A report of a panel on naval vehicles to the committee on undersea warfare of the National Academy of Sciences stated the issue. Forwarded in July 1962 to Admiral George W. Anderson, Jr., chief of naval operations, the report gave high priority to the development of lighter-weight propulsion plants. Bluntly, the panel declared its reservations about the part of Naval Reactors in the effort.

> [It] represents a larger body of practical experience in supervising the design and construction of reliable nuclear power plants, whether for propulsion or for energy generation, than any other comparable group in the nation. Their judgment has often been vindicated by experience when the weight of expert technical judgment was on the other side. Nevertheless, we must also recognize that a group which has pioneered and grown up with a new and successful technology is not usually the group best qualified to take the next major step forward, once this technology has come to maturity.[5]

Nothing came of this or other attempts to break the hold of Naval Reactors on the development of nuclear propulsion. A document drawn up in 1961 and kept in the Naval Reactors historical files gave Rickover's position. Design criteria for naval nuclear propulsion plants rested heavily upon operational experience. Submarines propelled by pressurized-water reactors had voyaged beneath Arctic ice and tropic seas as well as taking part in naval exercises and undertaking lengthy patrols. Even the shock of combat had been simulated by tests in which explosives were set off near ships underway. Lessons from operational submarines and land prototypes were factored into new designs and, if possible, into modifications of existing plants.

Reactor plant safety was the single overriding design criteria. Against this standard Rickover tolerated no compromise. Closely associated with safety was reliability: the ship had to be assured of the constant availability of propulsive and auxiliary power. The criteria called for spare capacity to be designed into the propulsion plant systems and components, and the plants were designed to allow the crew to carry out preventive maintenance and repairs. Finally, all the nuclear submarines had an independent means of propulsion for emergencies.

Rickover's approach was based upon his own service in submarines, his years at sea as a practical engineer, his experience as head of the electrical section in the Bureau of Ships during World War II, and his knowledge gained in developing nuclear propulsion. He remembered an early design proposed by the commission's Argonne National Laboratory that did not provide enough heat-transfer surface; he recalled a reactor control system proposed by Bettis that was far too complicated to be reliable, let alone allow adequate maintenance. He had studied and rejected plans which did not allow components of sufficient mass to transmit the designed energy. He opposed automation, particularly in systems that were vital to safety. Such controls were not absolutely reliable, and a failure, especially if undetected, could lead to a severe accident. He was willing to spend money for prolonged testing of equipment and systems. If something worked well, an engineer had to argue cogently and persistently to get approval for a design change. Having given his approval, Rickover followed the matter closely, prodding, advising, criticizing, and helping. To him nothing outweighed the acid test of actual operation.

He had not settled on the pressurized-water approach or continued its development without keeping abreast of other concepts. He had developed two sodium-cooled reactors—the *Seawolf* and its prototype—which proved inferior to the pressurized-water approach for ship propulsion. In 1956 Knolls Atomic Power Laboratory, operated by General Electric, had investigated an organic cooled and moderated reactor for a destroyer. Hoped-for advantages disappeared under close scrutiny and experiment. The next year Bettis completed a study of a gas-cooled reactor and an associated gas-turbine plant for a destroyer, but the approach had no savings in weight and perhaps, under certain circumstances, had an increase in hazards. The laboratory had also studied a boiling-water reactor and concluded it had serious drawbacks for naval propulsion. Naval Reactors continued to keep informed of these and other reactor approaches, as well as of progress in various areas of reactor technology. Pressurized-water reactor technology was not standing still, and there was no reason to think that other concepts were doing so.

His conservative philosophy influenced his approach to the design and development of propulsion plants that would propel a submarine faster. Speed was important because it gave a commanding officer a greater chance to engage, break off action, or evade an enemy. An increase in speed was not easy to attain, for the greater the velocity of a body through the water, the greater its resistance. Consequently, gaining a fraction of a knot at high speed demanded far more power than achieving the same fraction at a lower speed. The rate a ship moved depended not only upon the propulsion plant but upon hull design and other features associated with naval architecture.

Silence was also important in underwater operations. Sound betrayed a submarine. By other means of detection, the submerged ship was almost impossible to find. Visibility beneath the surface of the sea was so limited as to play only a small part in antisubmarine warfare. Radar, so effective in surface and air operations, was useless in water because the range of high-frequency electromagnetic radiation was merely a few feet. On the other hand, sound traveled vast distances under water, as far as 2,000 miles under certain conditions, and its behavior was hard to predict. Temperature, pressure, and salinity influenced its transmission, and these factors differed in various parts of the world, from one body of water to another, and even from one time of day to another. Despite all the variables, one thing was certain: postwar development had made it possible to hear a submerged submarine at long distances.

Roughly speaking, ship noises came from the movement of the hull through water and from the vibration of machinery, particularly those components having reciprocating or rotary elements. Steam plants, with their turbines, pumps, valves, and auxiliary systems, presented many problems. Of these, reduction gears were among the most important. Beautiful pieces of machinery, their function was to reduce the high rotary speed at which the turbine was most efficient to the much slower rotary speed that was best for the propeller. No matter how well made and how well engineered, they remained a major source of noise. Silencing a propulsion plant was a never-ending battle; no sooner was one component dampened than another took its place as the major culprit. Quiet operation was an essential element of a submarine force that had to depend on excellence instead of numbers.[6]

Rickover did not have a free hand in quieting propulsion plants. He was responsible for the entire propulsion system of a ship that was the first to use a particular reactor. For later ships he had cognizance only over the reactor and its associated systems; other parts of the bureau had responsibility for the remaining portion. Here they could make changes that Rickover might question and argue against, but which he had to accept as long as they did not affect the operation of the reactor. The division of responsibility allowed the introduction of some methods of quieting he accepted only reluctantly, but once they had proved their effectiveness, he became a strong advocate.

To sum up, a ship was the integration of several technologies, and a change in one affected the others. In many of these—sonar and weapons, for example—Naval Reactors had little direct influence. On the other hand, the size, weight, and power of a propulsion plant were strong factors determining the overall characteristics of the ship.

Silence—The *Tullibee*

Naval Reactors' effort to develop a quiet nuclear propulsion plant began early—even before the sea trials of the *Nautilus*—with the hunter-killer submarine *Tullibee* (SSN 597). The purpose of the hunter-killer was to ambush enemy submarines. As the mission of the ship was seen in the early 1950s, speed was less important than silence. By substituting an electric-drive system for reduction gears, Rickover hoped to reduce noise. In this approach a generator ran an electric motor. Varying the speed of the motor would achieve the same result as the reduction gear, but there would be a penalty; the electric propulsion system would be larger and heavier than the components it replaced.

On 20 October 1954, the Department of Defense requested the Atomic Energy Commission to develop a small reactor for a small hunter-killer submarine. The ship was meant to be the first of a large class. The commission, wishing to broaden industrial participation in the program, assigned the project to Combustion Engineering, Incorporated. The S1C prototype achieved full power operation on 19 December 1959 at Windsor, Connecticut. Congress authorized the *Tullibee* in the 1958 shipbuilding program, Electric Boat launched the ship on 27 April 1960, and the navy commissioned her on November 9 of that year. The ship was not small; although her tonnage, beam, and draft were less than the *Skipjack,* her length was greater. By the time the *Tullibee* was in operation, she was about to be superseded by the *Thresher* class.[7]

Superficially, the *Tullibee* appeared to be one of the blind alleys into which technological evolution occasionally wandered. Nevertheless, the ship was important. To get good reception, her sonar was placed far forward, as far away from the ship's self-generated noise as possible. Her torpedo tubes were moved aft into the midship section and were angled outward from the centerline—features that were incorporated in the *Thresher* submarines.[8] Finally, electric drive worked well; the submarine was the quietest nuclear platform the Navy had.

Silence—the Natural-Circulation Reactor

To many engineers in Naval Reactors, the natural-circulation reactor (S5G) was a more promising line of advance. In principle, the concept was simple. Two different temperatures in portions of a system set up a current, for the cooler, more dense water forced the warmer water to rise.

By using natural circulation to the maximum extent feasible, it might be possible to eliminate the large reactor coolant pumps. As the heat-transfer medium would still be water kept under pressure, the reactor would be a pressurized-water type. Beneath the attractiveness of the theory was one major uncertainty: no one could be sure that the system would operate at sea where a ship was subject to rolling and pitching.[9] To Rickover the natural-circulation reactor was attractive primarily because it promised simplicity. The silencing features were less important.

Bettis had completed preliminary thermal and hydraulic calculations for a small natural-circulation reactor by September 1956. Over the next two years the laboratory reached the stage where it was necessary to run tests to make sure that data taken from forced-circulation plants were valid for a natural-circulation system. Two years later Rickover brought Knolls more strongly into the effort, but with Bettis maintaining its main role. When the Department of Defense asked the commission on 3 September 1958 to develop and test a natural-circulation reactor for submarine propulsion, Rickover began pressing the commission for funds to undertake research, procure long lead-time items, and begin construction of a prototype at the Commission's National Reactor Testing Station in Idaho. In all his prototypes Rickover insisted that each consist of an actual reactor and propulsion-plant components arranged as if they were in a ship. The new facility would follow the same pattern, but added one important innovation. To make sure that the concept would work at sea, the prototype would simulate the motion of a ship in operation.[10]

The commissioners demurred. They were willing to order components that took a long time to manufacture, but they thought the technical data were too uncertain to commit themselves to prototype construction. To get an independent assessment, they called for a review panel. In two meetings in September, Naval Reactors and Bettis won agreement that even if detailed answers were not available for all the technical and engineering problems, enough was known to warrant going ahead. Unable to resist tweaking the commission, Rickover observed in February 1959 that in the past he had been criticized for not developing new reactors: now that he was doing so the commission was holding him up. The commission placed the item in its budget, and Congress duly authorized and appropriated the funds.[11]

With the project gathering momentum, Rickover called a meeting between Naval Reactors and Bettis. On 11 May 1959 he made sure that everyone understood the ground rules. Design had to be kept simple. He would approve no development work unless it was absolutely necessary. He wanted the principles of personal responsibility followed. In practice this meant he would not tolerate anyone hiding behind a title or organizational chart. That applied to his own engineers as well: technical recommendations had to be accompanied by the names of the people proposing them.[12]

Late that summer the work at Bettis received an unexpected blow. Without informing Rickover, Westinghouse took several key personnel out of Bettis and assigned them to a new laboratory to work on projects for the space program. Rickover was furious. He argued that the company was siphoning off individuals who had been carefully trained at unique government facilities. Furthermore, the company was casually breaking the ties of confidence that had been painstakingly erected between Naval Reactors and the laboratory. Loudly and vehemently he protested to the commissioners and the joint committee. Even though Westinghouse rescinded the action, Rickover took the natural-circulation project away from Bettis and assigned it to Knolls.[13]

Commander Willis C. Barnes, a veteran of the program and acting manager of the Schenectady Naval Reactors Operations Office, on 29 August 1959 officially requested Knolls to proceed urgently with the design, development, and construction of the prototype. Bascom H. Caldwell, the General Electric general manager of the laboratory, drew men from the submarine advanced reactor (S3G/S4G) and the destroyer reactor (D1G/D2G) projects and began a recruiting and training program.[14]

As Rickover saw it, Westinghouse had attempted a sharp and deadly thrust at a principle upon which the program was based. Although Naval Reactors made the technical decisions, it depended upon the laboratories for proposals, recommendations, advice, and work. He frankly considered the laboratory personnel as "his" people. He admitted—reluctantly—the right of the company to shift its personnel, but not unilaterally and not without offering qualified replacements for approval who, if they performed satisfactorily, agreed to serve for a number of years. Almost overlooked in the dispute was the swiftness with which General Electric and Knolls picked up the work—an indication of the high competence of both laboratories and their ability to work together.

May 1961 saw the beginning of construction of the S5G prototype with completion planned for 1963. The schedule had already slipped a year when Rickover briefed senior naval officers on 2 July 1962, urging them to include a natural circulation reactor submarine in the fiscal year 1964 shipbuilding program.

He told them that, in some respects, he considered the project's drive for simplicity a return to earlier engineering concepts. If the machinery was less efficient then, it had the compensating virtues of ruggedness, reliability, simplicity, and easy maintenance. These qualities were vanishing as the navy was installing complicated high speed machinery, often beyond the abilities of officers and men to maintain, in order to squeeze the most energy from every ounce of fuel oil. Rickover's strategy for reducing noise was to get rid of equipment; if that was impossible, to turn it off during quiet operation; to slow down the component; or to redesign the particular equipment to get rid of rotating components.

Naval Reactors was analyzing the design of the fluid systems in the propulsion plant and scrutinizing every valve to see if it could be eliminated. At the briefing Robert Panoff, assistant manager for submarine projects, went into details of how these aims were being achieved and I. Harry Mandil, chief, reactor engineering branch, explained the S5G reactor core. If the navy considered noise reduction important, Rickover summed up, it should get the ship to sea as soon as possible for evaluation—possibly by 1966.[15]

Much of his talk dealt with his engineering philosophy. In this context he brought into the discussion his full-scale wooden mock-ups, a device he had begun with the *Nautilus* and continued to use, as he was doing now with the S5G. They were fascinating. Built largely of cardboard and wood, they made it possible to trace every pipe in its actual size, see the location of every valve, and observe the overall arrangements of components. Rickover took a great deal of time in his frequent inspections of a mock-up, often remaining transfixed while he visualized the motions that men would have to make to maintain or repair equipment. The mock-up even showed whether lighting was sufficient to read instruments. Each component received a tag; one if its position was approved, another if it was still under consideration. The full-scale mock-up exposed problems that would not have been apparent from blueprints or a model. It allowed shipyard personnel—such as welders—to be sure they could perform their job in the ship wearing full working gear. One curious phenomenon that Naval Reactors field representatives had to watch for: frequently carpenters and woodworkers fell into the error of making their work more finished than it need be. After a mock-up had served its initial purpose, it still remained useful. If a plant had to be modified later, its mock-up could be used in training people, making sure procedures were correct, and ensuring that operations could be carried out as planned.[16]

Panoff, calling upon other Naval Reactors engineers, was applying to the entire S5G propulsion plant the same meticulous scrutiny and hard analytical thought that had served Naval Reactors so well in previous reactor development. They spoke of giving the design of each component "a fresh look" and "wiping the slate clean."[17] It was evident, however, that at this stage Rickover was still more interested in simplification and reliability than in noise reduction.

The schedule for the prototype continued to slip. Some of the problems were inherent in any large construction project with rigid specifications. In early 1963 Electric Boat was completing construction of the hull, beginning to install the piping for the reactor system, and building some of the off-hull facilities. The work showed the need for improved communications between the Idaho site and Groton, for speeding up the training of engineers, and for establishing a new and more vigorous system of quality control. The unique characteristics of some major components were leading to a host of manufacturing problems, and it took time to work out and bring into effect new fabrication techniques. Stringent testing of development items, if time consuming, was proving valuable and forcing some rethinking and many design changes. And there were other factors, among them a fire in a vendor's plant that destroyed a number of components.[18] The loss of the *Thresher* in April 1963, although the cause could not be associated with the reactor plant, gave renewed impetus to the drive for simplicity and reliability.

Toward the end of 1964 Knolls reported that the core was in the final stages of assembly. On 22 January 1965 a strike stopped the testing of the main engine at the General Electric plant at Lynn, Massachusetts, adding delay to a schedule already in trouble. March saw the reactor fueled, and May the arrival of the main engine at the site. Finally, on 12 September 1965 the reactor reached criticality and, to the satisfaction of Naval Reactors and Knolls, within close agreement with prediction. Months of testing followed, not only to determine the actual characteristics of the plant in physics, fluids, and hydrodynamics, but also for noise reduction. Power range testing began on 13 November, and once again operation verified theory. Manned by a Navy crew, in June 1966 the prototype successfully completed a simulated voyage from New London, Connecticut, to London, England; over twelve years earlier the nearby *Nautilus* prototype had made a similar run. A long series of crucial tests were begun in August: they determined that a natural circulation plant would in all probability work well at sea.[19]

Electric Boat laid the keel of the *Narwhal* (SSN 671), authorized by Congress in the 1964 program, on 17 January 1966. Launching came on 9 September 1967 and commissioning on 12 July 1969. Although the natural-circulation reactor was successful, the navy built no more ships of that class; that step was not necessary to incorporate the advances into future submarines.[20]

Quest For A New Attack Submarine—First Phase

The keel of the *Narwhal* had not been laid when Rickover, alarmed at growing evidence of an increasing Soviet submarine force, began to press for a new class of attack submarines to replace the *Thresher*. He was not alone on this issue; it was obvious a new class would be needed at some time. The ship he envisaged would have the speed to escort fast surface-strike forces and convoys, protecting them against hostile submarines, and to seek out and destroy enemy missile submarines. The escort function was new and one that provoked an adverse reaction from the officers of the surface fleet. Communications between a fast-moving surface ship and a fast-moving submarine were difficult, but he did not think they were insuperable.

He broached the concept to the House Appropriations Committee on 6 March 1964, and on April 6 he asked Electric Boat to begin the design of a high-speed submarine. When Robert S. McNamara, secretary of defense, visited Bettis on 24 April, Rickover urged him to request the commission to develop the reactor. McNamara, although finding the idea interesting, was unwilling to go that far. Rickover turned to the navy. He discussed the results of the Electric Boat study with Rear Admiral Eugene P. Wilkinson, director of the submarine warfare division in the office of the chief of naval operations. The first commanding officer of the *Nautilus* and an experienced submariner, Wilkinson knew well the value of speed. In July he agreed to request a study within the navy for a high-speed submarine.[21]

But a second project was beginning to take shape. In July 1964 Rickover motivated the ship characteristics board of the office of the chief of naval operations to ask the Bureau of Ships to study a submarine of the *Tullibee* type—an electric-drive ship—but with greater speed. Since its commissioning in November 1960, the *Tullibee* had performed well. In September 1964 Admiral David L. McDonald, chief of naval operations, asked for another study of an electric-drive submarine, one that would have enough speed to escort surface forces and incorporate a new sonar.[22]

On October 20, the two projects—no more than studies at this point—came together at Electric Boat. The Bureau of Ships asked the yard to begin design of propulsion plants of both types—a reactor and an electric-drive system, and a reactor with turbine and reduction gears.

For a time the high-speed and the electric drive projects traveled on parallel courses.

In March 1965 Knolls and Electric Boat and Naval Reactors agreed on the general features of the high-speed plant. On the surface all appeared normal, but troubling currents were stirring beneath the calm. Rickover was uneasy over his relationship with Electric Boat. From the beginning of the nuclear propulsion program, the company had been the lead yard for every new nuclear submarine propulsion plant: that is, it did the development work and prepared the detailed designs that other yards would follow. Electric Boat did good work, but Rickover never liked to depend upon a single source. Further, he suspected some costs were too high. Going to a second source was his answer.

Of all the yards, both navy and private, he thought Newport News could best assume the additional responsibility. It was already the lead design yard for nuclear propulsion plants for aircraft carriers and already experienced in building nuclear-powered attack and Polaris submarines. On 24 September 1965 he transferred the lead yard responsibilities for the propulsion plant of the fast escort submarine to the Virginia company.[23] As far as the propulsion plant was concerned, Naval Reactors, Knolls, and Newport News were the heart of the team.

During these same months the electric-drive project was running into trouble. It was becoming clear that the ship could not be fast. Changes in her military characteristics promised to reduce the speed even further. Nonetheless, the approach could be supported for the advances it might contribute to silencing submarines. The ship characteristics board wanted to place the submarine in the 1967 construction program. In forwarding additional information, Rear Admiral William A. Brockett, chief of the Bureau of Ships and his senior, Vice Admiral Ignatius J. Galantin, chief of naval material, agreed. On 8 January 1966, McDonald turned to Paul H. Nitze, secretary of the navy, to get support for the ship.[24]

An exceedingly experienced official, Nitze wanted to know why the navy wanted a submarine that was not as fast as the *Thresher* or *Sturgeon* classes—the latter, also driven by an S5W, was closely allied to the *Thresher* ships. The *Sturgeon* was only a few weeks away from launching, and sixteen other ships of her class were in various stages of completion. Into their design and construction had gone all the latest techniques of silencing. At this time it seemed to him far better for the navy to increase the number of *Sturgeon*s than to develop a new submarine. He must also have been aware that some officers were questioning the need for the ship. Wanting to make a better case before he saw McNamara, Nitze asked for more information.[25]

McDonald replied on April 4 that for the next two decades submarine silencing would remain one of the most crucial areas of development in undersea operations. The *Sturgeon* was a considerable advance, but the navy was nowhere near its ultimate goal and had to explore every avenue. Rear Admiral Edward J. Fahy, now chief of the Bureau of Ships, forwarded some technical data. He thought that if the electric-drive submarine proved superior in quietness but slower than the latest attack submarines, the navy would have reason to develop a more powerful electric-drive system. But only by getting the ship to sea could the navy assess its qualities.[26]

Men disagreed vehemently over the ship. It was becoming clear that the electric-drive ship would be one of a kind. Opponents argued that it offered nothing in speed, operational depth, or armament. Even for its advances in silencing, the ship was not worth building, for the bureau was developing several new techniques that looked promising. If Rickover wanted to try out electric drive, let him do so in an experimental ship.

Rickover rejected all the arguments. The sonar required more power than any existing propulsion plant could supply and needed more space than any existing hull design could provide. Because quiet operation was the most critical area of antisubmarine warfare, the navy should go ahead with the electric drive. He refused to try out the electric drive in an experimental ship, for he was convinced that only through operational experience could the plant be evaluated.[27]

Somehow the deadlock had to be broken. As director of defense research and engineering, John S. Foster, a young physicist, formerly director of the commission's weapon laboratory at Livermore, California, followed the controversy closely. On 10 May 1966 he sought a compromise. On the one hand, he proposed that the navy build one of its currently authorized submarines emphasizing noise reduction. In this ship he would place the electric-drive system, even if all the studies were not completed. Although the ship might not have the operational capabilities of other submarines, nonetheless, he expected that it would be an effective combat unit. On the other hand, he would push ahead with all research and development so that in three years the Navy would be able to build even quieter submarines.[28]

Foster's views on the electric drive paralleled those of McDonald. The chief of naval operations still hoped to get the ship in the 1967 program, although his chances were slim since that effort was already well along on its congressional road to authorization and appropriation. To gain more support for the ship, he approved some changes in the proposed operating depth and torpedo capacity. On May 19 he asked Nitze to raise the subject with McNamara. Before taking that step Nitze wanted information on funding, the availability of shipyard space, and the impact on the submarine construction program. With these questions answered, Nitze saw McNamara on July 1. The secretary of defense wanted an analysis that compared the proposed gains from other approaches with those expected from the electric drive.[29]

On 23 August Nitze furnished the data and made a strong case for the ship. In the opening paragraph of his argument he wrote:

> Because of the large number of Soviet submarines, anti-submarine warfare is one of the most important and difficult problems facing us. We believe our latest classes of nuclear submarines are superior and quieter than Soviet nuclear submarines. . . . We must exert every effort further to silence our submarines or we will lose the qualitative advantage we now hold.

He proposed funds for long lead-time procurement in fiscal year 1967 and for the rest of the ship the next year. In the final months of 1966 the Department of Defense and Congress gave their approval to placing the entire ship in the 1968 program.[30]

Sonar development was also influencing the fortunes of the high-speed submarine. The Bureau of Ships study begun in September 1965 showed that a ship based on the characteristics of the *Thresher-Sturgeon* classes and with the new sonar would be too slow. Consequently, McDonald cancelled that effort and in August 1966 called for a new study for a class of submarines that would be fast and able to serve as escorts as well as carry the advanced sonar. The chief of naval operations wanted to begin construction of the class in the 1969 building program.[31]

Rickover thought the plan was risky, for it committed the navy to building a class of ships when two critical components—the propulsion plant and the sonar—were still under development. It would be far more prudent to build one ship as a fast escort submarine with the high-speed propulsion plant, and construct the other ships in the 1969 program as *Sturgeons*. In this way the navy would have a fully proven propulsion plant ready when the sonar was available, and in the meantime would be adding more *Sturgeons* to its strength. And if the navy obtained funds for advance procurement, he could have the new plant ready for a ship in the fiscal year 1968 program.[32]

Rickover's plan was conservative, but it also meant that the design and development of the propulsion plant was the driving force behind the introduction of new types of submarines. As a result it clashed directly with another design philosophy. Called concept formulation, it had been devised by the office of the secretary of defense and was based upon constant evaluation of critical areas of design and technology as well as the potential enemy threat. One sentence illustrated the philosophy: "[It] provides first effort to establishment of a total system design procedure utilizing an integrated subsystem approach."[33]

Under concept formulation Rickover and the nuclear propulsion program would have less influence over the design and scheduling of new classes. Those functions would now be carried out by numerous studies of the enemy threat and the status of the various critical areas of technology. Concept formulation bore all the marks of a procedure that could lead to one study after another, each entailing delay. It was a system likely to diffuse responsibility.

For support Rickover turned to the senior officers of the submarine force. In a carefully prepared presentation on 7 March 1967, he painted a bleak picture. The navy did not have a strong submarine design organization nor did American industry have a strong submarine design capability. Recent organizational changes within the navy and the Department of Defense had only made the situation worse by adding the weight of an elaborate hierarchy. Blame for this state of affairs for the most part rested squarely upon the submarine force—it had not been able to adapt to the technological changes after World War II and could not cope with the increasingly complex organization of the defense establishment. Into this vacuum others had stepped. In the final analysis, he was their most effective voice in Washington. They should work to see that the navy established a submarine design capability; they should personally think through the characteristics needed in new submarines; and they should work with him to get new submarine projects. They should support trying out promising new concepts in one-of-a-kind submarines. The alternative was to do nothing or commit large numbers of combat submarines to unproven ideas. The navy had to evaluate new concepts now so as to have a firm basis for designing future nuclear submarines.[34]

At the end of the month Rickover considered the possibility of having distinct types of submarines. To Admiral McDonald he pointed out that the navy could not continue to design attack submarines to perform all missions; the result would be large and slow submarines that could do many things but few of them well.[35]

Rickover had more confidence in the future of the high-speed submarine when Admiral Thomas H. Moorer replaced McDonald. The new chief of naval operations agreed that the navy should construct a fast submarine as quickly as possible. In anticipation, Rickover defined the role of Naval Reactors. His organization would be directly responsible for the entire nuclear propulsion plant, propulsion plant control, and associated components. More specifically, these areas included reactor-plant fluid systems, steam-plant fluid systems, reactor-plant control and electric systems, as well as overall propulsion-plant control, steam-plant control and electric systems, reactor compartment arrangements and compartment containment requirements, shielding arrangements and details, reactor-plant water chemistry, steam-plant water chemistry, engine-room arrangements, ship-service turbine generators, and main condensers. His group had to concur in any proposed system or component design, structure, or arrangement that in any way affected propulsion-plant requirements, space, or shielding design.[36]

Rickover knew it was too late to get the ship into the 1968 program. He did not like what he heard of a new plan: fund advance procurement in 1969 and the rest of the ship in 1970. Although this arrangement was not unusual, it had its dangers, for dragging out the funding for two years gave a chance for political alliances to shift. Because Naval Reactors was at that stage where it had to get firm commitments from vendors, Rickover wanted complete funding in 1969. As the budget for that year was drawn up, it looked as if he had lost.[37]

The center of opposition was the office of the director of defense research and engineering. James K. Nunan, assistant director, analyzed the possible courses of action, and on 17 December 1967 sent his conclusions to Foster. In brief: the navy ought to get on with the job of designing a new class of submarines and stop working on one-of-a-kind ships. Within two years the navy could make a decision on facts that would probably lead to a considerably smaller, quieter, and faster ship requiring a smaller crew, using micro-miniaturized electronics, and costing far less money than the submarine Rickover was advocating. Funding that ship would be spending money "for the wrong boat, at the wrong time, for the wrong reasons."[38]

Electric Drive in Trouble

The electric-drive submarine was also in trouble, even if it were in the 1968 program. The difficulty was procurement. It was not the reactor that was at issue, for it was to be a modified S5W, but the design and manufacture of the main propulsion equipment for the electric-drive system. For that assignment Naval Reactors wanted Westinghouse or General Electric—not Bettis or Knolls, but the parent companies. In Naval Reactors' experience, Westinghouse tended to excel in meeting production schedules and General Electric in advanced development. Whichever company undertook the task would do so under a subcontract to Electric Boat. In the last months of 1965 the shipyard had requested that the two companies submit feasibility studies. General Electric replied that because of prior technical commitments it would not do so. In mid-1966 Westinghouse undertook the study, completing it in February of the next year.[39]

Design and manufacture of the main propulsion equipment was the next step. General Electric refused to bid, again citing its workload and prior commitments. Electric Boat wanted Westinghouse to redesign the ship-service turbine generator originally to be supplied by General Electric. Westinghouse could not do so for lack of technical information, but was willing to submit a bid for the remainder of the equipment. Once again, General Electric was the focus of the controversy.

On 8 March 1967 Rickover telephoned Donald E. Craig, vice president and general manager, General Electric Power Division, under whose responsibility the design and manufacture of the equipment would fall. Rickover had known Craig for years, had argued with him and come away with respect. Citing the importance of the project to national defense, Rickover asked Craig to reconsider General Electric's position. When the company official replied he could not, Rickover pointed out that the matter would have to come up before the highest levels of the government.

For several reasons General Electric held firm. It believed that the components would be difficult and expensive to fabricate. The company saw no market. It was convinced that the electric-drive ship would never be more than one-of-a-kind and that the technology for the propulsion system components would never have any commercial application. Already in a strong position, the company brought up another point. No specifications could ever be drawn up to cover every aspect of a highly complex technical system. In the past it had seen Naval Reactors tighten existing specifications and impose new ones, and by these changes take up time and facilities as well as add to the cost. If General Electric was to take on the assignment, it would insist that Naval Reactors limit its activities. Rickover fought hard, but the company would not move. Through arduous negotiations, a compromise was reached that satisfied him. The company was not setting a precedent, and General Electric signed a letter contract with Electric Boat on 22 August 1967.[40]

Although the major procurement problem had now been settled, the electric-drive project was in trouble on another front. The office of the secretary of defense questioned the value of the ship for submarine warfare. Nitze, now deputy secretary of defense, foresaw significantly increased cost. Worried about these and other issues, Foster also wondered if the ship was worth building.

Force Levels and the Russian Threat

As 1968 opened, the electric-drive and high-speed submarines, both projects for which Rickover was fighting hard, were mired in controversy. On January 3 he learned that McNamara had decided not to build the high-speed ship.[41] The decision was part of a long and bitter struggle with nothing less at stake than the future of the American undersea fleet.

Shortly after entering office McNamara found that establishing the number of attack submarines the navy needed was an exceedingly complex problem. Into its determination had to go various aspects of antisubmarine warfare, such as the effects of weapons delivered from the surface and air, the capabilities of allies and, above all, the comparison of American and Russian submarines. At his direction the navy undertook a number of studies of antisubmarine warfare, among them Cyclops I, II, and III, the latter forwarded to McNamara on 3 August 1966. The navy found them useful in bringing out some aspects of undersea warfare, but not for setting attack submarine force levels.

Because the navy could not come up with a force level based on an analysis satisfactory to the office of the secretary of defense, Doctor Alain C. Enthoven, assistant secretary of defense (systems analysis), undertook to do so by using the factors the navy had incorporated in its studies, by applying the law of diminishing returns, and taking into account the total antisubmarine warfare picture. Enthoven frequently used the employment of missiles to illustrate what he meant by diminishing returns. If one missile had a 50 percent chance of hitting a target, a second missile would raise that probability to 75 percent and a third to 87 percent. Each additional missile added less and less to the probability of hitting the target. At some point the increased effectiveness was not worth the cost of an additional missile. Determining the force level of attack submarines was admittedly far more difficult. Many more factors were involved, but the philosophy was the same.[42]

The results of the analysis, completed in 1967, were stunning. They showed American technical superiority so great that in war the Russians would lose about twenty-five submarines to every one the Americans lost.[43] From this conclusion it followed that the navy needed only a few more submarines than those already in operation, under construction, or authorized. Then construction could stop. These findings Enthoven forwarded to McNamara.

The secretary accepted them although the navy did not. At the end of 1967 he set the total approved strength of the submarine attack force at 105 ships. Of these, sixty-nine were to be nuclear-powered and thirty-six diesel-electric. As it was inconceivable that Congress would authorize any more diesel-electric submarines, the question focused on the nuclear ships. As of 1 January 1968, thirty-two were in commission, twenty-two were under construction, and another eleven authorized but not laid down. These totaled sixty-five. With the addition of only four more, the Navy would reach its full strength, and construction would stop.[44]

To Rickover and Naval Reactors the means by which the force level had been determined was systems analysis at its worst and most dangerous. As a student of history, Rickover was aware that at the outset of two world wars, the submarine had been grossly underestimated and had nearly been the weapon of victory. Some of his engineers, if not versed in history, were experienced in the intractable and unpredictable nature of technology, and they were convinced that so much had to go so well to obtain the postulated results. Not enough weight had been given to the rate of American obsolescence nor to a much greater speed of Russian progress than anticipated. Although they had little hard proof to back their contention, Rickover, Naval Reactors, and some officers believed it dangerously possible that the Russian submarine threat was growing far more swiftly than expected by those who had set the force level. Certainly the sheer size of the Soviet submarine program, demonstrating it held a high military priority, had to be a serious worry.

Finally, the termination of construction would be devastating. Probably at some future date it would be necessary to begin building again. But by that unspecified time all of those elements—construction yards, manufacturers, vendors, laboratories, and the trained manpower essential to develop, design, and build submarines—would be dulled by idleness or drawn into other markets from which it would be difficult if not impossible to recall and retrain them. Seldom if ever had a major part of national defense been subjected to so cavalier a proposal.

On 5 January 1968, less than a week after the secretary of defense had turned down the high-speed submarine, a handful of Americans with access to highly sensitive intelligence information learned suddenly, dramatically, and irrefutably that Russian nuclear submarines were far faster than anyone thought. That day in the Pacific a Russian *November* class submarine, in following the nuclear-powered aircraft carrier *Enterprise*, revealed a far greater speed than expected. Even more devastating, the *November* ship was not a new class. The Russians had put thirteen into service between 1958 and 1964.[45]

Quest for a New Attack Submarine—Second Phase

To Rickover, the high-speed submarine as a prototype for a new class of submarines was the only response to the astonishing Russian capability. He began a renewed campaign by turning to Paul R. Ignatius, secretary of the navy since 1 September 1967. An expert in military procurement, Ignatius had graduated with a master's degree in business administration from Harvard and had formed his own management consulting and research firm. He had a good background, for he had served as assistant secretary of the army (installations and logistics), under secretary of the army, and just before taking his new position, had been assistant secretary of defense (installations and logistics). He had another qualification of great importance. Like Nitze, Ignatius could work with the McNamara management system.

Rickover wanted Ignatius's support to procure long lead-time items for the propulsion plant of the high-speed submarine. His work was at the stage where he needed vendor commitments. Two factors were making this hard. Manufacturers could see all the uncertainty in the naval nuclear propulsion program and at the same time study predictions of a huge growth in commercial nuclear power. Vendors committed to nuclear propulsion would be less able to compete for commercial work. From all the information reaching him, he was certain that it was folly to wait for the development of a new sonar. Already the estimated weight, space, and power requirements were greater than those expected, and reasonably firm information on these points was probably some years off.

Writing to Ignatius on 15 January 1968, Rickover listed the objections to the ship that he had heard: he was stifling the development of new, smaller, and higher-powered reactors; the high-speed submarine was too large; it cost too much; and the navy had too many one-of-a-kind submarines. Finally, the navy should wait a few years until concept formulation could be completed. Angrily he concluded:

> It seems incredible to me that supposedly responsible Department of Defense officials could believe that studies such as Concept Formulation can result in a viable submarine with the required military characteristics and which at the same time is significantly smaller, cheaper, faster, and quieter

than the design proposed by those in the Navy knowledgeable in and responsible for submarine design.

The objections I have listed above may be the reasons why the High Speed SSN was turned down. If this is so, I consider it indefensible for those occupying technical positions in the Department of Defense to abuse their subordinates making capricious technical recommendations—recommendations which are not based on engineering facts and experience but on wishful thinking.[46]

Three days later Foster's office issued a draft of a development concept paper it had prepared for navy comment. The document stated that the high-speed submarine project had been deferred until concept formulation studies on high-speed attack submarines had been completed.[47]

Rickover and his engineers read the three-inch-thick draft report—and at that, some of the appendixes had not yet arrived—with great concern. The ship was to be propelled by two natural-circulation reactors (S5G), possibly redesigned for simplified control. Savings in weight were to come from lighter gears and increased propulsion efficiency from counter-rotating propellers. Finally, the ship was to have a hull as close to the ideal form as possible.[48]

The design made immense demands. The S5G reactor had achieved initial criticality on 12 September 1965, but the *Narwhal* was well over a year from commissioning. How the plant would behave at sea was unknown, although the operation of the prototype promised well. Two reactors on one submarine had been tried out successfully on the *Triton*, but two S5Gs with redesigned controls, some remotely operated, was a very different thing. Lighter gears were hazardous, for fewer parts of the propulsion system received greater stress or strain. Counter-rotating propellers were also highly developmental. They had been tried on the *Jack* (SSN 605), but were not a success. True enough, the counter-rotating propellers of the concept formulation ship were based on a different approach, but, nonetheless, it was a huge step forward. Finally, there were suggestions of substantial reductions in the crew. How these were to be accomplished was anything but clear.[49]

For the concept formulation ship so much had to go so well. A failure in any of the major areas could mean expensive delays at best, or a ship unable to meet its design specifications at worst.

On 23 January 1968, the arena shifted from the corridors of the Pentagon and the Naval Reactors offices at National Center in Arlington, Virginia, to a congressional hearing room. L. Mendel Rivers, chairman of the House Armed Services Committee, called a meeting to order to hear the testimony of Captain James F. Bradley, Jr., Naval Intelligence Command, and Rickover and two of his senior staff, William Wegner and David T. Leighton. A stunned committee saw satellite photographs of Russian building yards, heard estimates of how far the Russians were outspending the Americans on submarines, and finally the startling disclosure of the speed of a *November* submarine. In the next few weeks the Joint Committee on Atomic Energy and the Senate Armed Services Committee heard similar versions of the threat. All committees were strongly pro-Rickover, a fact placing advocates of the concept formulation approach on the defensive.[50]

The proposal of the joint committee after hearing Rickover on February 8 was evidence of his strength. The usual pattern for funding first-of-a-kind nuclear propulsion plants called for the commission to undertake the nuclear development work and the navy to procure the steam-plant components. On February 28 the joint committee asked the Bureau of the Budget to reprogram some of the commission's research and development funds to speed up the work on the propulsion plant.[51]

As director of defense research and engineering, Foster was carrying the brunt of the struggle to thwart the high-speed submarine project championed by Rickover. At the end of February, Foster declared he was willing to approve a high-speed submarine, provided the ship made a certain speed. Rickover refused to be drawn; he would do his best, but he could not guarantee the result.[52]

Foster could have gotten little hope from an *ad hoc* panel that Admiral Thomas H. Moorer, chief of naval operations, had established on the recommendation of Rickover. Under Rear Admiral Philip A. Beshany, director, antisubmarine warfare division, office of the chief of naval operations, the panel of high ranking officers—all of whom were experienced in nuclear attack submarine operations and design—met on 1 March. Their purpose was to assess the configuration of the high-speed submarine, evaluate missions, and examine the proposed equipment from the standpoint of space, weight, ruggedness, reliability, and maintenance. Foster had every reason to expect the panel to favor the Rickover ship.[53]

On March 19 Foster appeared before the preparedness investigating subcommittee of the Senate Committee on Armed Services. To a group of hostile legislators he tried to explain that he was not certain that the Rickover submarine was the one to build. For that matter he was not certain that the Russian threat had been sufficiently understood: it was so great that the navy had to be sure that it was making the right decision. For that reason he wanted time for more studies, among them the concept formulation submarine. He hoped to make a decision by June.[54]

Members of the committee were hardly rubber stamps, to be easily manipulated by Rickover or anyone else. But they were confronted with a choice between Rickover, a man they had known for years and whose achievements they respected, and a senior official in the McNamara defense establishment calling for time for further studies. They chose Rickover.

Nor did the *ad hoc* committee have any difficulty in reaching its conclusions. Although its report was not due until July 1, the panel on 30 April 1968 declared that their work supported the decision of Ignatius and Moorer to place the ship—it would have hull number 688—in the 1970 program. Although further study would lead to some refinements, they would not change the finding that the high-speed submarine advocated by Rickover was the ship to build. To get the speed, the panel sought every possible way to save weight. One method was to decrease the depth the ship could reach; the *688* would not be able to dive as deeply as ships of the previous class.[55]

The electric-drive and the high-speed submarine came together again briefly when Foster considered combining the best features of each into one ship, a hope that quickly proved illusory. Rickover saw Ignatius on May 27 to make the points that both the turbine electric drive and the high-speed submarines should be built—the first to improve technology in noise-quieting, the second to develop a higher-performance attack submarine. Both were essential to keep the American submarine force ahead of the Russians. Foster, complained Rickover, was holding things up by his questions and his requests for studies.[56]

The next day Foster acted. By memorandum he asked Ignatius to consider once again whether the electric-drive submarine should be built: in any event, he did not want funds committed to it until the whole situation was clarified. As for the high-speed submarine, Foster wanted the issues on that resolved as well, and in the context of the 1969 shipbuilding program, a phrase that could be interpreted that its existence was also in jeopardy.[57]

Decisions

Even as Foster wrote his 28 May 1968 memorandum, the pressures for a decision on the high-speed submarine were growing more intense. The Senate Armed Services Committee under John Stennis on April 10 had recommended two submarines of the *Sturgeon* class for 1969 and provided funds so that one of the submarines in the next annual construction program might incorporate the higher performance characteristics. The House committee had not yet reported on its bill, but there was little doubt that under the leadership of Rivers it would call for a strong construction program and the development of new classes of submarines.[58]

In early June 1968, to get a better understanding of the need for speed, Foster and a few members of his office boarded the *Dace* (SSN 607) of the *Thresher* class. He had chosen the submarine because under Commander Kinnaird R. McKee she had achieved an outstanding record. The ship was to undertake various exercises with the *Shark* (SSN 591), a slightly faster ship of the *Skipjack* class, playing the part of a hostile submarine. During the event only the most skillful maneuvering and handling, as well as the high state of training of officers and crew, enabled the *Dace* to maintain a slight edge. While McKee was not certain what impression the two-day operation had made, he was inclined to think it had been favorable.

Later in the month Foster decided. He recommended that Nitze request advance procurement for a high-speed attack submarine in fiscal year 1969 and funds for the entire ship the next year. He would review an accelerated submarine research and development program to identify those elements that could be incorporated into the ship and later submarines. The high-speed attack submarine was no longer one of a kind: the navy was to begin a new class of attack submarines, the *Los Angeles* (SSN 688) class, with the goal of increasing the force level to 100 nuclear submarines. Of these, the *Skipjack* class would be the oldest.[59]

Foster had not yet decided upon the turbine electric-drive submarine. He was troubled by changes in the military characteristics of the ship and the estimates of increased costs. Although the navy assured him that his information was incorrect and misleading, he was uneasy.[60]

The quieting features could benefit later submarines, and the exceptionally low noise levels could make the ship especially valuable for surveillance and intelligence missions. There would be increased cost, but the navy was willing to drop a destroyer escort from its program and shift the funds to the electric-drive submarine. Finally, the design division at Electric Boat was already hard at work on the project. Yet he was not certain that the benefit of the electric-drive system was worth the cost: maybe it would be better to put the resources into the *Los Angeles* class.[61]

Foster could not ignore the impressive support for the ship. Moorer saw the electric-drive submarine as a fundamental engineering approach the navy had to explore. Rickover continued to argue that the navy needed the lessons it could learn from the ship. Foster was aware that over the years two chiefs of naval operations, McDonald and Moorer, and two secretaries of the navy, Nitze and Ignatius, had supported the ship. And in his memorandum of 10 May 1966 to Nitze (then secretary of the navy), Foster had placed himself on record as favoring the ship. Also, the pressure from the armed services committees and the Joint Committee on Atomic Energy was intense.[62]

Clark M. Clifford succeeded McNamara as secretary of defense in March 1968. Few individuals knew more about politics and defense than Clifford. Almost two decades earlier as President Truman's naval aide and then as his special counsel, he had been a chief architect in drawing up legislation designed to unify the armed forces. In later years as friend and counselor to successive presidents, he remained in close contact with defense issues. Clifford shared Foster's doubts and wanted time to study the matter. He was well aware of the bitterness of the dispute over the ship, and at one time he had to defend Foster and Enthoven publicly against the personal criticism they had suffered. He was worried about the cost of the ship, but he also knew of the political pressure. On October 25 he announced the Navy would go ahead with the electric-drive submarine.[63]

NR-1—a Different Submarine

During the turmoil over the introduction of new types of nuclear propulsion plants and new classes of submarines, Naval Reactors was also working on a nuclear-powered deep-submergence research vehicle. Postwar technology had opened the ocean depths as never before to manned research. In 1948 the British *Challenger II* discovered the Challenger Deep, at 35,800 feet the greatest depth known to man: in 1960 Jacques Piccard and Don Walsh in the bathyscaph *Trieste* reached its bottom. Other research vehicles of different types and characteristics also explored deep waters, but although these craft could reach great depths they could not stay down long or cover more than a very small area.

Rickover saw nuclear propulsion as a way around the limitations of battery-driven submersibles. On 23 November 1964, on a flight back from Schenectady, he questioned Mark Forssell, the project officer for prototypes and advanced development, on the different capabilities and uses of the growing number of deep-diving research vehicles. Thoroughly intrigued by what he had learned, Rickover assigned Forssell the job of pursuing the possibility of applying nuclear propulsion to the exploration of the oceanic depths.

In a few weeks Forssell, working with the Bureau of Ships' submarine designers, finished a rough draft of guidelines for a preliminary design study for the submarine and propulsion plant. Because the purpose of the vehicle was nonmilitary, he could apply somewhat different naval architectural design principles from those that governed combat submarines. It was unnecessary to take noise reduction into account, and he could accept reduced shock standards, although the increased depth capability demanded the use of higher-strength materials to resist the greater hydrostatic pressures. To keep the crew as small as possible, Rickover accepted centralized remote control and operating stations, but he would not permit automated controls to reduce manning requirements. Despite the changes his philosophy remained the same: no compromise in reactor safety or plant integrity. The preliminary design study Rickover assigned to Knolls.[64]

By January 1965 the Schenectady laboratory had determined that a small pressurized-water-reactor propulsion plant was feasible. To no one's surprise, the study showed that the nuclear research submarine would be larger than non-nuclear research submersibles. The reactor compartment had to be a certain size to provide for space and shielding to reduce radiation levels. Shielding posed a special problem; it was not only heavy, but its weight was concentrated in a small area.[65]

At some point Rickover saw Harold Brown, director of defense research and engineering. Brown gave his approval and also helped overcome resistance in the Navy. On 28 January 1965 Rickover and several other officers briefed Admiral McDonald. Without doubt the characteristics of the propulsion plant would dominate the design.[66] As he had in past projects, Rickover decided to limit development to the propulsion plant, depending upon conventional technology for the oceanographic equipment. Sometime before the end of March 1965—he was to recall a late evening at the end of a busy day—he suddenly realized the vehicle had no name. Promptly he chose NR-1. The letters stood for Naval Reactors, the number for what he hoped would be the first of a class.

In May he assigned various responsibilities to his engineers. In general they followed their usual assignments. Forssell became the project officer, coordinating the efforts of Naval Reactors and outside agencies and ensuring overall coordination. Tom A. Hendrickson had the same functions for all the technical aspects of design. He was also in charge of fluid systems as well as propulsion and ship arrangements. The two men worked closely together—for in their jobs was a healthy overlap—and depended upon other Naval Reactors engineers for special areas: Jack C. Grigg for electrical systems and components; Edwin J. Wagner for main coolant pumps and steam generators; William M. Hewitt for steam plant components; Philip R. Clark for reactor vessel, core, and refueling equipment and procedures development; Edwin C. Kintner for refueling operations; James W. Vaughan, Jr., for shielding and radiation; Alvin Radkowsky for reactor physics; William Wegner for reactor safety, personnel assignment, and training; and Kenneth L. Woodfin for fiscal matters.[67]

On 18 April 1965, President Johnson at his Texas ranch announced that the navy and the commission were developing a nuclear-powered research vehicle, with Rickover responsible for the design and development of the propulsion plant. That same year Congress authorized construction of the ship. With growing concern, Naval Reactors reviewed the design work at Knolls and Electric Boat. Too many changes had been made to keep the vehicle small and light. A proposed computer system that would control more than 40 percent of the reactor power was unacceptable; it was too complex and too developmental. Rickover tightened his reins, allowing no development where existing component design had shown successful military or commercial application. Anything more than minor modifications to a successful design had to receive the written approval of Naval Reactors. The same philosophy he carried over to other

parts of the ship; the hull and installed equipment were to be nondevel-
opmental and within the demonstrated state of the art.[68]

Later he was to doubt the wisdom of this decision. Although adequate
for operations lasting a few hours below the surface, most components
could not meet the demands of prolonged submergence. Procuring, testing, and inspecting such equipment as sonars, television sets, and lights
took time and added greatly to the cost.[69]

Electric Boat began erecting the hull on 10 June 1967. During his
frequent visits to the yard, Rickover always took time to inspect the ship—
some company officials believed he took an even greater personal interest in the NR-1 than he did in other projects. Her crew was to consist of
two officers, three enlisted men, and two scientists. Her operational depth
would allow her to explore the continental shelf. The small pressurized-
water reactor would drive two externally mounted motors with propellers and provide power to four ducted thrusters to give her maneuverability. Television cameras and viewing ports offered views of the bottom
and the surroundings. Rickover decided the NR-1 should have external
wheels so that she could crawl along the bottom. Having no combat
features whatsoever, she was to measure about 150 feet in length, 12 feet
in diameter, and when submerged displace about 400 tons.[70]

Trident

The Polaris fleet faced a problem similar to that of the attack submarine—
when should it be replaced by a new class? Between 10 December 1959
and 1 April 1967 the navy had commissioned forty-one of the ships—an
average of one every two months.[71] Although the rate of construction had
given the United States a missile system that was almost invulnerable and
impossible to destroy in a preemptive strike, there was another side to
the picture. It was block obsolescence. If the United States was to continue
to have a submerged ballistic-missile system, at some time it would have
to have a new class of ships. These would not only have to pass through
all the stages that separated the drawing board from the building ways,
but they also had to win the approval and support of the navy, the
Department of Defense, the White House, and Congress.

Several factors accounted for the amazing swiftness with which the
Polaris fleet was built. The status of three crucial areas of technology was
one important element. The S5W propulsion plant had already been
developed and the industrial base established for multiple production.
The hull was, with important modifications, available. A ship of the
Skipjack class was cut apart on the building ways and a missile section
inserted: it was the work of a very capable group of Electric Boat design
engineers under the leadership of William Atkinson. Only the missile
was uncertain. With superb skill Vice Admiral William F. Raborn and the

Special Projects Office and its contractors, vigorously backed by Admiral Arleigh A. Burke, chief of naval operations, developed the missile and its launching and guidance systems. Another important key to the success of the effort was the strong personal interest of Presidents Eisenhower and Kennedy and the leading members of Congress.[72]

The Polaris program was not static. The *George Washington* (SSBN 598) and her four sister ships were based on the modified *Skipjack* design. The five *Ethan Allens* were specially designed for their mission, while the thirty-one *Lafayette/Benjamin Franklin* submarines were fitted with quieter machinery. The missile was also improved. The *George Washington* went on its first patrol with the A-1 missile that had a range of 1,200 miles. The *Ethan Allen* (SSBN 608) was the first to carry the A-2 missile with a range of 1,500 miles. Eventually all but three of the fleet were fitted with the 2,500-mile A-3 missile. The last major change came in 1969 when the *James Madison* (SSBN 627) began the conversion to the Poseidon, a missile with the same range as the A-3 but with a multiple warhead that could be directed at different targets. Significantly, the navy did not attempt to convert the *George Washington* and *Ethan Allen* classes: they were too old. Three strands marked the history of the Polaris program: quieter ships, longer-ranged missiles, and obsolescence.[73]

Obsolescence and Russian capabilities affected all American strategic missile systems. On 1 November 1966 McNamara opened the entire question of future missile systems by calling for a comprehensive study on basing the weapons at sea, on land, or in the air. STRAT-X, which he received in August 1967, recommended four possibilities—among them an undersea long-range missile system, soon known from its initials as ULMS. Naval Reactors had nothing to do with STRAT-X, but for ULMS provided on request a cost estimate for an NR-1 plant and later for an S3W and an S5W plant. The Strategic Systems Project Office (formerly the Special Projects Office, which had developed Polaris) and other parts of the navy undertook a number of preliminary studies for ships with missile ranges of 4,500 and 6,000 nautical miles. Some of the submarines would be huge, going from 30,000 to 50,000 tons, compared to a little over 8,000 tons for a Polaris submarine. Two ways of carrying missiles were considered: external to the ship, which, among other possible advantages, meant a smaller hull; and internal and vertical as in the Polaris ship. Because some of the technical aspects of the external mode were risky, the navy chose the internal upright version. With an extremely long range missile the submarine would have a huge area in which to patrol and yet be within target range; it would even be possible for it to operate in the coastal waters of the United States. Consequently, neither speed nor the ability to dive deeply appeared essential.[74] Because the S5W was already developed, there was no need for Rickover to get involved at all. He had been kept out of the Polaris program, and the same situation might work out with ULMS.

Believing that ULMS was never going to become a reality, Rickover had little interest in the project. That situation changed because he found it was going ahead and because he had under development at Bettis a very high-powered reactor, but with no ship in mind for it. His thoughts turned to the new missile ship. The high-powered reactor would provide speed to give a better chance of arriving more quickly on station or breaking away from an enemy. It would incorporate the latest silencing features. A more powerful reactor would be safer. The principal danger he saw came from the momentum gained by a huge and heavy submarine: an accident while submerged could very quickly bring the ship to crush depth unless she had the power to check her descent quickly. The reactor would also provide a margin of power for any later installation of new equipment. But it would require a large ship.

Now taking Trident seriously, as the project was named, on 12 May 1969 Rickover met with Rear Admiral Levering Smith, head of the Strategic Systems Project Office and Rear Admiral Jamie Adair, commander Naval Ship Systems (formerly the Bureau of Ships). Together they represented the three basic elements of Trident—the missile, the ship, and the propulsion plant. In the Polaris program only the missile required a major effort; in Trident none of the three constituents was a given. The three men agreed that representatives from their offices would meet regularly to establish a close working relationship, but would not be authorized to make contractual arrangements or change organizational responsibilities. An unknown chronicler in Naval Reactors observed: "From this time on NR was heavily involved. . . ."[75]

On 28 October 1970 Admiral Elmo R. Zumwalt, Jr., who had succeeded Admiral Moorer as chief of naval operations, decided that a ship driven by the high-powered reactor and carrying twenty-four missiles should be presented to the secretary of defense for review. Zumwalt was not enthusiastic about the ship; a few days later he set the decision aside and asked for more studies. He also set up a panel of officers who had commanded nuclear attack and Polaris submarines to consider the need for speed. While he had a good idea of the response, it would be valuable and represent the views of the submarine force. As he anticipated, the panel concluded speed was essential for several reasons. Of these the one he found most impressive was the one for safety.[76]

The Strategic Systems Project Office proposed selecting one of two ships for study: one with a high-powered submarine reactor, the other with an S5W. Some individuals did not see much choice. Because the larger plant would require a bigger ship, which in turn would necessitate extensive and expensive alterations to shipyards, refitting facilities, and ship research and development, the smaller version was likely to be selected. On 19 January 1971 before John W. Warner, under secretary of the navy, Zumwalt, Smith, and several senior officers, Rickover attacked the manner in which the effort was being handled. To him the Strategic Systems Project Office was taking far too much upon itself. By April 29 the Trident ship had been more clearly defined: it would have either twenty or twenty-four missiles, and in either case a new reactor—the S8G—was to be developed. Although not requiring as large a hull or having the horsepower of the high-powered submarine reactor plant, it had much more power than the S5W.[77]

Nontechnical forces were also affecting the effort. In late 1970 and early 1971 Nitze, while negotiating with the Russians on strategic arms limitation, found them anxious to learn of American intentions on replacing Polaris. He believed a new missile ship would show American determination to maintain its nuclear strength and perhaps also give leverage to the talks. As time went by another factor intruded: Trident should be well along to prevent an agreement that might limit its development.[78]

By the latter half of 1971, the Trident program was moving forward. An S8G would propel the submarine, but Rickover had not yet been given the word to proceed. On June 22 Robert A. Frosch, assistant secretary of the navy for research and development, recommended the twenty-missile ship to Foster. On September 14 David Packard, deputy secretary of defense, approved proceeding with the C-4 missile, later renamed Trident I, which had a range of 4,350 nautical miles and which could be placed in the Polaris and Trident submarines. The step was an interim measure, designed to give the Polaris ships greater range until the Trident submarines became operational. Trident I was also a step toward Trident II with a range of 6,000 or more nautical miles. On October 6 Packard approved proceeding with the development of the propulsion plant. To a query from Packard, Rickover replied that the ship could be at sea in 1977 if all went well.[79]

So far the program was faring well in Congress, partly because it had the support of two fundamentally opposed groups. Some legislators, such as Members of Congress for Peace Through Law, saw in Trident a chance to reduce or replace other weapon systems: others saw the effort as an additional and more effective nuclear deterrent.[80]

The uneasy coalition did not last long. Not only was the estimated cost bound to be huge, giving cause for concern in a period of tight budgets, but the diplomatic scene was also changing. In May 1972 the United States and the Soviet Union reached an interim agreement on strategic arms limitation. Promptly two views of Trident emerged. Senator Lloyd M. Bentsen of Texas argued that the interim agreement removed the urgency of the effort. Therefore, it was possible to save money by delaying the initial deployment and by stretching out the building program. Furthermore, a longer period of construction would prevent costly mistakes, and national defense need not suffer because the Trident I missile with its greater range could be fitted into the Polaris submarines. His opponents read a contrary message into the interim agreement. Trident had to be accelerated before further negotiations foreclosed its development. A slower rate of construction would not save money, for increasing inflation would levy its toll. Above all, they believed a slowdown gambled with the nation's future.[81]

The two factions fought in 1972 when the navy requested funds to continue engineering of the Trident I missile; initiate ship design; and procure long lead-time items, mainly propulsion plant components, for ten Trident submarines. The navy planned to deploy its first ship in 1978 and the others at an annual rate of three a year. Bentsen, acting chairman of the subcommittee on research and development of the Armed Services Committee, proposed delaying the program for a year, except for missile research and development. In full committee the vote was eight to eight with Stennis as chairman breaking the tie in favor of funds to accelerate the effort. On the Senate floor Bentsen introduced an amendment incorporating the subcommittee's proposals to delay. He picked up a number of co-sponsors—Clifford P. Case of New Jersey, John Sherman Cooper of Kentucky, Alan Cranston of California, Philip A. Hart of Michigan, Howard E. Hughes of Iowa, Hubert H. Humphrey of Minnesota, Jacob K. Javits of New York, Edward M. Kennedy of Massachusetts, William Proxmire of Wisconsin, Adlai E. Stevenson III of Illinois, and later in the debate, William V. Roth of Delaware. These men, six Republicans and five Democrats, were national figures.[82]

The opposition fought back. Stennis of Mississippi and Strom Thurmond of South Carolina buttressed their case by pointing to the experience and qualifications of Moorer, Zumwalt, Smith, and Rickover. The "father of the nuclear submarine" received special attention. Thurmond declared, ". . . when we have his opinion that the Trident will be successful on the accelerated schedule, who is there to contradict him?" John O. Pastore of Rhode Island, a stalwart member of the Joint Committee on Atomic Energy, read a letter from Rickover on the need for the Trident, the status of the effort, and the chance for success. The Bentsen amendment was defeated on 27 July 1972 by a vote of 47 to 39. A change of five votes and the amendment would have passed.[83] Undoubtedly, several factors coalesced behind the Bentsen amendment, among them the lack of firm answers to the project, the worry over cost and inflation, the unrest over the war in Vietnam, and the presidential election of 1972.

Tension was even greater in 1973. Under Thomas J. McIntyre of New

Hampshire, the subcommittee on research and development of the Senate Committee on Armed Services voted unanimously to cut the administration's request for $1.7 billion in half. On August 1 by a vote of eight to seven, the full committee accepted the proposal. Because Barry Goldwater declared his proxy had been miscast, the committee voted again—this time rejecting the recommendation. On the Senate floor the fight continued over McIntyre's amendment. The navy lobbied intensively, bringing to bear its most influential individuals: John W. Warner, secretary of the navy; Zumwalt; and Rickover. On 27 September 1973, in an exceedingly close vote of 47 to 49, the Senate rejected the amendment. In the final outcome the navy did not get all it wanted, losing only about $2 million—which was far better than losing the $885 million that had been at risk.[84]

Trident was to continue to run into congressional difficulties, but none quite so serious as those of 1972 and 1973. Rickover assigned the S8G to Knolls. Electric Boat began construction of the prototype at West Milton in July 1973, and the reactor reached full power in December 1979. The navy awarded a contract to the Electric Boat Division of General Dynamics Corporation on 25 July 1974 for the first Trident submarine, with an option for the next three ships. The contract called for a delivery date of April 1979 for the first ship.[85]

Controversy surrounded the type of contract. Some navy officials saw Trident as a highly developmental effort, too risky to warrant the use of the same sort of fixed-price incentive contract routinely used for ship construction. They advocated a cost reimbursement type contract in which the contractor could be assured of recovering all his costs plus a guaranteed profit.

Rickover believed that the developmental aspects of the shipbuilding contract were overstated—the development features of the Trident were primarily in equipment that the government would supply to General Dynamics—weapon-control systems, communications, and the propulsion plant. He viewed the shipbuilder's job of hull construction, equipment installation, and testing as not enough different from prior classes to warrant eliminating all shipbuilder risk as would be the case under a cost-reimbursement contract. The navy agreed. As a result the navy negotiated with General Dynamics a fixed-price ship-construction contract along the lines of prior new-construction ships, but with substantially more contingency built into the price in recognition of the uncertainty that did exist.[86]

Throughout his career in the naval nuclear propulsion program, Rickover held strong views on contractors and never hesitated to express them to a company, the navy, the commission, the Department of Defense, or Congress. A useful summary of these views he wrote in a lengthy memorandum to the general counsel of the navy dated 10 May 1971. The Trident contract was consistent with that philosophy.

For many years shipbuilders have been operating on what is, in effect, a noncompetitive basis. There is, and has long been, no compulsion, no requirement for them to develop effective cost controls, procurement practices, or concern about the efficiency of their operations. Generally, the attitude in these shipyards is that costs cannot be controlled and they will end up to be whatever they turn out to be. Wasteful subcontracting practices, inadequate cost controls, loafing, and production errors mean little to these contractors. They will make their profits whether the product is good or bad; whether the price is fair or whether it is higher than it should be; whether delivery is on time or late. Shipbuilders can let costs come out where they will and count on getting relief through changes and claims, relaxation of procurement regulations and laws, government loans, follow-on sole-source contracts, and other escape mechanisms. It necessarily follows that there is considerable inefficiency and waste in shipbuilding. In fact, current Department of Defense profit policies actually *reward higher costs with higher profits* and punish greater efficiency with lower profits.[87]

In his view a contract with a ceiling was better than one with no ceiling at all.

Rickover played a major role in the Trident effort, a fact made possible by the success of the technology developed in the naval nuclear propulsion program. The propulsion plant he proposed would have the latest techniques in silencing, allow for the power required for equipment that might be installed years later, and (as Zumwalt acknowledged) add safety to the operation of the ship. For Trident Rickover followed his practice of constructing a full-scale mockup of the reactor compartment and engine room. Not only did it allow assurance that the shipyard workers would be able to carry out their specialties in the close quarters, but it permitted designers to pre-test a new maintenance concept. In this approach large hatches allowed the replacement of questionable equipment and components. The ship could be back on patrol while these were being checked and repaired. It was an error to assert that the propulsion plant set the size of the ship: the dimensions and number of missiles determined that. Rickover had nothing to do with the technical aspects of the missile and preferred a twenty- to a twenty-four-missile ship, mainly on the grounds that the larger number was too great to place on one platform. The decision for twenty-four came from the White House. Assessing the weight of his views on senators and representatives is impossible, but turning over the pages of the *Congressional Record* reveals frequent appeals to his name and insertion of correspondence containing his views.

Harvest

Summarizing the development of nuclear propulsion for submarines at any time is a complicated task, but never more so than for the period considered here. Seventeen years separated the commissioning of the *Skipjack* with its first S5W plant from the *Los Angeles* with its S6G reactor plant; twenty-two years divided the commissioning of the *George Wash-*

ington with its S5W reactor and the *Ohio* (SSBN 726) with its S8G reactor. These same years had seen the commissioning of the *Tullibee* with its electric-drive plant on 9 November 1960; the *Narwhal*, with its natural-circulation reactor, on 12 July 1969; the *Glenard P. Lipscomb*, with its electric-drive system, on 21 December 1974; the *Los Angeles* on 13 November 1976; and the *Ohio* on 11 November 1981. The *NR-1* was placed in service on 27 October 1969.

All met their design standards. As Zumwalt, no admirer of Rickover, summed it up in 1976 ". . . one thing no one can say about him is that he ever produced a lemon."[88] The *Glenard P. Lipscomb* and the *Narwhal* contributed greatly to submarine propulsion technology; of the two, probably the *Narwhal* provided the most important advances, but an assessment depends upon knowledge that has not been made public. The *Los Angeles* and her sister ships were well on the way to becoming a mainstay of the attack submarine force. Rickover hoped that the *NR-1* would be the first of a small class, with the successors reaching greater depths. Expense and slow metallurgical development of hull steels made the realization impossible. The *NR-1* demonstrated her usefulness many times; the instance given most publicity was the assistance in recovering an F-14 fighter, which with its Phoenix missile, had slid off the deck of an aircraft carrier into the deep waters of an open sea. The *Ohio* was delivered to the navy about two-and-a-half years behind her original schedule and cost about $1.2 billion, 50 percent more than estimated. Several reasons accounted for the increase and delay, among them higher than anticipated inflation, contractor mistakes, labor difficulties, government changes, and problems with government-furnished equipment. With the successful operation of the *Ohio* and her successors, the tide of controversy ebbed slowly.[89]

Conclusion

A number of forces shaped the post–World War II submarine fleet of the United States. Only two were considered here: pressurized-water reactor technology—and Rickover.

From the time of the exhilarating sea trials of the *Nautilus*, it was certain that pressurized-water reactor technology would play a dominant role in propelling American submarines. Two later events prove the strength of the statement. After June 1957 the navy did not lay down any more diesel-electric submarines. After almost two years of operation, the *Seawolf* (SSN 575) returned to Electric Boat at the end of 1958 to have her propulsion plant converted from a sodium-cooled to a pressurized-water reactor. All American nuclear submarines were the pressurized-water type. If application is the measure of a mature technology, pressurized-water propulsion systems certainly qualify.

It is possible to divide the application, somewhat arbitrarily and with some overlapping, into three phases. In the first the *Nautilus* and the *Seawolf* demonstrated the feasibility of the technical concept. In the second, pressurized-water reactor technology was applied to the four submarines of the *Skate*-class, the radar picket *Triton*, and the *Thresher-Sturgeon* attack and the Polaris missile submarines. For these ships Rickover, Naval Reactors, and the other elements of the naval nuclear propulsion program were providing propulsion plants; the characteristics of the ships were largely determined by others. In the third phase, Rickover took a much larger part. He instigated and fought for the *Narwhal* with its electric-drive system, and the *Los Angeles* attack and Trident-missile submarines. To put it another way, in the third part Rickover was a major force in getting the ships authorized and funded.

Because the issues were not technical but political, he went to Congress. His key to getting strong support was the excellence he demanded and built into Naval Reactors, the research and development carried out at Bettis and Knolls, the procurement activities of the Plant Apparatus Division and the Machinery Apparatus Operations, and the countless contractors and vendors. Weighing heavily in congressional opinion were the reliability of the propulsion plants and the superbly trained officers and men. When so many military programs were in trouble and the results uncertain, the naval nuclear propulsion program was a welcome exception.

An ancient prayer of Breton fishermen runs, "O, God, Thy sea is so great and my boat is so small."[1] Its few words are a grim reminder of the weakness of man's works before the power of nature. For submarines the prayer is especially true, for no ship sails in a more relentless and unforgiving environment. No ship demands more from the men who design, build, and sail it.

CHAPTER THREE
Thresher

On 2 July 1956 Congress authorized six nuclear-attack submarines. Five were to be *Skipjacks*. The sixth, designated SSN 593 and to be named the *Thresher*, was to be the first of a new class. The convergence of several technologies—nuclear propulsion, naval architecture, electronics, weapons, and metallurgy—gave the navy a chance to create a superb instrument for undersea warfare, one that would be deadly against enemy submarines as well as surface ships. In addition, the *Thresher* would have several features that would be incorporated in the Polaris submarines beginning with the *Ethan Allen* class.[2]

Determining the general military specifications of a new ship—the desired speed, displacement, dimensions, and armament—was the job of the ship characteristics board, a group of officers attached to the office of the chief of naval operations. For views on the new class of submarine, the board turned to the chief of naval operations, the commanders of the Atlantic and Pacific Submarine Forces, and the officers of the technical bureaus. From these sources Rear Admiral Denys W. Knoll, staff director of the board, drew up tentative specifications for the new ship and on 14 June 1957 sent them out for comment. On July 26, the office of the chief of naval operations distributed the characteristics for a nuclear-powered submarine that combined high submerged speed, great underwater maneuverability, and endurance so that the ship would be able to employ advanced tactics. Perhaps most striking was the new depth at which the ship was to operate: it would be far greater than even the Skipjack class.[3]

Reaching the new depth depended upon HY-80, a low-carbon steel of superior strength and toughness developed by several companies after World War II. It was promising for ship construction, providing certain problems could be solved. Inability to make various structural pieces was one major difficulty; it was possible to fabricate flat pieces that could be rolled into plates, but the means for producing extrusions, forgings, and castings had yet to be developed. Furthermore, the shipyards had to install new machinery to roll HY-80 plates to proper shapes and sizes. Finally, the improved steel required better welding materials and techniques.

In all these areas progress was rapid. In 1951 and 1952 the navy used HY-80 to form pressure-hull plates for the *Albacore*; plating and framing for the hangar of the *Growler*, a Regulus submarine; and structural parts of the aircraft carrier *Forrestal*. Continued advances in fabrication and welding techniques reached the stage in 1955 where the navy decided to use HY-80 in all new submarines. The *Skipjack* was the first in which both the plates of the pressure hull and frames were made from HY-80. By 1957 improvements in fabrication techniques allowed the production of thicker plates that, combined with progress in welding methods, offered the promise of a submarine that could operate at greater depth.[4]

In its enthusiasm the navy was moving fast. When the ship characteristics board sent out its memorandum on 14 June 1957, the only nuclear ships in commission were the *Nautilus* and *Seawolf*. Although the navy had begun building its first classes of nuclear attack submarines, the lead ships—the *Skate* and the *Skipjack*—were still under construction. Electric Boat had launched the *Skate* on 16 May 1957 and laid the keel of the *Skipjack* on 29 May 1956.[5]

Rickover and his leading engineers had some reservations. Their official responsibilities were limited. Because the *Thresher* would not be the first to use the S5W plant, Naval Reactors' cognizance would extend only to the reactor and its supporting systems. It was not the technical aspects they doubted but the building schedule. It called for several of the ships to be under construction before the first was proving itself at sea. If deficiencies showed up during operation, it would be easier to correct them in the ships that were in the design stage rather than on the building ways. The same conditions held true for the Polaris ships; those incorporating some of the *Thresher* features would be under construction before the results of the *Thresher* operations were known. In the last months of 1957, Naval Reactors engineers explained the reasons behind the layout of the first S5W plant and offered assistance.[6]

Not yet an advocate of quieting machinery, Rickover was disturbed by the plans of the Bureau of Ships. To get quiet operation, the bureau intended to dampen machinery noise by placing major components on resilient mountings and by using flexible pipe couplings. Because improved hull design and better propulsion plants were making possible new maneuvers that placed heavy and dangerous stresses upon machinery, he and his engineers argued that more testing was necessary. They were dissatisfied with declarations that the bureau had alternatives if the development of the mountings failed; they believed the other approaches poorly thought out and the expense of using them underestimated. The explanation that the issues he raised had already been dealt with drew the caustic remark that he could not comment on designs he had never seen. Rickover, Robert Panoff, the project officer for S5W plants, and Howard K. Marks, responsible for submarine propulsion plant engineering, won agreement on 9 December 1957 that more work had to be done.[7]

Rear Admiral Albert G. Mumma, chief of the Bureau of Ships, chose the Portsmouth Naval Shipyard, located on the Piscataqua River between Maine and New Hampshire, to build the *Thresher*. By this assignment Portsmouth would become the lead yard for the *Thresher* class, preparing detail designs, working drawings, and specifications for the ship that other yards would follow as more of the submarines were authorized. Portsmouth had good claim to the honor. It had launched its first submarine in 1917 and eventually stood second only to Electric Boat in the number of submarines constructed. After World War II Portsmouth was the lead yard for the *Tang* class and had built the *Albacore*. In 1950 Rickover had tried to interest the yard in nuclear submarine construction, and although Portsmouth refused, in later years it acquired some nuclear experience. When Mumma assigned the *Thresher*, Portsmouth had launched the *Swordfish* and laid the keel of the *Seadragon*, but for these nuclear ships and for the *Skipjack* class, Electric Boat was the lead yard. With the *Thresher*, Mumma was giving Portsmouth a major job and broadening the navy's technological base.[8]

With the selection of Portsmouth, Rickover faced a new decision. If the yard was to do the detail design for the ship, perhaps it should assume the same responsibility for the reactor plant. To the bureau it made sense to concentrate both functions at Portsmouth. Panoff assessed the arguments. Although the yard would gain valuable experience, training personnel would place a tremendous burden on Naval Reactors. Furthermore, Bettis and Portsmouth had never worked together, and Panoff had definite reservations about opening the laboratory to the naval yard. Giving the yard access to Bettis could cause a host of annoying problems. More important than these factors, however, was the technical experience of Electric Boat. If Rickover made the private yard responsible for preparing the working plant for the *Thresher* reactor, he could rely on an existing organization of established competence and almost certainly save time and money. Rickover agreed. Briefly the bureau attempted to work out a scheme under which Electric Boat would do its job under a contract with Portsmouth, but Rickover refused to countenance a relationship that diluted his responsibility. On 24 January 1958 Electric Boat received official notification of its new assignment.[9]

Portsmouth laid the keel on May 28 without much ceremony. Rear Admiral Robert L. Moore, Jr., the shipyard commander, and a few of his officers and civilian engineers came down to the waterfront to watch a crane swing the first section of the ship onto the ways.[10]

Admiral Arleigh A. Burke, chief of naval operations, was well aware of the significance of the *Thresher* to the navy's entire submarine program. Wanting assurances that the technical base for the *Thresher* class was sound, Burke asked Knoll to investigate. From the bureau, the David W. Taylor Model Basin (which was testing hull forms), and Portsmouth came confident replies. Knoll reported to Burke on 13 January 1959 that the number of innovations incorporated in the *Thresher* design was not unusual for a prototype; indeed, the planning philosophy was conservative.[11]

The magnitude of the commitment represented by the *Thresher* was attracting much interest. To explain the design and development philosophy and to give a chance to answer questions, Knoll held a special meeting. Men from the fleet, shipyards, and bureaus on January 27 heard descriptions of the interior arrangements, model basin tests, resilient mountings, and various development work. HY-80 attracted a great deal of attention, but the problem of cracking did not appear insurmountable and was being solved by careful procedures and high-quality workmanship. Reaching the new test depth—a term meaning the greatest depth at which the ship could safely operate—required no breakthroughs, no lessening of safety factors, no new theories or techniques.

One of the many officers listening to the presentation, Captain Eugene P. Wilkinson, one of the few who had commanded a nuclear submarine, agreed that the goals of the new design were highly desirable. Nonetheless, it would be far better to build more *Skipjack*s while learning from the *Thresher*. By pointing out that the entire submarine program was not within the scope of the meeting, Knoll turned the issue back to the *Thresher*: did Wilkinson think the risks were too great? Not for an experimental ship, came the reply. Several voices disagreed—the ship was not experimental but developmental; a distinction that meant that the innovations were well within the state of the technology. On February 18 Knoll summed up the meeting for Burke. Two conclusions were particularly important. First, HY-80 could be welded safely as long as procedures were followed carefully; this was the judgment of shipyard commanders working with the metal. Second, the number of new development features to be built into the *Thresher* was not excessive.[12]

Toward the end of 1959 the picture changed. One yard after another complained of troubles in welding HY-80. Lieutenant Commander David T. Leighton, nuclear-power superintendent at Mare Island, was particularly vocal. He discovered that welds joining hull plates to the frame in a submarine under construction had cracked. In the process of checking how the welds could have been accepted as satisfactory, Leighton found that the yard's radiographic and quality-control practices were poor. Although the hull was not part of his responsibility, he informed Rickover who, with characteristic promptness, insisted upon a complete inspection of the hull surrounding the reactor compartment, even though to gain access some of the reactor plant had to be dismantled. For that section of the ship around the reactor compartment, he had all the welds replaced. For the rest of the hull, the shipyard sampled the welds and repaired only those in the sample that were defective.[13]

Although there was debate over the significance of the cracks, one fact was certain: welds that had passed inspection had cracked days and even months later. Some individuals had the eerie experience of being near a weld and hearing it crack. Repairs were difficult, costly, and time-consuming. Some welds had to be reworked six times before they were satisfactory. Obviously all submarines being constructed with HY-80 had to be examined.[14]

Rear Admiral Ralph K. James, now chief of the bureau, set up a special team of officers to visit the yards, consult naval and civilian scientists and engineers, and conduct a thorough literature search. On 5 January 1960 the group issued its report. The answer to the shipyard problems lay in promptly issuing uniform procedures for welding and fabrication. These were complicated, demanding, and required time to complete. A major uncertainty with HY-80 was fatigue; that is the tendency of the metal to crack under repeated cycles of stress. Not enough experience had been gained to know at what point the metal lost its resiliency, although in time that question would be answered. Nothing had been uncovered to overturn the decision to use HY-80.[15]

Because the advanced technology of the *Thresher* was to be incorporated in the urgent Polaris effort, on April 2 Burke gave the ship the highest priority in the submarine construction program. Puzzled by arguments over HY-80 and disturbed by differing views over the *Thresher* innovations and their application to other submarines, he sought a new appraisal. Instead of looking toward the bureau, Burke turned to Rear Admiral Francis D. McCorkle, president of the board of inspection and survey, an organization that inspected the navy's ships and reported directly to the chief of naval operations. McCorkle found it difficult to get consistent data, but he was convinced that HY-80 had to be used if the navy was to have submarines that could operate at the new test depth. On some features McCorkle proposed waiting for results from operations with the *Thresher* before building them into later submarines. On 23 April Burke discussed McCorkle's report with Rickover and several other officers. The next day he decided. He accepted McCorkle's recommendations on HY-80. Because of the importance of the ship to the entire submarine program, he wanted to get the ship to sea as soon as possible.[16]

Needing the data from the ship, the bureau pushed the schedule for initial sea trials ahead to 15 November 1960, recognizing that by doing so the ship in some respects would still be incomplete. Portsmouth would have to back off the work on other submarines and institute a six-day work week in some shops. Moore, now deputy chief of the bureau, on 9 May 1960 wrote Captain Henry P. Rumble, shipyard commander, that the *Thresher* was on the master urgency list and the secretary of defense had approved priorities for all urgently required components. It was up to Portsmouth. Rumble quoted paragraphs of Moore's letter in an information bulletin to the yard personnel, adding:

> The Portsmouth Naval Shipyard has been given one of the biggest challenges it has ever faced. It is a greater challenge than any other shipyard has. To meet it we must exceed any record we have ever made; we must "do better than our best."[17]

Exhortation was one thing; achievement another. Harrison S. Sayre, a civilian engineer in the Bureau of Ships, left Washington to examine inspection procedures for HY-80 hull welds at Electric Boat and Portsmouth. On June 13 he made his report. Electric Boat weld radiography was of high quality, the coverage good, and it was possible to trace back the individual radiographs to a specific weld. Qualified personnel manned the radiographic laboratory, and the shipyard evaluation officer and the office of the navy's supervisor of shipbuilding also reviewed the radiographs for defective welds—an arrangement that meant that the navy was inspecting the work it was paying for. At Portsmouth Sayre found a different state of affairs. The shipyard laboratory carried out radiography when requested, and although the techniques, processing, and control had been poor, the yard had improved somewhat. An example of the problem was the film taken of the hull welds of the *Thresher* and the *Abraham Lincoln*. If a reexamination of a radiograph showed a possible defect, the chances were that there was no way to identify the weld. Sayre concluded that Electric Boat procedures met bureau standards; those at Portsmouth did not.[18]

Nothing can rob a ship launching of its drama, particularly on a brilliant New England summer afternoon when flags and bunting are vivid, uniforms a dazzling white, epaulets and braid a bright gold, and band music loud, cheerful, and stirring. For a brief time the shipyard, normally filled with the loud and sharp sounds of construction, is at rest. Not even the dreariest of speeches nor the longest of benedictions can quench the mounting excitement. An instant of silence, a swing of a champagne bottle, and the ship, almost imperceptibly at first but with gathering momentum, moves down the building ways and hits the water. After a brief moment of freedom, tugs catch the ship and nudge it to a pier. July 9, 1960, was such a day when Portsmouth launched the *Thresher*. Because of the length of the ship and the depth of the water at the foot of the building ways, the submarine had been built facing the water. As a result the *Thresher* slid into the Piscataqua River bow first.[19] Once tied to the pier, yardmen clambered back on board, for months of work lay ahead. Yet the ship was now in its element, rising and falling with the tide and shifting slightly with the changing wind.

Piping

For Commander Dean L. Axene the launching ceremony was an event that comes rarely in a lifetime. As the ship's prospective commanding officer, he had reported to Portsmouth on 1 June 1960. His qualifications were impressive. He had been the first executive officer of the *Nautilus* during those exhilarating days when the ship was exploring the boundaries of nuclear propulsion. His next duty was in diesel-electric submarines: if the assignment was less exciting technically, it was a greater challenge professionally, for one of them became his first command. After he was selected for the *Thresher*, Axene spent an arduous year of additional training in Rickover's Washington headquarters.[20]

Axene found the pace at Portsmouth slow. In mid-August the yard put its best pipefitters and welders to work on the *Abraham Lincoln*. He thought the resulting lack of progress on the *Thresher* showed that the yard had trouble in working on two ships at the same time. He also found Portsmouth slow to organize for the meticulous preparations that Rickover insisted upon before bringing the propulsion plant into operation. Axene met with the shipyard commander and his senior officers several times to check off the work that had been completed and match the jobs to be done against the demands of the schedule. In September Axene was convinced that the ship was falling further behind. In October progress was better. The improvement he credited to Commander William E. Heronemus who had recently reported to the production department, that part of the yard organization that did construction work.[21] In November Axene—and the navy—received a sharp and grim warning of trouble.

On 30 November 1960 the Portsmouth-built submarine *Barbel*, under Lieutenant Commander Joseph J. Meyer, Jr., was two days out of Norfolk to take part in an exercise involving several submarines and surface ships. Meyer decided to submerge to test depth to check his ship, a practice he carried out whenever possible after leaving port. After ordering the crew to stations and to man the sound-powered telephones, he began the dive, cautiously leveling off at each hundred feet to recalibrate his instruments and to check for leaks.

At 10:03—almost at test depth—a voice crackled over the phone: "Flooding in the engine room, take her up fast."

Immediately Meyer ordered the bow planes on full rise, the engines ahead full speed, the flooding compartment isolated, and the main ballast tanks blown. Briefly the *Barbel* seemed to hesitate, then swiftly began to rise. Quickly Meyer learned that the flooding was under control: its cause was a leak in a saltwater line. Three minutes from the first alarm the ship broke the surface. Meyer went back to the engine-room compartment. A pipe had given way in a saltwater line at a silver-brazed joint. From rough calculations he estimated the ship had taken on board about eighteen tons of water.

Meyer had cause to be proud of the crew. No one had panicked and all reports reaching him had been clear and specific. He also had reason to congratulate himself on the precautions he had taken. Later investigation revealed that the shipyard had installed a pipe of the wrong material. Since her initial sea trials in May 1959, the ship had returned to Portsmouth several times to have deficiencies corrected and equipment repaired. Considering all that had gone wrong, Meyer stated to a board investigating the incident: "I believe that the number of casualties the *Barbel* has had borders on the unbelievable."[22]

Of all the piping systems on board a submarine, none were more dangerous than those containing salt water; yet because they brought cooling water to propulsion components, they were essential to the operation of the ship. These lines had to withstand the same force of the sea as the pressure hull, which was constructed of heavy plates of HY-80. Even a small leak was dangerous, for the seawater would form a fine spray, blinding the crew and threatening to short out electrical equipment. Water from a larger leak would ricochet off bulkheads and equipment so that the crew, buffeted from all directions, would find it difficult to find the source of the danger. The old adage that a chain was no stronger than its weakest link applied to saltwater systems, for these were no better than the weakest joint that linked sections of pipes, valves, and pumps.

For shipboard use the navy used two types of joints: silver-brazed and welded. In silver-brazing, two pieces of pipe were joined together and the brazer, a skilled workman who had been specially trained, applied heat. When the joint was uniformly heated to the proper temperature, a solid alloy composed mostly of silver and copper flowed into the gap between the two pipes. If the metal was clean, the temperature sufficiently high, and the alloy accurately applied and in the correct amount, the joint would be sound. In some instances silver-brazing was the best method for making joints between pipes of different materials. Good brazing demanded experienced and careful workmanship. A major drawback at this time was the lack of a reliable way to check the soundness of the joint.

Welding was a different process. Two pieces of metal were brought together and heated at the point of contact to above the melting point while a rod, or electrode, of solid metal of similar chemical composition was applied and also melted. At high temperatures the faces of the pipes and the intermediary molten welding rod became metallurgically a single piece. The mechanical properties of a properly welded joint were stronger than those of the best brazed joint. Furthermore, radiography could determine the quality of the welds; while the same technique could be used to examine brazed joints, it did not reveal certain types of defects. Welding was more expensive than brazing and could not be used to join pipes of certain different materials.[23]

All the yards were having trouble with silver brazing. In December 1960 the bureau recommended that Portsmouth cut out and inspect the *Barbel* joints that had leaked under pressure. Later that month the bureau directed the yard to replace all brazed joints over four inches in diameter. But other yards had the same problem. On 4 January 1961 a conference at Portsmouth attended by bureau personnel and the supervisor of shipbuilding at Electric Boat proposed developing some way of testing silver-brazed joints without cutting into them, as well as working out a better method of identifying material.[24]

Shortly after the *Barbel* incident, some silver-brazed fittings failed during a trial of the *Abraham Lincoln*. The deputy commander of the Atlantic submarine force on February 3 called for a reinspection of the saltwater systems of the two ships, but noted also the importance of meeting the dates for delivering the submarines to the operating forces. On March 24 the bureau required all the yards constructing submarines to certify that proper materials were being used in the saltwater systems. Since the sea trials of the *Thresher* were only a few weeks off, Portsmouth decided to divide the task into two parts: all saltwater piping accessible and not covered with insulation would be inspected between April 7 and April 23, and the remainder would be checked after the first sea trial and prior to delivery of the ship. (How much of the inspection was carried out in the first phase is not clear, but in May four pieces of improper piping were found.)[25]

At the Ingalls Shipyard at Pascagoula, Mississippi, six sections of pipe containing a total of twenty-four silver-brazed joints were removed from major saltwater systems of the *Snook* (of the *Skipjack* class) and subjected to hydrostatic pressure. Although the piping stood up well, cutting into the joints revealed several instances of poor brazing. To William Wegner, Rickover's representative, and to Commander Howard E. Bucknell, the prospective commanding officer, the results were not reassuring. Instead, they raised the question of whether hydrostatic testing was a sufficient measure of the soundness of the joints. These, after all, had to withstand vibration, temperature changes, and shock, which were an inherent part of the life of a combat vessel. They wanted more joints cut open and examined, not primarily for discovering the soundness of the joints, but for testing the reliability of the means of inspection. In their view the technical officers tended to believe that pipe failures such as the one that occurred on the *Barbel* were isolated events and not symptoms of a serious problem. On 4 March 1961 they began a long letter to the deputy commander of the Atlantic submarine force: "I believe that we have a problem of substantial proportions in the silbrazing of joints in submarine sea water systems."[26]

The bureau had already taken steps to improve the silver-braze situation. To the commanders of the submarine forces it had recommended examining all silver-brazed joints visually and replacing those that showed misalignments. It had begun an investigation into using mechanical and electrical resistance techniques for nondestructive testing. On March 1 Portsmouth issued a new booklet setting forth specifications and procedures for silver brazing. The yard concluded that recent tests showed with a high degree of assurance that the silver-brazed joints on ships in operation were adequate.[27]

Trials

As the time approached for the first sea trial of the *Thresher*, pipe joints were still a serious matter. Before that event the reactor would have to achieve initial criticality and undergo power range testing. Although officers and men of the ship's engineering force already had at least a year of nuclear training, Rickover would hold a pre-criticality examination, a very important exercise carried out when a reactor was first brought into operation. The first time, in December 1960, he and a few of his Washington staff had given a two-day preliminary examination. Now it was time for a more thorough investigation.

On Saturday, 7 January 1961, after the usual day of work, Rickover, along with Theodore Rockwell, Jack C. Grigg, David G. Scott, and Gene L. Rogers, flew to Portsmouth to interview the engineering department personnel of the ship and to find out if they were ready to operate the plant safely. Wasting no time, the group (known behind its back as the "hatchet squad") began its work. From 9:00 until 10:00 P.M. the members discussed the purpose of the examination with Axene and his executive and engineer officers. From 10:00 until midnight the visitors and the three ship's officers toured the engineering compartment. Work on Sunday began at 7:00 A.M. with a survey of the organization of the engineering department, its records, operating procedures, and training program. For the next twelve hours the group questioned all engineering personnel—officers and enlisted men—on their understanding of the reactor plant and its operation. From 10:30 until noon on Monday, Rickover and his staff discussed their findings with Axene, his executive officer, and his engineer officer. From their interviews the Washington team determined that the engineering department could operate the plant safely. They offered a few suggestions: officers should increase their theoretical knowledge of reactor operation; enlisted personnel should be thoroughly familiar with the details of all the equipment in the spaces where they stood watch; and some portable instruments should be obtained before initial criticality. But the *Thresher* was ready for criticality and power testing.

On March 10 the reactor reached criticality and two days later generated power. Rear Admiral Charles J. Palmer, the shipyard commander, slipped the date for beginning sea trials from April 23 to April 29 to make sure the ship would be ready. On the morning of April 25 the *Thresher* began its fast cruise, an exercise in which the submarine remained tied—or fast—to the pier, but was sealed up for a few days with only the officers and crew on board. Free from the distractions of yard workmen, Axene was able to drill his crew at their stations and to check the equipment and machinery.[28] Perhaps during the crowded hours Axene was able to give a moment's thought to one item on the trial agenda that he and Captain John J. Hinchey had talked about.

Hinchey was the nuclear-power superintendent. His job had a deceptive simplicity about it. Rickover held him responsible for all phases of reactor work in Portsmouth having to do with plant installation and testing. Hinchey had a strong background in submarines, engineering, and nuclear technology. Leaving the Naval Academy in December 1941, he spent most of the war in submarines. From 1945 to 1948 he took a postgraduate course in marine engineering and naval construction at the Massachusetts Institute of Technology. After two-and-one-half years at Portsmouth, he returned to MIT for an advanced course in nuclear physics. Rickover accepted him into the nuclear program in July 1951. In 1954 he left Washington headquarters for Schenectady and in August 1959 reported to Portsmouth.[29] As other men had found, Hinchey learned that duty as nuclear-power superintendent meant long hours in the yard and close contacts with Rickover. For reactor plant construction Hinchey drew qualified welders and pipefitters from the yard work force. Now that the *Thresher* was almost ready for sea, Hinchey was disturbed because the trial agenda did not call for special precautions for going to test depth.

During the war he had been in submarines that had gone below their test depth in order to avoid enemy attack, but then the limit was only a few hundred feet. Later the navy set a new test depth, but the increase was not large. With the *Thresher* the navy was going down to a significantly greater depth. The yard planned to instrument the hull with strain gauges to measure stress, but the dive itself would be routine. With Axene's support, Hinchey had tried to get into the agenda special procedures calling for the ship to submerge to test depth in increments. Others saw no need for the precaution. There was little more that Hinchey and Axene could do directly, for the agenda was the responsibility of the shipyard commander.

Rickover, however, was responsible for the initial sea trials for the propulsion plant. His practice, broken only twice because of serious illness, was to direct the trials in person. Unable to believe that the *Thresher* was going to test depth so casually, he asked Panoff to check around the bureau. To his anger and astonishment Panoff discovered that there were no special plans for that part of the trial. Rickover and Panoff were convinced that diving in increments alone was not sufficient.

The evening before the ship was to go out Rickover, Panoff, and Grigg flew to Boston where they were met by Axene. On the drive to Portsmouth the conversation immediately turned to the trial agenda. Arriving at the yard Rickover, now furious, demanded a procedure by which the ship would descend to its test depth in hundred foot increments. Against violent opposition, he and Panoff demanded a thorough check of the ship, at each stage of all saltwater piping systems, and a test of the crucial valves and pumps. That night he, Panoff, Moore, Palmer, Hinchey, Axene, and a few others stayed up until 2:00 in the morning working out details. A few points had yet to be settled when the ship got underway some hours later.[30]

A few minutes after eight on Saturday morning, 29 April 1961, the *Thresher* left the pier and steamed the short distance down the river to the Atlantic. For the first time the entire propulsion plant from the reactor to the propeller worked together to drive the ship. Surface trials—steaming ahead and astern, and tests of the steering apparatus—went well; so did the shallow dives. When it was time to descend to test depth, Axene put into effect the measures that had been worked out the night before. The best men were stationed at critical points, repair parties were standing by in the forward and after compartments, and the sound-powered telephones were manned. In stages the *Thresher* dropped farther and farther below the surface. Far deeper than submarines normally operated, but not yet at test depth, a strain gauge showed the hull was undergoing far more stress than anticipated. Recognizing that in all probability the gauge was at fault, Rickover nonetheless ordered the dive halted. Once back in Portsmouth it was clear that the gauge was in error.

But the propulsion plant functioned beautifully. Rickover rated the performance of the ship's company outstanding and the nuclear training of the officers and men satisfactory. He received a brief handwritten note from Admiral James congratulating him on the successful trials of the twentieth nuclear power plant at sea, along with the wish that other areas of the ship had done as well.[31]

The *Thresher* went out again for its test dive on May 23. Since the propulsion plant had already passed its tests, Rickover was not on board. At test depth a joint in a small saltwater line failed and filled the air with fine spray. A sailor stationed near a bulkhead saw the source and quickly isolated the system. Back at periscope depth, as the men were repairing the leak, they discovered another failed joint. Both were silver-brazed fittings. On the other hand, Axene reported to Rickover, the propulsion plant had operated "extremely well." So for that matter had the resilient-mounted machinery.[32]

The ship looked good. From every indication the navy had succeeded in building the first of a new class of submarines that would run fast, silent, and deep. Rear Admiral Lawrence Daspit, deputy commander of the Atlantic Submarine Force, congratulated Portsmouth on achieving new milestones in submarine operating depth and in quiet operation. He was certain the same dedication would solve the silver-braze problem before the ship left Portsmouth for evaluation by the Fleet.[33]

Double Standard

As the *Thresher* began operations at sea, the bureau continued to wrestle with the problem of silver-brazed joints. Having little faith in the bureau's corrective effort, Rickover decided to get rid of them where he could. After discussing the matter with Panoff in early June 1961, he decided he would use welded joints in those seawater systems for which he was responsible. While Electric Boat was working out the plans and procedures for the change, he went one step further. On September 7 he wrote in a change order: "Brazed joints should be eliminated from all *reactor compartments through piping which is subjected to submergence sea pressure. These piping joints should be modified to welded construction. . . .*" [emphasis added]. His reasoning was severely logical. Radiation limited access to the reactor compartment; therefore, piping had to be sound. Within a few months most submarines, both in commission and under construction, had been earmarked for the change to welded joints.[34]

A few days before he signed the change order, an event occurred that made him more certain than ever that silver-brazed joints in saltwater systems were exceedingly dangerous. On 28 August 1961, the *Snook* had gone out on sea trials. Because he was ill, Rickover had placed Panoff in charge. Early parts of the trial were routine. With the crew at diving stations and the damage-control parties in position, the *Snook*, leveling off at frequent intervals and cycling valves, descended to test depth. The dive ended without incident, and the ship climbed some hundreds of feet to undertake other tests, among them a four-hour run at full power.

Wegner, Bucknell, and a few others were in the wardroom when over the public address system came the words: "Emergency! Emergency! Flooding in the engine room." Bucknell sped to the control room, Wegner to the engine room, only to find his way blocked by a closed watertight door. Through the small porthole he could see that everything was under control and from the slant of the deck that Bucknell was driving the ship to the surface. The *Snook* broached, sank down again, and finally settled on the surface. The crew had been able to isolate the leak and, fortunately, no spray had reached any vital electrical equipment. An investigation showed that a mix-up of materials was the cause.

Panoff ordered a visual inspection of other silver-brazed joints, which uncovered another mix-up of materials in a larger saltwater system. Both it and the first joint had passed inspection. The *Snook* resumed her trials.

Wegner and Bucknell looked back for lessons. Frequent and thorough drilling of officers and crew was essential. Isolating the leak was crucial, but it had to be done intelligently. Cutting off all saltwater systems would be a bad mistake, for the action would deprive the plant of cooling water and cause a sharp loss of propulsion power when it was needed most.

The point was important. At deep depths the pressure was so great that a submarine gained buoyancy comparatively slowly when air was blown into the ballast tanks to force water out. Instead, the ship depended upon its speed and diving planes to get out of trouble. As some officers expressed it, at these depths the submarine was "flying." But to keep operating, the plant had to have cooling water, and that in turn depended upon saltwater systems. Wegner urged replacing silver-brazed joints with welded joints in all the larger saltwater systems; doing so would be a logical extension of the practice that Rickover had already adopted for the reactor compartment. For deeper diving submarines—and here Bucknell was referring to the *Thresher* class—all joints in saltwater systems should be welded.[35]

The submarine force was well aware of the danger. On September 13 Daspit sent a message to James listing the piping failures that were occurring with "alarming regularity." Since the *Barbel* incident, bad joints had shown up on the *Skate*, while the use of wrong materials had been found on the *Thresher* and *Snook*. Daspit called for action: the bureau should alert all concerned, impress on the builders the serious consequences of poor design and fabrication of piping systems, expedite efforts to get rid of improperly designed connections, design ways to shield electrical equipment from spray, and develop reliable nondestructive methods for testing silver-brazed fittings.[36] By this last measure the forces afloat could test the joints of the submarines in operation.

The bureau was trying to increase the reliability of saltwater systems, James replied on 15 September 1961. Unquestionably the integrity of the systems was a serious matter, and the bureau had already taken steps. Early in the year it had sent representatives to instruct all the submarine construction yards on ways to better quality control. On August 31—a few days after the *Snook* incident—the bureau called all the builders to Washington to discuss techniques for improving the quality of the submarine systems. Mare Island was evaluating ultrasonic test procedures for shipboard use. The bureau was studying changes in the design of saltwater systems and, in inviting bids for *Thresher*-class submarines in the 1962 shipbuilding program, was calling for cost data and technical feasibility of using all welded joints in certain saltwater systems.[37]

Although the silver-brazing problem was claiming an increasing amount of the bureau's attention, an improperly welded joint was no better. In mid-October 1961 Hinchey had his division undertake a review of radiographs of reactor plant welding that the Portsmouth material testing laboratory had accepted as adequate. The examination showed that a large number of radiographs did not meet bureau standards; some were so poor it was impossible to say with certainty that the welds were sound. Abruptly Rickover halted all reactor work at the yard and sent a task force of materials engineers from the nuclear program. For the first two days in November, these men conducted a wide-ranging survey and interviewed individuals ranging from welders to the shipyard commander. The Rickover group concluded that more technical control was imperative. A senior experienced welding engineer was needed along with more engineers who had the background and ability to become welding specialists. Portsmouth was considering consolidating all reactor-plant pipe welding in one shop to improve supervision and quality control: this action should be carried out quickly. The yard should institute a formal system for issuing procedures for welding and nondestructive testing—and make sure these procedures were followed. As for radiographs of the reactor-plant welds, the final interpretations and acceptance of radiographs—and therefore the welds—should be the responsibility of the nuclear power division.[38]

Rickover was handling the problem by his usual methods. If an organization would not do the job, he set up one that would. By establishing formal procedures and by fixing the responsibility upon Hinchey, he was making sure that a specific individual—not a faceless organization—would be held accountable. And he warned his superiors of the technical faults that forced him to act.

Palmer admitted that Portsmouth was having trouble meeting the welding standards. On 18 January 1962 he wrote James of the results of a review of the radiographs in the non-nuclear portion of the *Tinosa*, a submarine of the *Thresher* class under construction. Except in two instances—which were being redone—radiographs of pressure-hull joints met standards, although the film processing was not all it should have been. Radiography of non-nuclear pipe joints did not meet the requirements for sensitivity, and again the film processing left something to be desired. Even though the radiographs did not meet the standards, they appeared good enough to have revealed major defects.[39]

Two philosophies were clashing: one that efforts that came close to standards were sufficient, and one that standards were the minimum that had to be met. Rickover summed up the situation when he wrote James on 13 February 1962:

> Insofar as *Tinosa* is concerned, I do not see how the problem of its non-nuclear pipe welding can be lightly set aside. High integrity steam and salt water systems are equally as important in a submarine as the nuclear systems; all involve safety of the ship. Based on experience with the reactor plant welding, I recommend the shipyard be required to comply with applicable Bureau welding specifications.[40]

Thresher at Sea

The *Thresher* underwent additional tests after its initial trials. Occasionally equipment or components failed and required further work, but one part of the ship gave Axene no concern: "The propulsion plant functioned beautifully throughout the trials and has been a joy to operate." Commissioned on 3 August 1961, the *Thresher* was assigned for evaluation to submarine development group two of the Atlantic submarine force. Quickly the ship was sent south to the acoustic range in the Bahamas to determine the noise the ship gave off at different depths and speeds. Again the results were impressive, and in maneuvers with other submarines the *Thresher* proved outstanding.[41]

In December the ship was back in Portsmouth where Hinchey took advantage of the opportunity to replace most of the silver-brazed joints that were under Naval Reactors' cognizance with welded joints. After some weeks of exercises the *Thresher* entered the yard at Electric Boat on 16 April 1962 to prepare for more tests. During that time the yard replaced more of the silver-brazed joints in the reactor plant.[42]

The yard was preparing the ship for shock tests. By studying the effect of underwater explosions, the navy sought to improve the design and construction of its ships, machinery, and equipment. The history of shock testing began in the 1860s with the introduction of ironclad ships and steam propulsion. During World War II, Rickover visited all the battle-damaged ships he could to improve the design of the electrical equipment for which he was responsible. When the *Nautilus* was under construction, he shock-tested various components on board the *Ulua*, a submarine not yet completed as the war ended and set aside for the purpose. Atomic bombs brought a new dimension to the problem. Operation Crossroads, the first peacetime test of atomic weapons, took place in 1946 in the Bikini lagoon. One aerial and one submerged weapon dealt devastating effects to an armada of unmanned and anchored ships of various combat types. In 1958, however, the Hardtack weapon test series at Eniwetok revealed that the navy could do much to protect its ships. In later tests the navy detonated conventional explosives against a number of surface combat ships and submarines; among the latter were the diesel-electric submarines *Trout* and *Bonefish* and the nuclear submarines *Skate* and *Skipjack*. As the first of a new and large class, the tests of the *Thresher* were of great importance.[43]

Months of preparation went into the effort, for several organizations needed the data; the Bureau of Ships, the Bureau of Naval Weapons, the Naval Research Laboratory, the Naval Engineering Station, the yards of Portsmouth and Electric Boat, several contractors, and the submarine force of the Atlantic Fleet. As the time approached, the ship was heavily instrumented with high-speed motion picture cameras, accelerometers, velocity meters, and strain gauges. The schedule called for no more than one shot a day; then the ship would head for Key West. At that point only the possibility of gross damage could be assessed; the time and effort of many skilled individuals from several disciplines were needed to study the data and apply them to other ships.[44]

On 20 May 1962, the *Thresher* left Electric Boat and steamed south for more exercises. On June 3 at Cape Canaveral the ship ran into minor trouble. Because she was unwieldy and hard to handle on the surface, Axene relied on tugs when the submarine was in close quarters. Two tugs were pushing the *Thresher* to her dock when a mistaken engine-room order caused one tug to surge ahead and gash a three-foot hole in the ballast tank below the waterline. Damage was slight, but since the schedule called for the shock tests, the submarine headed back to Electric Boat for repairs. By June 17 the ship was off Key West and ready.[45]

From June 17 through June 29 the *Thresher* went through its ordeal. For each shot the procedures were much the same. An explosive charge, carefully calculated as to strength, was precisely positioned at an exact depth. The fleet tug *Salinan* controlled the detonation while the submarine rescue vessel *Penguin* steamed slowly nearby to provide assistance, if that should be necessary, and to warn other vessels off the range. With radio contact established, the *Thresher*, at periscope depth, steered a course that would bring it between two orange buoys. The prepositioned movie cameras were turning; an officer at the ship's public address system began the countdown. Everyone was at his station wearing a hard hat, standing with flexed knees, watching intently his assigned component or instrument—and waiting. As the *Thresher*, its slender periscope trailing a graceful feather of white water, glided between the two buoys, the *Salinan* fired the charge. Under the impact the submarine bucked and shuddered. To the men on board, no matter how well prepared, for a brief moment reality was more terrifying than anticipation.

A degree of immediate assessment was possible. Some gauges and instruments had failed, some components had refused to start and had been badly shaken on their foundations. Twenty-eight silver-brazed joints had given way, but only one—a pinhole leak in a non-saltwater system— was in the reactor compartment. One analysis was particularly interesting. Just prior to the tests a number of silver-brazed joints had been inspected ultrasonically, a new technique in this application. Those joints found below standard by the ultrasonic tests had been replaced. None of the joints that had passed the ultrasonic probing had failed.[46] It looked as if the navy had found a nondestructive means to determine the soundness of silver-brazed joints.

The navy was proud of the ship. The tests off Key West appeared to confirm the hopes for the *Thresher* class. Axene thought the ship had acquitted itself extremely well and, looking back over the record since the submarine had gone to sea, considered that the *Thresher* was a major and outstanding step forward in submarine development. Daspit, assessing the test results, was extremely pleased. There were design problems, of course, and these had to be overcome, but compared to the achievement the deficiencies were minor. He awarded Portsmouth the naval accolade of "Well Done."[47]

Return to Portsmouth

It was time for an overhaul. The *Thresher* arrived at Portsmouth on 11 July 1962. The yard was busy with building the *Tinosa* and *Jack* and the Polaris submarines *John Adams* and *Nathanael Greene.*[48]

Rear Admiral Charles J. Palmer, the shipyard commander, had about 9,000 people working for him. Most were civilians under civil service regulations, but he did have a small group of officers specialized in particular technical areas. For the *Thresher*, the planning and production departments were the most important parts of the yard organization. Under Captain William D. Roseborough, Jr., the planning department was responsible for plans, specifications, and procurement of materials. The production department, under Captain John G. Guerry, Jr., was charged with seeing that the work was done in an orderly, timely, economic, and efficient manner and met specifications. Although Guerry had a broad engineering background, he lacked experience in submarine construction, and he depended heavily on Captain William E. Heronemus, the shipbuilding and repair superintendent in the production department who saw that the assigned tasks were completed. He had attended a three-year postgraduate course on construction engineering at MIT and had worked on the design, repair, construction, and conversion of sub-marines at Mare Island, the Bureau of Ships in Washington, and Ports-mouth.[49]

The nuclear propulsion division was somewhat different. Because both planning and production were involved in the nuclear work, Hinchey reported to Roseborough and Guerry, but his primary responsibility was to Rickover.[50] By insisting that the yard meet the nuclear standards, Hinchey at times got into disputes with other officers and civilian offi-cials. At times the bitterness took an ugly turn and carried over into social relations, a situation that was neither unique to Hinchey nor to Ports-mouth.

Work on the *Thresher* did not begin at once. Axene used one day to take the submarine out for two brief dependents' cruises—occasions when wives and families had a chance to get acquainted with the ship that played so large a part in their lives. On July 20 yard and ship officers conferred on the work that had to be done. The yard knew about the major jobs, for its representatives made a practice of visiting ships before they arrived, and experience gained from years of overhauling subma-rines gave them an idea of many others. Still, there was the need to get more information and to rough out a schedule. Generally speaking, the work could be divided into three categories: repairing damage from shock tests; fixing and adjusting equipment and systems that, because of an unusually long and arduous operating period, had seen hard service; and installing new equipment. By far the greatest number of these jobs would be minor, but a few, such as those involving the hydraulic system and an experimental sonar, were not. Not much had to be done to the reactor plant. All in all, the yard estimated it would be finished with the *Thresher* in about six months. Counting from mid-July, the completion date would be about mid-January 1963. On July 23 Portsmouth began its work.[51]

Yardmen with their gear tramped through narrow passageways which, once immaculate, became grimy and dirty. Compartments, once neat, orderly, and quiet, were festooned with cables and filled with shrill noises as drills bit into metal, while the acrid smell of flame cutters filled the air. Living spaces once having personality were dead. The ship's company—those members who did not live near the yard—were quartered in a barge moored close by. For months the *Thresher* was a gutted and lifeless hulk.

Installing new sonar required changing a maze of piping; modifying the hydraulic system proved a more difficult job than anticipated. Palmer kept himself informed of the progress of the work in his yard by holding daily conferences Monday through Friday, or more often, if necessary, with Roseborough and Guerry; by weekly reports from Guerry's planning department on those jobs that were controlling schedules; and by peri-odic inspections. In addition, he held a meeting once a week in which the *Thresher* alone was the topic of discussion. Heronemus had close contact with the *Thresher* and other submarines. A young officer was assigned to coordinate the various efforts on the ship.[52]

As the weeks went by, it was clear that Portsmouth could not complete the work on schedule.

Never-Ending Challenge

In the fall of 1962 the *Thresher* was hardly one of Rickover's major concerns. The sheer size of the nuclear program was straining the abilities of his organization. Using October 1 as a date for a rapid survey, the navy had twenty-six nuclear submarines in operation; another thirty in various stages of construction between keel laying and commissioning; the aircraft carrier *Enterprise* and the guided-missile cruiser *Long Beach* in operation; and the frigate *Bainbridge* only a few days from commissioning. The total number of reactors represented by these ships was sixty-nine, to say nothing of Shippingport, five prototypes in operation and one under construction, as well as the improved reactor types he had under development. With a program of this magnitude, he was in a strong position to assess the ability of industry to meet the high standards demanded by the new and potentially dangerous technology. Disturbed by what he saw, he accepted an invitation to address the forty-fourth annual National Metal Congress.[53]

On the morning of October 29 at the Hotel Biltmore in New York City, about 700 people settled back to listen to a speaker already known as "the father of the atomic submarine." As he often did on such occasions, Rickover began in a philosophic vein. Progress, like freedom, he observed, was desired by nearly all men, but not everyone understood the cost. The price of progress, whether it was in culture, science, or technology, was more exacting standards. In any advancing society, some groups accepted the benefits of innovations, but ignored the obligations—an attitude that hampered progress. In his experience nuclear power was the best example of the confrontation of technology and society. Safe operation of nuclear power plants demanded highly competent and rigorously trained people. Bringing them into an established organization challenged personnel policies, engineering practices, and management procedures. But if society was to reap the advantages of nuclear power, present ways had to change. It was not only social patterns that had to adapt, but the technical products of that society had to be improved. Heat exchangers, pressure vessels, and valves, as well as turbines and generators were designed and manufactured according to long-established procedures, but these conventional components did not live up to specifications and were less reliable than the nuclear reactor itself. In his own organization, most of his senior engineers spent much of their time solving problems in the design, materials, and workmanship of the conventional components. If successful civilian nuclear power plants were to be built at reasonable cost and in reasonable time, the whole plateau of workmanship, engineering inspection, and quality control had to be raised far above the present level. That was the job of management.

One particular nuclear plant steam system had ninety-nine carbon-steel welds. The manufacturer stated that the welds had been radiographed and met specifications. But an investigation using correct procedures and proper X-ray sensitivity showed that only 10 percent met standards set by the American Society of Mechanical Engineers; 35 percent had defects in excess of the standards; and 55 percent had such rough external surfaces that interpretation was uncertain. Only because he insisted that manufacturers meet the standards that they themselves had accepted in the contract, did the bad situation come to light. Poor workmanship was part of the cause, but the underlying problem was the failure of management to enforce standards. The fault also lay directly with the technical associations who established the standards and with customers who accepted inferior work.

Radiography was another troublesome area. Because the technique had been in existence for over thirty years, Rickover had assumed that it was well understood and that the sensitivity requirements of the ASME and navy specifications were being met. This was not the case. The requirements had been violated, and large numbers of radiographs were of no use. One reason was that the specifications were thought to be a desirable goal rather than a firm requirement. Another was a lack of understanding as to what the specification requirements actually were and why it was important that they be met. At times an individual manufacturer changed a specification without informing the customer. In other instances, meeting the particular specification was thought unnecessary, but often the customer was not notified.

Modern technology demanded strict quality control, but here, too, the record was bad. Recently he had learned that a stainless-steel fitting had been welded into a nickel-copper alloy piping system for a submarine. The fitting had been certified by the manufacturer as nickel-copper and had all the required certification data. Indeed, the words "nickel-copper" were etched into the fitting. But it was the wrong material. The piping system was to carry salt water; had it been placed in operation, the stainless-steel fitting could have corroded away, and a serious casualty could have occurred. It turned out that other customers of the manufacturer had also received fittings of the wrong material. Rickover himself had been in a submarine far below the surface when a saltwater system failed because a fitting was of the wrong material. "But for prompt action of the crew, the consequences would have been disastrous."

He could not offer any sweeping solutions. More effective management and engineering attention had to be given to routine and conventional aspects of technology. Nothing could be taken for granted. Management had to get into details, had to look at the hardware, had to uncover the cause of troubles and take prompt corrective action—all the while taking nothing for granted. Technical societies could play an important role by seeing that specifications of high technical quality were developed, and consistently and rigorously enforced. Recognizing the influence of industry, he warned that technical societies had to guard against becoming "kept" organizations.[54]

Rickover drew prolonged applause. The press agreed that the issues he raised were important. The *New York Times* carried stories on the speech twice and featured a quotation from it in its column "Ideas and Men." Other leading newspapers and magazines—the *Washington Post*, the *Christian Science Monitor*, the St. Louis *Post-Dispatch*, *Time*, and *Business Week*—also had accounts. His reference to technical societies as complacent captives of industry was particularly goading. R. David Thomas, Jr., president of the Arcos Corporation of Philadelphia and a former president of the American Welding Society, issued a statement that his industry had overcome the problem of welding nuclear components.[55]

There had been progress, but claiming solution was going too far. Arcos was a leader in the development and manufacture of welding electrodes and the Naval Reactors rated their product better than most. The corporation, by accepting Naval Reactors–induced military standards, was helping to raise the level of the welding electrode industry. Still, as late as 1966 some cans supposedly containing Inconel material in fact held steel welding wire. In 1968 in another speech, "Who Protects the Public?" delivered before the Materials Engineering Congress and Exposition of the American Society for Metals, Rickover charged industry with deficiencies in safety codes. Again, he focused his attack on the failure of technical societies and business organizations to meet their responsibilities.[56] To Rickover, making individuals aware of the consequences of their actions was, as he titled his speech to the National Metal Congress, "The Never-Ending Challenge."

Making Ready for Sea

If the quest for safety and reliability had no end, at times there seemed to be milestones of achievement. One appeared at the beginning of 1962 when it looked as if Mare Island, with assistance from Electric Boat, had developed ultrasonic testing to the stage where it could be used in nondestructive testing of brazed joints. The improved technique even rejected a few good ones along with the bad, but this could be considered as a margin of safety. Ultrasonic testing would give the means to examine the submarines in commission. Now the bureau could check them as their schedules permitted.[57]

Portsmouth was to test the Thresher's silver-brazed joints ultrasonically, but the extent of the effort had not been settled. With all the work that had to be done on the ship, the yard was eager to hold testing to a minimum. In drawing up the schedule, Portsmouth proposed to inspect only those joints that had been repaired as a result of shock damage, arguing that the others had been examined earlier and the tests had proved them sound. The bureau disagreed. Before the test, it pointed out, 8 out of 115 joints showed irregularities. A visual inspection of all saltwater systems was needed. Again Portsmouth demurred. Not only was the examination unnecessary, but it would also be impossible to carry out in the time the ship was in the yard. On 20 July 1962 the yard and ship officers reached a compromise. All silver-brazed joints two inches and larger that were not covered by wrapping or insulation and were readily accessible should be examined visually.[58]

Still not satisfied, on August 28 the bureau directed Portsmouth to use at least one ultrasonic test team on the Thresher for the rest of the time the ship was in the yard. The team was to test as many of the joints as possible and to keep a complete record of every joint checked. Because the effort was a pilot project, the bureau wanted comments, suggestions, and recommendations.[59]

For the yard, ultrasonic testing—difficult and time-consuming to perform—was an additional burden imposed when the Thresher was already falling behind schedule. Portsmouth had underestimated the extent of some of the work and accepted additional jobs. On November 29 the quality assurance division summed up the results of testing. Of 145 pre-overhaul joints on saltwater systems two inches and larger, 13.8 percent did not meet minimum bond requirements. If the bureau's directive was to be carried out, insulation around some piping would have to be removed. On December 4 the yard stopped ultrasonic testing on additional old joints. The shipyard commander and the production officer were aware of the action; the bureau was not. Portsmouth had neither informed it of the decision nor forwarded the results of the work it had done.[60]

Axene was troubled by the use of silver-brazed joints in saltwater systems. He made the point in a report he submitted on 16 November 1962 to the chief of the Bureau of Ships. Axene thought the Thresher was the most effective antisubmarine warfare weapon afloat. Although difficult and dangerous to handle on the surface or at periscope depth, the ship behaved beautifully at greater depths. He gave high marks to the propulsion plant and its resilient mounting, but he considered many systems needlessly complex. Flooding at test depth was the greatest potential danger. Somehow the bureau had to cut down on the amount of piping and flexible hoses in saltwater systems subject to full sea pressure, particularly in areas where silver-brazed joints were involved.[61]

Much to his regret, in January 1963 Axene received orders to report as prospective commanding officer of a *Polaris* submarine. He did not want to leave, at least at that time. Not only had he found duty on the *Thresher* exciting and challenging, but he also wanted to take the ship back to sea. His request for delay was turned down, for the navy was critically short of nuclear-trained officers at a time when the nuclear fleet was expanding rapidly. That same month his executive officer, William J. Cowhill, was also transferred.[62]

Axene knew his replacement, Lieutenant Commander John W. Harvey, for the two men had served together on the *Nautilus*. Axene had been executive officer and Harvey a junior officer. After graduating from the Naval Academy in 1950, Harvey served in a carrier for about a year before reporting for submarine duty. He was in the diesel-electric submarine *Sea Robin* when Rickover accepted him for nuclear propulsion. Although not one of the original *Nautilus* crew, Harvey was present when the submarine reached the North Pole. He was sent to Windsor, Connecticut, for training on the S1C, the prototype for the *Tullibee*. Later he became the engineer officer of that ship. His next assignment was the *Seadragon*. He was executive officer when that ship crossed the top of the North American continent and participated in polar exercises with the *Skate*. The *Thresher* was his first command.[63]

Harvey was in a difficult position. The *Thresher* was far behind schedule, and the deputy commander of the Atlantic submarine force was growing impatient, for the delays were affecting his operational commitments. On 19 January 1963, the deputy commander wrote to the commander-in-chief of the Atlantic Fleet and the chief of the Bureau of Ships. Certainly, Portsmouth might not have been able to foresee some additional work, he admitted, and some was beyond the yard's control. But the need for better planning, scheduling, and use of manpower was clear. He expected the yard to expedite.[64]

Perhaps even more troubling for Harvey was the personnel situation. He and his executive officer were new to the ship. Of the eleven officers, only five were qualified in submarines; the others were learning. Of the eleven, three, including himself, were qualified in the nuclear plant. Only three officers had been with the *Thresher* for any significant time. Learning that more transfers were in the offing, Harvey asked the Bureau of Naval Personnel to delay. He won agreement that no more of his officers would be shifted until sometime after the *Thresher* was back at sea.[65]

At last there were signs that the long stay at Portsmouth was ending. For five days, beginning on February 23, the propulsion plant operated on shore steam. On March 15 the reactor reached criticality, supplying steam for the next two days. Harvey began his fast cruise on March 23, during which he conducted drills and tested equipment. He found too many things going wrong in both areas. On the morning of March 26 he called his officers into the wardroom to tell them he was cancelling the rest of the fast cruise. He had counted 456 deficiencies, of which 186 had to be corrected before he would consider the ship ready for sea.[66]

The yard was astonished. Heronemus had set up a watch in a field shack at the end of the dock in case anything was needed, but had heard nothing until his office phone rang at noon. Normally blunt and outspoken, Heronemus was angry. Of course the deficiencies should be corrected, but he did not think them serious enough to justify interrupting the fast cruise. But that, he recognized, was Harvey's business.[67]

At eight o'clock on Sunday morning Harvey resumed the fast cruise. Twenty-four hours later it was over. One valve casualty would require some days to fix, but nothing else had occurred that was critical. The crew needed more training: during a drill simulating a flooding casualty, it took twenty minutes to isolate the leak.[68]

On April 1 tugs moved the *Thresher* to an acoustic basin for further work. The next day Harvey issued the agenda for the approaching sea trials. Responsibility for the schedule belonged to the shipyard commander, but the ship's commanding officer had a strong voice in the matter. The trials could be divided into three parts.

Once clear of the river mouth and on the way to the initial dive area, such equipment as the fathometer, radio transmitters, radar, and navigational equipment would be tested. Harvey would build up to flank speed—the maximum speed forward. When the propulsion plant was in a stable condition at flank speed, he would reverse the engines and gradually build up power until the ship was backing at emergency full speed. After testing the engines at these two extremes, he planned to go to all ahead flank, to emergency reverse, and from maximum speed astern to ahead flank—maneuvers that placed a heavy strain on the propulsion train of turbines, reduction gears, and propeller shafting.

The first dives would come about three hours out of Portsmouth. For the most part these would be at periscope depth. The crew would check for leaks and test the periscope, underwater communications, torpedo tubes, and snorkel. After another interval on the surface of about an hour and a half at full power, the *Thresher* would submerge again for a sixteen-hour shallow dive, during which it would run at full power for four hours, test various combinations of rudder and diving planes, and try out the sonar while the ship was traveling at various speeds. By this time the submarine would be beyond the continental shelf and in deep water.

The *Thresher* would be about twenty-five hours out of Portsmouth when the first deep dive was to begin. In two hours the ship was to descend to test depth and return to the surface for an examination of all the fittings that might have been damaged by pressure: running lights, sonar, antenna, searchlights, and other navigational equipment. Two hours later the second dive to test depth would begin. For almost six hours the ship would be hundreds of feet below the surface, operating at various speeds and rudder angles and testing equipment. Halfway to test depth and again at test depth, the crew would try out the main seawater valves and the auxiliary seawater systems.

All told, the ship would complete the last dive about thirty-five hours out of Portsmouth. The trials would be over. No tests were planned for the trip back. Harvey intended to cover most of the distance submerged; the ship was far more comfortable below the surface, and the tired officers and crew, as well as yard and contractor personnel, would gain some rest.[69]

With only a few days to go, Harvey called Lieutenant Commander Richard A. Claytor, Rickover's engineer who was following the work. A few problems were yet to be solved, Harvey reported, but none concerning the reactor plant. In that case, replied Claytor, no one from Rickover's organization would be on board.[70]

On April 4 tugs eased the *Thresher* into the dry dock for some last-minute work. On the morning of April 8, the submarine was floated and moored to berth 11 bravo. That afternoon yard and ship officers met in the wardroom to go over the uncompleted items on the work list. None were serious—touching up some paint in officers' country, a small job in the torpedo room, and a few other matters. In the midst of the discussion, an officer representing the Atlantic submarine force entered to announce that the escort vessel *Skylark* was ready to sail. Based in New London, the *Skylark* had to sail before the *Thresher* in order to reach the test area on time. As commanding officer it was Harvey's job to determine when his ship was ready. The first step in the immediate process was the *Skylark*. Harvey decided: "Tell her to sail."[71]

The Loss

A few minutes before 8 o'clock on Tuesday morning 9 April 1963, the *Thresher* was ready. The submarine was crowded, for in addition to its complement of 108 officers and men, the ship was carrying a member of the staff of the deputy commander of the Atlantic submarine force, three officers and thirteen civilians from the yard, and four representatives from two electronics companies. Only a few men in orange life jackets were on the low-lying rounded deck to handle the lines. Alongside, a yard tug waited to add its power to maneuver the unwieldy submarine into the river channel. At 8 o'clock came a flurry of orders. The men cast off the lines to the pier, and beneath the stern of the tug the water broke into turbulence as the propellers took hold. Out in the river the tug turned the *Thresher* downstream. Soon the men on deck cast off the lines to the tug, and the ship proceeded under her own power. Because the channel was narrow and tortuous the tug followed, turning back only after it had passed the light at the mouth of the river. Now alone, the *Thresher* steamed past the Isle of Shoals, into the Gulf of Maine, and toward the test area.[72]

At 9:49 A.M. the *Thresher* met the *Skylark* in shallow water east of Newburyport, Massachusetts. The submarine rescue ship had already had a moment of fame, for it had accompanied the *Nautilus* when it first got "underway on nuclear power." Built in 1946 as a fleet tug, the *Skylark* was converted the next year to its present role. Equipped with radio, sonar, radar, and an underwater telephone, the escort vessel was to keep in contact with the submarine at all times. It also had a team of divers and a submarine rescue chamber. The ship looked powerful and businesslike: a high pilothouse and bridge offered excellent visibility, a foremast carried radar, a short, stubby stack housed the diesel exhausts, a mainmast supported heavy booms, and a long afterdeck free of obstructions gave plenty of working space.[73]

But appearances were deceiving. The rescue chamber could go down only 850 feet; the *Thresher* would be taking its test dives in far deeper water off the continental shelf. The underwater telephone was the most effective means of communication between the surface ship and submarine, but it had serious drawbacks. Under good conditions, voice contact was possible up to three or four thousand yards, but even then surface waves, underwater sounds, or the motion of the two ships could distort the words. If voice transmission was poor, the operator could send his message in Morse code by sound impulses. Although that method took more time, it gave greater range and clarity.[74]

Lieutenant Commander Stanley Hecker had been captain of the *Skylark* since 8 January 1963. On graduating from the New York Maritime College at Fort Schuyler, New York, he received an ensign's commission in the naval reserve. In 1950 he was called to active duty and served in the diesel-electric submarines *Tench* and *Perch* and later was assigned to the *Skylark* as navigator. Hecker had done well as commanding officer. In March his ship received an official commendation for ingenuity, tenacity, and superb seamanship for towing a complicated target array under adverse wind and sea conditions. In April, only a few days before her present assignment, the *Skylark* had undergone an operational readiness inspection and received the grade of excellent. Although Hecker knew in general the *Thresher*'s intentions, he had not been furnished with a copy of the trial agenda.[75]

The first day ended without incident. The *Skylark* had sighted some discolored water that looked as if it came from the *Thresher*. Upon investigating Hecker could not determine its origin, but it looked like a muddy bottom disturbance. At the end of the day the two ships separated, each proceeding independently to a rendezvous over 200 miles off Cape Cod where the water was deep.[76]

At 5:45 in the morning of 10 April 1963, the two ships found they were about ten miles apart. The sky was overcast, visibility was about ten miles, and the sea was calm. In order to calibrate its sonar, the *Thresher* radioed the *Skylark* to circle. At 6:35, the submarine, through its periscope, sighted the escort at a distance of about seven miles. Harvey requested Hecker to lay to while the submarine approached to get in range of the underwater telephone. Still at periscope depth, the *Thresher* stopped at 3,400 yards southeast of the *Skylark*. Two minutes later, without surfacing, Harvey announced he was beginning his first dive to test depth. The water was 8,400 feet deep.[77]

The *Skylark* signaled that it would maintain just enough speed so that the ship could answer its rudder. The *Thresher* replied that the escort could maneuver as it wished so long as it remained in its present area. At 7:50 the *Skylark* asked for a "Gertrude" check every fifteen minutes. The check was a brief message—perhaps only a single word—that the *Skylark* would send and the *Thresher* would acknowledge or repeat; in this way the two ships would know if they were in contact with each other. Two minutes later the submarine was 400 feet below the surface, pausing to check for leaks. A few more messages passed, and at about 8:07 the *Thresher* announced it was proceeding to half its test depth. By expressing its intention in these terms, rather than in feet, the submarine was minimizing the chance of any unauthorized person learning the depth at which American submarines could operate. At about 8:35 the *Thresher* telephoned it was descending to test depth less 300 feet.[78]

On the *Skylark*'s bridge and pilothouse the routine was normal. Hecker was present. Lieutenant (junior grade) James D. Watson, the navigator, was at the plotting table, the officer of the deck was standing forward of the binnacle, and the junior officer of the deck was close at hand. An enlisted man was at the helm, another was standing by as messenger, and the quartermaster of the watch was present. Roy S. Mowen, Jr., a veteran of four years on the *Skylark*, was operating the underwater telephone while Wayne H. Martin, radioman third class, kept the log of the underwater telephone messages. Martin, more accustomed to the format of the radio log, occasionally erred in making his entries so that a message from one ship was ascribed to the other. The underwater telephone had a loudspeaker; consequently, everyone in the pilothouse heard the message of 8:53, "Proceeding to test depth."[79]

From the course changes the *Thresher* sent, Hecker could tell that the submarine was descending in a spiral. Near test depth Mowen found a transmission hard to understand. A few minutes later the two ships exchanged a Gertrude check. About 9:13 the men in the pilothouse heard a calm voice state: "Experiencing minor difficulties. Have positive up angle. Attempting to blow."[80]

The wording was puzzling. "Positive up angle"—if those were the words—was not standard phrasing. "Positive" and "up" were redundant. "Blow" meant Harvey was trying to add buoyancy by using compressed air to expel water out of the ballast tanks. At least "minor difficulties" was reassuring, and the calm tone of the unknown voice transmitting the message was not alarming. Nonetheless, Hecker took certain precautions. Realizing that the *Thresher* might have to surface, he took over the telephone to report that the area was clear of shipping and gave his own position. He got no reply to his request for the range and bearing. Coming up directly under the *Skylark* was a small but dangerous possibility. Hecker had been operating with one engine. He ordered the other three cut in, as they could give him more speed if he should need it. The *Skylark* received at least one message, perhaps more, but they were so garbled that they made no sense. Hecker repeatedly asked, "Are you in control?" One more transmission came over the loudspeaker, but only the words "test depth" could be understood. Hecker was certain he heard the submarine blowing its tanks.[81]

One agonizing minute stretched into another. Hecker clung to the hope that communications equipment had failed. He tried to make contact by Gertrude check, sonar, and radio. He brushed aside one officer's suggestion that he send a message to shore that the submarine was missing. At 10:40 he ordered hand grenades thrown over the side in groups of three, a recognized signal requesting a submarine to surface. Five minutes later—more time had gone by than he realized—he sent his first message to shore. Earlier that day transmission had been good; now, perversely, it was not. Not until the early afternoon—12:45 P.M.—did New London get the word that the *Thresher* was missing.[82]

There was nothing that Hecker or anyone else could do. The depth was almost 8,000 feet deeper than the rescue chamber could reach. As planes overhead sought traces, other ships gathered: the salvage rescue vessel *Recovery*, the frigate *Norfolk*, the destroyers *Wallace L. Lind*, *Blandy*, *Yarnell*, *Samuel B. Roberts*, *Warrington*, *The Sullivans*, the *Sunbird* (another submarine rescue ship), and the oceanographic research vessel *Atlantis II*. Later more ships came to assist. Beneath the surface the nuclear submarine *Seawolf* and diesel-electric submarine *Sea Owl* probed with sonar and called the *Thresher* on the underwater telephone. There were no results. Except for an oil slick, a piece of plastic, and two rubber gloves, nothing could be seen on the surface. The weather was growing worse. Winds gusting up to 40 knots were building seas 5 to 9 feet high. On the night of April 10 Admiral George W. Anderson, chief of naval operations, made the now inevitable announcement: the *Thresher* was overdue and was presumed missing.[83]

Investigation

The navy had to investigate. Not only was there the moral obligation to the families of the missing, but there was also the need to determine insofar as possible whether the tragedy held lessons for the construction and operation of other submarines. In its long history the navy had devised various means to probe disasters. For one of the magnitude of the *Thresher*, a court of inquiry was the proper forum, because it had the power to subpoena witnesses. Fred Korth, secretary of the navy, with Admiral Anderson, chief of naval operations, and the judge advocate general, determined the membership. Vice Admiral Bernard L. Austin was named president, with Rear Admiral Lawrence R. Daspit, Captain William C. Hushing, Captain James B. Osborn, and Captain Norman C. Nash as members and Captain Saul Katz as counsel.

Austin had wide service experience. Graduating from Annapolis in 1924, he was assigned briefly to the Bureau of Ordnance and later to the battleship *New York*. He had experience with older diesel-electric submarines, having served on the *R 10* and *R 6*, and having commanded the *R 11*. He had been an instructor for three years in electrical engineering and physics at Annapolis. When the United States entered the war, he was a naval observer in London. Later he saw combat in destroyers off the coast of North Africa and in the South Pacific. At the time he was selected to head the court, he was president of the Naval War College. Not only was that assignment prestigious, but it came under the office of the chief of naval operations, not under one of the fleet commands. The point was subtle but important, for it meant that Austin could deal directly with officers in military commands.

He had not selected the other members of the court but he was pleased to have them. Daspit had also commanded submarines, and during much of the time the *Thresher* was in operation and in overhaul, he was the commander and deputy commander of the Atlantic submarine force, a somewhat equivocal position because he had been impatient to get the *Thresher* out of the yard. Hushing, an engineering-duty-only officer, had been supervisor of shipbuilding at Electric Boat since 1960 and was winning recognition in the service for his contributions to speeding up Polaris submarine construction. Osborn was the only member with experience in nuclear propulsion, for he had been the first captain of the *George Washington*, the first Polaris submarine. Because of his training, he felt a special responsibility to the court. Nash had attended the Naval War College and was qualified to command submarines. In his present position as commander of Service Squadron 8 in the Atlantic Fleet, he was thoroughly familiar with problems of damaged ships and salvage operations. Katz, a highly intelligent legal officer, had held a command; not many of the navy's lawyers had done so. His job was to see that the court was prepared to ask the proper questions of the witnesses, and that the members knew ahead of time the areas of experience or technical knowledge of the men they were examining.

Austin's orders called for convening the court at New London at 10 o'clock on the morning of April 11 or as soon thereafter as possible. As it turned out, not until 8:25 in the evening could Katz take the official steps of reading the orders appointing the court and begin examining the first witness. Austin had already determined the strategy the court would follow. It would hear first those witnesses who knew something about the immediate circumstances of the loss of the ship—such as the officers and men on the bridge of the *Skylark*—for their impressions would fade quickly. Then the court would turn to other individuals who might offer valuable information on the design of the *Thresher* and the work done on the ship at Portsmouth. Insofar as possible the sessions would be open to the press, but because the court would have to get into secret matters such as submarine construction and operating procedures, a good deal of testimony would have to be heard behind closed doors.[84]

Two civilians—John T. Conway and Edward J. Bauser—were present when Austin began the proceedings. Senator John O. Pastore, chairman of the Joint Committee on Atomic Energy, had sent Conway, the executive staff director, and Bauser, also a staff member, to attend both opened and closed sessions of the court. Pastore had two purposes in mind: one was to get the facts necessary to fulfill the committee's legal responsibility to keep fully informed of the nation's atomic energy program; the other was to forestall attempts of other congressional committees to seek headlines by launching their own investigations. Conway, a reserve officer during the war and a former FBI agent, possessed degrees in engineering and law. Bauser was a retired navy captain of twenty-two years' service who had been in Rickover's program from 1952 to 1958. He was at the Idaho reactor testing station when three soldiers were killed while working on a small reactor the army was using for training purposes.[85] Bauser had not been impressed with the investigation of the Idaho accident.

Relations were strained at first. Some members of the court thought the two outsiders would leak information to Rickover, who would try to influence the findings. Conway and Bauser, on the other hand, thought the navy might try to whitewash the disaster. Conway decided that both he and Bauser should be present at every session, or if one had to be absent, another staff member should attend. In that way two representatives of the committee could check their impressions against each other and lessen the possibility of misunderstanding. A moment of tenseness came when Austin called for a closed session. While the visitors left the room, Conway and Bauser remained. For a few moments the court hesitated before going on with its work.

After hearing the testimony of the officers and crew of the *Skylark*, on April 13 Austin moved the court to Portsmouth, still concentrating on those men whose memories of the *Thresher* just before the ship went to sea might hold some clue. As time went on, much of the initial stiffness between the court and the congressional staff wore off. Conway and Bauser admired the decisive way that Austin ran the court, while he, in turn, recognized that by keeping the staff members fully informed he could ease the navy's relations with Congress. On the other hand, the two civilians always kept a certain distance. Even though they were staying at the same motel, they did not dine or mingle with Austin and other members of the court.

In the evenings the six officers frequently discussed what new evidence the day had brought forth. Osborn felt himself the technical expert and was willing to explain nuclear operations to the others. After dinner he and Nash would occasionally go back to the yard and board the nearly completed *Tinosa*. The two officers would walk through the compartments, trying to visualize what had happened from the scanty evidence they had.

In the mornings the court assembled. Before each session the members and counsel would go over the schedule for the day, discussing who was appearing, what evidence they were likely to contribute, and what they would be asked. As time went on each member compiled a notebook of various records; these, too, became a source of questions.

Rickover Testimony

Austin followed the same strategy at Portsmouth as he had at New London, hearing those individuals who had firsthand knowledge of the condition of the ship just before it went out on trials, and only then turning to those people who had technical knowledge of submarine design and construction.

Rickover had been hard hit by the tragedy. He knew the officers, some of the men, and the ship. To families he penned personal letters of condolence. He saw the inquiry as both an opportunity and a danger to the nuclear propulsion program. It was a danger because over the years he had antagonized the bureau concerning many technical matters—not just the *Thresher*—and he had strongly criticized Portsmouth work. But there was another dimension besides technical issues. As the transfer of Axene and Cowhill showed, the navy was desperately short of nuclear-trained officers qualified for command. Many diesel-electric submarine officers had been anxious to enter the program, but he had refused to accept them for training. He had rejected them because he had concluded that many of these officers, bold and skillful operators during the war, would be unable to adapt to nuclear technology. In a way it was one more instance of individualism giving way before the imperatives of technology. Rickover was certain that his standards for selecting officers for training would be attacked once more.

On the other hand, the inquiry could be an opportunity to show how the technical standards that he had insisted upon should be applied to other work. As he had pointed out in his letter to James of 13 February 1962, "High integrity steam and salt water systems are equally as important in a submarine as the nuclear systems; all involve safety of the ship."[86] As Rickover saw it, the navy had embarked upon a technological revolution in many areas. Probably the exact cause of the loss of the *Thresher* would never be known, but the tragedy could serve as a scythe to cut down outmoded practices and organizations.

Rickover's testimony could help—if he were allowed to testify. From contacts, he heard rumors that he might not be asked to appear. He believed it was human nature to seek a scapegoat. He was convinced that in the ranks of both the engineers and the seagoing officers were many individuals who would be pleased to see the blame foisted upon the reactor plant and his authority and prestige curtailed. What to do was not an easy question. If he were ignored he would have no opportunity to present his views. If he were asked by the court to testify, it could be interpreted as an admission that evidence had been discovered that pointed to the involvement of the reactor plant. On the whole he and his senior staff decided he should testify, but it should be soon. Furthermore, although less important, he had scheduled a trip abroad.

While some individuals did not want Rickover to appear at all, Austin and others on the court realized he had to testify. It was inconceivable that the court could launch an investigation in which the chief of the Bureau of Ships and other high-ranking officers would have to appear, and not include Rickover. For the court it was a matter of timing; Austin was still anxious to hear first those individuals closest to the event. On 17 April 1963, Austin telephoned Rickover to set a date. Both men agreed there was no urgency. That soon changed. Pressed by his own commitments and an increasing concern over rumors circulating that he was not to testify, Rickover called Austin and told him of an impending trip overseas on official business. Austin still wanted to delay. On April 22 Rickover went to Korth, who asked Austin to change his schedule. The result was an agreement for Rickover to appear on Monday morning, April 29.[87]

The day began awkwardly. The court had arranged to have Rickover met at the airport on Monday. However, he had flown in on Sunday, been picked up by Hinchey, and brought through a back gate into the yard, where he stayed overnight. Until it was time for him to appear, he waited in Hinchey's office. For a few minutes he and the court met privately. Rickover wanted to know how the transcripts were made. Austin explained the procedures, and the two men turned to how the session would begin. The first part would be open. Austin would announce that the court had asked Rickover to appear and would state that the court, to date, had found no evidence that the reactor plant was responsible for the loss of the ship.

In the open court under the agreement reached with Austin, Rickover began by detailing his responsibilities. With this in the record, Austin stated that so far there was no evidence that the reactor plant had any direct causal relation to the loss of the ship. Rickover repeated the facts that he had already released to the press shortly after the loss of the *Thresher*; these described the inherent safety of the reactor, its construction, and its materials. Ships monitoring the area as late as the day before had been unable to detect any unusual radioactivity.

So that he could give his views in more detail, the court went into closed session. He saw a fundamental cause of the disaster.

> I believe the loss of the THRESHER should not be viewed solely as the result of failure of a specific braze, weld, system or component, but rather should be considered a consequence of the philosophy of design, construction and inspection, that has been permitted in our naval shipbuilding programs. I think it is important that we re-evaluate our present practices where, in the desire to make advancements, we may have forsaken the fundamentals of good engineering.

Since the *Thresher*, he had taken other steps aimed at further simplification of the plant, and he and his organization had gone even further in making sure that component manufacturers had established strict quality-control measures. He thought it would be wise to restrict the operating depth of submarines temporarily to a few hundred feet, and he proposed an examination of all submarines as their schedules made them available. He recommended a thorough examination of one submarine from each yard for integrity of hull, saltwater, hydraulic, and high-pressure-air systems. For those ships under construction, he thought the designs should be changed to specify welded saltwater systems. He also suggested that the yards be inspected to see if they were complying with specifications and were not granting waivers on their own initiative. Only the Bureau of Ships should have that authority.[88] Rickover left the court, promising to help in any way he could and somewhat disturbed that the members had so few questions to ask him.

Rickover's testimony carried the burden that the navy must reform to meet the demands of advancing technology. Other officers agreed that changes had to be made, that serious problems existed in the shore establishment and in the forces afloat.

Rear Admiral James, chief of the Bureau of Ships, spoke of his difficulties. Although shipbuilding appropriations had almost doubled in recent years, the bureau had been ordered to reduce its civilian personnel and engineering duty officers by 20 percent. Portsmouth was running significantly below its authorized strength of engineering officers. James's testimony reinforced the position that other yard officers had taken earlier; the lack of personnel was causing long hours of overwork, growing fatigue, and increasing possibilities of error.[89]

Vice Admiral William R. Smedberg III, chief of naval personnel, spoke bluntly before the court of the shortage of nuclear-trained personnel in the submarine force. The navy was producing Polaris submarines faster than it could find officers and crews to man them. The scarcity was particularly acute in commanding and executive officers; that was why the two officers had been transferred from the *Thresher*. The Bureau of Naval Personnel nominated its best and most seasoned diesel-electric submarine officers for nuclear training so they could qualify for such responsible positions as the command of a nuclear submarine. Of the numbers that Rickover interviewed, few were chosen. Smedberg expressly recognized Rickover's responsibility for the safe operation of the nuclear plants, but nonetheless, rigid standards of acceptance had caused two serious and undesirable conditions. One was overworking the nuclear-trained officers in the fleet so that they were being deprived of opportunities for staff duty and other assignments that would broaden and fit them for higher command. The other was the drop in morale of experienced diesel-electric officers who had done exceptionally well and now found themselves virtually foreclosed from entering one of the most promising programs of the navy.[90] Stripped to its essentials, Smedberg's position was that the navy should handle nuclear propulsion like any other complex technical program and not as a unique and uncompromising entity with standards of its own.

Behind Smedberg's testimony was the history of a clash with Rickover, for the two men were at odds at nearly every point. Rickover found that officers with the greatest experience in diesel-electric submarines were most often imbued with the habits and attitudes that were unpromising for the self-discipline and hard work required to operate nuclear ships. The argument that these men had spent years in command had no appeal to him, for these officers often represented an older tradition that had to be broken if the navy was to make the greatest use of nuclear propulsion. Younger officers were more adaptable and if properly trained, could handle responsible positions. Moreover, because they were young, the navy would have the benefit of their training longer. Rickover was willing to go beyond the ranks of submarine officers in the search for personnel, but this recommendation, while it might help ease the shortage, did not solve the problem of what to do with the diesel-electric submarine officers. Yet in Rickover's view, they had the chance to qualify. They were interviewed by him and his senior staff, and some, after all, were accepted for training—Axene, Harvey, and Wilkinson were examples. He would not compromise his basic philosophy—the navy had to adapt to a new technology. It could not be the other way around. The *Thresher* illustrated that point.[91]

Reconstruction

On 5 June 1963 at 9:20 A.M., the court began its last day—the forty-fifth day since they had first met—and one minute later they adjourned to consider all the evidence. Since 8:25 P.M. on April 11 the court had heard testimony from 121 individuals. The court had little enough evidence from which to reconstruct the last few minutes of the *Thresher*. From the testimony of the officers and men of the *Skylark* and of the Portsmouth officers and civilians who knew the condition of the ship when it left for sea trials, from entries in the radio and telephone logs of the *Skylark*, from knowledge of operating procedures, and from data acquired by the acoustical system that monitored the coast of the United States, the court drew up its conclusions, which it divided into three sections: 166 paragraphs of findings of fact, 55 paragraphs of opinions, and 20 paragraphs of recommendations.[92]

The *Thresher* began its final dive at 7:47 A.M. From 9:09 to 9:11 the ship might have blown its ballast tanks. At 9:11 the propulsion plant might have stopped or shifted to a lower speed. At about 9:13 the ship reported it was experiencing minor difficulty and was attempting to blow its ballast tanks. From 9:13 to 9:14 the ship might have blown its ballast tanks again, and at 9:18 came sounds that the navigator of the *Skylark* identified as those of a ship breaking up.[93] These events and these times—even if approximate—gave what the court believed was a framework upon which to conduct their investigation.

The court thought it probable that the ship was at test depth when a leak in the engine room occurred—possibly from a silver-brazed joint. As the ship attempted to blow ballast, it telephoned that it was experiencing minor difficulties. Water from the leak could have short-circuited the electrical equipment and caused the reactor to shut down. With no propulsion power except a small electric motor—which took time to energize—there was not enough force to drive the ship to the surface. One more attempt followed to blow the tanks, but by this time the submarine was probably too heavy and had gone beneath its test depth. Admittedly, the reconstruction was tentative, but it appeared logical and consistent enough for the court to draw up a chronology of probable events to run on a computer.[94]

But why had attempts to blow the ballast tanks failed? That question bothered Panoff. The blow system of the *Thresher* was complicated. Because of the requirement to operate at great depth, the bureau had designed the ship to store air at high pressure. To lessen the strain on the ballast tanks, the air had to pass through valves to reduce the pressure. Blowing ballast tanks was not an evolution that was performed at test depth. The reason was that the added buoyancy could bring the ship to the surface almost out of control. The usual practice, one which Axene followed, was to drive the ship up to periscope depth, look around to see if the area was clear, and then blow tanks. Almost never were the tanks blown at full pressure. Yet at test depth and in trouble, the *Thresher* had probably tried to do so, and something had gone wrong. Panoff thought blowing the tanks on the sister ship *Tinosa* might be enlightening. He approached one of his contacts. On April 19 the court carried out tests on the submarine. At full blow the valves froze.[95]

The reducing valves had strainers to keep out particulate matter. The strainers had not been required by the bureau, but the manufacturers had added them over and above specifications. Under certain conditions, moisture in air flowing at high pressure would form ice at constricting points.[96] In all probability, Harvey had tried to blow his way to the surface and the valves iced up. The pattern of an initial clogging, a few seconds in which the air passed through the strainer, and then a final blockage bore a close resemblance to what seemed to have occurred on the *Thresher*.

The court found that there was no requirement to design the valves to prevent blockage from the formation of ice. There were no dehydrators to remove moisture. Tests showed that the mesh strainers in the valves on the *Tinosa* were blocked and ruptured by the formation of ice in about thirty seconds. The *Thresher* had suffered some damage during shock tests. Although main power had not been lost nor the hull ruptured, a number of joints, fittings, bolts, rivets, and some machinery foundation elements had been disarranged. Even during the final stages of the stay at Portsmouth, items damaged by the test were discovered. The yard record on silver-brazing was poor. The bureau had directed Portsmouth to use an ultrasonic test team through the time the ship was in the yard to examine the maximum number of silver-brazed joints. By November 1962, 145 old joints had been tested ultrasonically with a rejection rate of 13.8 percent. After 29 November 1962, no more old silver-brazed joints were tested. The bureau was not informed either of the results of the surveillance or of the decision to stop testing. In the Findings of Fact the court stated laconically "that Portsmouth Naval Shipyard management and workers exhibited a high degree of confidence in the sil-braze joints in THRESHER's piping systems. . . . workers and management . . . [were] not in all cases adhering to the process and procedure documents. . . ."[97]

In the court's opinion the *Thresher* in all probability was lost because a flooding casualty in the engine room short-circuited the electrical system, causing the reactor to shut down. Operating procedures were inadequate to minimize the combined effects of flooding and the loss of reactor power. A poorly designed air system, susceptible to freezing, compounded the difficulties. The underlying cause of the disaster was the rapid change in material requirements called for by the accelerated pace of submarine technical development in the last decade. The court found that responsibility for the loss could not be placed on any one person or group of individuals.[98]

In its final recommendations, the court called for several detailed measures to be applied to the *Thresher*-class ships, other operating submarines, and those to be built. As was to be expected, seawater systems and silver-braze joints received a great deal of attention. Some joints of particular systems were to be replaced by welding, and all those remaining were to be thoroughly inspected and certified. In addition, for the *Thresher* class certain tests of the air system were prescribed, and the strainers in the reducing valves—those that had frozen up on the *Tinosa* and probably on the *Thresher*—were to be eliminated. On a broader issue, the Bureau of Ships was to require submarine builders to adhere to specifications and to obtain waivers where compliance was impracticable. And the bureau should increase its audits of yards to make sure that specifications were being met for construction, overhaul, and repair.[99]

The Joint Committee

Although the court had finished, the joint committee still had its commitment to Congress to keep. On 24 June 1963, the committee received a copy of the transcript of the testimony, the findings, opinions, and recommendations. Two days later Pastore called a hearing at which Korth described the measures the navy was taking as a result of the disaster, Austin explained the court's findings, and other officers dealt with such matters as brazing, welding, and air systems. The next day, June 27, Rear Admiral John H. Maurer testified. As director of the submarine warfare division of the office of the chief of naval operations, he was the spokesman for the officers of the submarine fleet. He believed Rickover's procedures and regulations could have been a factor in the loss of the *Thresher*.

> . . . there were specified operating procedures in connection with the nuclear plant, and these were hard and fast and rigid procedures. These were the ones that the boys were operating on. When the plant scrammed, assuming that it scrammed, the plant remained shut down until they had gone through these definitive steps to bring the plant back. . . .

By that time it was too late, and the ship was plunging to her death. Pastore summed up the argument: the ship might have surfaced had it not been for the reactor procedures. Perhaps, admitted Maurer, although of course other factors might have been involved.[100]

Computer Studies

Rickover had also received the court's testimony and conclusions. They clearly involved the reactor plant and operating procedures. Moreover, during its investigation the court had asked a team of specialists to analyze the acoustical evidence. The analysis appeared to indicate that the reactor plant had slowed down or stopped. Some of this data the court turned over to a computer group. From several computer runs the court selected three. Two were on the edges of probability, but the third, the court believed, was the most probable approximation of the events of those last few minutes. In each run several minutes elapsed from the time the reactor plant slowed down or stopped and the collapse of the ship.[101] That was why Maurer's charges of slow recovery time and rigid procedures were so important.

Rickover and Panoff acted quickly. Their first job was to gain access to the acoustical evidence. With the support of Rear Admiral William A. Brockett, now chief of the bureau, and over the initial reluctance of some officers, Rickover and Panoff, and Paul W. Hayes and Peter S. Van Nort—two other engineers from Naval Reactors—discussed the evidence with the technical specialists on July 8 and 9. It soon became apparent that the evidence was very unsubstantial as far as the reactor plant was concerned. It was impossible to tell whether the reactor had slowed or not. Admittedly, at some point the ship had lost power, but other factors could have accounted for that. The data considered by the specialists did not jibe with the information offered by the *Skylark*'s logs. After reexamining their analysis, the specialists prepared a memorandum containing new conclusions that, based on acoustical evidence not earlier made available to them, great care should be taken in assigning undue certainty to the evidence that they had been asked by the court to study.[102]

Next, Rickover, Panoff, Van Nort, and Hayes met on July 19 with Captain Samuel Heller and Captain Donald Kern, who had participated in the computer studies. Portsmouth had carried out a number of these studies on flooding rates, blowing capacities, as well as acoustical evidence. Heller repeated what he had previously testified before the court.

Portsmouth had made its computer runs based on figures and assumptions provided by the court. The computer personnel had never been requested to comment on these assumptions.

In addition, the meeting revealed that no computer run had ever been made that completely matched the case that the court designated as most probable. It was clear that the court had extrapolated from some computer studies and patched together fragments from others. Perhaps even more serious, the court had adjusted some of the times and assumptions to make the sequence of events more consistent. On the other hand, the court had never claimed certainty in its analysis of the disaster. It had explicitly stated that the specific nature of the loss of the *Thresher* could not be determined by assumptions and computer solutions based on those assumptions. All it was trying to do, the court pointed out, was to determine the parameters of various factors.[103] Unfortunately, however, the description of the studies in the court's conclusions lent a hard edge of actuality that the members never intended.

Portsmouth made new computer runs of the court's most probable case, but added some elements, substituted times from the *Skylark*'s log, and took into account certain factors affecting the buoyancy of the submarine. When Rickover walked into the joint committee hearing room a few minutes before 2:00 P.M. on 23 July 1963, he had received the new results. They showed that the submarine would have surfaced. If nothing more, the new run indicated that there was not enough tangible evidence to draw a hard and fast conclusion.[104]

It was not his intention, Rickover began, to defend the reactor plant, but Maurer as the navy's chief submarine officer, and James and Moore as two of the leading engineers, had stressed the possibility of reactor failure. Of course, that possibility could not be ruled out, but the evidence for that interpretation was tenuous. Even worse, the underlying problems of design, manufacture, inspection, quality control, and operating procedures were being ignored. These had to be corrected to prevent more disasters. He was looking at the reactor area to see what improvements he could make but: ". . . the real lesson to be learned is that we must change our way of doing business to meet the requirements of present day technology."[105]

That his procedures for reactor plant operation were so rigid as to be a factor in the loss of the ship was an incomprehensible argument. To believe that reactor operators were so thoroughly indoctrinated that they would not violate these procedures in the face of imminent danger was nonsense. For all normal conditions, standard procedures were mandatory. They reflected years of experience and, if properly followed, usually kept the machinery and operators out of trouble. In an emergency, the operator had to take whatever steps he thought necessary to save the ship. The operators were not robots, blindly following procedures when the safety of the ship was at stake. "Common sense tells you this is not so." He himself had added to the reactor procedures the statement that the instructions referred to normal operations and were not "intended to restrict . . . the actions which a Commanding Officer may . . . take in an emergency involving the safety of his ship."[106]

Recognizing that it was impossible to design equipment that would never fail and equally impossible to devise procedures that would cover all contingencies, the only logical course was to train the operator so that he would have a thorough understanding of the plant and its capabilities. That was the reason Rickover had worked out a comprehensive interview system—in which his senior staff took part—to select officers who were intelligent, capable of understanding complex phenomena, willing to undergo rigorous training, and able to grasp the essential element that in confronting a technical problem there could be no equivocation or evasion. A reactor operator had to be able to integrate the information flowing to him and use his knowledge of the plant to handle the situation. He could not depend on memorizing procedures. He had to know. Where Maurer saw the procedures and training as rigid and prohibitive, Rickover saw them as the basis for intelligent action in an emergency.[107]

Nothing angered Rickover more than the statement that it took the loss of the *Thresher* to convince him that the ship and its crew were more important than safeguarding the reactor plant. After the loss of the submarine, he had reduced the time to restart the plant, but this was part of a continuing effort that went back to the first voyage of the *Nautilus*. As reactor technology improved and as operating experience accumulated, he had decreased the start-up time. He had also cut down on the number of factors that could cause the reactor to shut down. On sea trials he personally witnessed the watch sections—not just the officers but the men at the controls—start up the reactor after a sudden shutdown. The loss of the *Thresher* added momentum to decreasing recovery time, but it had not begun that effort.[108]

Rickover's fundamental charge was that the navy was failing to keep up with technology. It asked for high-performance submarines that demanded the utmost in design and construction. The court found that the nuclear portion of the ship had higher standards of design and quality assurance as well as more strict administrative control than other parts of the ship, although, he observed, the conclusions did not refer to this superiority. From several witnesses the court learned that expense was the reason why nuclear standards were not applied to the rest of the ship. Rickover declared the answer specious: it required more money, for example, to repair welds than to do them right the first time. That principle held true for other parts of ship construction: good design, carefully thought out procedures, and well-trained people saved money. Careful work did not necessarily add to the construction time. Throughout his testimony, and in discussion with the committee, one point was paramount. The ramifications of the disaster were greater than the tragedy itself. The navy had to improve—drastically—the practices of both government and private yards. It had to upgrade the design activities, fabrication techniques, and inspection methods. It had to get rid of transient management. The navy had to adapt to the technological demands being placed upon it.[109]

Finding the Ship

When the court held its last meeting on 5 June 1963, the *Thresher* had not yet been found, although enough debris had been discovered on the ocean floor to leave no doubt that the wreck was somewhere in the area where it had begun its last dive. On June 14 the navy-owned oceanographic research ship *Robert D. Conrad* photographed broken piping, an upright compressed-air bottle, and some perforated metal and attached insulation. Ten days later the *Atlantis II*, a research vessel operated by the Woods Hole Oceanographic Institution, dredged up a damaged battery plate of the type belonging to the *Thresher.*[110]

Dredging and photography in 8,400 feet of water was extremely difficult and time-consuming, but help was near. The navy had brought the bathyscaph *Trieste*—a manned craft that had descended to the deepest known point in the Pacific, far deeper than it would have to go to search for the *Thresher*—from the West Coast through the Panama Canal to Boston. On June 24 the *Trieste* made its first dive. It found nothing, partly because its electric motors gave a very limited radius for searching, while the extremely cramped space made every descent extremely uncomfortable. On June 27 the *Trieste* found a rubber shoe-cover worn when working in a radioactive area. Although the letters "SSN" could be seen, the cover was tantalizingly folded over so that of the three digits only the "5" was visible. In subsequent dives more debris was discovered, but the hull was as elusive as ever. Some scientists had speculated that the submarine might have plunged into the bottom with such force that it was buried under hundreds of feet of silt. The increasing amount of wreckage, however, was mute evidence that the ship had broken up on its way down and could not have had the momentum to bury itself.

On August 28 the break came. From out of darkness and into the glare of lights came a large amount of twisted and torn metal. To Lieutenant Commander Donald Keach, commanding the bathyscaph, the area looked like a junkyard. Navigation was dangerous, for visibility was limited and objects were distorted. For a moment the *Trieste* hovered while a mechanical arm picked up a piece of pipe. Very carefully the bathyscaph rose to the surface. Swimmers from the escort ship seized the pipe. On board the ship it was examined eagerly. Crudely etched on the surface were some numbers and "593 boat." More dives revealed structural parts that clearly came from the *Thresher*, but not much could be learned from the remains. On September 5 Korth announced that the navy was ending its search.[111]

In May 1964 the navy began a new effort to locate more of the wreck. Rickover favored the idea, for he thought it possible that some lessons might yet be learned. In this attempt the bathyscaph—greatly modified and renamed the *Trieste II*—operated with the naval oceanographic ship *Mizar*. The *Trieste II* proved disappointing, but the towed cameras from the *Mizar* located major parts of the wreck. During one dive the bathyscaph actually settled on a large piece of wreckage. In this and the other descents the craft found no evidence of radioactivity that could be attributed to the *Thresher*.[112]

Aftermath

Shortly after the loss of the *Thresher*, the navy took several steps to improve the safety of its submarines. To Conway it was part of the joint committee's responsibility to know what those measures were. Moreover, he was not satisfied with all the information that had been developed at the hearings of June and July 1963. Particularly startling was the revelation that radiographs for the non-nuclear portions of the *Thresher* and *Tinosa* had disappeared at Portsmouth. Furthermore, he was deeply convinced that the navy owed itself, the families of the men who had died, and the nation a public account of the disaster. He and Bauser had been greatly disappointed with Korth's decision that none of the transcripts of the joint committee hearings could be declassified and that to release excerpts would run the danger that these might be read out of context and damage public confidence in the navy. Senator Clinton P. Anderson, chairman of the committee's subcommittee on security, found the navy's position astonishing, particularly since an article by Hanson Baldwin in the *New York Times* dealing with the influence of the *Thresher* loss on submarine design contained information that could only have come from naval sources. As time went by, the situation remained unsatisfactory to the joint committee; the hearings were still classified, and the navy was silent on what it was doing to prevent another disaster. On October 1 Bauser warned that the navy's stand was preventing the committee from meeting its legal responsibilities, and it might not be able to prevent other congressional committees from launching their own investigations. Under these circumstances the committee might have to hold more hearings. Paul H. Nitze, Korth's successor, was less reluctant to see that a declassified version of the hearing was prepared, and Conway, Bauser, and other members of the staff worked closely with the navy to make sure that as much of the transcript as possible would be released. On 1 July 1964 the committee held its final hearing concerning the *Thresher*.[113]

Vice Admiral Lawson P. Ramage, who had directed the earliest search for the *Thresher* and who was now deputy chief of naval operations (fleet operations and readiness), spoke of the measures taken in the submarine forces as the result of the loss. Submarines were operating under temporary procedures that restricted the depth to which they could dive and the speed at which they could maneuver at various depths. They were operating with positive buoyancy; that is, with the ship trimmed so as to be lighter than the water surrounding it. The training procedures had been modified to simulate flooding and other casualties. The submarine force was assuming greater responsibility for testing new submarines by instituting rigid inspections and determining that the officers and crew were adequately trained. Force commanders had changed the trial procedures; test dives took place in water shallower than the crush depth of the hull. All new submarines were authorized to make three controlled dives to test depth; one to check system integrity, another to test blowing the main ballast tanks, and a third dive, after post-shakedown availability, to test the first two items again. On these occasions a submarine rescue vessel was present, but was now equipped to tape-record all communications. On 18 February 1964, the secretary of the navy had established a submarine safety center at Groton with the task of improving operational procedures as well as collecting and disseminating information on safety. The navy, concluded Ramage, had learned valuable lessons from the tragic loss of the *Thresher*. Chet Holifield of the joint committee remarked that it was sad that it took the loss of 129 lives to demonstrate the need for safeguards.[114]

The technical measures to improve safety could be divided into two categories: those to be incorporated in new submarines, and those to be applied to existing submarines so that the restrictions on their operations could be removed. Most of these modifications stemmed from the recommendations of the court and the *Thresher* design-appraisal group, a small body of experts set up shortly after the disaster and placed under retired Vice Admiral Andrew I. McKee, the navy's leading authority on submarine design. Despite the wishes of Korth, Rickover refused to be a part of the design-appraisal group, explaining that to join would involve him in bureau matters in which he had no responsibility, but he promised his organization would be available for consultation and advice. To pull all the proposals together, on 3 June 1963 Brockett established within the Bureau of Ships the submarine safety or "subsafe" program and a submarine safety steering task force to administer the effort.[115]

The subsafe program was complicated. Its goal was to determine those changes that had to be made before the bureau could certify the submarine for safe operation at test depth. Generally, critical piping systems had to be welded and radiographed or, if silver-brazed, ultrasonically tested. Certain types of castings, pipe connections, and fasteners (studs and bolts) had to be carefully inspected and replaced if found deficient. Remotely operated seawater valves were added along with a simple emergency main ballast-tank blow system. Some components were relocated to provide better access during an emergency. Diving-plane controls had to be carefully inspected. Finally, specific requirements for records and plans were established to make sure that no component or system vital to the safety of the ship had been overlooked, improperly tested, or was below standard.[116]

Not the least of the difficulties was that criteria for safe operation had to be developed for several classes of submarines already in operation as well as for those under construction and on the drawing board. The immediate goal, as far as the ships in the fleet were concerned, was to make those changes so that operation at test depth could be resumed. Other changes that would add a further margin of safety had to be postponed for a scheduled overhaul. For submarines under construction, the problem was complicated by the fact that the ships were in various stages of completion. Those nearly finished would have but few modifications and would have to return to the yard. Others not so far along were in better condition for alterations. For ships under design, the goal was to eliminate all but the essential internal seawater systems, reduce the number and size of hull penetrations, and decrease the number of pipe joints. The program was expensive.[117]

Rickover still had reservations about the trend of submarine development. He was certain that the desire for improved tactical performance had not been weighed sufficiently against the risks, and he believed a reassessment was necessary. He was convinced that shipboard automation was dangerous, for it led to complicated rather than simple systems. Admitting the good qualities of HY-80, he still worried about its propensity to crack, particularly in areas where inspection was difficult. He noted that the bureau was now issuing written procedures in ship construction; he had always required written procedures for the nuclear plant. The bureau was now going to audit shipyard performance; he had always had audits. The bureau was going to have the yards keep records; he had always kept records. He had all the radiographs for the nuclear work; once he kept them for three years, now he kept them for seven years. The shipyards were still permitted to deviate from bureau standards for non-nuclear work; he never permitted deviation without an official Naval Reactors approval. The loss of the Thresher, he repeated, was a warning—made at great sacrifice of life—that the navy had to change its ways.[118]

As for personnel, that situation too was changing. The bureau policy was to keep engineering officers in one activity as long as they were effectively utilized. The optimum tour of duty was about four years. Of course, death and resignation could alter the pattern. Rotation for the sake of professional development was not a prime consideration in an officer's assignment. As for nuclear-trained personnel in the fleet, Rickover saw improvement. He was now taking about 400 young officers into the program each year. He had trained or was training about 1,500 officers and 10,000 men. Ramage thought there was still a shortage of nuclear-trained officers in certain ranks, but the problem was becoming less acute. Rickover pointed out that he did not take any enlisted man into the training program who had been in the navy over four years, and few officers who had over two or three years of commissioned service. Therefore the navy could get a lot of use out of the people he was training. He was proud of his record. With the 1 July 1964 hearing the joint committee completed its role in the *Thresher* investigation. The staff prepared an unclassified version that, even with substantial deletions, remained the most complete and useful account of the tragedy available to the public.[119]

In years to come the subsafe program changed. Originally the effort was intended to end after the specifications had been established and the ships brought up to them. Experience showed that continual scrutiny was necessary, not just to make sure that the safety standards were maintained, but because as a submarine grew older, additional areas had to be watched. Certification became a matter for each individual ship and was good only for a specific period of time. Inevitably, as more ships were built, instances of poor workmanship and improper use of material occurred, but these were now recognized for the dangers they were.

Operating below the surface would always be dangerous, a truism that the subsequent loss of the *Scorpion* only emphasized. On 27 May 1968, the navy announced that the ship was overdue on a voyage from the Mediterranean to Norfolk. The wreckage was finally located in deep water off the Azores. Rickover never relaxed his vigilance. In 1973 he discovered that because of a faulty depth gauge the *Greenling* was operating far below its indicated depth. Another gauge of a different type worked properly. However, the location of the instrument was poor, and even though it was more reliable, its reading was ignored. Although not his responsibility, Rickover got the situation made right. He continued the struggle to improve quality control, but as late as 1980 a serious mixup of materials and welding problems was uncovered at Electric Boat.[120]

The loss of the *Thresher* remained unsolved. To revert to the sequence of events: the ship began its deep dive at 7:47; about 9:11 the propulsion plant was either stopped or slowed; at 9:13 came the message "experiencing minor difficulties. Have positive up angle. Attempting to blow." Then came the sound of air under pressure, then silence. At 9:17 a garbled message, possibly containing the words "test depth," was followed by the sounds of the ship breaking up.

It is difficult to believe that a leak at test depth that would cause the reactor to stop at about 9:11 would be characterized two or three minutes later as a "minor difficulty." At or near test depth something did happen that seemed minor—and therefore was not a failure of the reactor plant or a major break in the watertight integrity of the ship. Harvey might have tried to slow his speed, but was unable to stop his downward movement. As a last resort he attempted to blow his ballast tanks—an action that was rarely tried at deep depth. The valves froze, freed themselves momentarily, and then froze again, just as they were to do days later on the moored *Tinosa*.

It is the nature of a few disasters that their cause can never be known. There are no witnesses and no survivors, and too many possibilities exist either singly or in combination. They include those related to personnel: the failure of leadership and training. They include those related to technology: the failure of design, materials components, and systems. In the case of the *Thresher*, Rickover never claimed he knew the cause, but he was certain that, in the absence of data to pinpoint a cause, the proper course was to return to the fundamentals of good engineering. It was easy to take that conclusion as an eloquent but empty phrase of pious exhortation. He did not mean it that way. Determining the fundamentals of engineering for a new and expanding technology required experience and hard thought. Keeping them from being obscured by management and administration required obsessive attention.

The Nautilus *and other early nuclear-powered submarines proved the value of the new technology by steaming long submerged voyages at high speed, by becoming an integral part of the nation's nuclear deterrent, and by penetrating polar regions that previously had been inaccessible. For surface ships the case for nuclear*

CHAPTER FOUR
Surface Ships— First Battles

propulsion was less compelling. Although they could steam long distances at high speed without refueling, they cost more to build, man, operate, and maintain than their oil-fired counterparts. Even before the first surface nuclear ships had been approved, defense officials, naval officers, and legislators questioned whether more should follow.

The nuclear surface fleet also was caught up in the congressional shift from annual appropriations, which covered only the orders to be placed that year, to the so-called full-funding concept, in which the total estimated cost of a construction project had to be appropriated at the outset. Under the full-funding approach, aircraft carriers and other weapons with an initially high cost and a long construction period became the focus of increased congressional attention.[1]

The application of nuclear propulsion to the surface fleet stood in sharp contrast to that of the submarine fleet. The future of nuclear propulsion was secure in submarines; for surface ships, it was always in doubt. The arguments were less technical—although technical problems were severe—than political. This chapter, which traces the story through the Eisenhower administration, is the first of three on the subject.

The application of nuclear propulsion to the surface fleet apparently had begun well. In three consecutive fiscal years the Eisenhower administration had requested and Congress had approved three different types of nuclear-powered surface ships: the cruiser *Long Beach* in 1957, the attack carrier *Enterprise* in 1958, and the frigate *Bainbridge* in 1959.[2] Each was a major warship.

Without doubt the aircraft carrier was the capital ship of the surface fleet. Crammed into its hull were the living quarters for over 4,000 officers and men of many skills and professions, elaborate and sophisticated machine shops, as well as hangars, magazines, stores, and tanks for aviation and ship propulsion fuel. Whatever the training of the officers and men or the function of the compartment, all had one purpose: to serve the 90 to 100 aircraft whose mission was to attack the enemy and defend the ship.[3] To many individuals the attack carrier, moving at tremendous speeds and launching and recovering its planes with swift and sure precision, was the embodiment of sea power. To others the ship was an expensive relic, a reminder of a recent and glorious past that was being outstripped by the atomic bomb, jet aircraft, nuclear submarines, and missiles.

Cruisers had a long and distinguished history stretching back to the beginning of the steam navy. The *Long Beach*, however, was to be something special. It was the first cruiser designed by the navy since the end of World War II. Not only was it to be nuclear powered, but the *Long Beach* would also be the navy's first large ship armed only with missiles. Talos and Terrier surface-to-air missiles would provide air defense, while Regulus, an air-breathing surface-to-surface missile, would strike at targets several hundred miles away.[4]

The frigate* had evolved after World War II to meet the needs of the navy for a surface ship large enough to serve as a destroyer squadron leader and flagship, and to carry missiles, guns, and antisubmarine weapons. The result was a ship only slightly smaller than a cruiser. It had several functions; screening high-speed task forces, covering amphibious landings, or operating independently.[5]

It could be argued that the three nuclear-powered ships were a promising attack upon the serious problem of obsolescence. Almost half the ships on the active list had been built during World War II. The navy estimated an average life of twenty-five years for large warships, twenty for small warships, and thirteen to fifteen for submarines. Assuming an overall life of twenty years, about half the fleet was midway through its active life. It was not simply a matter of years: new weapons, aircraft, radar, and sonar were speeding up the pace of obsolescence. To prolong

---

*In 1975 the term "frigate" was replaced by "cruiser" and nuclear frigates that had been designated DLGNs became CGNs. In these pages "frigate" is retained because it appears in congressional testimony and other official documents during the period covered in these chapters.

the life of its ships, the navy had embarked upon a vigorous modernization program. Attack carriers were receiving angled flight decks and steam catapults to make the handling of jet aircraft easier and safer. Cruisers and destroyers were being fitted with new ordnance and electronic equipment. But the smaller the ship the more difficult it was to make improvements, for the requirements for space and power were hard to meet. Some parts of ships were easier to modernize than others; it was simpler to install new radar or even a missile system than to make major changes in the propulsion plant.[6]

Senior officers had given much thought to the future fleet. On 13 January 1958 Admiral Arleigh A. Burke, chief of naval operations, approved distributing "The Navy of the 1970 Era," a study that had been three years in preparation. The navy would be large, consisting of 537 major warships—410 surface ships ranging from destroyer types up to attack carriers—and 127 submarines, of which 52 would be missile and 75 would be in the antisubmarine forces. Adding 200 smaller combatant ships and 190 noncombatant ships brought the total of the active fleet to 927. Prospects for the new propulsion technology for the surface fleet looked good: six of twelve carriers; twelve of eighteen guided-missile cruisers; and eighteen of fifty-four guided-missile frigates would be nuclear powered.[7] With a fleet of this composition the navy could have six all-nuclear-powered task forces consisting of an attack carrier, two guided-missile cruisers, and three frigates.

The Technical Background

When Burke approved the long-range study, the fundamentals of nuclear propulsion had been well established and demonstrated, for the navy had the *Nautilus, Seawolf,* and *Skate* in commission and four other submarines on the building ways. However, nuclear propulsion for surface ships posed its own set of tough technical difficulties. Carriers, cruisers, and frigates had a much greater tonnage than submarines and required far greater shaft horsepower to drive them at high speed. Going to higher power meant facing new problems in physics, metallurgy, and other areas of reactor technology. Because each ship would have more than one reactor—the *Bainbridge* and *Long Beach* would have two and the *Enterprise* eight—the propulsion plant layouts demanded careful thought. For surface ships Rickover was following the same strategy that had proved successful in submarines: he assigned a project to Bettis or Knolls and used one laboratory to check the work of the other. And he built land prototypes.

Construction of the first surface ship prototype reactor, the A1W, began in April 1956 at the commission's National Reactor Testing Station. As the designation suggested, it was the first reactor plant designed by

Westinghouse for an aircraft carrier. Obviously, it was impractical to build on the Idaho desert a full-scale eight-reactor plant such as would power the *Enterprise:* instead the facility was to consist of two reactors and the associated steam equipment to drive one shaft. Where possible, Naval Reactors and Bettis were using the A1W to test and develop different reactor materials. The prototype had another purpose: its data would be used for the design of the C1W plant for the *Long Beach.* To anticipate, the first reactor reached full power on 17 January 1959 and the second on September 4 of the same year. Both operated together at full power for the first time on September 15.

The ships themselves were already under construction. The Newport News Shipbuilding and Dry Dock Company, after enlarging its major dry dock by cutting a huge notch at one end for the bow of the ship, had laid the keel of the *Enterprise* on 4 February 1958. At the Quincy, Massachusetts, yard of the Bethlehem Steel Company, the *Long Beach* had completed the first year of a troubled construction history.

As was to be expected, work on the *Bainbridge* was not as far along. Rickover had assigned to Knolls the design and development of the D1G, consisting of a reactor and the steam plant equipment for one propeller shaft. The facility was in the very early stages of assembly in the 225-foot-diameter Horton sphere that had once contained the S1G, the sodium-cooled prototype for the *Seawolf.* Again to anticipate, the D1G did not reach full power operation until 9 May 1962. Bethlehem at Quincy was to lay the keel of the frigate on 15 May 1959.[8]

Maintaining the balance between work at a prototype and a yard was never easy. Endeavors at both areas were complicated and had demanding and interwoven schedules. In some respects the situation at the prototypes was easier in that Rickover was in charge, for they were commission-owned and were built and operated under commission contract. At the shipyard circumstances were different, for several technologies, many of them the responsibility of other parts of the navy's organization, came together on the building ways. Reports from the yards were showing a nearly universal trend. Construction costs were going up rapidly, whether the ship was oil-fired or nuclear-propelled.

The Threat Of Rising Costs

Two forces were driving up the costs of construction. One was the introduction of more elaborate and sophisticated weapons and equipment. Missiles, radar, sonar, and nuclear propulsion could provide military capabilities far beyond those of only a decade earlier. Concerning weapons, for example, the ordnance for a World War II light cruiser had cost $17.6 million and its largest gun had a range of 12.8 miles. The missiles for the *Long Beach* were estimated at $44.5 million, with the short-range missile reaching out 20 miles and the Regulus having a range of 1,200 miles. In addition, other costs were also going up. Statistics gathered toward the end of 1957 showed that between 1945 and 1956 wages for shipyard labor had increased 62 percent. For skilled labor the gain was much more: wages of welders had gone up over 90 percent. Over the same period, the composite index for shipbuilding materials showed a rise of 118 percent, while steel had increased two and a half times. To some extent the civilian economy shared the same trend. From 1941 to 1945 the average car with typical accessories cost $900 at the plant. In 1956 the average car with typical accessories cost $2,350 at the plant, an increase of 2.6 times.[9]

Before Congress, naval witnesses spoke of their anxiety over increasing costs. In the early months of 1959 Thomas S. Gates, secretary of the navy, and Burke appeared before the armed services and appropriations committees. The major item in their proposed fiscal year 1960 program was a new attack carrier. The ship they asked for was non-nuclear. Gates admitted that nuclear propulsion promised the ability to steam great distances without refueling, but the advantage did not seem worth the extra cost of $120 million. Burke, Vice Admiral Wallace M. Beakley, deputy chief of naval operations (fleet operations), and others hammered over and over again at the same point: it was the carrier that was important—not the propulsion plant.[10] To the aircraft taking off it was the flight deck that mattered—not how it got there.

To these men naval air power was an indispensable element of sea power, and since the end of World War II carriers had proved themselves in the Korean War and in other international crises that might have led to conflict. To meet its commitments the navy wanted fifteen modern attack carriers. It had made good progress toward this goal, for in every construction program from 1952 to 1957 Congress had authorized a *Forrestal*-class carrier. The last carrier to receive approval was the *Enterprise* in the 1958 program. A glance at the cost of the *Forrestal* class showed what was happening. The *Forrestal* herself cost $218 million. The successive ships cost less because the shipbuilders were gaining experience, a phenomenon known as the "learning curve." The *Independence,* the fourth of the class and which was completed in April 1959, cost $189 million. With the *Enterprise* estimated at $314 million—which might be low—the picture looked grim.[11]

The navy did not get its carrier. Neither of the armed services committees authorized the ship. On the other hand, the Senate Appropriations Committee proposed a nuclear carrier, and in conference, the House and Senate appropriations committees compromised and approved money for long lead-time items—those components that took years to design, fabricate, and test. But without authorization, the action was hardly a strong measure, and the Department of Defense did not release the funds.[12] It could be argued that Congress was more interested in a nuclear carrier than the administration.

The outlook for a second nuclear-powered carrier was dim. There was no reason to think that the Eisenhower administration would ask for one in its next budget; it was far more likely to repeat its request for an oil-fired carrier. Conceivably, the *Enterprise* might be the first and last nuclear carrier. If that were the case, the prospects for the application of nuclear propulsion to the surface fleet were slim.

Because the entire building program was in trouble, Burke embarked upon a vigorous campaign to stem the rising tide of construction costs. In June 1959 he pointed out to Rear Admiral Ralph K. James, chief of the Bureau of Ships, that more thorough effort in the research and engineering phases of new developments had to be carried out before placing them in a ship. Building time had to be cut, changes to a ship had to be held to a minimum, and only those accepted that promised significant improvement in performance. The *Long Beach* was the most notorious example of the problem—an original estimate of about $80 million had soared to $250 million.[13]

In his scrutiny of all bureau operations James included nuclear propulsion. Was it possible to make some reductions, perhaps by decreasing the inventory of spare parts and by transferring some costs to research appropriations? He could have gotten scant satisfaction from Rickover's reply. Reducing spare parts was risky and would yield little savings, for most had been purchased and were being manufactured. Even if that were not the case, decreasing the number of spare parts was dangerous, for the failure of some component without any in reserve could wreck the construction schedule. As for research, funds for the development of nuclear propulsion came from the commission—not the navy.[14]

A new factor threatened to drive up costs of the *Long Beach* even further. From information reaching him John A. McCone, chairman of the Atomic Energy Commission, believed that the Russians were having trouble in completing their nuclear-powered icebreaker *Lenin*. If this were so and if the Americans sped up the work on the *Long Beach*, the United States could have the first nuclear-powered surface ship—an achievement to place beside the first nuclear submarine and the first nuclear power plant.[15]

The idea did not last long. As the schedule stood, Quincy was to finish the ship in mid-October 1960, except for the missile systems. By cutting back even more on the degree of completion, it might be possible to get the ship to sea in July 1960. In the new timetable the propulsion plant would be the pacing item, but Rickover thought he could meet the goal with an additional $1 or $2 million. His inspection of the *Lenin* during his trip to Russia with Vice President Nixon's party gave him confidence in his view. In July 1959 Burke and McCone drew back. Burke suspected that the effort would take more funds than anticipated; McCone felt the chance of success too slim to warrant the extra expenditure.[16]

Rickover knew that speeding up the work on the *Long Beach* would be tough. Over the years Quincy had gotten a poor reputation for its work, labor relations, material control, and management. He thought the cost of the work high and the accounting practices lax. Several times he had complained to the management about the shortage of competent engineers and the lack of aggressive supervisory personnel, but corrective actions had been sporadic and short-lived.[17]

Late in the year he sent four of his own engineers to Quincy. All were topflight; all had somewhat different backgrounds; all were from different offices. Panoff was from the Washington headquarters, John W. Crawford, Jr., was the Naval Reactors representative at Newport News, James W. Carpenter was the Naval Reactors representative at Electric Boat, and John T. Stiefel from Westinghouse was the manager of surface-ship projects at Bettis. For thirteen days at Quincy they studied the yard's organization, observed work, and with the permission of management, interviewed individual supervisors. The conclusions were grim. Quincy personnel appeared to be lower in caliber, competence, and potential than to those of other yards. The material control system was antiquated, responsibility was fragmented, and communication between levels of management was poor. It was hard to find anyone who had a complete picture of the work to be done. The length of time Rickover allowed his men to be away from their jobs showed the depth of his concern.

One observation was unusually interesting. Management did not feel it was doing a bad job, but thought the unique demands of nuclear propulsion were the main source of the difficulties. To the Naval Reactors team the troubles lay elsewhere—in such conventional areas as poor welding and brazing and inadequate planning. Were these done properly, Quincy could be on top of the job.[18]

Nothing in the report surprised Naval Reactors. Its experience had shown that too often technical specifications and standards were regarded by workmen and management as useful goals that need not actually be met. While this attitude might have been tolerated in the past, it was clearly not acceptable for the new technology. The key to cutting costs lay in improving ordinary construction techniques. In a meeting with Burke on 1 December 1959, Rickover recommended sending a small group of officers to Quincy to see how Naval Reactors supervised its work and compare that effort with other areas of construction.[19] Doing the job right the first time was a lot cheaper than going back and redoing it.

The Hubbard Investigation

Burke decided to send an *ad hoc* committee to Quincy to examine the *Long Beach* and to Newport News to investigate the *Enterprise*. To lead the group he selected Rear Admiral Miles H. Hubbard. Although not an engineer, Hubbard had served briefly as chief of the Bureau of Ordnance. Other members included a captain from the Bureau of Ships, a supply officer, and Captain Eugene P. Wilkinson, prospective commanding officer of the *Long Beach*. In one vital aspect the job of the committee differed from what Rickover had proposed. Instead of looking into the causes of poor construction, the committee was to examine the reason for the escalating cost of nuclear-powered ships.[20]

For twelve days beginning on 4 January 1960 at Quincy and for three days beginning on January 20 at Newport News, the Hubbard committee talked to individuals ranging from senior management to supervisory personnel on the working level. At each yard Rickover made available to the committee the Naval Reactors representative and his report. Hubbard kept the sessions informal. All he wanted was information voluntarily offered him; he was neither conducting a formal investigation nor taking statements under oath.[21]

The Hubbard report came out on February 25. The committee investigated the number of changes that had been made in the specifications for each ship and traced the cost history, breaking it down into categories of construction plans and construction, electronic equipment, nuclear propulsion equipment, post-delivery work, and ordnance. For both ships every category showed an increase except one—the exception was ordnance for the *Enterprise;* in order to keep costs down, a weapon system had been deleted. The original estimate for the total cost of the *Long Beach* was almost $85 million; the latest projected cost was $313 million, an increase of 3.7 times. The original estimate for the nuclear propulsion equipment was $26 million; the latest projected estimate was $41 million, an increase of over 1.5 times. The original estimate for the *Enterprise* was $314 million; the latest projected cost was $472 million, an increase of a little over 1.5 times. The original cost of the nuclear propulsion plant equipment was $90 million; the latest projected cost was $133 million, also an increase of a little over 1.5 times.[22] The blunt fact was that the cost of everything was going up, and judging by the example of the *Long Beach* and *Enterprise,* the rate of increase for nuclear propulsion was not out of line.

The committee reached several conclusions. Of the two yards, Newport News was doing the better work. Quincy had been plagued by inefficient management, poor supervision in the lower levels, bad labor relations, resistance to efforts to improve productivity, and a lack of pride in workmanship. A problem in both yards was Rickover's tight control over the nuclear work. Admitting the need for close supervision, the committee found that the exercise of authority was so great that the builders seemed to be working for two masters: the supervisor of ship-building, an officer who represented the navy at the yard, and Rickover's representative. The committee heard that because the Naval Reactors representative bypassed the supervisor during technical discussions and kept him informed after the fact, the supervisor was not able to coordinate the efforts of the government. Nor was this all. The gap between the supervisors and the Naval Reactors representatives reflected the situation within the bureau where "the same schism . . . bears bitter fruit at all operating levels."[23]

The Hubbard committee saw no reason to push ahead and build more nuclear-powered ships until those now building were thoroughly tested at sea. There was little hope that pressurized-water reactors would ever be competitive with oil-fired plants; the technology was too expensive and the propulsion plants too heavy for the horsepower they provided. The committee reached the conclusion that the navy needed surface ships with greatly increased antiaircraft and antisubmarine warfare weapons and sensors; so long as cost was a factor, these should take priority over nuclear propulsion.[24]

Although angry, Rickover was not surprised at the report. He already knew that the purpose of the committee was not what he had proposed. Furthermore, by concentrating on nuclear propulsion the committee had inadvertently caused rumors that it was out to get Rickover. As for having two organizations at the shipyard, Rickover pointed out that it had been the usual practices and procedures that had allowed the situation to develop in the first place and had failed to correct it. With some irony he observed that the committee had found that new technology demanded new standards of control; these were exactly what he was providing for the nuclear work. The techniques and efforts made by Naval Reactors showed what could be done.[25]

There was never any chance that Rickover would decrease his role in the yards: indeed, the lesson of Quincy was that he could not. Perhaps the most significant part of the report was the committee's extreme reservations about the future of nuclear propulsion for surface ships— until some lighter and cheaper reactor was developed than that based on pressurized-water technology.

The *America* (CVA 66)

Doubts about nuclear propulsion for the surface fleet appeared also in the final months of 1959 as the budget for fiscal year 1961 was in preparation. The navy had asked for a nuclear carrier, but had been turned down by Secretary of Defense Neil H. McElroy and his successor Thomas

S. Gates. Hearing rumors of the decision, McCone reacted vigorously. If the navy was not interested, the commission could save money by reducing its naval propulsion program, stopping work on the destroyer reactors, and finding different uses for Bettis and Knolls. By passing these thoughts on to Rickover, McCone got a quick response, even if one not completely satisfactory. William B. Franke, secretary of the navy, replied on December 2 that the navy still wanted to convert the fleet to nuclear propulsion as quickly and extensively as the technology and funds permitted. The propulsion effort had to be seen in the long-range perspective, not from the short view of the annual shipbuilding programs.[26]

Testimony before the congressional committees in 1960 was even more bleak. Gates admitted that all future attack carriers might be oil-fired. Franke reported that initial enthusiasm over nuclear propulsion for surface ships had waned. No longer did the navy believe that the new technology would transform surface operations as radically as it had undersea operations. Burke and Beakley, while not going quite so far as their civilian chiefs on nuclear propulsion for future carriers, emphatically did not want one now. For Burke, it was cost; for Beakley, the advantages were vastly overrated. Beakley admitted the nuclear ship would have more space for bombs and aviation fuel, but this was no great advantage. Independence from logistics required some definition: an oil-fired carrier could operate its air groups four days without replenishing them, the nuclear ship five or six.[27]

The result was a foregone conclusion. Congress authorized and appropriated funds for the oil-burning *America*. Although there were some allusions that by appropriating funds for long lead-time items in the previous fiscal year Congress had indicated its will, there was no great controversy. Rickover believed that had the navy fought for a nuclear-powered carrier, it would have gotten one, but there was no way to prove the assertion. For the second straight year, however, the navy's construction program did not contain any nuclear surface ships.[28]

The Single-Reactor Plant—D1W

Rickover and Naval Reactors were convinced from the operating experience accumulating from the prototypes and ships, from closely following reactor development and other commission installations, and from some work at Bettis and Knolls, that there were no breakthroughs that offered a small, light, cheap reactor for ship propulsion. To reduce costs of the propulsion plant, Rickover and his engineers concentrated on refining and improving the pressurized-water reactors and on increasing the life of the reactor core so that a ship could operate longer between refuelings. Another path that might lead to lesser costs for surface ships was the development of a single-reactor plant.

Immense technical difficulties stood in the way of achieving a single-reactor plant for a surface ship. The power had to be high and its performance as flawless as possible, for a surface ship with a single reactor had no place to hide in the event of failure.

Under Rickover's stimulus, Burke in mid-June 1960 began the process of getting a single surface-ship reactor formally established as a commission project. On August 1 over the signature of James H. Douglas, acting secretary, the Department of Defense asked the commission to develop a low-cost, simple, lightweight single-reactor plant for a destroyer. It asked the commission to give the project a high priority so that the navy could place the ship in a construction program as soon as practicable. During a trip to Idaho with McCone to inspect the A1W, Rickover paved the way for the project. Reluctantly, the chairman and his colleagues, frankly disturbed and disappointed by the slowness with which the navy was moving in nuclear propulsion for surface ships, agreed to go ahead.[29] Rickover assigned the project to Bettis, where it was to become known as the D1W.

By establishing the D1W project Rickover had accomplished two things: he had an official statement that the navy was maintaining its interest in nuclear propulsion for the surface fleet, and with that declaration he had an answer to McCone's doubt whether the commission should continue to commit its funds and facilities to that goal.

Catapults for the *Enterprise*

As Rickover was bringing into existence the new D1W project, he was also bringing to an end a long battle over the type of catapult for the *Enterprise*. The origin of the struggle between Naval Reactors on the one hand and the Bureau of Aeronautics on the other went back several years. By the end of World War II, the navy had found increasing operational advantages in launching carrier-based aircraft by catapult. With the introduction of heavier aircraft after the war, the navy searched for better catapults. After experimenting with various approaches such as compressed air, fly-wheel, and hydraulic power, in 1952 the navy adopted the British-developed steam catapult.

Steam drawn out of the propulsion plant system was stored in an accumulator and fed through launching valves into catapult cylinders beneath the flight deck. The cylinders carried the piston that in a few hundred feet towed the aircraft from at rest to a speed great enough for it to take to the air. All the *Forrestal*-class carriers had steam catapults, and some carriers of the earlier classes had been fitted with them during modernization.[30]

In 1952 the Bureau of Aeronautics began to develop a catapult that promised to weigh less and deliver less shock to the aircraft. Because its power was to come from igniting a mixture of gas and air, the new approach was called the internal-combustion catapult. As a backup, the bureau also had under development a compressed-air catapult. The Bureau of Naval Weapons (formed by the merger of the old Bureaus of Aeronautics and Ordnance) and the Bureau of Ships agreed that the *Enterprise* would be fitted with the internal-combustion type.

Rickover and Shaw, his engineer who handled nuclear propulsion for surface ships, worried. In their view the navy was making the performance of one of its most important ships hostage to one untried development backed up by a second untried development. On principle Rickover thought it was dangerous strategy, but he also had a practical interest in the choice. If he could be sure that the internal-combustion approach would work, he could design the *Enterprise* steam plant to meet one set of conditions. Although assured that the internal-combustion development was proceeding well and he did not need to take into account demands for catapult steam, Rickover determined otherwise. On 26 October 1955 he decided to design the plant to handle the requirements of the steam catapults.

Two months later the experimental internal-combustion catapult at the Naval Air Station at Lakehurst, New Jersey, exploded. Shaw visited the installation. To him it was all too clear that much had to be done before the approach could meet its design objectives. Sponsors of the project, however, saw the incident only as a setback that could be made up in time. The specifications for the *Enterprise* continued to call for internal-combustion catapults. On 21 February 1956 Rickover won agreement that he was to design the steam system so that the ship could use either steam or internal-combustion catapults.[31] Design of the ship was to provide for either approach.

The Bureau of Naval Weapons was still expressing confidence in the success of the internal-combustion approach, although Shaw found it increasingly difficult to get details of the project. In July 1960 the A1W showed by a series of tests that it could more than meet the steam catapult requirements. By that time the internal-combustion approach was failing to meet specifications. The Bureau of Naval Weapons proposed to substitute the compressed-air type.[32]

Time was pressing hard. Newport News launched the *Enterprise* on 24 September 1960. Two days later the Bureau of Naval Weapons and the Bureau of Ships agreed to use steam catapults and to set the steam requirements. With these established, Rickover arranged a demonstration in the A1W. On November 10 Shaw led a group of eighteen high-ranking officers and civilians through the facility. He had the plant operated at several power levels, including ahead flank and astern full. Carefully, he allowed plenty of time for questions and discussion. When everybody was ready, he began the demonstration. In outward appearances the test was not dramatic. No significant changes in the A1W had been necessary. Only a valve had to be installed to remove steam from the system in the quantities and intervals needed for sustained catapult operations—those conditions the Bureau of Naval Weapons had set for a "maximum" strike while the ship was operating at full speed.[33] But the results were impressive. They showed that the nuclear propulsion plant could more than meet the requirements of any of the postwar carriers in operation, as well as those under construction and in the design stage.

To Rickover the struggle over the catapults illustrated a key principle: never be at the mercy of another's development project. In the case of the *Nautilus,* he had fended off some non-nuclear innovations that he feared would break down and hamper the ship's true purpose of illustrating the military advantages of nuclear propulsion. In the instance of the catapults, he saw other aspects as well. Considering the importance of the ship to the navy, it would be very hard to admit to Congress, the White House, and the public that the ship was inferior to oil-fired carriers in handling aircraft, and it would be hard to argue that the ship should be the first of a kind. He was sure that had the internal-combustion or compressed-air catapults been installed and found wanting, the blame would have been placed upon the nuclear propulsion plant and himself. He was convinced that an inferior *Enterprise,* regardless of cause, would have strengthened the hand of those individuals who opposed nuclear-powered carriers.

The Treatise

Although prospects for nuclear propulsion for the surface fleet were gloomy in the first half of 1960, they brightened during the remaining months. Not only was the D1W established and the long and often bitter fight over the catapults for the *Enterprise* finally ended, but a new administration—led by either Richard Nixon or John F. Kennedy—would also take a fresh look at the issue. Even before the voters made their decision, government routine called for the old administration to draw up the budget that would be presented—although probably changed in some respects—to Congress by the new. For the 1962 construction program, the navy asked the office of the secretary of defense to include two nuclear frigates.

To make the case for the ships, Naval Reactors and other elements of the bureau were drawing up cost comparisons between the nuclear frigates and their oil-fired counterparts. On 20 October 1960 the bureau forwarded to Burke the first approximations. Roughly speaking, three oil-fired frigates cost about the same as two ships of the *Bainbridge* class. After taking into consideration costs of construction, fuel, personnel, maintenance and operation, and a twenty-year life, a more elaborate analysis in late October confirmed the ratio that a nuclear frigate cost 1.5 times as much as a conventional frigate.[34]

The office of the secretary of defense deleted the two frigates on the grounds that one nuclear frigate cost twice as much as an oil-fired ship of the same type. Furthermore, until the *Bainbridge* was completed and was acquiring operational experience, the navy was premature in requesting the nuclear ships.[35]

Possibly the election of Kennedy, who had campaigned vigorously for a greater effort in national defense, was one consideration in Burke's mind when he called for a conference to discuss nuclear propulsion—especially its application to surface ships. He wanted a wide-ranging meeting to cover all aspects— operational, technical, and financial. Above all he wanted a completely open exchange of views and frank statements of differences. From the meeting he hoped would come a common position. Rickover, he added, would attend.[36]

In the conference room of the chief of naval operations on November 25, Rickover declared that the status of the nuclear surface-ship program was like that of the nuclear submarine effort when the *Nautilus* went to sea. What was needed was the follow-through. For that reason the two deleted frigates were crucial to the future of the surface fleet, for only by getting a number of these ships at sea could their full potential be discovered. It was not necessary to wait for the operation of the *Bainbridge* before going ahead; two years of successful operation of the A1W had proved the technology was ready. The navy should not delay until the single-reactor plant was operating. While that project was aimed at simpler, more reliable, and less expensive surface-ship plants and while the reactor would be the highest-powered Naval Reactors had yet attempted, the development was just beginning.[37]

Although no minutes of the meeting have been located, other evidence shows that from Rickover's view the session was hardly a success. On 5 December 1960, Douglas informed the commission that the Department of Defense would not include a nuclear frigate in the budget. Nonetheless, he expressed satisfaction that the commission was proceeding with the single-reactor plant. A summary Rickover had drawn up for Burke to distribute to senior naval personnel was severely toned down. The office of the chief of naval operations excised the urgency—phrases like "The time has come to enlarge the Navy's nuclear combatant surface fleet. . . ." were altered to "The Navy should enlarge its nuclear combatant surface fleet. . . ." The declaration that including a nuclear-powered frigate similar to the *Bainbridge* was a key step in the nuclear surface-ship program was drastically changed to read that the Department of Defense would not support the ship in the fiscal year 1962 program.[38]

A few days after the meeting Burke asked for a treatise to cover surface-ship nuclear propulsion from all angles—the positive as well as the negative—and to take up operations, logistics, maintenance, and personnel. The treatise could furnish a common denominator for preparing congressional testimony, for writing magazine and newspaper articles, and for giving background briefings. He assigned the project to Rear Admiral Robert H. Speck in the office of the chief of naval operations.[39] Speck worked closely with Naval Reactors, especially Shaw. In early 1961 "A Treatise on Nuclear Power in Surface Ships" was ready.

By dividing the material into four main parts—informative, favorable aspects, limiting aspects, and considerations—the treatise came to grips with its subject. The first section admitted that nuclear propulsion would not revolutionize the operation of surface ships the way it had submarines. Nonetheless, it gave surface ships significant military advantages. As for costs, available data made realistic if imprecise estimates showing that nuclear ships cost 1.5 times their oil-fired counterparts. It was important to recognize that the increase would be felt not only in construction but also in appropriations for personnel as well as maintenance and operations. In order of priority, destroyers and frigates stood to gain most from nuclear propulsion, for they steamed greater distances than the larger ships; next came cruisers and carriers.

Virtually unlimited high-speed endurance ranked first in the section dealing with favorable aspects. Nuclear propulsion gave a higher average speed of transit from one area to another. The nuclear ship did not need to replenish its fuel tanks from an oiler; it did not have to accept increased vulnerability by narrowly restricting its movements during refueling. By not requiring oilers, nuclear ships reduced the requirements for replenishment ships and the need to protect them.

Nuclear propulsion had other advantages. Because a reactor delivered steam at a lower pressure than an oil-fired plant, the steam-system components could be simpler and more reliable. Over its life a ship received new equipment that almost always demanded more power. An oil-fired ship had to meet those requirements from its limited supply of fuel, but a nuclear propulsion plant could be designed so that new equipment could be installed without affecting the ship's ability to steam at high sustained speeds. Nuclear propulsion eliminated stack gases that made turbulent air currents a problem around carriers, corroded exposed surfaces, and were particularly damaging to antennas. One fact was seldom considered: nuclear cores could be manufactured and stockpiled in an emergency; they were not radioactive, took up relatively little room, and could be transported fairly easily.

The section on limiting aspects turned at once to cost. The cost factor of 1.5 meant that the number of ships within a given monetary level was reduced on a two by three ratio; that is, the navy could buy ten nuclear-powered ships or fifteen oil-fired ships of the same type for the same total sum. As pointed out earlier, the ratio of 1.5 would have an impact on other parts of the navy's budget besides construction. The top speed of nuclear-powered ships was slightly lower than their oil-fired counterparts because of reactor limitations; the maximum sustained speed was about the same, but the endurance of the nuclear-powered ship at these speeds was greater by far.

The final portion of the treatise stated the navy's policy toward nuclear propulsion for surface ships, and in doing so made clear the grounds for conflict. National interests determined the size of the navy. When provided with adequate fueling facilities, oil-burning ships were able to meet the navy's commitments. The undeniable advantages of nuclear propulsion did not permit the navy to reduce its number of combatant ships.[40] Whatever else it was, the treatise was no ringing endorsement of nuclear propulsion for surface ships.

"A Treatise on Nuclear Propulsion in Surface Ships" contained little of the optimism that marked "The Navy of the 1970 Era." The years between the two documents showed the slow pace in the application of nuclear propulsion to surface ships; the 1960, 1961, and the proposed 1962 construction program did not contain any nuclear surface ships. The reason was cost. Three ways existed to attack that problem. The first was to search for a breakthrough that might reveal small, light, cheap reactors—but Rickover, Naval Reactors, and the laboratories saw no signs of its existence. The second was to build upon the accumulating pressurized-water technology to develop higher-powered reactors with long core life—along this course the program was already pressing hard. The third was to build ships and gain savings through experience. That way had been blocked by the Eisenhower administration, but its successor had campaigned hard for a stronger national defense. Perhaps the new administration might overturn the decisions of the old.

President John F. Kennedy appointed a strong and aggressive secretary of defense, Robert S. McNamara. Under him, nuclear propulsion for surface ships was a bitterly controversial issue. Debates in the Navy Department, the Department of Defense, and in congressional committees were not about the excellence of

CHAPTER FIVE
Surface Ships—The Alliance with Congress

nuclear-powered ships, but about how many the fleet should have. Rickover argued that all major combatant ships should be nuclear-powered; McNamara would agree only to one nuclear-powered carrier and a few nuclear-powered escorts. In the struggle over the propulsion plant for the carrier John F. Kennedy, McNamara chose the oil-fired plant and won the battle. His victory was costly but indecisive for determining future application of nuclear power to the surface fleet.

Secretary of Defense McNamara fit well into the mold of an administration of young and vigorous leaders. Born in San Francisco in 1916, he was well-educated, graduating in 1937 from the University of California and receiving his master's degree two years later at the Harvard School of Business Administration. After a brief stint with an accounting firm, he returned to Harvard to become an assistant professor. During the war he had served as a civilian consultant to the War Department on a statistical control system for the Army Air Forces and later was in uniform in England, India, China, and the Pacific. Up to this point his career had been that of a precocious and brilliant young man occasionally found on the campuses of major universities, but the immediate postwar years showed a different trend. In 1946 he joined the Ford Motor Company, then in the throes of a long-overdue reorganization. He rose rapidly, becoming president of the company on 9 November 1960, the day after the Democratic victory. It was a goal achieved by ambition, a hunger for power, a passion for hard work, an appetite for detail, and a conviction that the key to the most stubborn management problem lay in scientific analysis. McNamara had been head of Ford only thirty-four days when he agreed to become secretary of defense. He was convinced that the secretary had to take an active role in resolving defense issues. He had the authority he needed: the reorganization of the Department of Defense in 1958 gave him that.[1]

The new secretary of the navy, John B. Connally, had a very different background. A young but skillful and astute politician, he was closely associated with Vice President Lyndon B. Johnson. During the war Connally had served in Washington in the office of the chief of naval operations, in the office of the under secretary of the navy, and overseas as a member of the group planning the invasion of Italy. In the Pacific he was on the carrier *Essex* as radar and radio officer and later in the demanding job of fighter direction officer.[2]

Glenn T. Seaborg, the new Atomic Energy Commission chairman, was a brilliant chemist and a Nobel laureate whose experience with atomic energy was almost as old as the program itself. He was best known for discovering the element plutonium and devising a chemical process for its extraction. He was also the co-discoverer of nine transuranium elements, the author of several books and innumerable articles, and deeply interested in education. He was chancellor of the University of California at Berkeley when asked to become chairman. His nomination won wide acclaim, and his confirmation by the Senate was never in doubt.[3]

Rickover did not know McNamara or Connally at all, but he had met Seaborg several times. The new chairman had been one of the original members of the General Advisory Committee, established to advise the commission on scientific and technical matters. In those early years Seaborg had been favorably inclined toward nuclear propulsion, believing it might be a good way to bring industry into atomic energy.[4]

By accelerating the Polaris submarine program, Kennedy left no doubt where he stood on that issue. Placing Polaris missiles on surface ships was another matter. The Eisenhower administration had cancelled the further development of Regulus, which had been one of the weapon systems planned for the *Long Beach*. Shortly before the Kennedy administration took office, Admiral Arleigh A. Burke, chief of naval operations, had won approval to install Polaris on the nuclear cruiser, provided the navy could find the funds. McNamara decided that installing the missile on the *Long Beach* was not worth the cost. There was nothing a Polaris surface ship could do that a Polaris submarine could not do better. Not only was the surface ship more vulnerable than the submarine, but its deployment during a period of tension or limited war could also lead to a dangerous misunderstanding. Kennedy accepted the recommendation:

the ship was to be completed with her armament consisting only of Talos and Terrier surface-to-air missiles. But McNamara left intact the surface ship program proposed by the departed Eisenhower administration. It called for seven oil-burning frigates to add to the twenty-three (including the *Bainbridge*) the navy already had in operation or under construction.[5]

The *Truxtun*—The Second Frigate

The opening moves before the congressional committees in 1961 contained no surprises. Burke admitted that nuclear ships were superior but cost more. Beakley declared that the navy had not placed a nuclear frigate in the budget because Rickover had a single-reactor plant under development that perhaps would be ready for use in small ships in a few years. The deputy chief of naval operations called the *Bainbridge* an "exploratory ship."[6] Whatever he meant by the term, it was clear Beakley believed the navy needed no more *Bainbridge*s.

Rickover was upset by the navy's position. At the meeting of 25 November 1960 in Burke's conference room he had argued—obviously unsuccessfully—that the navy did not need to wait for the operation of the *Bainbridge* before building more ships of that class. Furthermore, the navy was placing itself in a poor position by basing nuclear propulsion for destroyers and frigates upon the development of a highly advanced reactor.

Outside the hearing room other forces were at work. It was no secret that Gates had dropped from the budget two nuclear frigates that the navy had requested. At some time and in some manner Rickover and certain members of Congress came together. By 19 March 1961 their plans were sufficiently firm for Rickover to telephone Burke, stating that the legislators wanted to know if the chief of naval operations really wanted the frigates. Burke did: if he could not have them this year, he wanted them the next.[7]

For some weeks Rickover had wanted to brief the secretary of the navy on the nuclear propulsion program. On April 18 he did so, emphasizing especially the critical state of the surface ship effort. Delaying construction in the hopes that a technical breakthrough would lower costs was unrealistic; the only way to achieve that goal was a steady construction program that would create and maintain the skills in vendors and shipyards. Citing the bureau studies that two nuclear frigates cost about the same as three conventional frigates, Rickover proposed taking two of the seven requested and making them nuclear. Although the navy would get six instead of seven ships, the two nuclear frigates would be superior and give the surface ship program the continuity it needed.[8]

He convinced Connally. Rickover raised another point. He was certain that he would soon be asked to testify: could he state that Connally approved including two nuclear for three oil-fired frigates? He could.[9]

At ten minutes past ten on the morning of 24 April 1961, Carl Vinson called the House Armed Services Committee to order. No congressman knew more about the navy than Vinson. Elected to the House in 1914, he had been assigned to the Naval Affairs Committee. He became chairman in 1932, just as the navy was embarking upon a major expansion program. After World War II the Naval Affairs Committee was merged into the new House Armed Services Committee, a change resulting from defense reorganization and military unification. Consequently, it was a very senior and powerful congressional leader who observed in his opening remarks that committee member William H. Bates of Massachusetts had proposed to substitute two nuclear for three oil-fired ships. Vinson had changed the hearing schedule so the committee could hear Rickover.[10]

The groundwork had been carefully laid. Rickover had already talked with Vinson to outline the points he wanted to make. Bates, James E. Van Zandt of Pennsylvania, and Melvin Price of Illinois were also members of the Joint Committee on Atomic Energy. Even though this was Rickover's first appearance before the House Armed Services Committee, he had every reason to think his reception would be friendly.

After describing the advantages of nuclear propulsion for surface ships, Rickover turned to the present situation. The single-reactor plant was far from ready for a ship, and it was a mistake to hold up the program for that project. Reactor technology forced restrictions on the application of nuclear propulsion for surface ships: he drew a line at 8,000 tons displacement. A nuclear plant in a smaller ship took up too much space; in a larger ship nuclear propulsion gave unparalleled advantages. L. Mendel Rivers of South Carolina was loud, emphatic, and enthusiastic in his praise of Rickover. Vinson hoped the committee report would state that nuclear propulsion should be considered for all combatant ships over 8,000 tons.[11]

From every indication Rickover's intervention had been successful. On April 28 Vinson and a few other congressional leaders met with McNamara to discuss several budget items, among them the two nuclear frigates. It made sense, Vinson observed, to adopt the substitute program. McNamara did not object. In his memorandum to the president the secretary of defense forwarded the proposal, recommending approval, but observing that he was not taking a stand on nuclear propulsion for the surface fleet. That subject, McNamara noted to Kennedy, he was just beginning to study.[12]

Although Rickover had not known about the Vinson-McNamara meeting, he as well as several other people soon learned the results. If encouraging, they were still tentative, for the Senate Armed Services Committee had yet to be heard from. As the Bureau of Ships began drawing up preliminary plans for the ships, Rickover urged great care. The future of the nuclear surface fleet depended upon the navy making a good construction record; that meant holding costs down. Therefore, the bureau should think of the new ships as copies of the *Bainbridge* and stay away from rearranging components or trying out new equipment. Even if the ships should have different armament, the bureau should hold to the original ship lines and the structure of the machinery space. As an additional measure to keep down costs, only yards experienced in nuclear work should build the ships. In his view Quincy and Newport News alone were qualified, but he deemed it likely that the Ingalls Shipbuilding Corporation of Pascagoula, Mississippi, and the New York Shipbuilding Corporation of Camden, New Jersey, might claim that constructing nuclear submarines fitted them to build nuclear surface ships.[13]

Connally was eager to know the bureau's plans. James's reply contained ideas paralleling those Rickover had offered; hull and propulsion plant to duplicate the *Bainbridge,* but armament to be improved. He intended to award the ships to qualified builders by competitive fixed price contracts. The bureau had already begun to prepare specifications and contract plans; these should be finished in September and the contracts let in the next six months.[14]

Although the bureau was moving into high gear, Congress had yet to complete its task. The first sign that all might not be well came in the House. On May 24 Vinson presented the report of the committee. It included the two nuclear and four conventional frigates, but neither the text of the document nor Vinson's remarks on the floor were as strong as the views he had expressed at the hearing. Neither contained an explicit reference to 8,000 tons. To cover the omission Van Zandt declared on the House floor that the committee held that no surface combatant ship over 8,000 tons should be built unless it was nuclear-powered. His colleagues showed no great enthusiasm for the idea.[15]

The real blow fell when the Senate Armed Services Committee called for the seven oil-fired frigates. In conference, the two houses reached an agreement authorizing the navy seven frigates, one of which was to be nuclear-powered. Vinson, studiously vague when he explained the compromise to the House on June 12, remarked that in a fifteen-member conference it was difficult to say precisely why any particular action had been taken. Nonetheless he found the compromise acceptable: one nuclear frigate had been deleted for reasons of economy, one conventional frigate restored for reasons of national security. Passage of the legislation was without incident: Kennedy signed the authorization bill on June 21 and the appropriation bill on 17 August 1961. The New York Shipbuilding Corporation, not a company Rickover rated highly, was awarded the contract for the ship and laid the keel at Camden, New Jersey, on 17 June 1963. The frigate was to be named the *Truxtun.*[16]

With good reason Rickover and his congressional allies could claim credit for the ship; why the Senate committee refused to follow he never knew. On the other hand, the *Truxtun* had not faced tough opposition: that was because McNamara had not made up his mind on nuclear propulsion for surface ships.

Surface Ship Reactors

The *Truxtun* was to be driven by a two-reactor D2G plant similar to the one Knolls was developing for the *Bainbridge*. The new frigate was important for the continuity of the program and as an addition to the surface fleet, but she was not a great step forward in propulsion-plant development. The A1W core 3 and the D1W were the major efforts in that direction. The A1W core 3 at Bettis was intended to provide data for improved cores for the *Long Beach* and *Enterprise* plants. Core 3 was to be installed in the A1W prototype when core 2 was depleted in 1963. Philip N. Ross, general manager of Bettis, had assigned the project to Ellis T. Cox, the general manager for surface ship projects, a logical move since he was responsible for the A1W and its various offshoots. By November 1961 Bettis had reached the stage where core design was reasonably firm.[17]

The A1W core 3 was advancing beyond its objectives. It promised to make possible a four-reactor plant that would produce about as much power as the eight-reactor plant of the *Enterprise*. By halving the number of reactors and by using many components and supporting systems already developed, Rickover hoped to reduce costs and stimulate new interest and support for nuclear carriers. As the A1W was the prototype and the A2W the *Enterprise* plant, the A3W became the designation of the new project.

At the same time, Bettis was developing the D1W, the single-reactor plant for the destroyer. Ross had assigned that project to Alexander Squire, a veteran who had directed the design of the Bettis facility that had produced zirconium for the *Nautilus* prototype in Idaho. He had also led the team that designed the S3W and S4W plants for the *Skate*-class submarines. At Newport News, engineers under John L. Redpath III began designing the reactor plant and steam plant arrangements, electrical system, and shielding. Redpath was assuming that the lines of the ship would be the same as for the *Bainbridge,* an indication that the single-reactor ship would be the size of the frigate.[18]

In the fall of 1961 the D1W was running into trouble. Studies at Bettis showed no advantage for the reactor over the two-reactor plant in space or weight. Analysis at Newport News disclosed a center of gravity that was higher than desirable. To see what could be done, in September Rickover formed a task force of senior engineers from Bettis and Newport

News, adding some from Electric Boat because of the company's experience in laying out steam plants within the restricted space of a submarine. At the end of the month the task force produced a layout that was somewhat less in length and weight than the *Bainbridge* plant. However, the question of plant reliability—crucial for a single-reactor surface ship—was proving troublesome.[19]

In November Rickover took a new tack, asking Bettis to study a D1W that would have a much higher power-rating—half again that originally planned. On 27 and 28 December 1961 he focused the entire D1W effort on the new approach. Newport News and Electric Boat had already begun to design a ship that would displace about 2,000 tons more than the *Bainbridge*. By his action he put an end to the work on a single reactor for a destroyer and to the idea that nuclear propulsion could be applied to surface ships smaller than that frigate, which, when fully loaded, displaced 8,500 tons.[20]

Surface Ship Trials

As Bettis was driving ahead with the second generation of surface-ship reactors, the first of the first generation was getting ready for sea trials. At the beginning of 1961 the propulsion plant of the *Long Beach* had been ready for almost a year; it was the weapon system that was holding things up. Rear Admiral John T. Hayward, deputy chief of naval operations (development), urged getting the cruiser to sea to provide the technical data for the *Bainbridge* and the single-reactor destroyer plant. He warned Burke that it might be very hard to convince Congress that the navy was really serious about nuclear propulsion if it did not get the ship to sea as soon as possible. Connally, agreeing that the trials should take place in July, was discouraged to learn that the ship would have to return to spend a lengthy period in a yard to finish the installation of the weapon systems. That too, he pointed out, did not look good.[21]

At 6:30 on the morning of 5 July 1961, the *Long Beach* was moored in the Fore River off the Quincy yard. For Rickover and Captain Eugene P. Wilkinson, the commanding officer, getting the navy's first nuclear-powered surface ship underway must have brought back memories of the *Nautilus* trials that had occurred six and a half years earlier. Then, too, Rickover had been in charge and Wilkinson had been the commanding officer.

Once past the Boston Lightship the cruiser began a long and complicated series of tests. That evening the main engines were shut down in order to clean the main condensers of the marine growth that had accumulated during the long time the ship had been at its dock in the yard. In addition, the sea chests had taken in a number of fish while the cruiser was passing through shallow water; these had to be removed. Shortly after midnight the *Long Beach* began its four-hour run at full power. Just as the ship completed that evolution, a heavy fog closed in, cutting down visibility at times to 200 yards. Occasionally the fog lifted enough for Wilkinson to carry out various maneuvers to determine the ship's characteristics. With visibility still poor, on 7 July the *Long Beach* steamed into dry dock. The ship had been at sea for about fifty hours and had steamed roughly 820 miles, a part of which had been over 30 knots. The propulsion plant had performed beautifully.[22]

Successful trials off New England augured well for those to be held farther south off the Virginia capes. Unlike Wilkinson, Captain Vincent P. de Poix, prospective commanding officer of the *Enterprise,* had no previous shipboard nuclear experience. An aviator who graduated from the Naval Academy with distinction in 1939, he won his wings shortly after the Japanese attack on Pearl Harbor. In 1960 Rickover selected him for training. A few days before the sea trials of the *Long Beach,* de Poix reported to Burke that the reactor plant testing in the *Enterprise* was moving along smoothly, and its performance was highly successful. All eight reactors had achieved initial criticality with no difficulty, the dock tests of the main engines had been completed on three of the four shafts, and he hoped that the entire propulsion plant could be tested as an integral unit at the dock later in July. Changing the catapult system from internal combustion to steam was controlling the schedule. Within recent weeks, however, Newport News had made excellent progress. Personnel was a headache; allowances established over a year ago were proving inadequate, especially for supporting the air group and for the propulsion plant and electronics systems. Nonetheless, de Poix believed the ship could be ready for trials at the end of October.[23]

Rickover worried about the proposed organization of the ship's engineering department. Regulations called for it to be responsible for the entire propulsion plant. With eight reactors the *Enterprise* contained the most powerful nuclear plant in the world. He believed it would be far better to concentrate responsibility for the nuclear portion of the plant into a separate reactor department headed by a reactor officer. That officer would have fewer personnel to administer and would be free from the distraction of supervising non-nuclear work. Rickover had his way, but the opposition was intense, both inside and outside his organization. It was based on the argument that splitting the engineering department would divide responsibility and lead to inefficiency.[24]

On 29 October 1961, at 9:14 A.M., the tide was right. Men on the docks and on the ship singled up the mooring lines.[25] The harbor pilot gave an order to the engine room before all the lines were cast off, a usual practice because in most ships it took time for the propulsion plant to respond. Not so for the *Enterprise.* As Rickover had warned, the nuclear plant responded immediately. The ship moved, snapping one huge hawser. If nothing else, the incident marked the beginning of a record-breaking voyage.

Spectators lined the banks of the James River as the ship, dwarfing the accompanying tugs, steamed toward the open sea. To one observer it seemed as if a part of the city's skyline was floating downstream. The carrier displaced 85,000 tons and drew 37 feet of water; the flight deck was 1,101 feet long and 252 feet broad, giving an area of four and a half acres.[26]

At sea the destroyer *Laffey,* the assigned escort, met the carrier. Completed by the Bath Iron Works in 1944, the destroyer had seen hard service. After the invasion of Normandy, she took part in the closing campaigns in the Pacific. Off Okinawa she survived a kamikaze attack that caused heavy casualties and great damage. Rebuilt and returned to service, the ship resumed an active life. Just prior to the sea trials, the destroyer had taken part in NATO exercises. It was a proud veteran that greeted the nuclear carrier with the insouciant message: "WELCOME TO THE BRINEY DEEP."[27]

For much of the first part of the trials, the carrier steamed at slow speeds, maneuvering engines, testing components, and gaining a base for later calculations. Certain compartments had been set aside so men from Naval Reactors, along with others from the Bureau of Ships, the laboratories, the major contractors and vendors, and various naval commands could monitor the tests. Scratch pads, slide rules, calculators, schedules, blueprints, cups of cold coffee, and half-consumed cans of Coca Cola cluttered table tops. Cables for telephones, buzzers, bells, and warning lights crisscrossed the deck, overhead, and bulkheads. Engineers moved constantly in and out of the compartments, sometimes to check on the progress of a test schedule or a change in the trial agenda, to fill out forms and record data, and sometimes to bicker over the interpretation of some of the findings.

Gradually the *Enterprise* built up full power, driving steadily through the sea at over 30 miles an hour. At that speed huge waves flanked the bow, while another powerful wave surged in angry pursuit at the stern. At the end of the run but still at full power, de Poix ordered the scheduled sharp turns. To an unbelievable extent the ship heeled over. Below decks, unwary personnel who had disregarded warnings found cabinet doors swinging open, disgorging their contents, which slid across the deck, first in one direction, then in another. Within the makeshift test headquarters the engineers made their calculations: no other ship had poured so much power into the ocean. The *Laffey,* outpaced, signaled: "FUEL GONE, TOPSIDE SALTED, CREW WET AND ENGINES TIRED. NEVERTHELESS HONORED TO BE FIRST SMALL BOY WITH WORLD'S NEWEST AND GREATEST."[28]

The *Enterprise* steamed up the James River to the yard with a huge broom—the time-honored symbol of a clean sweep—lashed to the highest antenna. In his report to the commission and the navy, Rickover wrote that the ship had been underway about thirty hours and had steamed 629 miles. Plant, officers, and men had passed their tests successfully. In Washington, Admiral George W. Anderson, Jr., chief of naval operations, informed senior officers: "Her maneuverability is reported as nothing less than spectacular, for any ship, regardless of tonnage. Her quick reverse from ahead and vice versa must be seen to be believed."[29]

Troubled Future

Despite the sucessful trials, the future of nuclear propulsion for the surface fleet remained in doubt. On 22 September 1961 McNamara sent to the service secretaries and joint chiefs of staff the budget assumptions for fiscal year 1963. They were devastating. Although accepting the navy's needs for a force of fifteen attack carriers, and although approving funding new carriers in fiscal years 1963, 1965, and 1967, none were to be nuclear powered. He would approve one more nuclear-powered frigate. With this ship and the ones previously authorized, the navy would have an austere nuclear-powered task force to be used on those occasions when endurance was necessary.[30]

The nuclear-powered frigate McNamara was proposing for the 1963 program was to be the first of a new design built around the Typhon. An elaborate and sophisticated weapon system, Typhon was to defend a carrier force against weapons coming into operation after 1965. It would be able to handle more targets, detect them at greater ranges, and react more quickly than any existing system the navy had. It could provide the ship with a greater degree of air control of antiaircraft and antimissile missiles than ever before.[31] It made sense to put the system in a ship that could provide plenty of electric power and steam at high speed for a long period of time without refueling.

The commission was disturbed to learn that the application of nuclear propulsion to the surface navy was to be limited to a single task force. Seaborg found himself confronting the same situation McCone had faced: reconciling the commission's development of naval reactors for ships the navy was not going to build. Commissioner Robert E. Wilson, a chemical engineer who had been chairman of the board and chief executive officer of the Standard Oil Company (Indiana), thought the problem might be Rickover and his tight grasp on naval nuclear propulsion development. Maybe it was time for the commission to seek a new leader for the program. By asking the navy to review its plans for nuclear-powered surface ships and the commission to study different reactor types, something might turn up to break the deadlock and in the process uncover a replacement for Rickover.[32]

Seaborg had no interest in replacing Rickover—the naval nuclear propulsion program he considered well-led—but he and his colleagues could see the merit of a briefing. On 29 December 1961 Rickover and senior Naval Reactors engineers explained their position. Their main theme was the necessity for the propulsion plants to be rugged and reliable, characteristics that placed stringent constraints on design and development. Based on its knowledge of reactor technology and experience in naval propulsion, Naval Reactors knew of nothing that promised to be superior to the pressurized-water reactor in the foreseeable future. Seaborg was impressed: he found Rickover objective and his arguments persuasive.[33]

The navy, too, was disturbed by McNamara's stand. Admiral Anderson, a distinguished naval aviator who had held some of the navy's most important commands, thought maybe it would be less expensive converting ships to nuclear propulsion than building them new. Rickover took as an example the *Ranger,* a *Forrestal*-class carrier completed in 1957. Conversion was possible, but it would take time and money. Putting a four-reactor plant in the *Ranger* would take about three years: building the *Enterprise* from keel-laying to commissioning had taken three years and nine months. Installing the propulsion system in the *Ranger* would take about $25 million more than placing it in a ship designed from the beginning to be nuclear powered. Smaller ships had the added disadvantage that they could not be converted without a great penalty to their military worth.[34]

Developing a small, light, cheap reactor was a constant refrain from those seeking to lower costs. On 3 February 1962, Rickover, I. Harry Mandil, Robert Panoff, and Theodore Rockwell explained to a large number of naval officers and officials that reducing costs by cutting weight and size and maintaining performance was hardly a new idea. Rickover recalled the *Marlin* and the *Mackerel,* small submarines built in the late 1930s, the smaller hunter-killer submarines constructed in the 1950s, the compact high-speed diesel engines developed for submarines, and the ambitious *Timmerman* project, a destroyer with a propulsion plant designed and developed to save weight and space. All had been failures—some because of poor design and unwarranted confidence in technical advances, and others because a decrease in size had led to a drastic decline in the ability to carry out military missions. To sum up, the development of small, light, cheap components was troublesome and often unsuccessful. Nuclear propulsion was no different. Essential qualities such as ruggedness, reliability, and safety did not lead to small cheap reactors.[35]

Fred Korth listened to the briefing with great interest. A Texan, a lawyer and banker, and a close friend of Vice President Johnson, Korth had succeeded Connally on 11 December 1961. In congressional testimony he confined his remarks on nuclear propulsion to the bland, obvious, and noncontroversial statement that the subject was continuing to receive attention. Anderson was troubled. Before the Senate Committee on Armed Services he hailed nuclear propulsion as perhaps the greatest achievement in the history of the navy. Reluctantly, he was willing to wait until additional operating experience was acquired before asking for more nuclear-powered surface ships.[36]

Possibly the secretary of defense was not so adamant. On February 27 Korth received a request from Roswell Gilpatric, deputy secretary of defense, a lawyer with wide governmental background, for information on the naval nuclear propulsion program, including its history, status, and plans for developing compact propulsion plants. As an interim reply Korth sent notes of the briefing. In his covering memorandum to the amplifying report of March 30, he pointed out that the navy's policy called for moving ahead with nuclear propulsion and not waiting for technological breakthroughs. Building ships was the best way to cut costs.[37]

Anyone studying the testimony of Korth and Anderson would have had little trouble gaining the impression that the navy was shifting its attitude toward nuclear propulsion for surface ships. The operations of the *Long Beach* and more particularly the *Enterprise* were actualities and promises fulfilled. Both men were coming to the conclusion that the navy needed nuclear-powered surface ships and that the only way to get them was not to wait for a technological breakthrough to lower costs, but to embark upon a steady construction program. That way put the secretary of the navy and the chief of naval operations on a collision course with the secretary of defense.

Mobilizing the Joint Committee

Inevitably, Rickover turned to the Joint Committee on Atomic Energy. That body closely followed the nuclear propulsion program and had even held some meetings at sea: 20 March 1955 on the *Nautilus,* 11 April 1959 on the *Skipjack,* and 9 April 1960 on the *George Washington.* On each occasion the committee and its staff had a chance to inspect the ship, see her in action, question officers and men, and talk with Rickover and Naval Reactors engineers. In early 1962 it was clearly time for a meeting on the *Enterprise.*[38]

On the afternoon of March 31, the *Enterprise* left Guantánamo Bay, Cuba. Rickover and David T. Leighton, Shaw's successor as the Naval Reactors project officer for surface ships, gave a tour of the ship to a strong contingent of the committee: Representatives Chet Holifield, Melvin Price, Wayne N. Aspinall, Craig Hosmer, Thomas G. Morris, and Jack

Westland, and Senators Clinton P. Anderson, John O. Pastore, and George D. Aiken as well as James T. Ramey, John T. Conway, David R. Toll, Edward J. Bauser, and George F. Murphy of the committee staff. The ship's guests learned that the propulsion plant could drive the ship at full speed and still provide enough steam for the catapults to launch the navy's heaviest aircraft with no trouble. Leighton pointed out that the *Enterprise* had recently arrived in Guantánamo with only five minor deficiencies in the propulsion plant. A comparable figure for an oil-fired carrier would have been about one hundred.[39]

That evening at 6:45 in the flag officer's cabin, Holifield called the meeting to order. Because night was fast approaching and operations would soon demand his presence on the bridge, de Poix was the first witness. He spoke of the demonstrated superiority of nuclear propulsion for aircraft carriers. The ship could accelerate and decelerate quickly, enabling the rapid maneuvers necessary when the ship was launching and landing different types of aircraft. The quick response to orders changing speed made possible the rapid return to the base course so that at the end of a given time, the ship would be farther along toward its intended objective than an oil-fired carrier. De Poix listed other advantages: absence of stack gases, which disturbed the air and corroded equipment, high sustained speed, and long endurance so that the ship would arrive and remain in an operation area unlimited by the supply of ship's fuel.

Against the whine of jet engines and the thud of catapults, Rickover pointed out that the cost of nuclear surface ships was deterring the navy from building them. A nuclear carrier would always cost more to construct and operate, but dwelling on monetary comparison obscured the real issue—the military advantages of nuclear propulsion. In the discussion that followed Rickover came to his main argument: by exerting pressure the joint committee could decide the future of the surface navy. Indeed, unless it did so, the United States would not have a nuclear-powered surface navy.[40]

Holifield issued a press release on his return from the two-day trip. He declared the *Enterprise* an impressive weapon and an achievement in atomic energy of which all could be proud. He praised de Poix, his officers and crew, and lauded Rickover and his organization for new developments and for maintaining with undiminished vigor the standards essential to the safe design and maintenance of nuclear power plants. The release did not mention building more nuclear-powered surface ships—for that was the responsibility of the authorization and appropriations committees—but it left no doubt where the powerful joint committee stood.[41]

Cuba

The visit of the joint committee was only a brief incident in the busy schedule of the *Enterprise*. Later she took part in a naval review during which Kennedy visited the ship. In August she joined the Sixth Fleet in the Mediterranean, returning to Norfolk on 11 October 1962.[42]

At two-thirty on the afternoon of October 19 the *Enterprise* put to sea with an escort of four destroyers. The approach of Hurricane Ella was the excuse, but to a city as wise in the ways of the navy as Norfolk, the cover story seemed pretty thin; it appeared more likely that the Cuban crisis was the reason. That afternoon off North Carolina plane after plane landed on the *Enterprise* until the ship was carrying more aircraft than had ever been on board a single carrier. Later the *Enterprise* and the carrier *Independence* moved through the Windward Passage to take up station off southern Cuba. The two carriers, each with four destroyers, were about 120 miles apart. Between the two groups was a replenishment force of an ammunition ship and two tankers. In the early evening of October 22 Kennedy, speaking to the nation and the world, announced the presence of Russian missiles in Cuba. For all mankind began days of agonizing uncertainty.

Hayward assumed command of Task Force 135 on October 24. Its planes were prepared to launch air strikes against selected targets, support the defense of Guantánamo Bay, and cover the forces allocated to reinforce that base. Strongly convinced of the need to apply nuclear propulsion to the navy, Hayward was anxious to see what the *Enterprise* could do.

He set up alternate days for each carrier group to refuel. Prudence and not need dictated the frequent refueling; he wanted his force as near peak readiness as possible. Because of increasing signs of Russian submarines, Hayward moved his forces farther south, first into the area of the Jamaica Channel, and then to the shallow waters off the south and southwest coast of Jamaica. At night the carriers moved swiftly, steering evasively and zigzagging to reach new positions at dawn.

On October 28 Kennedy announced Khrushchev's decision to dismantle and remove missiles as well as other offensive weapons. The *Independence* left the area on November 22; the *Enterprise* reached Norfolk on December 6. During the forty-three days the ship was away from the United States, the *Independence* consumed about five and a half million gallons of oil. The *Enterprise* burnt none.[43]

As far as the application of nuclear propulsion to surface ships was concerned, the Cuban crisis provided no answer. Of the three nuclear surface ships in operation, only the *Enterprise* could take part. The *Long Beach* was in the Philadelphia Navy Yard undergoing the lengthy process of missile installation, while the *Bainbridge,* commissioned on 6 October

1962, had not yet worked up to be an effective combat unit. The *Enterprise* had performed well; her nuclear plant proved reliable and able to meet the tactical demands of the ship and the requirements of her aircraft. But the Cuban crisis did not call for sustained speed—the ability to steam fast over long distances for long periods. In the particular circumstances of the Cuban crisis, nuclear propulsion had no way to show its most significant advantage.

The Loss of the Typhon Frigate

Nothing in the operation of the *Enterprise* before or during the Cuban crisis changed McNamara's mind that all the navy needed, at least for the present, was a small nuclear-powered task force. He had included the Typhon frigate in the 1963 program to round out that force.

The Bureau of Naval Weapons was finding the Typhon system far more difficult to develop than anticipated. In May 1962 it had proposed substituting a *Bainbridge* for the Typhon frigate, placing an oil-fired Typhon in the 1964 program, and reviewing the Typhon effort to make sure that in performance, cost, and size it would be suitable for a large number of ships. Furthermore, the navy lamely proposed a single-reactor destroyer with a modified Typhon.[44]

On 26 November 1962, McNamara cancelled the Typhon frigate of 1963 and permitted no substitutes. A third *Bainbridge* was not what the navy needed, and the navy had no operating experience with a single-reactor surface ship. He proposed that the navy spend its available funds on correcting the deficiencies of the Terrier, Talos, and Tartar surface-to-air missiles. Here the secretary was touching upon a sore point, for the performance of the missiles during Kennedy's review of the fleet had been so bad as to evoke the intervention of the president himself. McNamara pointed out that the rejection of the Typhon frigate, a third *Bainbridge,* and the single-reactor destroyer was not to be construed as opposition to nuclear propulsion for these ships. He would consider the matter again in the next year.[45]

The CVA 67

The fiscal year 1963 carrier, known from its type and hull number as CVA 67—later to be named the *John F. Kennedy*—had been authorized and approved as an oil-burning ship. As pointed out earlier, the attack carriers scheduled for the 1965 and 1967 programs were also to be conventionally propelled. By the end of 1962 Rickover sought to reopen the question of the CVA 67, for Bettis had made significant advances in the development of a four-reactor A3W plant. Not only was the power rating increased from a year ago when the four-reactor plant was proposed for the CVA 67, but preliminary calculations also showed it could fit in the space allotted for propulsion machinery. It was not a matter of simple substitution, for the two propulsion systems differed radically in their arrangement and weight distribution. The decision had to be made soon before the ship was very far under construction and preferably before that stage. As yet the Newport News Shipbuilding and Dry Dock Company had not laid the keel.[46]

On 8 December 1962 Rickover asked the bureau's ship-design division to study the feasibility of installing the plant in the CVA 67. On the last day of the year Rear Admiral Ralph K. James, chief of the Bureau of Ships, forwarded the results to the chief of naval operations. The change was feasible, but would require extensive redesign. The four-reactor plant would have only slightly less power rating than the eight-reactor plant of the *Enterprise*. A nuclear-powered CVA 67 would cost an estimated $113 million more than its oil-fired counterpart; of this amount $32 million was for the initial fuel loading—which would last about seven years—and the remainder was for the design, procurement, installation, and testing of the plant. James did not go so far as to endorse the four-reactor plant for the CVA 67, but he recommended that it be considered for future aircraft carriers.[47]

With the bureau's favorable opinion on the technical feasibility established, Rickover sought support for the change. He could count on the joint committee. In October it had published an unclassified version of the hearings held on the *Enterprise*. In the foreword Holifield praised the tremendous strides nuclear propulsion had made under Rickover and declared that it was time to convert the surface fleet to the new technology.[48]

Korth was willing to take a stand. His year in office had converted him to nuclear propulsion. He was impressed by the *Enterprise* and by the operation of the nuclear-powered submarines, by his contacts with Naval Reactors and Rickover, and by the views of other people whose opinions he respected. Recognizing the need for a strong statement from an experienced flag officer, he turned to Hayward.

On 2 January 1963, in a letter clearly intended for publication, Hayward wrote that his experience with the *Enterprise* off Cuba and in the Mediterranean convinced him that the advantages of nuclear propulsion in surface combatant ships far outweighed the extra costs. The *Enterprise* was outperforming every carrier in the fleet. Her planes were easier and cheaper to maintain because they were not exposed to corrosive stack gases. The ruggedness and reliability of the propulsion plant gave her a high sustained speed and the ability to maneuver readily that enhanced air operations. In her first year the ship had 10,000 landings, a record no other carrier had achieved. Hayward strongly believed that nuclear propulsion would be badly needed in the years ahead. For that matter he was deeply disturbed that the navy was not exploiting every technological advance fully. Weighing the advantages of technology in dollars and cents now could cost victory later.[49]

The Atomic Energy Commission was another element to mobilize. On 18 December 1962 three of the commissioners, Seaborg, John G. Palfrey, and James T. Ramey, held a meeting on board the *Enterprise*. Palfrey, a former law professor at Columbia University, and James T. Ramey, formerly executive director of the staff of the joint committee, were both recent appointments to the commission. Ramey, deeply interested in reactor development, admired the achievements of Naval Reactors and liked Rickover. After hearing Hayward and de Poix, they listened to Rickover describe the four-reactor plant. It was still possible, he declared, to install it in the CVA 67. He urged the commission to support the conversion of the surface fleet, not only to improve national defense, but also to advance power reactor technology.[50]

The commission swung into position. On 7 January 1963 Seaborg wrote McNamara that the commission had recently reviewed its eight-year-old surface ship program. Within the last eighteen months the *Enterprise, Long Beach*, and *Bainbridge* had joined the fleet, and from every report reaching the commission the propulsion plants of these ships had proved reliable, had met the navy's design objectives, and had shown a state of technical maturity and promise that justified increasing the number of nuclear surface ships. Yet apart from the *Truxtun,* no nuclear ships had been authorized. From this background Seaborg came to his major point. Because of the improvements in the proposed four-reactor plant, the commission asked McNamara to reconsider his decision on the CVA 67.[51]

Reopening the question provoked mixed reactions. Admiral Claude V. Ricketts, vice chief of naval operations and second in command, saw nothing in Seaborg's letter to alter McNamara's decision. The cost of going to nuclear propulsion was still sizable. As a practical matter, changing at this stage meant a complete redesign of the hull; it was too late, too costly, and too time consuming. However, the four-reactor plant should be considered for future attack carriers. Other officers felt differently. Admittedly, changing the CVA 67 would upset the carefully balanced shipbuilding program, but for $113 million—Rickover's figure—the navy would be getting an increase in combat effectiveness almost impossible to measure. Rumors sweeping through the navy corridors of the Pentagon held that James H. Wakelin, office of the assistant secretary for research and development, and Kenneth E. BeLieu, assistant secretary of the navy, wanted a nuclear carrier, and Korth was leaning in that direction. In the Department of Defense, Harold Brown, director of defense research and engineering, and Charles J. Hitch, assistant secretary of defense (comptroller), reportedly were favorable. Rickover's knowledge of Congress was unsurpassed, and he was understood to report that while the legislators presently preferred a nuclear ship, they might not remain in this mood long. The question was McNamara.[52]

Anderson saw no chance of changing McNamara's mind. The two men had not worked well together. The chief of naval operations distrusted McNamara's method of reaching decisions and his downgrading of professional advice during the Cuban crisis. He had every reason to think he would be relieved in August after the completion of his two-year term. On 10 January 1963 Anderson had told his staff that the CVA 67 would stay conventional.[53]

As he was driving to the airport to fly to New London, he heard Rickover present his case. Over the next few days he met again with Rickover and Leighton. Perhaps the major session with the Naval Reactors engineers came on January 16 when they reviewed the progress at Bettis. The laboratory had improved core design so that the total power rating of the four reactors was equal to the eight of the *Enterprise*. A four-reactor CVA 67 based on the *Enterprise* hull could have several advantages over a conventionally powered counterpart, including the ability to carry seven instead of six squadrons, store 50 percent more aircraft fuel, and stow 50 percent more aircraft ammunition.[54]

Impressed with the arguments, Anderson turned to the Bureau of Ships. James replied that a four-reactor *Enterprise* could be delivered late in the calendar year 1967, providing full funding and authorization were available on February 1. The date was important, for the navy was scheduled to issue an invitation on February 11 for bids to construct the conventional ship.[55]

On 23 January 1963, in a letter to McNamara that took five days to write, Korth reviewed the benefits of nuclear propulsion, the importance of keeping alive technical and manufacturing processes, and the need to maintain the interest of the Atomic Energy Commission. He asked McNamara to reconsider his decision on the CVA 67.[56]

The Decision

On February 2 McNamara replied to Seaborg, acknowledging the technological advances that had taken place and promising to reconsider the decision on the CVA 67. His reply to Korth on February 22 was more complicated. Phrases Korth had used about the need to ". . . utilize the most advanced proven technology, . . ." and to move ". . . further along the road to the nuclear Navy we envisage for the future," McNamara found unpersuasive, and until he had the answers to the fundamental questions on the place of nuclear propulsion in the navy, he could not decide the type of propulsion for the ship.[57]

He wanted a comprehensive quantitative study. It should analyze the impact of nuclear propulsion on the composition of a task force and on the number and types of escort vessels. It should consider whether nuclear submarines could defend a carrier force against hostile submarines. It should examine the matter of supply ships to see if they, too, should be nuclear powered. It should assess the effect of nuclear propulsion on fleet deployment and if its application would permit a reduction in the total number of carriers or carrier task forces. The study should also provide the navy's ideas on how to achieve the transition to nuclear power. Answers to these and other questions should be based on the understanding that the goal was to obtain the most efficient naval force possible, defining efficiency as achieving the most beneficial military results for a given expenditure. If the new technology increased military efficiency, then the navy should take advantage of it. But first he needed a proper evaluation of the possibilities.[58]

He was asking for a great deal. The navy was blocked until it could answer, to McNamara's satisfaction, his questions on nuclear power and the navy. His request was a good example of applying the technique of systems analysis to military force structure. Alain C. Enthoven, a young scholar who had a strong background in economics and who had been appointed assistant secretary of defense (systems analysis) in October 1962, defined the discipline as ". . . the application of quantitative analysis and scientific method, in the broadest sense, to the problems of choice of weapon systems and strategy." Without doubt, systems analysis was valuable in cutting through deeply parochial vested interests to provide information on comparable approaches as, for example, the effectiveness of the total missile strength of the United States, regardless of which military service owned the weapon. The difficulty was applying systems analysis in "its broadest sense." It leaned heavily on economics and tended to discount professional experience.[59]

The navy was already building its case. Vice Admiral Charles D. Griffin, deputy chief of naval operations (fleet operations and readiness), alerted Hayward on January 25 that the CVA 67 question was active. Hayward, commander of Carrier Division Two and flying his flag from the *Enterprise,* sent Rickover a photograph of his ship and the *Bainbridge* as they met on February 7 in the Atlantic; it was the first rendezvous of two nuclear-powered surface ships. The picture was only a memento of an historic occasion. More important, Hayward noted that the weather had been so bad that he had not been able to refuel his oil-fired destroyers for forty-eight hours and had been forced to slow down to conserve fuel.[60]

Under Captain Raymond E. Peet, the *Bainbridge* had passed her initial sea trials on 2 September 1962. The next February she began her deployment with the Sixth Fleet. Peet had been gunnery and executive officer of a destroyer that was a proud member of "31-Knot" Burke's "Little Beaver Squadron" during World War II in the South Pacific. From actual combat he knew how every destroyerman worried about the amount of oil in his fuel tanks. In contrast, the experience with the *Bainbridge* was exhilarating.

> Our transatlantic trip was extremely rough. RADM Hayward had more than his share of problems trying to fuel the other DD's. Anyone who witnessed that operation would think nuclear power is not only a bargain, but an operational necessity for the Navy. . . .

He felt his assignment as flagship to the commander of a destroyer squadron had not really given the ship a chance to show what it could do. Still, Hayward was about to use the *Enterprise* and *Bainbridge* in exercises in the Eastern Mediterranean. Maybe it would be possible to prove that the *Bainbridge* was worth two or even three oil-fired frigates.[61]

The navy was determined to move as soon as McNamara gave the word. On March 7 Griffin sent the characteristics of the oil-fired CVA 67 to the Bureau of Ships with a request to begin immediately an alternate design of a nuclear-powered CVA 67 in an *Enterprise* hull. Rear Admiral William A. Brockett, chief of the ship design division in the bureau, planned to have the alternate design by mid-April, but he warned that delivering the ship late in calendar year 1967 would be tough. In mid-March Rickover discovered that the office of the chief of naval operations was imposing a draft limitation on the ship. Although it was part of established policy, because the more water a ship drew the fewer ports and bases it could enter, it had been breached before. Rickover got it set aside, for enforcing it on the nuclear CVA 67 meant a serious reduction in aviation fuel and ammunition capacity. He seized the incident to declare a general principle: all fixed limitations on ship design should be examined to make sure no arbitrary restrictions would prevent the navy from gaining the most from nuclear propulsion.[62]

Completing the study asked for by McNamara was obviously impossible without delaying the construction of the carrier. On April 4 Korth and Anderson agreed to send to the secretary of defense the information that had been gathered. It was difficult to put a dollar mark on the significant military advantages that nuclear propulsion gave to large ships—there was nothing with which to compare them. The *Enterprise, Long Beach,* and *Bainbridge* had proved the outstanding capabilities of nuclear propulsion and the reliability of these plants for surface ships. Based on these considerations Korth and Anderson supported nuclear propulsion for all new major combatant surface ships larger than 8,000 tons—the chief of naval operations had issued a revised policy statement to that effect on

March 28. All future attack aircraft carriers, beginning with the CVA 67 and those planned for fiscal years 1965 and 1967, should be nuclear powered; all future frigates should be nuclear powered beginning with the lead Typhon in fiscal year 1965 and continuing with the two guided-missile destroyers in fiscal year 1968.[63]

Leighton waited impatiently. Reports of Korth's letter had begun to appear in the press, and Leighton, as he circulated a few copies to key personnel in the division, warned that there must be no discussion outside the office. On April 9 he gathered some information for Rickover to use in a talk with division personnel. The maximum program could go as high as five attack carriers, fourteen frigates, and twenty-three destroyers—a total of forty-two new ships—representing a total of ninety-four reactor plants, all to be in operation by 1975.[64] It was an exhilarating prospect.

McNamara replied on April 20. The information was not what he wanted. It did not tell him the magnitude of the increase in effectiveness or possible reduction in force. The navy was asking him to approve an additional expenditure of at least $600 million to the five-year shipbuilding program, but not giving him the ultimate result of the outlay. Although recognizing that the question was hard to answer, he wanted to know what nuclear-powered force would be the equivalent in effectiveness to a conventional force. Comparing the two could be revealing.

> In suggesting equal-cost forces, let me reassure you that the intent is not to force an arbitrary budget ceiling on the Navy. Rather the problem is this: Of course nuclear-powered ships are better than conventional ships, costs not considered. But cost has to be considered because it is a measure of what is being given up elsewhere—elsewhere in the Navy, the Department of Defense, the Federal Government, and the economy as a whole. The absence of arbitrary budget ceilings does not mean that resources are unlimited. I need to know whether nuclear power for surface warships is a sensible expenditure as part of any budget, or whether your proposal merely makes sense if the implied reductions in other capabilities are neglected.

He set down column headings for a table he wanted filled in. He also wanted to know about the possible loss of military effectiveness in a period of transition. The advantages of nuclear task forces had been described, but only in qualitative terms. Using scenarios would allow application of quantitative analyses.[65]

For the next several months the navy gathered data to meet Mc-Namara's request. On 26 September 1963 Korth again pressed for a decision. Once more he pointed to the advantages of virtually unlimited endurance at high speed. It meant increased tactical flexibility, enhanced opportunity to use evasive transit tactics, improved capability to operate in bad weather or to take alternate routes to avoid storms, the ability to extend an attack along a greater perimeter, reduced vulnerability to submarine and guided-missile attack and freedom from dependence upon replenishment in areas of high threat, greatly reduced dependence upon mobile logistic support, and the ability, under severe threat situations, to operate from distant bases completely free of logistic dependency, cycling in rapid transits for ammunition and aviation fuel. Again he remarked that the increasing shipboard electric power requirements for new radars, sonars, and missile systems could be accommodated by nuclear reactors without reducing the range of the ship during operational deployments. As for the quantitative aspects, a study still under review showed that five task groups with nuclear-powered CVA 67s would have the combat effectiveness of six conventional task groups with oil-fired CVA 67s. Korth urged McNamara to decide to construct the ship with nuclear propulsion.[66]

McNamara replied on October 9. Agreeing that nuclear ships were superior, their greater cost was a serious penalty, especially in construction. Because building the CVA 67 with an oil-fired propulsion plant would not lead to any loss of effectiveness, Korth was to proceed with construction as soon as possible. The decision was not setting a policy; the question would be further reviewed when the navy finished its study of the application of nuclear propulsion to escort ships and carriers.[67]

To all intents and purposes the matter was settled—at least for the CVA 67 and probably for all surface ships. The loss of future nuclear surface ship construction would mean the loss of the carefully trained workmen in the yards and vendor facilities along with the investment in special equipment that the technology required. Rickover and his senior personnel—those few individuals from whom he sought advice on nontechnical issues—had no faith that continued studies would provide much more data than that already available. They suspected, correctly or not, that in this instance systems analysis was an excellent technique to buttress a decision already made. From that standpoint Naval Reactors saw systems analysis as a political weapon and chose the political arena in which to continue the struggle.

The Joint Committee

Of all the individuals in Naval Reactors, Rickover and Leighton were the two most deeply involved in the struggle: Rickover as head of the program and Leighton as project officer for surface ships. Both men recognized that the mission of Naval Reactors was to develop nuclear propulsion and that surface ship application was a major field. But they were also firmly convinced that the military advantages were worth the cost. The two men agreed that if the joint committee would hold hearings on the CVA 67 issue, the decision might yet be overturned.

They moved swiftly, turning first to Senator John O. Pastore, chairman of the Joint Committee on Atomic Energy. He promptly wrote McNamara on October 9, calling attention to press reports that the decision had been made not to install nuclear propulsion in the ship and asking if the stories were true. He announced that he intended to hold hearings in the near future emphasizing nuclear propulsion for surface ships.[68] The next day Rickover and Leighton saw Korth. He was willing to act and was surprisingly relaxed. He wrote McNamara, expressing surprise at the decision to go ahead with the conventionally powered CVA 67 and asking for reconsideration of the question. Not until a few hours later did they learn that Korth, involved in the TFX issue—a plane McNamara hoped would meet the requirements of the navy and the air force—had also written injudicious letters on official stationery. More important, clearly out of step with McNamara's management approach, Korth had decided to resign.

The response to Pastore's letter came first. On October 11 Roswell Gilpatric wrote the senator that the decision on the CVA 67 had not been made, and the department would be happy to cooperate in hearings dealing with the general question of nuclear propulsion. As soon as a decision was made, Pastore would be informed. That same day Pastore issued a press release that he would hold hearings. The heading of the release ". . . Pastore Wants Defense to Consider Atomic Propulsion for Aircraft Carrier" revealed that the committee chairman saw nuclear propulsion and the CVA 67 as the main purpose of the hearing.[69]

McNamara began preparing. On October 12 he saw de Poix, who spoke of his experience with the *Enterprise*. On October 15 he talked to Rickover and Seaborg, who repeated the familiar arguments in favor of nuclear propulsion. McNamara replied that for months he had been trying to find out from the navy the impact nuclear propulsion would have on size, cost, and composition of the fleet—so far without success.[70]

On October 21 Rickover assessed the situation. He knew the commission and the joint committee favored a nuclear surface fleet and the nuclear CVA 67 because of the contribution they could make to reactor technology. He was less certain of others. He believed that Jerome B. Wiesner, the president's scientific advisor, supported nuclear propulsion because of the importance of American application of advanced technology in all fields, and he heard that Harold Brown, director of defense research and engineering, was sympathetic. The chief of naval operations and the secretary of the navy had certified that nuclear propulsion provided more combat capability at less ultimate cost than conventional propulsion. On the other hand, the office of the comptroller of the secretary of defense was apparently opposed—not on the grounds that money was not available, but that the nuclear ship was not worth the extra cost. To Rickover the issue raised a matter of principle: who was to decide whether the armed services should have a tested and proven weapon—professional officers or military analysts? In the coming joint committee hearings, Rickover thought, the proper course was for the navy to hit hard at the issue of the military advantages.[71]

By the end of the month events were moving swiftly. Pastore wrote Brown on October 22 that the hearings were to be held on October 30. The next day, October 23, Pastore announced his intentions through a press release. On October 25 McNamara finally answered Korth's memorandum of October 9: the secretary of the navy was directed to proceed with the construction of the conventionally powered ship. The assistant to the secretary of defense for legislative affairs sent the news to Pastore. It arrived in his office late in the afternoon of October 25. Pastore felt the committee had been badly used, but he was determined—perhaps more than ever—to go ahead with the hearings.[72]

On October 30 at 10:00 A.M. Pastore called the meeting to order: eleven of eighteen members were present, an unusually high attendance. The list of witnesses was impressive: from the navy was Korth; Admiral David L. McDonald, chief of naval operations; Rickover; de Poix; Wilkinson; Peet; and several other officers. Seaborg and three of his colleagues and a few staff members, among them Leighton, represented the commission. From the Department of Defense the main witness was Brown. McNamara was not present: he was to testify at a later date.

In the meantime the committee heard Korth state McNamara's position that he was not setting policy on nuclear propulsion for surface ships. Angry that the decision of the CVA 67 had not been held up until the committee had completed its hearings, Pastore remarked: "It still smells like a rose." McDonald emphasized that the military advantages already demonstrated and those anticipated made it most desirable to move ahead with the application of nuclear power to the surface fleet as fast as the budget permitted. Rickover declared that he could have the four-reactor plant available for the carrier when it was needed. Hayward, Wilkinson, Peet, and de Poix gave their perspectives. Brown admitted that such ships were better: a year ago he had recommended that the CVA 67 be nuclear powered, but thought his view should be replaced by analytically thought out conviction.

The committee members left no doubt where they stood. Pastore wondered how the Department of Defense could disregard the views of experienced officers. Senator Henry M. Jackson observed that the department had its priorities reversed: the navy of the future should evolve from technologically advanced equipment—not studies. He did not see how going ahead with a second nuclear carrier should interfere with the plans the navy had for 1970 and 1975.[73]

On the second day of the hearing, Kennedy at his press conference announced that the navy would get an oil-burning carrier because that was what the navy needed. A final decision on nuclear power for major ships would come later. A carrier required a number of ships to accompany her, so the total investment was large. He was not certain what the ship would be used for: limited war or strategic attack—apparently the president thought of the ship in one category or the other. He firmly supported the decisions of the secretary of defense on the matter.[74]

Because of turmoil in Saigon, McNamara testified on November 13, almost two weeks after his original schedule. Again, eleven of the eighteen committee members were present to hear him. McNamara had no prepared statement. He began by remarking that he and his associates had always enthusiastically endorsed nuclear propulsion. He saw two questions before the committee: the future of nuclear propulsion in the navy and the CVA 67. As for the ship, Congress had authorized a conventionally powered carrier. He thought the legislators had considered the matter fully and properly, and he knew of no information or evidence that would warrant his return to Congress. Indeed, the opposite had occurred: some things had arisen that raised doubt as to whether the navy needed another attack carrier at all.

The budget was not a factor in his thinking: the nation was wealthy enough to buy whatever it needed for defense, but it was essential to procure the maximum defense for any given dollar. Defense should be given the best equipment in relation to the requirement: a nuclear carrier was unquestionably superior to a conventional carrier, but the better of the two ships would not strengthen the United States against the Soviet Union. In the total defense effort a carrier had low priority. He drew an analogy: a farmer had a truck that would move his grain at 30 miles an hour. He could get a better truck that would move his grain at 80 miles an hour: why should he pay more for the faster truck when the slower one met the need?

Although the *Enterprise* performed well in the Cuban crisis, it had not met—could not meet—the most serious problem that the United States faced during those days—the lack of escort and patrol craft. Probably there were instances where nuclear-propelled carriers were superior, but he thought such occasions would be rare. However, that issue the navy was studying. He hoped the continued development of nuclear propulsion would permit its application to all larger ships for the navy.[75]

He neither impressed nor convinced the joint committee. It analyzed the testimony, and on 11 January 1964 found that nuclear propulsion provided significant military advantages for surface ships, that the increased cost attributable to nuclear propulsion was minor, that the CVA 67 should be nuclear powered, that all future first-line surface ships should be nuclear powered, and that research and development on nuclear propulsion for surface ships should continue. The joint committee observed that it was not getting into shipbuilding programs—that was the domain of other committees. Every new warship of a type for which reactors had been developed should receive them.[76]

Reverberations of the conflict continued. On 21 December 1963, Pastore wrote to President Lyndon B. Johnson, nearing the end of his first month in office, that the decision on the CVA 67 could adversely affect national security and that the committee hoped Congress would take action in the coming session. McNamara replied for the president on 15 January 1964. While agreeing that the issues were complex, just as the committee had problems in understanding his position he had difficulty in understanding the navy's logic. In the House of Representatives as it met in 1964, a dozen bills were calling for nuclear propulsion for the ship. There they languished, explained Representative Gerald R. Ford, for lack of votes. Senator Jackson prepared for a new round, asking the navy for a specific comparison of the oil-fired and nuclear-powered CVA 67. On April 3, Rickover wrote to Paul H. Nitze, the new secretary of the navy, that recent developments since October had increased even further the capability of the four-reactor plant. Again Rickover urged action while there was still time.[77]

To many in the hearing room and to others reading the excerpted version of the testimony, McNamara had failed to make his case against nuclear propulsion for future carriers. Although the navy declared that in its professional judgment five nuclear-powered task forces were superior to six oil-burning task forces, McNamara asserted that he was absolutely certain the opposite was true. He cited a study that showed that nuclear-powered forces were superior to conventional forces of equal cost. (Later investigation showed that the study itself had a troubled history and could not be relied upon for either side of the question.) Perhaps most important, McNamara never answered probing questions from the legislators on why nuclear carriers were not worth the extra costs.[78]

Before the committee McNamara had been careful to point out that his decision on the *John F. Kennedy* did not preclude nuclear propulsion for the small number of other large carriers that might be built in the next few years, but that the real future for propulsion technology was in the "literally tens of major ships we will be building." Realization of the full potential of nuclear propulsion, however, depended upon reducing the size, weight, and cost of the reactors.[79]

Trip to Bettis

Undoubtedly, politics would have a strong influence on the application of nuclear power to the surface fleet. The commission was eager to show

McNamara the work that Naval Reactors was doing, particularly for aircraft carriers. For that purpose few things were more impressive than a visit to Bettis. On 24 April 1964, schedules meshed. The commission intended to put its best foot forward. McNamara flew to the Allegheny Airport outside Pittsburgh with Seaborg, Commissioners James T. Ramey and Gerald F. Tape, along with Rickover. A good crowd had gathered at the airport to see President Johnson, who was visiting the area in his "War on Poverty." Almost unnoticed, the McNamara group was whisked to Bettis where Mandil, Leighton, and the laboratory officials waited.

One fact emerged clearly during the briefing and tour of the laboratory: McNamara would not accept the four-reactor plant. With quickened interest he heard Ellis T. Cox, the laboratory general manager for surface ship projects, give a presentation on the D1W two-reactor plant. He learned that the two-reactor as compared with the four-reactor plant would require less personnel to operate, fewer components to fabricate, and would be able to drive a carrier larger than the *Midway* but smaller than the *Forrestal*. McNamara urged further development and asked for studies.[80]

Rickover and Leighton looked quickly at each other. They had not expected the reaction. Later they surmised that the secretary of defense saw in the two-reactor plant a way to accept nuclear propulsion for carriers without reversing his decision on the four-reactor plant. At that moment the proposed four-reactor plant was the best of the two. The number of reactors in itself was an advantage, for the sudden shutdown of one out of four would have less impact on the total power than one out of two. In a two-reactor plant, each would have to produce enough power to operate the carrier at a high speed and provide enough steam for the catapults. Achieving this power rating would be difficult. Moreover, although a two-reactor plant would require fewer components, some of these would be very large—pumps and valves among them—and would need greater development and testing. But it was the two-reactor plant or nothing.

McNamara returned from Bettis filled with enthusiasm. He had new officials with whom to discuss his visit. A thoroughly disgruntled Anderson had left in August 1963 to become ambassador to Portugal. Admiral David L. McDonald was his successor. An aviator who had held several important commands, he had not wanted to become chief of naval operations, preferring to stay out of Washington. Soon after taking office, he realized that one of his chief problems was the relationship in the Pentagon between the navy and the office of the secretary of defense: some men were not speaking to each other. Paul H. Nitze replaced Korth at the end of November. In fifteen years of public service Nitze held many positions, most recently as assistant secretary of defense for international security affairs. He was more inclined to favor nuclear propulsion, but had strong doubts about Rickover, particularly over his close ties with Congress. McNamara turned to Nitze for a study to see if a two-reactor carrier smaller than a *Forrestal* would be of interest. On May 1 Nitze asked Rickover to prepare information on the availability, cost, size, weight, design criteria, and fuel costs. He wanted the data by May 15.[81]

Rickover could not meet the deadline. The reactor was in the preliminary conceptual design phase, and at this stage nothing was certain.[82] He, his engineers, the laboratory, and the shipbuilder had only rough ideas of what the actual plant would be like. As yet, they did not know how much space the propulsion plant would occupy nor did they know how much it would weigh. Ship design was impossible without reasonable estimates of space and weight. They did not know, for example, the size of the main coolant pumps, and they did not know the arrangement of the plant components.

They did know that each reactor would be the most powerful of any that had been developed in the naval propulsion program. That meant designing, developing, and setting up production lines for some first-of-a-kind components. Moving into higher power levels could present new and unexpected phenomena in physics. With so many uncertainties, Rickover wanted to avoid giving out information that could be translated into meaningless estimates and could cause disputes and recriminations in the years ahead.

The navy was in a tight position. Earlier building programs had called for an attack carrier in the 1963, 1965, and 1967 programs. Controversy over the *John F. Kennedy*, the 1963 ship, had caused the schedule to slip seriously, and the next carrier—which might be propelled by a two-reactor plant—had slid back to fiscal year 1967. In providing tentative guidance on the number of attack carriers the navy should have, McNamara wrote on May 16 that he could not approve nuclear propulsion for the 1967 carrier until the navy gave him its current study of nuclear surface ship propulsion.[83] Once again the controversy over nuclear propulsion was threatening the construction schedule for carriers.

Three days later Rickover told Nitze and McDonald that Naval Reactors could develop a two-reactor plant for a carrier about the size of the *Midway*. That ship, laid down twenty years earlier during World War II, was smaller than the *Enterprise* and would carry fewer planes and less aviation fuel. However, he was certain he could have the propulsion plant ready on time. Or Naval Reactors could develop a more powerful two-reactor plant for a carrier the size of the *Forrestal* or *Enterprise*. That was the plant McNamara had seen at Bettis. However, Rickover was not sure he could have the plant ready for a fiscal year 1967 ship, although he believed that with a quick and firm decision and with funding he stood a good chance. McDonald promptly asked for a study to answer the first possibility: did the navy want a small nuclear-powered carrier?[84]

The Bureau of Ships completed its study of a small carrier on June 17. Compared to the larger ship, it would have two instead of four catapults, three instead of four aircraft elevators, and a hangar deck with an over-head three feet lower than that called for in postwar designs. Furthermore, with one reactor out of operation the ship's ability to launch and land certain types of aircraft was marginal at best.[85] The navy had no interest in a two-reactor small carrier.

Even before the study had been completed, the tide was running in favor of the larger ship. On June 8, three days after visiting Bettis, Nitze learned that the larger of the two reactor plants could be ready for a fiscal year 1967 ship if the decision was made soon and funding was available. Although the ship would have a flight deck about the size of the *Kennedy* and a hull about the size of the *Enterprise,* these characteristics did not need to be determined now. But it was important to get the commission officially at work on the plant. On July 16 Nitze recommended to Mc-Namara that he take that step. Rear Admiral Thomas F. Connolly, assistant chief of naval operations for fleet operations and readiness, sent a copy of the memorandum to Rickover with a brief handwritten note: "Hope this does the job with McN!"

Nitze was going further in his thinking. After reading studies on tactical warfare, he concluded that the navy needed at least fifteen attack carriers and recommended funding one each fiscal year beginning with 1967 and ending in 1973. "I am of the opinion that future new-construction CVAs should be nuclear-powered."[86]

McNamara, while not ready to go that far, agreed it was time to request the commission to develop the plant. Before doing so he wanted to inform the joint committee. For that task he chose Harold Brown, director of defense research and engineering. Meeting on August 6 with Pastore and Price, and with Rickover and Leighton present, Brown explained his mission. He referred to the decision on the *Kennedy* and, in words later recalled by Rickover, Price, and Leighton, said, "Let's face it, Bob made a mistake." During the discussion the committee members warned that the next carrier would be nuclear or there would be no carrier. Brown agreed, noting, however, that McNamara had not decided to ask for a nuclear carrier for the fiscal year 1967 program.[87]

The next day McNamara asked the commission to develop the reactor plant within a schedule permitting its use in an aircraft carrier tentatively scheduled in the fiscal year 1967 program, although he was willing to consider some delay. In a covering note to Nitze, McNamara observed he was not yet prepared to make the fiscal year 1967 ship nuclear powered, for the navy had not completed the studies. At his news conference of

September 5, President Johnson announced that the commission and the Department of Defense were proceeding to develop a two-reactor plant. The two reactors would have about the same power rating as the eight reactors of the *Enterprise* or the four proposed for the *John F. Kennedy*. The effort, added the president, would be under the direction of Rickover. On 22 October 1964 McNamara stated in his meeting with the press that the chances were good that the next carrier would be nuclear.[88]

A reporter asked if the recent circumnavigation of the world—Project Sea Orbit—had influenced his thoughts on nuclear propulsion for surface ships. Under the command of Rear Admiral Bernard M. Strean and organized as Task Force 1, the *Enterprise, Long Beach,* and *Bainbridge* had passed through the Straits of Magellan to arrive home on the East Coast of the United States on October 1. They had made the trip independent of logistical support and had been host to several foreign dignitaries who had witnessed air operations and to thousands of visitors during brief stays in port. Although Sea Orbit made little impression on McNamara, had the ships' performance been less than flawless, they could have damaged the arguments of those fighting for the application of nuclear power to the surface fleet.[89]

Studies
In February 1964 McDonald had asked the Center for Naval Analyses to study nuclear propulsion for surface ships with primary emphasis upon carriers. Because the possibility of a two-reactor ship threw off its schedule, the center on September 26 issued an interim report examining the relative effectiveness of nuclear and conventional power in selected attack carrier task groups to be built by 1965 for a given total investment and operating budget. In addition, the report considered the logistical requirements of the different groups under combat conditions. Because it was the thirty-third study conducted by the naval warfare analysis group, Pentagon jargon quickly christened it NAVWAG 33.[90]

The study group assumed that three carriers could be built by 1975, and they would be needed at least until 1990 because of possible conflicts requiring the presence of tactical air power that could remain in troubled areas. The analysts compared five different ships: a four-reactor *Enterprise*, a two-reactor *Enterprise*, a two-reactor *Kennedy*, an oil-burning *Kennedy*, and an oil-burning carrier with the approximate load-carrying ability of a four-reactor *Enterprise*.

The analysis was difficult. To compare the effectiveness of nuclear and oil-burning carriers with equal-cost forces, the study group increased the cost of the conventional task group by adding to its logistical strength to make it about equal to the nuclear group. Twenty-six appendices compared several technical areas, among them ordnance capacities, ship fuel-consumption rates, carrier-wing composition, aircraft-sortie rates, and replenishment times. In sustained operations the naval warfare analysis group found that the capability of a two-reactor *Enterprise* with oil-burning escorts exceeded that of an oil-burning *Kennedy* by about 10 percent. In an emergency unsupported response range, the nuclear ship was superior by over 100 percent. For sustained operations, a conventional carrier group required more replenishment than a nuclear carrier with the same escorts. To attain capabilities approaching those of a nuclear carrier, considering only sustained operations and response range, a 30-knot hypothetical ammunition-oiler had to accompany the conventional carrier group, replenishing it en route to and in the strike area. To support the conventional carrier and its fast oiler required one or more additional replenishment oilers. To sum up, the two-reactor *Enterprise* cost less or was essentially comparable (depending upon the method of calculation) to a *Kennedy* plus a fast ammunition-oiler and a replenishment fleet oiler.[91]

McDonald believed the study had important limitations. It assumed no losses to the carrier strike forces or their logistical support forces. By not considering a combat environment, the study did not place sufficient value on the reduced requirement for logistics that nuclear propulsion made possible. Most of all, it did not take into account the military value of greater freedom to move far and fast—a new order of capability that nuclear power provided and that oil-burning carriers could not match. But it confirmed Nitze's 16 July 1964 recommendation to the secretary of defense that a two-reactor plant be developed for a carrier in fiscal year 1967.[92]

The conclusions of the final report, issued 22 February 1965, did not change those of the first, and found additional advantages to nuclear propulsion when the vulnerability of logistical support ships was taken into account during sustained operations. To McDonald, it was clear that placing a nuclear carrier in the fiscal year 1967 and subsequent programs could give commanders of naval forces the ability to meet situations calling for resilience, flexibility, and endurance. Nitze forwarded the report to McNamara on May 26, observing that it bore out his conviction that the fiscal year 1967 carrier should be nuclear powered. Neither man was ready to recommend a program for escorts—that issue was under study.[93]

Decision for the Future

Within the office of the secretary of defense the decision on nuclear propulsion for carriers seemed stalled. On August 11 Brown telephoned Seaborg, proposing that the chairman write McNamara stating that the two-reactor plant could be ready for the ship. A few days later Charles J.

Hitch, assistant secretary of defense (comptroller), in a memorandum of August 26 summed up the pros and cons of nuclear carriers and asked if those scheduled in the 1967, 1969, and 1971 programs should be nuclear. In each instance McNamara wrote "Yes."[94]

What McNamara had done was to give a schedule to carry out a decision already made. When, over a year before, he returned from Bettis, it was clear that the next carrier would be nuclear powered. The White House announcement that Rickover was in charge of the project and the formal request by the secretary of defense to the chairman of the Atomic Energy Commission to undertake the development made that fact even more certain. Only the constant pressure of Congress kept the ship in the 1967 program. The political cost of not going ahead was far too high for the administration to pay.

Secretary Robert S. McNamara's initial decision to limit the nuclear surface fleet to an all-nuclear task force, at least until less expensive nuclear propulsion plants became available, meant that the surface fleet would consist of the Enterprise (CVAN 65), Long Beach (CGN 9), Bainbridge (DLGN 25)—all in commission by the

CHAPTER SIX

Legislating Nuclear Power into the Fleet

end of 1962—the Truxtun (DLGN 35)—laid down in 1963—and perhaps one frigate. His reversal in the fall of 1965 that led to nuclear carriers in the 1967, 1969, and 1971 programs again raised the issue of escorts.[1]

The question was important. The navy needed escorts for the carriers, but had to take several factors into account. How many were needed? How should they be propelled—by conventional steam plants or by nuclear propulsion plants? How should they be armed to protect a task force from air, surface, or submarine attack? How should construction of the ships be scheduled? How should their building programs be fitted in with other ships the navy needed? How could budgets be maintained against the ravages of inflation?

Because political pressure had finally overcome the opposition to nuclear carriers, it was natural for Rickover to turn again to Congress. This time, however, there was a significant difference. He was to try to use legislation to settle once and for all the place of nuclear propulsion in the navy.

In its interim report of 17 September 1964, the naval warfare analysis group of the Center for Naval Analyses paid most of its attention to analyzing types of carriers and kept the question of escorts to a secondary role. The analysis gave each carrier the same escort force, usually four oil-burning ships, but for purposes of testing the sensitivity of their analysis the group studied carriers with six conventional escorts and a mix of two conventional and two nuclear escorts. If two of the four were nuclear powered and assigned to an oil-burning carrier, the increase in response range was less than 20 percent. If two of the four were nuclear powered and assigned to a nuclear carrier, the increase in response range was about 90 percent.[2]

The study went to Paul H. Nitze, secretary of the navy since 29 November 1963. Understanding and accepting the principles of the McNamara philosophy, Nitze was able to present the navy's case with an effectiveness his predecessors lacked. For the moment Nitze was not concerned with a mix of two nuclear and two oil-burning escorts. Instead, he accepted McNamara's earlier position that the *Enterprise* needed one more nuclear escort to complete an all-nuclear task force. On 13 November 1964, he proposed the ship for the 1966 program. The new frigate, equipped with advanced sonar, would provide optimum effectiveness against attacks from above and below the surface. It could handle attacks from air or submarines without leaving its position and reducing readiness while refueling. Tanks in the *Enterprise* could be used for jet fuel, increasing the carrier's ability to carry out continuous air operations. Five days later he wrote to McNamara, again reemphasizing the importance of the frigate, and observing that the navy considered the ship one of the most important items in the fiscal year 1966 budget. The secretary of defense disagreed. In his mind modernizing and converting certain missile ships demanded higher priority.[3]

The failure to include a nuclear frigate in the 1966 program raised storm warnings of a struggle in Congress. Chet Holifield, vice chairman of the joint committee, took up the administration's challenge. At the launching of the *Truxtun* on December 19 at the yard of the New York Shipbuilding Corporation at Camden, New Jersey, he declared that if capital ships of the navy were necessary for national security, they should be nuclear powered. Congressman L. Mendel Rivers, now chairman of the House Armed Services Committee, warned the administration on 22 January 1965 that his committee was going to look into the navy's plans for nuclear propulsion. On February 19 Holifield pledged his support to Rivers, citing the joint committee recommendation following the CVA 67 hearings that the United States adopt a policy of using nuclear propulsion in all future major surface warships. He pointed to Operation Sea Orbit as a clear demonstration of the ability of nuclear-powered warships to go anywhere, deliver their combat load, and return—all without logistic support.[4]

That same day McNamara was testifying before the House Armed Services Committee. He was not going to propose a frigate to round out the *Enterprise* task group. If the carrier needed more defense, the better course was to add a surface-to-air missile system as had been done with the *Forrestal* class. Not until nuclear propulsion was cheaper should the navy build more nuclear escorts.[5]

An angry Rivers was not an antagonist to be taken lightly. Strong-willed, impatient, determined, and irascible, perhaps some of his flamboyance came from his humble origins in rural South Carolina. He left no doubt that he intended to be a strong chairman. He was fond of pointing out that Article I Section 8 of the Constitution gave to the legislative branch the authority to raise and support an army and to provide and maintain a navy. The key words of the article and section he had engraved upon a plaque fixed to the podium behind which he sat, dominating the hearing room. As witnesses testified, Rivers gestured to the plaque to remind them where the Constitutional authority rested. He had taken Rickover's measure at the committee hearing of 24 April 1961 and liked what he saw.

The report the committee issued on 29 April 1965 was a blunt declaration of no confidence.

> The committee feels, and has felt for all too long, that the Department of Defense has both procrastinated and vacillated in its approach to nuclear-powered surface ships. It has been an in-and-out game, with nuclear propulsion recommended one year and a return to conventional power the next year—and for the same general type of ship.[6]

Rickover did not take a prominent role. He did not testify before the committee, but he did appear before the House subcommittee on defense appropriations where, on 12 May 1965, he gave one of his wide-ranging discourses on nuclear propulsion and the state of the navy. He referred to the action of the House Armed Services Committee and remarked that if Congress approved the ship, it would be the only surface ship, destroyer size or larger, authorized in the last three years.[7]

Possibly he was being overconfident by not taking a more active part. While the House committee had come out strongly for the ship, the Senate committee had not. In conference the difference was settled in favor of the House. Before the appropriations committees, the frigate did not fare so well. Arguing that she would be the first of a new class, neither of the committees saw the need for full funding. Preliminary design was not scheduled to be completed for some months nor contracts to be awarded until spring of the next year. Funding the entire ship at this time could lead the navy to commit the entire amount, causing the hasty preparation of essential designs, plans, and specifications, which would only lead to expensive changes later. Therefore, the best thing would be to appropriate money for advance procurement for long lead-time items, such as the reactor plant, and not fund the rest of the ship until the design was firm. Advance procurement and more realistic and careful contracting procedures should not delay the ship's entry into the fleet. The legislation signed on 29 September 1965 appropriated funds for the long lead-time items.[8]

To a certain extent the situation was like the old adage: a half a loaf is better than none. The reports of the appropriations committees made clear the intent of Congress. The House report declared that the committee expected the Department of Defense to proceed with the preparation of contract plans and specifications and procurement of the long lead-time items for the frigate during the fiscal year 1966 and to budget for its construction in the next fiscal year. The Senate report, if less vigorous in its language, urged the Department of Defense to budget the construction of the ship in fiscal year 1967, for it was the view of the committee that it was necessary to get on with the building of more nuclear-powered surface ships for the navy.[9]

To McDonald the future looked good. For the next year he hoped to get the remaining funds for the 1966 frigate, another nuclear frigate, and a second nuclear carrier. That was a great deal to run through the gauntlet of the navy, the office of the secretary of defense, the White House, the committees of Congress, and Congress itself. At least it seemed certain that the idea of an austere nuclear task force was dead. The chief of naval operations was now thinking of nuclear carriers accompanied by two oil-burning and two nuclear escorts. That seemed a logical compromise.[10]

Mandatory Language

Rivers began his campaign for nuclear surface ships in the 1967 program shortly after President Johnson signed the 1966 program into law. As an opening shot, the committee chairman wrote to McNamara on 18 October 1965, asking when the contracts were to be placed for the long lead-time items and when the frigate was to be delivered to the fleet. He could draw scant comfort from the reply. McNamara stated on November 2 that the department was reviewing the entire long-range shipbuilding program as a step in preparing the fiscal year 1967 budget. Until that had been reviewed and approved by the president, the secretary of defense could not say when—or if—the contract would be let nor when—or if—the ship would be laid down or delivered to the fleet. Rivers followed up with letters to Admiral McDonald and President Johnson. Holifield added his weight. In his address at the keel laying of the *Narwhal* (SSN 671), he called for the construction of a nuclear surface fleet—and noted how the Department of Defense was paying no attention to the will of Congress.[11]

In the final days of formulating the administration's program, McDonald found that McNamara wanted to slip the carrier back a year and replace the nuclear frigates with two oil-burning destroyers. Getting McNamara's permission and telling him what he was going to say, in December McDonald flew down to the Johnson ranch in Texas to argue for the nuclear ships. It was difficult to know which influence prevailed, but the program the administration presented to Congress called for the nuclear carrier (the *Nimitz*, CVAN 68) and two oil-fired destroyers but no nuclear frigates. The funds for the long lead-time items in the 1966 program the secretary of defense had refused to release.[12]

Rivers called the committee to order on 8 March 1966. The first day was peaceful, mostly taken up by an elaborate exposition of defense issues and world affairs—a survey that had become a hallmark of McNamara's annual appearances before the armed services and appropriations committees. The next morning saw some tension. Rivers declared that Congress had authorized advance procurement for a ship the chief of naval operations said he needed: was Congress being irresponsible when it appropriated money for this end? Congressman Porter Hardy, Jr., thought the Department of Defense was arbitrarily overriding the will of Congress. McNamara replied that it was clear the executive branch in certain cases had the legal right not to expend funds in accordance with that authorization. Both sides drew back: the right of the executive branch to impound money voted by the legislative branch was a thorny constitutional issue.

March 10 saw more sparring. Questioned by Rivers and William H. Bates, a Republican from Massachusetts and a member of the joint committee, McNamara admitted that no major surface ships—nuclear or oil-burning—had been requested, authorized, or funded over the last few years. Bates proposed changing two of the large destroyers to nuclear frigates. Doing so would enable the navy to make the most effective use of its nuclear carriers. McNamara admitted:

> There is no sense of having a carrier that is nuclear-powered if you can't realize the full potential of the nuclear power in the carrier because you don't have a nuclear-powered escort fleet. I think we have such a fleet: if we don't, I want to have one, because I fully accept the point that we ought to balance off these advantages we paid so heavily for.[13]

Rickover was hopeful. Early in the year he had begun collecting information on the performance of nuclear ships off Vietnam, asking their commanding officers to let him know of instances in which nuclear propulsion proved particularly advantageous. To Vice Admiral John T. Hayward, he wrote on 20 April 1966: "It has taken us many years to win the fight for nuclear power in aircraft carriers. I truly believe we can get over the top on the acceptance of nuclear power in major fleet escorts."[14]

He had reason for optimism. On April 22 Nitze wrote McNamara that the concept of two nuclear and two oil-burning escorts per nuclear carrier was sound. On April 28 Rivers declared he would add two nuclear frigates to the two destroyers (one frigate was the completely funded 1966 ship, the other was new).[15]

Much earlier Rickover had agreed to appear after all the navy witnesses had finished: that way he could counter the arguments of others. Although the administration's official program included two conventional destroyers and no nuclear frigates, Rickover decided to testify that nuclear escorts were best, and to recommend that the committee authorize the two nuclear frigates and the two destroyers, but giving priority to the frigates. To Rickover the time to press for the frigates was now; to other officials Rickover's foray might jeopardize the navy's hopes of getting five nuclear and fifteen conventional escorts over the next five years.

Rickover began his testimony on May 2 by urging Congress to resume the powers it had let slip to the executive branch. The prevalent pattern called for the executive departments to decide what they needed and to ask Congress for the funds. Should Congress venture to modify that request, the executive branch would not carry out the change. After all, Congress was an elected body and was responsible to its constituents; in the administration, except for the president and vice president, the officials were appointed. Rickover proudly admitted—as he often had—that he was a creature of Congress, for without its intervention he would not be appearing before them. And it was Congress who forced the navy into nuclear propulsion. As it usually did, the opening drew an exchange of compliments, nonetheless sincere even if framed in the stilted terms of congressional courtesy. Rickover proposed that Congress take a strong stand and withhold funds for certain items. That course would be difficult, but by it Congress could make its will felt.

As for the frigate, it was superior to either of the proposed destroyers. Its greater size enabled it to carry twice the number of missile launchers and magazines; it had better helicopter facilities; it had accommodations for a screen commander and a more complete naval tactical data system; twice as many torpedo tubes—and all the advantages of nuclear propulsion.[16]

The report Rivers submitted to the House on May 16 began in the usual format by stating the provisions of the bill and providing statistical summaries. These out of the way, it sharply called attention to the constitutional responsibility of Congress to provide for defense. In a wide-ranging commentary of which nuclear propulsion was but a part, the committee spoke of brilliance and misdirection in the Pentagon, of difficulty in getting information on military projects, and of allegations that sound military decisions had been overridden by the secretary of defense. One third of the report took up the issue "do we start now to have all nuclear task forces." That section summarized the Soviet submarine threat, the logistical dependence of the steam-propelled ships upon oil, the superior military effectiveness of nuclear-powered ships, and the policy statements of several secretaries of the navy and chiefs of naval operations favoring nuclear propulsion for the surface fleet.

The committee called for two frigates and inserted in its bill language to which it called particular attention:

> Notwithstanding the provisions of any other law, the Secretary of Defense and the Secretary of the Navy shall proceed with the design, engineering, and construction of the two nuclear-powered guided-missile frigates as soon as practicable.

The committee made its intent clear.

> If this language constitutes a test as to whether Congress has the power to so mandate, let the test be made and let this important weapons system be the field of trials.[17]

The two armed services committees did not agree. The Senate deleted the two destroyers and kept one nuclear frigate, observing that the Navy had only the *Long Beach, Bainbridge*, and *Truxtun* to accompany the *Enterprise* and the second nuclear carrier called for in the present program. Construction of the new frigate would permit each carrier to have an escort of two nuclear ships. In conference the differences were resolved by completing the funding for the 1966 frigate (*California*, DLGN 36) and including funding for long lead-time items for another frigate. The conference also softened the mandatory language: contracts for the *California* "shall be entered into as soon as practicable unless the President fully advises the Congress that its construction is not in the national interest." The legislation President Johnson signed on 13 July 1966 included the conference agreement on the ship as well as the revised mandatory language. As far as the ships were concerned, the appropriations committees followed the lead of the authorization committees.[18]

The navy had done well in the 1967 nuclear propulsion program. Not only did it get the *California* and long lead-time items for another frigate, but it also got the *Nimitz*, the second nuclear carrier. No sooner had President Johnson signed the appropriation legislation on October 19 than Rivers renewed his pressure. He wrote Nitze, McNamara, and Johnson asking when they were going to let the contracts for the frigates in compliance with the law. On that same day and the next, Holifield, in letters to the same individuals, pledged the support of the joint committee to the House Armed Services Committee. The mandatory language provisions appeared to work: the navy received the fiscal year 1966 money for the *California* on 27 January 1967 and the balance on March 27.[19]

On the other hand, the navy did not get funds for advance procurement for the other frigate (*South Carolina*, DLGN 37). That ship was embroiled in a new controversy.

Escorts and Studies

McNamara did not release funds for the *South Carolina* because he saw no need for the ship. He was reluctantly willing to go ahead with the *California* so that each of the four nuclear carriers would have one nuclear escort. Besides the *California* he included in this total the *Long Beach*, *Bainbridge*, and *Truxtun*. In his view the navy had a greater need for destroyers and destroyer leaders to replace those that were growing obsolete. He had the navy studying the feasibility of escorts of a new design—oil-fired—which might achieve substantial economy in design and construction. By using modular units, it might be possible to install, maintain, and remove major components as entities, allowing easier repair and modernization. Two types of ships were involved, both having a strong degree of commonality. One, a destroyer, was designated for the study as a DX; the other, a guided missile ship, was referred to as the DXG. The "X" was used to show that not all the characteristics had been determined.[20]

As another step toward modernization of the navy, McNamara wanted two new guided missile destroyers in the 1968 program. Not only would they incorporate an improved missile system, radar, and other electronic and communication equipment, but they would also be driven by a gas-turbine propulsion plant. Gas turbines offered a quicker response time, going from a cold engine to full power in a matter of minutes compared to a steam plant which, whether the heat source was a reactor or a boiler, took a few hours to warm up. In addition, gas turbines promised to be easier to maintain and to require less personnel to operate.[21] Without doubt, that propulsion system would be a strong candidate for the ship under study.

Introduction of the gas turbine threatened to be stormy. To McDonald and Admiral Horacio Rivero, vice chief of naval operations, the decision was premature because the navy lacked experience in operating gas turbine ships. Having failed to convince Nitze of the risks of too quick a move to gas turbines, McDonald accepted the inevitable. The 1968 program fell into two parts: a request for two gas-turbine destroyers and funds to study a new destroyer (DX) and a guided-missile destroyer (DXG). Not only would the study consider the latest technological gains in antiair warfare and antisubmarine warfare systems, but it would also look into the best propulsion plant—steam, gas turbine, or nuclear. The total number of ships would be large, and they would be built over a number of years.[22]

To Rickover and Naval Reactors, nuclear propulsion plants were far superior to gas turbines. On 3 February 1967 Rickover forwarded to Nitze a study that Naval Reactors had just completed. It compared two-reactor escorts with gas turbines, each having the same armament. The study showed that an all-nuclear carrier task group built around the improved capabilities of the *Nimitz* was superior to those reported to the secretary of defense in any previous study. In an all-nuclear task group all the tank capacity of the carrier could be allocated to aircraft fuel. It was the supply of aircraft ordnance and aircraft fuel that would determine the need for replenishment. He recommended that the navy adopt the policy of providing nuclear carriers with all-nuclear escorts.

One paragraph in particular summed up a major part of Rickover's argument.

> No matter how many tradeoffs we study of other ways to spend the money we need to pay for nuclear propulsion, we will always be faced with comparing unlike things; none of the tradeoffs accord freedom from logistic support for propulsion fuel which is provided by nuclear propulsion. *The other tradeoffs provide additional defense protection to the CVAN, but none of them increase the offensive capability of the CVAN as well—as does nuclear propulsion in the escorts.* To compare a larger number of conventional escorts with a smaller number of nuclear escorts at equal cost is not to compare alternate ways of achieving the same capability; it is merely to compare two different capabilities that can be achieved with the same amount of money.[23]

McDonald supported the conclusion that all nuclear carrier escorts should be nuclear powered. He did not find it inconsistent with his earlier stand that each nuclear carrier should have a mix of two conventional and two nuclear escorts, for that was a pragmatic determination based on the initial cost of nuclear ships and limited appropriations. At any event he believed the Rickover study emphasized the need to implement the navy's previous program of at least two nuclear-powered escorts per nuclear carrier.[24]

Nitze found several flaws in the study. It made the chief index of merit the time on line before replenishment. The secretary felt that the index would be significant only if the force could not be replenished or only if the navy had not planned to engage in sustained operations. He thought several other questions affecting the sustained fighting capabilities of the task group required analysis. He believed that under repeated attacks the requirement to replace "out of action" escort ships might be a more compelling problem than exhaustion of fuel or air-to-ground ordnance. He agreed that the study should be sent to those individuals analyzing the navy's need for major escorts—the DXs and DXGs.[25]

Rickover replied with a detailed rebuttal and then warned of the possible impact of the course the navy was taking. It was committing itself to the position that it must not make any decisions on the matter until the major fleet escort study was completed. That had begun in January 1967 and was due in April but would probably be late—very late if it was to cover all that was originally intended. This delay could be used to further postpone the construction of major fleet escorts. Nuclear propulsion for naval striking forces had been studied several times. In 1966 all five congressional committees—the two armed services committees, the two appropriations committees, and the joint committee—concluded that the navy should have nuclear escorts for nuclear carriers. Congress might well be affronted if, after all the navy's experience with nuclear propulsion, it did not have the military knowledge to know whether it should support all-nuclear escorts for nuclear attack carriers, or, for that matter, if the navy had to tell Congress that more studies were necessary before taking a position.[26]

On 20 March 1967, the Senate Armed Services Committee approved the two gas-turbine destroyers and ignored the *South Carolina*, for which long lead-time items had been appropriated the previous year. Possibly the House committee might overturn the position. Over a breakfast with Rivers on April 11, Rickover agreed to testify. He informed Nitze. The secretary was worried that Rickover might endanger the favorable action the Senate committee had taken on the gas-turbine ships. Rickover replied that he had been asked for his personal views and he would have to give them.[27]

On April 18 Rickover took his place in the familiar hearing room. After making the record clear that Rickover was going to give his own opinions and not those of his superiors, Rivers moved at once to ask for comments on the DX and DXG and on five other issues. Should the committee substitute two nuclear-powered frigates for the two non-nuclear destroyers? Should all nuclear-powered carriers have nuclear-powered escorts? Should the DXGs under study be nuclear propelled? Were more studies necessary before a proper decision could be made on new major fleet escorts? Had the admiral received any letters from commanding officers of nuclear ships that cast light on the operational advantages of nuclear-propelled ships?

Rickover had no difficulty in answering the questions. Interspersed among his answers were gibes at studies. Whoever believed in them forgot the difference between what people thought was going to happen in war and what actually happened—a difference that was proportionate to the interval between the wars. Situations did not repeat themselves nor could they be foreseen with sufficient precision by economic and mathematical models, as useful as those might be for certain purposes. Wars dealt with unknowns that studies could not reveal. Therefore, the weapons had to be flexible. The navy had made enough studies. He cited

Bret Harte's poem, "Caldwell of Springfield," which recounted an episode in the Revolutionary War. When the Americans ran out of cannon wadding, the Reverend James Caldwell, whose wife had just been killed, brought from his church an armload of hymnals by the theologian Isaac Watts. Caldwell urged the troops, "Now put Watts into them boys! Give 'em Watts!" Rickover declared that in all previous wars Americans had fought with the weapons on hand. In the next war officers would be exhorting their men "Now put studies into 'em boys. Give 'em studies."[28]

The House committee changed the two gas-turbine ships to nuclear frigates by authorizing the remaining funds for the *South Carolina* and full funds for a second frigate (the *Virginia*, DLGN 38). While granting funds to study the DX/DXG ships, the committee barred their use in the design of any major fleet escort that was not nuclear powered. And again the bill contained the proviso that contracts for the two ships were to be placed as soon as practicable unless the president fully advised Congress that their construction was not in the national interest. In conference the House views prevailed. Once more Rivers threw down the gauntlet to the secretary of defense:

> Can the appointed Secretary of Defense thwart the exercise of the constitutional powers of the Congress to provide and maintain a Navy?[29]

Changes in Personnel

The summer of 1967 saw changes in key personnel. On June 30 Nitze became deputy secretary of defense, second only to McNamara. John T. McNaughton, assistant secretary of defense for international security affairs, was to become secretary of the navy, but was killed in a plane crash before he could take the oath of office. Paul R. Ignatius, assistant secretary of defense (installations and logistics) became the new secretary of the navy. A graduate of the University of California, a lieutenant in the naval reserve during World War II, and possessor of a degree in business administration from Harvard, Ignatius had founded a management consulting and research firm specializing in military supply and procurement.

Admiral Thomas H. Moorer replaced Admiral McDonald as chief of naval operations on 1 August 1967. Like his predecessor, Moorer was an aviator who had won distinction during World War II and had risen in rank and positions of responsibility. During one of his Washington tours of duty he had drawn the task of studying the military advantages of nuclear propulsion. It became obvious to him that the military advantages of the technology could not be measured in dollars. Every effort had to be made to keep costs down, but military factors should be the basis for decisions on nuclear propulsion. He thought Rickover had a valid argument in stating that major combatant ships over 8,000 tons should be nuclear powered. He knew Rickover was not always easy to get along with, and he shared his distrust of systems analysis. He respected Rickover's constant pressure on his own people to do better.

Major Fleet Escort Study

Under Rear Admiral Elmo R. Zumwalt, chief of the analysis division of the office of the chief of naval operations, the first volume of the major fleet escort study was completed and forwarded to the secretary of the navy on 5 August 1967. Volume I (two other volumes completed during the year were appendices) analyzed the number of escorts needed to defend the naval forces programmed for the 1970s in a major war. The study derived the economically efficient number of escorts on a cost and effectiveness comparison basis; that is, it used a marginal analysis to trade off incremental expenditures on escorts against expenditures on the forces escorted. The study not only provided an analytical basis for missile ship force levels; it also gave a total escort force level and an illustrative building program.[30]

Taking several factors into account, the study concluded that approximately 242 escorts were needed. Of these, at least 107 should be missile ships—these would be the DXGs—and the others the DXs. But of the 107 DXGs a minimum of 67 should be escorts for carrier task groups. In deriving the ship characteristics, the study investigated four general areas: antiair warfare weapon systems, antisubmarine warfare weapon systems, number and types of guns, and "other." The latter category considered the propulsion plant, its endurance, and the speed at which it could drive the ship. The analysis of the type of propulsion plant was issued in a separate supplement on endurance on September 15. This analysis Zumwalt thought was of little value, and he undertook it mainly to stave off Rickover's efforts to stultify the study. However, preparing the supplement at least gave a chance to explore the issue.[31]

The endurance supplement compared conventional and nuclear escorts for a nuclear-powered carrier task force consisting of a carrier and four escorts operating in the North Atlantic. It quantified and credited to the nuclear escorts the ability to transit long distances at high speed without logistic support, the reliability of nuclear propulsion plants, and the ability to maintain high speeds for extended periods on strike station without increased logistic support. The supplement did not take into consideration such factors as the ability to conduct independent surveillance, scouting, barrier, and intercept missions. It did not consider the ability of a nuclear-powered task force to operate free from the need to replenish in areas of high threat and in unfavorable combat situations. It did not take into account the ability to avoid bad weather and to remove from concern the loss of fuel-oil facilities, whether at the source, at prepositioned depots, or en route to the refueling rendezvous.

The supplement found that, considering only those advantages that could be quantified, the cost differential of nuclear and conventional escorts of equal capability was so marginal that the choice between them depended upon the many nonquantifiable military factors and other considerations. Under the assumptions, between fourteen and eighteen nuclear frigates could be justified.[32]

Rickover discussed the proposed escort building program with Moorer on 7 September 1967. The new chief of naval operations was eager to begin the effort. He planned to recommend nine conventional DX escorts, two nuclear frigates, and advance procurement for four additional nuclear escorts in fiscal year 1969. He also planned to include the balance of the funds for them in the next fiscal year. Rickover had never advocated nuclear propulsion for the DX because of the expense of the nuclear propulsion plant. He believed that any nuclear escort should have both antisubmarine and antiair weapon systems, and not just antisubmarine warfare capability as was being considered for the frigates and guided-missile destroyers. He was worried over two arguments that he had heard were being prepared to buttress the case for the conventional ships. One was that it was not technically feasible to build the large number of guided-missile escorts the navy needed with nuclear propulsion; the other was that the guided-missile destroyer—the DXG—was too small for nuclear propulsion. Neither argument had merit. The naval nuclear propulsion program could provide reactors for the forty-nine guided-missile escorts as well as meet its commitments for nuclear carriers and submarines. Rickover and Moorer both agreed that the near-term goal was to obtain sixteen nuclear escorts. With the *Long Beach, Bainbridge, Truxtun,* and *California,* that number would give each of the four carriers five nuclear escorts.[33]

Leighton cautioned senior engineers, and fiscal and administrative personnel of Naval Reactors that their planning had to take into account the possibility of a sizable increase in the surface-ship program. Not only had the chief of naval operations gone on record recommending the effort, but several influential members of Congress had also stated that in the future no nonnuclear major combatant surface ships would be authorized or appropriated.[34]

Rivers Threatens

Rivers was certainly one of the key congressmen Leighton had described. In what was now almost an annual event, a few weeks after the president had signed the appropriation legislation, the committee chairman asked the secretary of the navy when he would carry out the act and award contracts for the *South Carolina* and *Virginia.* Ignatius had already raised the subject with the secretary of defense, who replied that neither ship was in the five-year defense plan and, furthermore, he was reviewing the entire program in the light of the recently completed major fleet escort study. On 24 October 1967, Ignatius informed Rivers.[35]

On November 6 McNamara made a tentative decision: he proposed to build five nuclear frigates based on the characteristics of the DXGs. For the first of these ships he would apply the funds appropriated for the *South Carolina*, seek authorization for two more in fiscal year 1969 and another pair in 1970. The ships would be ordered as soon as a satisfactory design was completed using the procedures of contract definition. Furthermore, the procurement contract would contain an option for up to ten more.[36] The Navy, if all went according to plan, would get a new class of fifteen nuclear frigates.

Rickover thought the proposal was flawed. Concept formulation and contract definition were meant primarily for acquiring large numbers of ships. Under concept formulation the navy would determine the mission of the ships it needed and would work with industry to draw up the general characteristics. These were to be used as the basis for decisions on design and production. Under contract definition preliminary design and engineering studies were verified, contracts let, and management planning begun. Accepted by the navy under heavy pressure from the office of the secretary of defense, the entire approach depended heavily on systems analysis. Rickover and his senior engineers saw a great danger, believing that it would take so long to get agreement on a "satisfactory design" that the ships might never be built.[37]

The new class would have inferior armament—for its ships would carry only one surface-to-air missile system, while the *South Carolina* and *Virginia* would have one forward and one aft. The first arrangement was called the "single-ended" ship, the second the "double-ended" ship. Analysis had shown that against the expected threat the single-ended ship was the best of the two. Again Rickover disagreed, believing that the better-armed ship was capable of more missions and was a more flexible fighting unit.[38]

The proposed program ran head on into the mandatory provisions of the law. Rivers challenged President Johnson on 13 November 1967. Congress clearly wanted the ships it had authorized and funded. Unless the president determined that their construction was not in the national interest, they should be built. Rivers said he was not naive; he realized that the new program could be an excuse to delay constructing the frigates for several years. "Unless awards are made for these two nuclear-powered frigates by January 1968, I can assure you that the Committee on Armed Services will unquestionably reanalyze the manner in which it authorized major Defense procurement items."[39]

As lines were forming for battle, McNamara resigned. Much of official Washington knew before Johnson's announcement of November 29 that the secretary of defense wanted to leave.[40] He had held that position far longer than any of his predecessors, had worked long and exhausting hours, had seen his country enter the most unpopular war in its history, and had suffered the pain of hearing it called "McNamara's War."

Rickover had clashed too often with McNamara to have any regrets, and he was too realistic over the uncertainties of the future to feel much elation. While he could not judge the impact of McNamara's policies on the air force and army, on the navy he thought it had been bad. Rickover thought systems analysis was dangerous and never hesitated to say so publicly, although in private he recognized its limited value in attacking well-defined problems. Also, by concentrating the authority of the defense establishment in the office of the secretary, McNamara had created a massive bureaucracy. Inevitably, lower levels of an organization reflected the complexity of the upper levels: bureaucracy begat bureaucracy. Rickover and others believed engineers could no longer do their technical work; instead, they were entangled by red tape.[41]

Before Congress he gibed at bureaucracy, suggesting that each day for a week all latecomers should be fired or that bureaucrats be paid their salary to stay away from the office. He tried through friends in Congress to get the navy organization simplified—the Naval Material Command was a favorite target—and to reduce the number of flag officers. In these efforts he had little success. What he urged most strongly was continuity—breaking the pattern of rotation in which an officer or civilian left an assignment or job for another every few years. Continuity would not guarantee that a person could master a job, but it gave him a chance to do so.

Rivers continued to concentrate his fire on the White House. On December 13 he sent a telegram to Johnson, repeating his threat to disrupt procurement. From the floor of the House he was even more blunt.

Mr. Speaker, unless contract awards are made for the two nuclear-powered frigates, to which I have referred, by January of 1968, I am contemplating asking the Committee on Armed Services that no authorization of any major items be approved by the Congress next year, unless the President makes a finding required by law.

I am sick and tired of having the Committee on Armed Services and the Congress of the United States treated like little children. We represent the people of the United States.

Not a single member of the Department of Defense has been elected by the people. The people I represent, the people the Committee on Armed Services represents, and the people the House represents want two more nuclear-powered frigates in our fleet. They want them started now.

I will not tolerate any further delay by the arrogance of one man who seeks to thwart the will of Congress and I herewith and hereby serve notice.[42]

On December 18 McNamara, to be replaced by Clark M. Clifford on March 1, answered Rivers's telegram for the president, replying that the nuclear escort program was still under review. Furious, Rivers announced to the press that the Department of Defense was flagrantly disregarding the will of Congress and brazenly violating the law.[43]

Compromise

McNamara had no intention of backing down. He argued that the single-ended DXGN would cost less than another *California*. Furthermore, with five DXGNs, and the *California*, *Truxtun*, and *Bainbridge*, the navy could have two all-nuclear carrier task groups. On 20 January 1968 he proposed that Johnson fulfill the requirements of the law by determining that construction of the *South Carolina* and *Virginia* was not in the national interest.[44] The president signed the letter, but did not send it. The mounting unrest over Vietnam could well have been a source of anxiety; getting into a battle with someone as powerful as the chairman of the House Armed Services Committee was not to be undertaken lightly.

Before the Senate Armed Services Committee on February 5 McNamara presented his program. Three days later, before the joint committee, Rickover argued strongly in favor of the *South Carolina* and *Virginia*. That same day Ignatius called on Holifield to persuade him that the administration's program was really great progress for the navy. The veteran legislator disagreed. On February 9 the *New York Times* carried a story by William Beecher that a constitutional showdown pitting Congress against the executive branch was near. Holifield seized upon the article, reminding Johnson of an earlier promise that McNamara and Clifford would call. Neither had done so. A few days later Johnson asked Clifford to talk to Holifield.[45]

Clifford telephoned the congressman on 27 February 1968 that he would study the matter. The next day McNamara, about a week from the end of his long tenure, informed Johnson that the estimated cost of the nuclear frigates was increasing. Perhaps the new secretary might want to reconsider the entire guided-missile surface-ship program. That point made, McNamara telephoned Holifield that action on the frigate had been frozen. At least, thought Holifield, Congress had gained time.[46]

Two ships at issue offered the possibility of a compromise. On March 25 Clifford proposed building the *South Carolina* as a *California*-class ship and the *Virginia* as the first of the DXGNs. The administration made its moves. Clifford released funds for advance procurement of the *South Carolina* on May 9 and the balance on June 20, thus placing the ship in the 1968 program. For fiscal year 1969 Congress authorized and appropriated funds for advance procurement for the two DXGNs—the *Virginia* and the *Texas* (DLGN 39). Rivers hailed a new atmosphere—an "ambience of cooperation."[47] The propulsion plant for both classes was Knolls's D2G.

Admiral H. G. Rickover standing on fantail of the USS *Nimitz* during her initial trial, March 1975. (U.S. Navy)

USS *Skipjack* (SSN 585) on sea trials, 1 April 1959. (U.S. Navy)

USS *Skipjack* (SSN 585) with her S5W reactor plant combines nuclear power and the streamlined *Albacore* hull for high sustained speed submerged. (U.S. Navy)

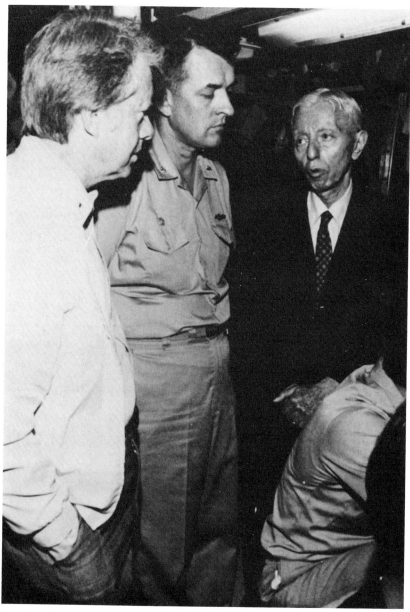

President Carter inspecting the USS *Los Angeles* (SSN 688) on 27 May 1977. With him are Admiral Rickover and Captain J. C. Christianson. (U.S. Navy)

NR-1 nuclear-powered research vehicle completes sea trials, 18 August 1969. (U.S. AEC-69-8619)

The first Trident missile submarine USS *Ohio* (SSN 726) underway, September 1981. (U.S. Navy)

Portsmouth Naval Shipyard launches USS *Thresher*, 9 July 1960. (U.S. Navy)

USS *Thresher* (SSN 593) undergoes most severe shock test ever conducted on an operating submarine as of July 1962. (U.S. Navy)

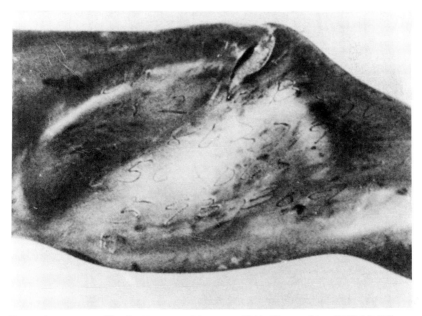

Brass pipe recovered by the *Trieste* on 28 August 1963. The marking "593 BOAT" identifies the pipe as belonging to the *Thresher*. (U.S. Navy)

The first nuclear-powered task force — the USS *Enterprise* (CVAN 65), USS *Long Beach* (CGN 9) and USS *Bainbridge* (DLGN 25) in the Mediterranean on 30 June 1964. (U.S. Navy)

A leading figure in the struggle for a nuclear-powered surface fleet Chairman of the House Armed Services Committee L. Mendel Rivers attends keel laying of the USS *South Carolina* (DLGN 37). (Newport News Shipbuilding and Drydock Company)

Launching of the USS *Nimitz* (CVN 68) at the Newport News Shipbuilding and Drydock Company on 13 May 1972, at the end of. years of struggle to obtain nuclear-powered carrier. (AEC-72-9818)

Admiral Rickover and President Kennedy discussing the Multilateral Force and education, 11 February 1963. (Courtesy White House)

Admiral Rickover speaks to midshipmen at the Naval Academy (U.S. Navy)

Near the end of his navy career, Admiral Rickover, with Mrs. Eleonore B. Rickover and Secretary of the Navy John F. Lehman, Jr., inspect the Trident submarine USS *Ohio* (SSBN 726) at her commissioning at Groton, Connecticut, on 11 November 1981. On the preceding day Mr. Lehman had informed Admiral Rickover that he had recommended his retirement to Secretary of Defense Caspar W. Weinberger and President Ronald Reagan. (U.S. Navy)

Admiral Rickover at the commissioning of the USS *Ohio* (SSBN 726). As usual, the admiral is in civilian clothes. Beside him is Admiral Harry D. Train II, Commander in Chief, Atlantic. They are followed by Vice Admiral Steven A. White, Commander, Submarine Force, Atlantic, and Admiral Thomas B. Hayward, Chief of Naval Operations. Under construction in the background is the USS *Georgia* (SSBN 729). (U.S. Navy)

Dr. Glenn T. Seaborg, chairman of the Atomic Energy Commission from March 1961 to August 1971, thought the Naval Propulsion Program under Admiral Rickover's leadership was well run. He urged nuclear propulsion for the aircraft carrier USS *John F. Kennedy* (CVN 67). (Atomic Energy Commission)

John S. McCone, chairman of the Atomic Energy Commission from July 1958 to January 1961, thought the navy slow in applying nuclear propulsion to the surface fleet. (Atomic Energy Commission)

President Richard Nixon congratulating Admiral Rickover on receiving his fourth star, 3 December 1973. (U.S. Navy)

Admiral Rickover and President Jimmy Carter, who had served under Admiral Rickover as a young officer, talk with the press on board the USS *Los Angeles* (SSN 688) 27 May 1977. The controversial ship was the first of a new class of attack submarines. (U.S. Navy)

Talking with allies on the Joint Committee on Atomic Energy on 11 April 1959 in the *Skipjack* (SSN 585). Vice Admiral Rickover with Senator Clinton P. Anderson on the left and Senator Henry M. Jackson on the right. (General Dynamics)

Congress authorized the *Virginia*, changed from its earlier design to a double-ended ship, for the fiscal year 1970 program; the *Texas* for 1971; the *Mississippi* (DLGN 40) for 1972; and the *Arkansas* (DLGN 41) for 1975. That gave the navy enough for two all-nuclear carrier task forces. On 30 June 1975 all the nuclear frigates were reclassified and designated "CGNs," guided-missile cruisers, joining the *Long Beach*; nuclear attack carriers, previously "CVANs", became "CVNs."[48]

Congress and Carriers

Rising costs, inflation, and unrest over the defense program affected all parts of the navy and threw off the schedule for the aircraft carrier. The plan that McNamara had approved in 1965 called for one of these ships in each of the 1967, 1969, and 1971 programs. The first ship—the *Nimitz*—was funded on schedule, but the second—the *Dwight D. Eisenhower* (CVN 69)—was not. The Nixon administration stretched out advance procurement for the *Dwight D. Eisenhower* over the 1968 and 1969 programs. While requesting funds to complete the *Dwight D. Eisenhower* in fiscal year 1970, the administration wanted to defer advance procurement for the third carrier—the *Carl Vinson* (CVN 70).[49]

Extending the construction period posed serious problems for the nuclear propulsion program. It jeopardized the possibility of taking advantage of multi-production of some components for the ships. Although the three carriers were of the same class, stretch-out raised problems and caused uncertainties among the vendors. If some of them dropped out, Naval Reactors, Bettis and Knolls, and the Plant Apparatus Division and Machinery Apparatus Operations—the latter two dealing primarily in overseeing the production of nuclear components—would have to take the time and effort to find, train, and equip new suppliers. Stretching out the effort could cause difficulties for Newport News, the only shipyard that had the facilities and experience to build nuclear-powered carriers. Delay would disrupt and disperse the highly trained work force.[50] Slipping the schedule raised another risk: Congress might decide not to go ahead with the ships.

That hazard, always a possibility, took on a new urgency on 3 July 1969 when the Senate Armed Services Committee recommended complete funding for the *Dwight D. Eisenhower*. Debate on the Senate floor revealed that the two ships were embroiled in challenges to the entire defense effort—including the antiballistic missile system, contractor studies, and biological warfare. On August 12 the navy received a blow. Walter F. Mondale, Democrat, and Clifford P. Case, Republican, introduced an amendment withholding funds for the *Dwight D. Eisenhower* until Congress received a study of the ship's usefulness that was to probe the navy's rationale for maintaining fifteen carriers and the duplication of carrier-based and land-based aircraft. To conduct the study the two senators proposed the comptroller general of the United States. As head of the General Accounting Office he reported to Congress.[51]

The navy was not completely surprised. Earlier a study group headed by Senator Mark O. Hatfield of Oregon had proposed much the same thing, but the reception of the Mondale-Case Amendment showed that sentiment against the carriers ran deep. Believing the navy had a good case, Rickover suggested to Moorer that the Navy publicly answer the many questions on the size of the carriers and their vulnerability. He furnished Secretary of Defense Melvin R. Laird with facts for a luncheon meeting with Senator John L. Stennis, chairman of the Senate Armed Services Committee. To a request from Stennis, Rickover wrote a several-page letter, inserted into the *Congressional Record* on September 10, on the need for a strong military defense and on the impact of deferring funds for the *Dwight D. Eisenhower*.[52]

Mondale and Case modified their amendment on September 9 and again on September 12. It now permitted full funding of the *Dwight D. Eisenhower* because Congress, by authorizing and appropriating advance procurement for the last two years, had made its intent clear on that ship. However, the amendment denied funds for advance procurement of the *Carl Vinson* until the Senate and House Armed Services Committees completed their study, due by 30 April 1970. In the late afternoon the weary senators, after spending some minutes untangling parliamentary procedure, voted 84–0 in favor of the amendment.[53]

The joint subcommittee of the two armed services committees began hearings on 7 April 1970 against a confusing background. The administration, while asking for advance procurement for the *Carl Vinson*, would not delegate those funds until the National Security Council had made its own study. By its action the administration had muddied the waters. Stennis did not see how the subcommittee could take a position until it knew the conclusion of the National Security Council. Nonetheless, he thought the subcommittee should proceed with its task.[54] Several witnesses, among them Rickover; Case; Mondale; Moorer; Secretary of the Navy John H. Chafee; General Earle J. Wheeler, chairman of the joint chiefs of staff; and Rear Admiral James L. Holloway III who, as director of the strike warfare division in the office of the chief of naval operations, was charged with preparing much of the navy's presentation. On April 22 eight of nine members of the subcommittee recommended authorizing the long lead-time items for the ship.

But if the administration had wanted to confuse the situation and maintain its initiative, it succeeded. On July 14 the Senate Armed Services Committee denied authorization. Under Rivers the House Armed Services Committee took a drastically different course. To put greater pressure on the White House he wanted the House to refuse to authorize constructing any naval vessels until it had the views of the National Security Council. Otherwise, Rivers explained, there was no guarantee that the study would be completed during the calendar year.[55] Never before had he gone so far.

Although he had the strength to get the amendment into the House bill, he lost it in the conference with the Senate. The conference reaffirmed the conclusion of the joint subcommittee that the ship was needed. But the administration in its "singular treatment" of the carrier had not budged from its position of making the construction dependent upon the National Security Council study. Consequently, the conference did not authorize advance procurement for the *Carl Vinson*. On the House floor Rivers told his colleagues that it was impossible to change the minds of the Senate conference when they were faced with an administration unable to make up its mind.[56]

Rivers died of heart failure on 29 December, 1970 at the University of Alabama Hospital at Birmingham. Rickover had gotten along well with him. Frequently the chairman had taken him behind the legislative scenes and shown other marks of confidence. The new chairman was F. Edward Hébert, Democrat from Louisiana. With him relations were to be good, but not as close as they had been with the flamboyant congressman from South Carolina.

Title VIII

Ever since he had first appeared before the House Armed Services Committee in 1961, Rickover had been seeking a way out of the endless arguments over the application of nuclear propulsion to the surface fleet. Then he had proposed a cutoff line of 8,000 tons for combatant surface ships; those below that tonnage were too small, but those larger could derive significant military advantages. The separation point had the merit of being based upon the technology, and it remained in Rickover's mind as a reasonable dividing line.

The sea-power subcommittee took up the idea. Established in 1968 by Rivers, the subcommittee was unique—the Senate had no counterpart—and its job was to focus upon naval affairs. Two members were particularly strong advocates of nuclear propulsion: subcommittee chairman Charles E. Bennett of Florida, an army combat veteran of the Pacific theater who had served in Congress since 1949; and Bob Wilson of California, also an army veteran who had become an advertising executive after the war and was elected to the House in 1952.

On 16 January 1974 at the Atlantic Fleet Compound at Norfolk, Virginia, Bennett called the subcommittee to order. It had already visited destroyers, frigates, a nuclear attack submarine, a replenishment ship, and an aircraft carrier, as well as witnessing an amphibious landing. With this background the subcommittee was to learn the navy's problems and requirements from Admiral Ralph W. Cousins, Jr., commander-in-chief, Atlantic Fleet, and his staff, and on the next day from John Warner, secretary of the navy; Admiral Elmo R. Zumwalt, chief of naval operations; and Rickover. One factor in the discussion was the oil embargo the Arab nations had imposed upon the United States since mid-October of the previous year. Cousins warned that the Mediterranean and Atlantic fleets would be faced with a severe fuel crisis by April unless the navy got more funds.[57]

Wilson was interested in the 8,000-ton limit, asking Zumwalt and Warner if, in fact, it was an arbitrary dividing line, and if nuclear propulsion ought not to be introduced more quickly and widely into the surface fleet. When it came his turn, Rickover, noting the origins and technical reasons for the cutoff line, observed that by far the greatest majority of the navy's surface ships had to be conventionally propelled: because of its expense, nuclear propulsion should be used only in first-line combat ships. On February 25 before the joint committee, Rickover spoke of the difficulties of getting nuclear ships for the navy.

> Until Congress passes . . . a law, we will be subject to the foibles of every official that gets into the Navy Department and decides to institute his pet transitory ideas, thus doing away with the advantages we can get from nuclear power.[58]

The thought of a legislative foundation was present in Rickover's mind when he flew with Wilson to give a speech, "Nuclear Warships and the Navy's Future," at the San Diego Press Club on March 8. When Wilson asked what he could do that would assist the nuclear propulsion program, Rickover replied that a statement of policy would help the most. In wide-ranging testimony before the sea-power subcommittee on March 21, Rickover observed that Wilson had suggested the need for Congress to establish a long-range policy. That was exactly what Rickover thought. Congress ought to take the lead in deciding what the navy ought to be and not let it be changed each year. There ought to be a permanent program that had been argued out in Congress, that had received congressional approval, and that had been put into effect.[59]

Behind closed doors the House Armed Services Committee worked fast. On May 10 Hébert submitted his committee's report to the House. The committee told how Congress had dragged the navy and the Department of Defense into the nuclear era. In perhaps no other area had Congress been so profoundly correct. The oil crisis resulting from the October war in the Middle East had increased the price of oil, making meaningless the vast comparative studies so laboriously prepared in the Pentagon. Consequently, the committee recommended to its colleagues that Title VIII be added to the authorization bill.[60]

Title VIII was a statement of national policy calling for modernizing the strike forces of the navy by constructing nuclear-powered major combatant vessels. It defined these ships as all submarines, aircraft carriers, and combatant ships that operated with an aircraft carrier, and strike forces operating independently when high-speed operations would be a significant military advantage. Title VIII required the secretary of defense to send written plans for the nuclear navy to the Congress with the annual submission of the budget. No further non-nuclear first-line combatant ships could be requested from Congress unless and until the president advised that construction of nuclear-powered vessels would not be in the national interest. Even this report would have to include an alternative program of nuclear-powered ships with appropriate design, costs, and schedule information.[61]

In the debate beginning on May 20 Hébert gave Bennett and Wilson credit for Title VIII. Bennett pointed out that the language did away with an arbitrary weight limitation. Wilson thought the provision one of the most important the committee had drafted in over two decades, although he admitted the Senate might not see it that way. Hosmer, Holifield, Price, and Stratton, all veterans, argued in its favor. Against little opposition, seven days later the House passed the bill: 358 yeas, 37 nays, 38 not voting.[62]

The House-Senate conference refined and clarified Title VIII. Several members of the conference were advocates of nuclear propulsion: from the House were Hébert, Price, Wilson, and Stratton; and from the Senate were Jackson and Thurmond. Both houses passed the legislation handsomely: the House on July 29 with 305 yeas, 38 nays, and 91 members not voting; the Senate the next day with 88 yeas, 8 nays, and 4 members not voting. President Nixon, only a few days before his resignation, reluctantly signed the legislation on August 5, remarking that he had several reservations about some of its provisions, particularly Title VIII. He intended to recommend nuclear propulsion only when national interest justified the cost.[63]

Title VIII never fulfilled the hopes of its proponents. At a round-table discussion held by the American Enterprise Institute for Public Policy Research on 6 October 1977, Bennett gave his reason: the president was against the approach, and the Senate was too parsimonious. One school of thought in the navy, represented by Zumwalt, saw an imperative need to produce a number of ships to ensure a balanced force capable of meeting the Soviet challenge. Building too many nuclear-powered ships blocked the goal. The navy had many missions that could be met with less expensive non-nuclear ships. AEGIS was another point of contention. Named after the shield that protected Zeus, AEGIS was an extremely elaborate and sophisticated shipborne system for defending carrier forces.

On the one hand it made sense to place the system on a nuclear-powered cruiser. On the other hand, for slightly more money it might be possible to build two non-nuclear AEGIS ships that together would exceed a single nuclear-powered AEGIS ship in tactical flexibility. The navy hoped for a mix between the two, but it was the nuclear version that gave way. To some observers, it was a travesty to have one of the most important ships defending a carrier task force dependent upon others for fuel.[64]

The Senate was never as strongly in favor of Title VIII as the House. In 1977 the Senate Armed Services Committee proposed repealing the section, but the House committee was successful in defending it. The following year the Senate committee again returned to the battle, and after eleven formal conferences and numerous meetings, a subcommittee of the conference committee hammered out new language. Title VIII became less restrictive, stating that the policy of the United States was to modernize the combatant forces of the navy through the construction of advanced, versatile, survivable, and cost-effective combatant ships. (Modernization of the navy by the construction of nuclear-powered major combatant ships was dropped.) In making his request for authorization of any ship for the combatant forces, the president had to recommend whether the ship should be nuclear or conventionally powered. For these changes the Senate backed the House in authorizing a fifth carrier, the *Theodore Roosevelt* (CVN 71). However, President Jimmy Carter vetoed the bill, asking that two billion appropriated for a nuclear carrier be applied to other defense needs. The new legislation, which Carter signed on 20 October 1978, contained the new language replacing Title VIII.[65]

To sum up, the *Theodore Roosevelt* was authorized in fiscal year 1980 and the *Abraham Lincoln* (CVN 72) and the *George Washington* (CVN 73) in 1983. When all were commissioned the navy would have seven nuclear carriers. The number of nuclear escorts would be far below those of the optimistic plans of earlier years. The *Texas, Mississippi,* and the *Arkansas* with their predecessors and the *Long Beach* came to only nine ships.[66]

The Naval Nuclear Propulsion Program and Congress

After he left the naval nuclear propulsion program, Rickover occasionally reflected upon the different responsibilities of legislative and executive branches. Unlike most students of the American political structure and procedures, he had a unique vantage point for his assessment and an unusually long time for close observation and participation. Like most practical men in government service who had commitments to meet, he found it difficult to draw sharp lines between the two branches.

As the highest ranking naval officer, the chief of naval operations was responsible for determining the forces the navy needed, although his opinions and those of the secretary of the navy were often modified by the secretary of defense, whose job it was to mesh the requirements of the navy with those of the army and the air force. But as Rivers frequently pointed out, Article I Section 8 of the Constitution declared: "The Congress shall have Power . . . to raise and support Armies . . ." and "to Provide and maintain a Navy. . . ." To fulfill its role Congress had to have access to different opinions; not just those offered by the administration. Rickover borrowed an idea from Wilson to explain the part Congress had to play. The representative had said, "I look at Congress as a grand jury."

Patricia Schroeder, representative from Colorado, was not sure how the individual lawmakers could sort things out to make a decision. Rickover replied that if they were not familiar with an issue—and on technical matters they probably could not be—they had to put most reliance on the qualifications and record of the witness. They had to be careful, for an expert in one field might not be an expert in another—the scientist might not be sound in engineering, or the engineer in science. But politicians were necessarily shrewd observers of human nature and could judge the credibility of a witness. The work of a member of Congress was exceedingly difficult, but no important job was ever easy.[67]

The stately old-fashioned tributes with which the chairman of a congressional committee introduced Rickover, and the candor—even brashness—of his testimony tended to obscure for an onlooker a vital element in the relationship that neither he nor the legislators ever forgot. Projects of the naval nuclear propulsion program worked. Perhaps they were expensive, although it was impossible to put a price tag upon high-speed endurance and reliability to meet a crisis that might occur tomorrow or the next decade. Nor was it only the reactors that compiled an astonishing record of accomplishment: from headquarters to the laboratories, to the yards and the contractors across the country, the program had a remarkable record of safety. It was not his personal relationships, although he counted many legislators as friends, nor the philosophy or the historical anecdotes he wove into his testimony that were the source of his strength with Congress: it was his success with the technology.

Throughout military history the sudden introduction of new weapons has caused intense concern among rival states. In the modern world, where development is often costly, a significant military and diplomatic policy issue is how to disseminate the information to strengthen friendly nations and how to keep it out

CHAPTER SEVEN
Technology and Diplomacy: The Multilateral Force

of the hands of potential enemies. The naval nuclear propulsion program was no exception to this pattern.

Admiral Rickover was in a strong position to influence the formulation of policy. A leader whose influence extended far beyond the confines of his official duties, he played a major part in determining which nations could be helped and which could not.

Much of the complex story of the diplomatic aspects of nuclear propulsion is still too sensitive for publication. This chapter therefore focuses on a single episode: the effort to create an international force of nuclear-armed and nuclear-propelled ships.

The six years of World War II had revolutionized warfare. Radar, missiles, the proximity fuse, and the atomic bomb, foreshadowed before the conflict, were realities at its end. More than ever before technological strength was a measure of a nation's power; more than ever before technology was a part of diplomacy. Nowhere was this relationship more evident than in the part played by atomic energy in the foreign relations of the United States.

The North Atlantic Treaty Organization was by far the most important of the international structures built by the United States in its search for security. The alliance, signed in Washington on 4 April 1949, declared that in the North Atlantic area an attack on one was an attack upon all. The treaty linked a victorious United States and a weakened Great Britain to a France that had spent years in occupation, to a defeated Italy, and to a subjugated and truncated Germany as well as to smaller countries. With its industrial resources, manpower, strength in the air and at sea, and with the atomic bomb, the United States held unquestioned leadership. Yet the situation was not static. As Western nations recovered from devastation, they regained a self-confidence and a willingness to explore more independent policies. Russian technological achievements in atomic weapons and missiles brought additional strain to the alliance.

To Americans who shaped foreign policy, whether they were in the White House, the Department of State, the Department of Defense, Congress, or simply private but influential citizens, atomic energy was one means of holding the alliance together. Although the existence of the nuclear shield provided by the United States protected NATO Europe, European members of the alliance were concerned that the United States might not respond swiftly and adequately to a Soviet attack against Europe if American territory were not in immediate danger. While the Europeans sought to find ways to safeguard against this possibility, the Americans were interested in means to reassure their NATO partners. Among the various possibilities was making available to the allies information assuring better integration of nuclear weapons in NATO defense, and sharing with them nuclear propulsion technology.

Keeping control of weapons might be more acceptable if other aspects of atomic energy—among them nuclear propulsion technology—were made available to allied nations. Seen in this context, atomic energy might not only tighten the bonds between the members, but it might also—and here was a generous dash of American idealism—transform the alliance. What was now a number of independent nations working together might become a supranational organization that would submerge old rivalries and antagonisms that had twice brought European civilization to the edge of an abyss.

The possibility of releasing naval nuclear propulsion technology to other nations involved Rickover. In practical terms the only source of the technology was Naval Reactors and the naval nuclear propulsion program—the laboratories, facilities, contractors, and shipyards he had brought into the effort and the people he had trained. As leader of the effort and with strong ties to Congress, his views were important. Because of the attention paid to atomic bombs, air power, and missiles, he did not believe the military significance of nuclear propulsion was fully recognized; instead, it was seen as a remarkable technical achievement but of secondary military value. Insofar as it lay within his power, he was determined that the issue be thoroughly considered.

The struggle over the release of naval nuclear propulsion technology has another interest. A frequently studied theme in history is the diffusion of ideas and technology. An example from recent naval history is the *Dreadnought*. Several existing technologies, including ordnance, range finding, fire control, steam turbines, and ship design, had converged to make the new battleship possible. Commissioned by the British in 1906, the first all-big-gun battleship made all other battleships obsolete. Those states that could not build them bought them, and within a few short years navies were ranked by the number of *Dreadnought*s each possessed. Nuclear propulsion was far different. Nuclear ships were not only extremely expensive, but demanded costly facilities, sophisticated instruments, a broad industrial base, skilled manpower, and access to uranium. Only a few nations could build a nuclear navy. For others, the course to nuclear propulsion lay through the shifting seas of diplomacy. That fact conditioned the dispersion of nuclear technology.

Offer to NATO

The Russian space triumphs—the first on October 4 and the second on 3 November 1957—reinforced President Eisenhower's conviction that NATO had to be strengthened. Offers by the United States to participate in the American nuclear program was one method; the best forum was the meeting of the heads of the NATO governments scheduled to be held in Paris in December. From hurried conferences among the staffs of the commission, State, Defense, and the White House came a number of proposals to give information needed for training and for planning military operations so that, for example, American nuclear weapons were compatible with allied delivery systems.[1]

Despite a minor stroke that had temporarily deprived him of speech, Eisenhower was determined to go to Paris. Although he had largely recovered, he was exposing himself to an arduous schedule and the risk of embarrassment, partly to see if he could still stand the rigors of the presidency, and partly because of the importance of the Paris meeting. At the opening session on December 16, and at the first business meeting later in the day, Eisenhower spoke simply but eloquently of the imperative need for unity, not only in defense but in economic and political matters as well. John Foster Dulles, following immediately after the president at the business meeting, set forth the American proposals. In brief, the United States would share with NATO some information on the military aspects of atomic energy. Of course, Dulles declared, the Atomic Energy Act would have to be amended; this was the task of Congress. It was with an observation on the congressional role that he began one significant paragraph.[2]

> In one important new area we are planning to seek necessary legislative authority to permit cooperation. I refer to the atomic submarine, which has proven its tremendous capabilities over thousands of miles of operation by the

Nautilus and *Seawolf.* If the necessary legislation is obtained, we will be able to cooperate with interested members of NATO in the development, production, and fueling of nuclear propulsion and power plants for submarines and other military purposes. This action will also greatly facilitate cooperation in the promising field of nuclear merchant-ship propulsion.[3]

Eisenhower moved quickly to make good his pledge. On 9 January 1958 he delivered his State of the Union message in person. Among the many goals he listed was the prompt enactment of legislation to permit the exchange of scientific and technical information with allies—particularly the NATO states. In no other way, he declared, could Congress demonstrate so clearly American unity of purpose.[4]

Rickover and Naval Reactors had not been aware of the offer to NATO nor was there any reason why they should have known. Eisenhower and Dulles, had they thought about it at all, could only have considered Rickover as an extremely successful leader of a complex technical program, hardly an individual to consult on foreign policy. To the president and secretary of state it was Congress that mattered, for it alone could amend the Atomic Energy Act of 1954 to implement the promises made at Paris.

Amending the Act
On 27 January 1958, Lewis L. Strauss, chairman of the commission, sent the administration's proposed amendments to Congressman Carl T. Durham, chairman of the joint committee. He and Senator John O. Pastore, chairman of the committee's subcommittee on agreements for cooperation, introduced the legislation on the floors of the House and Senate the next day.

The background was complicated. The act authorized the sharing of information in several areas, among them atomic weapons and submarine propulsion reactors, with friendly nations and regional defense organizations. The information was carefully defined in the case of weapons so that American allies would know enough to help in military training, planning, and defense, but not learn any important information on the design and fabrication of atomic weapon components. The act did not permit the transfer of propulsion reactors or their fuel.

The legislative package on which Pastore's subcommittee began hearings in executive session on January 29 was designed to facilitate greater cooperation, especially with the British but with other nations as well. With the British, the intent was to coordinate the two atomic-energy programs so that they would support each other rather than duplicate efforts and squander scarce and expensive resources. Other allies, although not gaining the same status, could have more information and assistance. As for propulsion reactors, the administration proposed to allow their transfer, with the fuel, to friendly nations. Blunt exchanges between Strauss and Senator Clinton P. Anderson showed that the administration would have a difficult time in getting this part of its bill through the committee. Angrily, the senator charged that in giving information earlier to the British the commission had been acting in bad faith and had been barring the joint committee from exercising its responsibility. Although Strauss and Anderson each had their version of the event, which was to be submitted as part of the published record, what counted was the senator's declaration that the scars of the controversy would mark the committee's consideration of the proposal on propulsion.[5]

Rickover testified in executive session on February 27. Many of the questions dealt with the British. Rickover was thoroughly familiar with the subject, for he had toured their facilities in August 1956, May 1957, and as recently as late January and early February 1958. Pastore pointed out that the administration had based its offer to NATO and its request for new legislation on the argument that the Russians already had the information that would be given to the allies. What were Rickover's frank views? Was the United States about to give something away that would jeopardize national security? Without hesitation Rickover answered. Until it was certain that the Russians had nuclear submarines, the United States should be cautious. From available evidence the Russians were not far advanced in nuclear-reactor technology. Despite propaganda, the small power plant that went into operation near Moscow was a pretty primitive affair. Therefore, the Soviet Union could learn a great deal from the American program. The greater the number of nations having access to the technology, the greater the risk of its ending up in the Kremlin.[6]

Congressional action was never in doubt, and Eisenhower signed the legislation on July 2. The amendment established an elaborate procedure for cooperation in certain areas with other countries. The commission and the Department of Defense had to negotiate the agreement and submit it, with their recommendations, to the president. The two organizations had to state that they received a guarantee that any material or any sensitive atomic-energy information would not be transferred to unauthorized persons. The president had to determine in writing that the proposed agreement would "promote and . . . not constitute an unreasonable risk to the common defense and security. . . ." He then had to submit it to the joint committee. That group would have sixty days while both houses were in session to consider and deliberate. Congress could block the measure by a concurrent resolution.[7]

Technically, the legal road was open for Eisenhower and Dulles to redeem their pledge to NATO. But none of the witnesses appearing before the subcommittee could have had any illusions about the role the joint committee intended to play: it would scrutinize any agreement on nuclear propulsion with great care.

Russian Interlude

Rickover was convinced that the Soviet Union could gain much if it could get access to any information on American nuclear propulsion technology. In the summer of 1959 he had an unexpected chance to assess the Russian program firsthand. The opportunity came about as Eisenhower and Premier Nikita S. Khrushchev were cautiously easing the tension between the two countries. As part of the thaw Frol Kozlov, the first deputy premier and heir apparent to Khrushchev, came to New York to open a Russian exhibit.[8]

Shippingport was one of the American atomic-energy installations Kozlov was to see. On July 11 after a half-hour briefing, Rickover took the deputy premier and his entourage on a tour. The Russian was impressed. At one point he refused to believe the plant was in operation because it was so quiet. Both men got along well and to the delight of reporters egged each other on. Once Rickover patted the portly Kozlov on the stomach and observed that the Communist official was fat, but the capitalist admiral was thin because he worked so hard. For a moment Rickover thought he had gone too far, but Kozlov grinned and the banter continued. When Kozlov suggested that an exchange of nuclear experts would be a good idea, Rickover agreed. At the airport before the press, Kozlov declared that it was fine to have been able to spend so much time talking about peace. Rickover replied, "It's all right to talk about peace. Now you go home and do something." The idea caught on. The *New York Times* chose to headline its story: "Rickover to Kozlov on Peace: Do Something."[9]

With Kozlov's return to Russia, preparations for a trip by Vice President Richard M. Nixon to open an American exhibit at a fair in Moscow later that summer swung into high gear. Under the principle of reciprocity, the Russians would show some of their atomic-energy installations, among them the nuclear-powered ice breaker *Lenin* under construction in Leningrad. Cheerfully and candidly admitting he knew nothing about the technical aspects of atomic energy, Nixon wanted someone with him who could assess the Russian technology. For his part, John A. McCone, now chairman of the commission, saw in the visit to the *Lenin* a golden chance to look at an example of Russian nuclear propulsion technology. He suggested three candidates: Manson Benedict, a professor of nuclear technology at the Massachusetts Institute of Technology who had played a major role in the atomic-energy program during the war; Harvey Brooks, dean of engineering and applied physics at Harvard; or Rickover.[10]

Without hesitation Nixon chose Rickover. The vice president did not know the admiral except by reputation, but picked him for several reasons. Rickover was well qualified to understand the Russian program. Further, Nixon hoped to negotiate an agreement—or at least to take steps in that direction—to exchange atomic-energy information. For that purpose he needed someone who knew the American effort thoroughly. A third reason was more complex. Knowing that he would return through Poland, Nixon thought the Polish-born Rickover could demonstrate as no one else the possibilities of American life. The final factor was more subtle. The navy warned Nixon that Rickover was brash, outspoken, and hard to control—qualities that could endanger the diplomatic objectives of the trip. Other officers, it was suggested, would be more amenable. Nixon, who admired men who had bucked the system and won, was determined more than ever to take Rickover.

The American party was so large that the two men did not talk much to each other on the flight to Moscow. On July 25, the second full day of the visit, Nixon took Rickover to the Kremlin and announced to Kozlov that Rickover was empowered to negotiate on the peaceful uses of atomic energy. On behalf of the United States Rickover offered information on all land power reactors including Shippingport; the fissionable material production reactors; a dual-purpose reactor that could generate power and produce plutonium; the aircraft propulsion reactor effort; and the merchant ship *Savannah*—all in exchange for the Russian equivalents. He proposed that Russian engineers attend the engineering school at Shippingport.[11]

It was an astonishing offer; the production and dual-purpose reactors were built to produce fissionable material for weapons; and the aircraft nuclear propulsion program, although far from fruition, was based on advanced technology. Even if Shippingport and the *Savannah* were unclassified, they were important examples of American nuclear technology. About all that Rickover held back were the reactors of the naval program.

Not surprisingly, he found that conversations with the Soviet officials were futile. They could have had no inkling of what he was going to offer. Rickover had, indeed, no authority except that given him by the vice president. As the commission and the State Department had not been informed of the proposals, neither was prepared to follow up on them. Furthermore, the commission and State Department, moving along the lines of more conventional diplomacy, were negotiating with the Soviet Union for cooperation on the peaceful uses of atomic energy, an effort that resulted in an agreement that was to be signed on 24 November 1959.[12]

On 22 July 1959, the Americans were in Leningrad, where among other things they would see the *Lenin*. To Rickover's surprise and anger they were hurried through the yard to the ship, shown a twenty-minute propaganda film in the wardroom, and given a perfunctory tour. Rickover and Nixon were furious; Rickover received Nixon's permission to stay behind.

The Russians claimed they could not find the key to the reactor compartment, and the workmen had gone home. Rickover refused to be put off with such nonsense. For some time he and the Russians argued. After the Leningrad officials called Moscow, Rickover was allowed to enter the compartment for a brief survey. He stayed two or three hours.

Now willing to talk more readily, the Russians told him the *Lenin* was to go to sea at the end of the year. To Rickover the plant looked rugged, but poorly designed and laid out. The propulsion system consisted of three pressurized-water reactors that would provide heat to the steam plant for four turbine generators. They would provide electric power to three propulsion motors, each driving a propeller. Rickover thought placing all the reactors in one compartment was bad, for a radiation leak in one could make the others inaccessible. The location of the heat exchangers was poor, and the way the piping ran made some plant components difficult to reach.[13]

After his return home, Rickover testified behind closed doors to a deeply interested joint committee. He thought work on the *Lenin* was not moving fast; he thought the United States, if it put sufficient effort into the *Long Beach,* could have the world's first nuclear surface ship. But on a deeper level Rickover was disturbed by the impression he gained, not of the *Lenin* but of Russian society. He intensely disliked its form of government, but it could decide on a course of action and quickly mobilize the necessary resources. In nuclear propulsion the Americans held the position of leadership; however, there were no grounds for complacency.[14] Convinced that the Russians were far behind, but were able and determined, Rickover saw more reason than ever to protect the technology.

The Multilateral Approach

The United States was still seeking a way to strengthen NATO in the face of Russian missile strength. After the 1957 heads of government meeting in Paris, the Supreme Headquarters, Allied Powers, Europe, studied the problem of meeting the Russian threat. In the absence of an American long-range intercontinental ballistic missile, the answer seemed to be in increasing the number of medium-range missiles in Western Europe. Making them mobile by placing them on barges, railway cars, and trucks offered a high degree of protection from Soviet attack, but it made them liable to seizure by the national forces of one country. Therefore, the mobile missiles had to be manned by mixed forces from several nations. The solution found no acceptance in the American, British, or French governments.[15]

To find a fresh approach, Christian A. Herter, succeeding Dulles as secretary of state in 1959, asked Robert R. Bowie to study the problem. A professor of international relations at Harvard and a director of the famous Center for International Affairs, Bowie had a good background for the task, for he had been a special advisor to the American high commissioner of Germany and had held important planning positions in the State Department. With the help of a small staff drawn from several agencies and institutions, Bowie finished in August "The North Atlantic Nations: Tasks for the 1960's."

Bowie saw two basic goals for the North Atlantic nations: to shape the basic forces at work in the world so as to create a viable world order, and to prevent the Sino-Soviet bloc from undermining that order or from dominating non-Communist countries. To achieve these ends the Atlantic nations had to assure their own defense, assist lesser-developed areas, create a common strategy toward the bloc, mobilize their resources, and create a political framework within which they could work together to achieve their goals. In pursuing these tasks the Atlantic community had to rediscover the cohesion and sense of purpose that marked its creation.

No longer could NATO count on American supremacy in strategic and tactical nuclear weapons. The growing Russian nuclear-missile capabilities were eroding the credibility of the threat of a strategic nuclear response to a less than all-out Soviet attack. Consequently, the European members of the alliance could become vulnerable to threats of limited aggression and blackmail. Bowie saw that a NATO strategy for the 1960s had to do two things: strengthen the non-nuclear capability of the NATO forces to resist attack by Soviet ready forces, and substantially reduce the dependence on nuclear weapons and enable NATO to mount nuclear retaliation against larger threats without an American veto. The latter point was the heart of the report.

Bowie argued that the Americans would have to provide most of the strength for deterrence, but NATO had to have its own strategic deterrent to assure its members that they had sufficient means under their control to deter a Soviet all-out attack on Western Europe. National nuclear-weapon programs did not meet the need; they were too expensive, too inefficient in their uses of scarce resources, and they raised old fears of nationalism that might shatter the alliance. A NATO strategic force under the command of the Supreme Allied Command, Europe, would meet many of these concerns and be free from many of these drawbacks.

At this point Bowie introduced a new element, one that was a significant change from the mobile missile systems studied by the Supreme Headquarters, Allied Powers, Europe, after 1957. Bowie proposed a sea-based NATO force using nuclear submarines and Polaris missiles—the same system that the United States was almost ready to bring into operation. Polaris submarines promised less vulnerability, less likelihood of creating political issues or public concerns, and greater security against seizure by national forces in peacetime. The NATO Polaris force should be created in two steps. The first would be an interim force of American-manned ships under full control of the Supreme Allied Commander, Europe. While the interim force was in operation, the United States would assist NATO in creating a multinational submarine missile force under common financing and ownership and manned by crews of mixed nations. The latter stipulation was required to prevent any ally from seizing the submarine and using it as a national force.

Maybe not all the NATO states would join, but Bowie warned that enough had to participate so the force would be truly multinational in character and control. This was indispensable: the United States should not accept anything less.

He acknowledged the help of many contributors to the study: representatives of the chiefs of missions to the European Community and the Federal Republic of Germany, the RAND Corporation, the Princeton Center for International Studies, the President's Council of Economic Advisors, the Central Intelligence Agency, the International Cooperation Administration, the Department of Defense, and the President's Science Advisory Committee, although these men served as individuals and not as members of their organizations.[16] Bowie did not list any naval officer—anyone experienced in nuclear submarine command—although perhaps he had their views through liaison with the Department of Defense and the military services.

Bowie briefed Eisenhower on the multilateral force sometime during the final months of the president's administration. The president was enthusiastic. Through hard-won experience he had learned the strengths and weaknesses of alliances, and he wanted something better for NATO. He saw the multilateral force, though, with a tinge of romanticism: it would be like the French Foreign Legion, which took into its ranks men of many nationalities and backgrounds and made them professional soldiers. The multilateral force would be an active agent in converting an alliance of nations into a new state rising above the old and bitter national rivalries.

At Paris on 16 December 1960, Secretary of State Herter proposed that the allies consider creating a special force to operate a NATO medium-range ballistic-missile system. As the United States saw it, the force would be truly multilateral in financing and control and would include mixed manning. A multilateral force offered the best means of providing a collective basis for common action in this area and might serve as a precedent for similar actions in other areas. The United States was willing to commit five Polaris submarines to NATO before the end of 1963 as an interim multilateral force, provided NATO committed a specific number of medium-range ballistic missiles to the Supreme Allied Commander, Europe, by the end of 1964. For that purpose the United States was prepared to sell the missiles and the vehicles with the understanding that they would become part of the sea-based multilateral force. Herter emphasized that he was presenting the concept for discussion. The Americans had to gain the approval of Congress, and the NATO allies had their own parliaments to consider. In the meantime a multilateral force could be discussed and its ramifications explored. There was little else he could say: he could not predict the will of Congress nor the approval of the new Democratic administration.

The New Administration

Determined that the president-elect not misunderstand the joint committee's position, on 16 November 1960, eight days after the electoral victory, Senator Clinton P. Anderson wrote to Kennedy. After a casual "Dear Jack," the senator referred to press reports of the offer of Polaris missiles and submarines to NATO. Admitting that prime responsibility for conducting the nation's foreign affairs belonged to the president, in nuclear matters the joint committee also had an obligation. The new administration, he warned, should not be entrapped by commitments made by the old.[17]

The new administration viewed the multilateral force cautiously. Kennedy did not share Eisenhower's enthusiasm, seeing in the scheme difficult problems of control and also a misunderstanding of the real needs of the alliance. That was the note he struck before the Canadian Parliament on 17 May 1961. He pledged five Polaris submarines to the NATO command, subject to agreed-upon guidelines on control and use. He saw them as the harbinger of a NATO sea-based force, truly multilateral in ownership and control—should that be found desirable and feasible—once NATO's non-nuclear goals had been achieved.[18]

A fundamental premise of the multilateral force was that it made nuclear-weapon programs of allied nations unnecessary; the Americans would provide the submarines and missiles. National programs might serve national ambitions, but they were likely to create tension and increase the chances of war—a reasoning not always accepted in European capitals, for some national leaders felt they had to have their own deterrent. The Americans also pointed out that weapon systems based on advanced technology such as Polaris were enormously expensive. Events at the end of 1962 demonstrated this argument.

Between the United States and Great Britain existed a "special relationship," a legacy of World War II. The two countries worked closely together in many areas of military technology. Although the British had developed their own nuclear weapons and the aircraft to deliver them, the rapid development of missiles had become a very heavy burden. In 1960, Prime Minister Harold Macmillan was forced to cancel work on two missile systems. Needing something to take their place, he reached an agreement with Eisenhower to buy the American Skybolt. Still under development, Skybolt was an extremely ambitious project. The missile was to be launched from a plane moving at high speed at a target 1,000 miles away. With Skybolt the British could prolong the life of their strategic bombers. Failures in several important tests raised the question in American minds whether the development was worth continuing, particularly after Polaris and Minuteman were successful. On 7 November 1962 McNamara abandoned Skybolt.

Although senior British officials in Washington and London were aware that Skybolt faced technical difficulties, the abrupt cancellation caught them by surprise. The British public was shocked and angered, and a wave of anti-Americanism swept the country. For some time Macmillan and Kennedy had planned to discuss several common problems at Nassau. Now the meeting took on a new urgency.[19]

Skybolt dominated most of the conversation at Nassau from December 19 through December 21. Macmillan, aware that many individuals around Kennedy wanted to use the cancellation of Skybolt to force the British to give up their independent nuclear deterrent, was relieved to find that the president did not share this view. Macmillan wanted Polaris. Even before the failure of Skybolt, the sea-based missile seemed a better deterrent.

Kennedy and his advisors hesitated. Although consenting to Macmillan's proposal would prolong the life of the nuclear deterrent of a close ally and save from embarrassment a political leader and statesman whom Kennedy liked personally, the situation had a complication. The British were applying to join the Common Market, a step the Americans felt highly desirable. The key to British acceptance was France. It was common knowledge that Charles de Gaulle felt the British were far too close to the Americans to make good Europeans. Selling Polaris to the British could only confirm de Gaulle's suspicions.

Through hours of discussion, sometimes heated, the two sides hammered out a compromise. The United States would sell the missile to the United Kingdom, which would provide its own nuclear warheads and nuclear submarines. These ships would be assigned to NATO, although the precise meaning of "assigned" was vague. To the Americans it could be taken as a step toward a multilateral force. To Macmillan it meant something less: it was British assistance to NATO. Kennedy offered assistance to France so that it could participate in a multilateral force.[20]

At his press conference on 14 January 1963, de Gaulle rejected British entry into the Common Market (even before Nassau Macmillan thought he would do so) and French participation in the multilateral force.[21]

The Americans had been poorly prepared for the Nassau meeting, not having thought through the implications of cancelling Skybolt or offering Polaris to the British. George W. Ball, undersecretary of state, believed the decision to continue to help the British maintain a nuclear deterrent was unwise and contrary to the best interests of American policy, but the personal liking of Kennedy and Macmillan for each other and the long tradition of the "special relationship" between the two countries were too strong to allow a candid appraisal of the situation. General Maxwell D. Taylor, chairman of the joint chiefs of staff, observed that neither government brought with it representatives from their chiefs of staff, an indication that neither staff felt the meeting had military significance.[22] The multilateral force, largely dormant since Kennedy took office, now had a new lease on life.

With the United States and the United Kingdom taking steps toward a multilateral force, even with so much left yet to be defined, it was necessary to approach other NATO states. A study by State, Defense, and the commission recommended creating as soon as possible a multilateral force consisting of the United States and at least three other nations. Germany, Italy, and Belgium were possible candidates, for they had shown willingness to discuss the matter. Probably the Europeans were more interested in submarines than surface ships.

The reasons were not hard to find: the Nassau agreement set a precedent, and the Americans were relying upon Polaris submarines—factors that made surface ships seem second best. Furthermore, adopting submarines as missile platforms might make it easier at a later time to move all the submarines of the alliance into a multilateral force. Mixed manning would be far more difficult to work out on submarines, but as long as three nationalities were on board—a number chosen so that no one group could predominate—the political requirements could be met. Because the idea of the multilateral force, although American in origin, would have to be accepted by the NATO states, they should be the ones to choose between surface ships and submarines. Several legislative hurdles would have to be cleared away before the United States could participate.[23]

Removing the legislative obstacles meant mainly the joint committee. On 18 January 1963 Kennedy met with its leaders to keep them informed and prepare them for future steps. After that meeting he saw Seaborg: the commission chairman thought it very important that the president see Rickover and enlist his support. Kennedy agreed.[24]

Interview with the President

The results of Nassau surprised Rickover; like many others he had no inkling that the multilateral force was suddenly to assume a major part in America's foreign policy. Although certain the scheme was not in the best interest of the United States, he told Admiral George W. Anderson, Jr., on 17 January 1963 that if the decision was made to go ahead, he would do all he could to help. He thought mixed manning for submarines was not safe. If it had to be accepted, the navy should insist that the commanding officer and the officers and men operating the propulsion plant be of the same nationality.[25]

Once again the tide was moving fast. On January 24 the White House issued a statement naming Livingston T. Merchant, Gerard C. Smith, and Rear Admiral John M. Lee to negotiate with the NATO states. It was a strong team. Merchant was an experienced diplomat. Smith, a former assistant secretary of state for policy planning, and Lee had been members of an earlier mission to NATO on the multilateral force.[26]

The growing momentum worried Rickover. In the Pentagon he found the idea generally accepted that the initial force would consist of three Polaris submarines, each manned by crews drawn from three nations. If, the argument ran, NATO would pay for the three ships and their missiles, the United States could reduce its Polaris fleet by the same number. Rickover heard that some individuals were hailing the Nassau agreement as another Magna Carta, while Kennedy was reported to have declared that the Nassau meeting was as important as the original NATO treaty. But was the expression of presidential support true? Rickover doubted it.[27]

Admiral Anderson was also skeptical. In an effort to inject a shot of realism into the discussion, he wrote Nitze on February 5 of some factors to be considered. The joint committee had to be consulted, and he was certain it would not tolerate any lowering of safety standards. Much of the navy's record for safety resulted from the careful training both officers and men received on commission-owned prototypes. It was doubtful that the commission would permit foreign nationals to use the prototypes, because these were also used for secret research and development. Another matter was liability in case of a nuclear accident, a subject Congress would certainly want to explore. Again Congress would want assurance that the participating states understood the cost of building and operating a Polaris fleet. He, too, was worried about classified information, not only on the technical aspects but on operational procedures as well. A break in secrecy on the operation of Polaris submarines could be devastating to American defense.[28]

Kennedy had scheduled a press conference for the afternoon of 7 February 1963. Because it would be the first since the announcement of the membership and mission of the Merchant team, he could anticipate getting some questions on the multilateral force. Seaborg suggested to Kennedy that it would be good politics if he could say he expected to see Rickover soon. The White House called Rickover and scheduled him for noon, February 11. As it turned out, although the subject of the multilateral force was raised during the press conference, no one brought up the question of Rickover. That did not matter, for it was still important to get his views.[29]

At twenty-two minutes after noon on February 11 Rickover was ushered into the Oval Office. He did not know how he would be received. He told a few of his closest associates he might return without a job. To his relief he found the president interested, courteous, and seeking information. Rickover explained why mixed manning was dangerous. Nuclear propulsion depended upon highly intelligent, specially trained officers and men. Differences in language and background were bound to increase the chance of accidents. Still, if necessary, mixed manning could be made to work. The greatest objection from Rickover's perspective was the risk to national security. He was certain it would be hard to protect information given to the multilateral force.

Kennedy was noncommittal. He spoke of the need to keep NATO alive and to prevent the proliferation of nuclear weapons. Then he turned to other subjects. To Rickover's surprise, the president had read his two books on education and promised to see that he got certain periodic reports from the Office of Education. For a few moments the two men talked about their childhoods and upbringing. The president ended the discussion, and Rickover left at 12:55 P.M. He did not know what impression his arguments had made. Every sign, at least, pointed to an immediate decision.[30]

The next day he got a telephone call from Edward R. Murrow, head of the United States Information Agency. Formerly a leading television commentator, Murrow had interviewed Rickover several times and found his candid replies refreshing. As a result, the two men had become friends. Murrow relayed the news that the president had found Rickover's arguments convincing: if there was a multilateral force, it would consist of surface ships. Two days later Rickover received a call reporting that the president at a National Security Council meeting declared Rickover had persuaded him that for reasons of simplicity, time, and security, surface ships were best. The president had also mentioned the difficulty in getting congressional approval for submarines. New instructions given to Merchant on February 13 reflected the change. To the NATO alliance he was to make clear the American preference for surface ships, at least for the initial stages.[31]

But Kennedy was still hesitant and doubtful. He felt other nations did not want the multilateral force—the British and French were opposed, the Italians uninterested, and the Germans, even if presently favorably inclined, would probably change their opinion once they studied the proposal and realized how little it offered them. He did not want the Americans to push too hard for a policy that might fail.[32]

McCone, now director of the Central Intelligence Agency, raised one last flurry. He thought the risk of using submarines for the force had been overstated, and the opposition of the joint committee was not nearly as great as claimed. Quickly Kennedy called for a new analysis by the

Defense Department and the Central Intelligence Agency, the results to be in his hands before the Merchant team left, a date tentatively set for February 22. Rickover and representatives from several agencies considered the McCone memorandum. The atmosphere was very different from that of a month earlier when the attitude was to devise an acceptable approach. Now one individual after another cited technical area after technical area in which American superiority could be jeopardized by a multilateral force. On February 27 McNamara sent a memorandum with McCone's concurrence recommending that the instructions to Merchant remain unchanged. Finally, it seemed the issue was settled.[33]

Yet the concept of using submarines still clung to life. Merchant found a strong preference for these ships among the NATO capitals, particularly among the Italians and Germans. The French were not interested in participation at all, and the British were at best lukewarm. Reports from other sources reaching Washington observed that a multilateral force with submarines was more likely to win acceptance than one with surface ships. If this was so, one way to save the scheme was to devise a two-phased approach with nuclear surface ships as the first step and submarines the second. Congressional opposition would be less for surface ships, and once the multilateral force was established and in operation, the question of submarines could be raised again.[34]

On 21 March 1963, Gerard Smith of the Merchant team called on Rickover to describe the two-step plan. Rickover and Theodore Rockwell, who followed international activities for Naval Reactors, listened. Rickover thought that the European states would hardly accept surface ships if they were to get submarines later. Rockwell remarked that the only way to see if the NATO states really wanted a multilateral force was to declare that they would never get submarines and then see who would still join. Smith declared he wanted all the help he could get to "float the multilateral force." Rickover replied that he was not ready to "sink the submarines" for that purpose.[35]

Without enthusiasm Kennedy was willing to see the negotiations continue. A multilateral force based on submarines was dead. If the Europeans would not accept surface ships, the United States should abandon the idea entirely. Rather than drop the plan immediately, the president accepted a trial of mixed manning.

The *Claude V. Ricketts*

Kennedy suggested using a guided-missile destroyer to demonstrate the feasibility of mixed manning, apparently more to gain time than anything else. The allies could hardly reject the multilateral force during the demonstration, and while it was in progress the United States could reassess its position. Under his successor, Lyndon B. Johnson, preparations for the experiment continued. The navy selected the steam-powered *Biddle,* a guided-missile destroyer commissioned in 1962. Representatives from the several navies worked out a memorandum of understanding. The ship was to operate first off the coast of the United States and then in European waters as a member of the Sixth Fleet. The demonstration would begin around June 1964 and end in December 1965.

The first foreign contingent reported on board in mid-May 1964. The ship was renamed in honor of Admiral Claude V. Ricketts. A strong advocate of the mixed-manning experiment, Ricketts had recently died of a heart attack. Through the rest of the year personnel from other navies arrived until the manning was half American, with Germans, Greeks, Italians, Dutch, and British making up the rest. The captain and executive officer were American; so were the communications officer and his men—that part of the ship's complement dealing with codes and cyphers—and the organization and procedures. After working up in January 1965 off Guantánamo, the *Claude V. Ricketts* deployed first to the Mediterranean and then to the participating countries of northern Europe. In July the ship returned to Norfolk and for the next several months visited Gulf and Caribbean ports. On 1 December 1965 formal ceremonies at Norfolk ended the demonstration.

Officers from the participating navies thought the experiment was successful. It had provided extensive experience that would be useful for a mixed-manned surface force. At the annual competitive exercises among Atlantic Fleet destroyers, the *Claude V. Ricketts* won an overall rating of excellent. Of course, several factors had been helpful. The very fact that it was a demonstration placed the ship's company on its mettle. Furthermore, as a unit of the United States Navy, the ship was able to count upon an existing headquarters and staff, a large logistic network, and well-equipped bases.

On the other hand, a voyage of a Polaris surface ship would be long and tedious, unlike the lively activities characteristic of destroyers. Different ethnic, cultural, and naval backgrounds had caused some problems, but these could be overcome. Common standards would have to be established. Pay scales, for example, should be set so men of the same rating received the same pay, regardless of what they got in their own service. Although the *Claude V. Ricketts* had very little personnel trouble, a common disciplinary code was essential. A common uniform would help weld the force into an entity.

Language was the real problem. At first, foreign personnel made rapid progress in mastering English, but soon reached a plateau beyond which there was little improvement. An ability to pass courses in technical and professional phrases was not enough to establish proper relationships between officers and men nor, above all, handle emergencies. Instances had occurred when, in spite of drill and training, people had to be pushed aside because they could not express themselves clearly and quickly.[36] Such conditions were dangerous enough in surface ships and would have been intolerable in submarines. Ultimately, these practical problems and the lack of continued political support overcame the initial diplomatic enthusiasm for mixed manning. It never was tried on any nuclear-powered ship.

A Matter of Responsibility

The multilateral force was an effort to fuse several diverging forces: the American desire to prevent the proliferation of national atomic-weapon programs, to strengthen the bonds of NATO by giving its members a greater share in the nuclear deterrent, and to make available to other states some of the nuclear technology that had been developed in the United States. Robert Bowie would never forget Eisenhower's eager interest in the submarine-based multilateral force, a zeal that was almost religious. To him—and to others in his administration and that of Kennedy—the new international force offered a bright future that might dissipate the shadows cast by national rivalries, uncertainties, and the growing Soviet menace.

Rickover did not oppose the multilateral force as such, although he had reservations about it, but he was against basing it in submarines for two reasons: safety and the compromise of sensitive information. His own role was to make sure that those charged with the responsibility of formulating national policy had all the points of view. He had no trouble in making his convictions known to the joint committee. Not knowing of Seaborg's suggestion to Kennedy to seek his views, Rickover went to the White House determined to speak out.

His particular strength was the unparalleled knowledge of the vast effort it took to develop nuclear propulsion. That achievement included many things besides the design, development, and manufacture of the reactor and its auxiliaries; it also included the layout of the conventional part of the plant as well, the arrangements carefully planned to provide safety, reliability, and maintenance. In a very real way, the success of the American nuclear propulsion program depended less on physics than on Rickover's application of the principles of engineering. Nor could engineering excellence be separated from the thorough training given to officers and men in schools he established and in the prototypes he operated—training in which he, his engineers, and contractors devised the curriculum, and in which he took a deep personal interest. Together these elements constituted a vital component of American sea power:

together they gave the United States a naval capability unmatched by any other country. It was his responsibility to make sure these facts were understood.

He considered the multilateral force unsound. He had read widely in history and biography, had studied and written upon the submarine and international law, and had more than a usual understanding of the strengths and fragilities of international organizations. Alliances were obviously necessary in a troubled world, but they should be based on enlightened self-interest. The multilateral force would not be an alliance among nations but a supranational organization, an elaborate edifice constructed by clever and sophisticated reasoning, but separated from the real world that had been fashioned by centuries of national experience.

He feared that the creation of the multilateral force would be undertaken without full consideration of all the responsible parts of the government. He was aware that the White House and State Department were strongly disposed to use nuclear propulsion as a diplomatic pawn, and that the Navy Department and the Department of Defense were acquiescent. On the other hand, Congress should be considered. The joint committee had a legal role to play in any arrangement involving atomic energy and a foreign power or organization. He was worried lest the committee be trapped by a situation in which negotiations had gone so far they could not be broken off. But if the decision had been made to help other nations or to establish the multilateral force, he would have done his best to make the arrangement work. He said so to President Kennedy, to Congressman Holifield, and to Admiral Anderson, chief of naval operations.

One source of his strength was the intense certainty of his beliefs. At a commission meeting, discussion turned to helping a nation on one aspect of nuclear propulsion. In years to come more than one individual was to remember the moment when Rickover exclaimed: how would the American people vote if they understood that the intent was to release information on a technology that was an integral part of their defense? At a congressional hearing in which a State Department representative was speaking in support of giving the propulsion technology to another country, he took his tie clasp, shaped like a Polaris submarine, and handed it to the witness so that "at least you have some idea of what you are talking about." He arranged to brief naval attachés before they went overseas to warn them that their job was not to be accommodating to their hosts; in their new assignments they would be subjected to subtle and sophisticated pressures that would be personally ingratiating and flattering, but they should recognize these gestures for what they were and never forget they were to represent the United States. To interpret these instances as skillful tactics was to miss the underlying conviction behind them.

Rickover was convinced that the multilateral force was dangerous to the security of the United States. It placed at risk too much technical and operational information. Furthermore, he was certain that mixed manning of nuclear-powered submarines was incompatible with safe operation. He had frequently asserted that technology does not obey military orders. He had no reason to think it would be any more amenable to the reins of diplomacy.

On 31 May 1953, the atom first produced power that could be used to drive machinery. The reactor was the land prototype for the Nautilus; the place was a desert in Idaho; the leader of the effort was Admiral Rickover. Because of his success he was soon assigned the job of developing and building the world's first full-scale central station nuclear power plant.

CHAPTER EIGHT
Shippingport

At the Shippingport Atomic Power Station, named after the small town in Pennsylvania where it was located, Admiral Rickover made three major accomplishments. The first was demonstrating the feasibility of using pressurized-water reactor technology for civilian application. The second was showing how pressurized-water reactors might be converted to breeding—a process by which more nuclear fuel was produced than was consumed. The third was 4pplying strict discipline over the operation of the civilian reactors to ensure safe and effective operation. It was an example Admiral Rickover hoped other civilian nuclear power plants would follow.

On the morning of 2 December 1977 Rickover was in the Oval Office at the White House. With him were his civilian superior, James R. Schlesinger, secretary of the Department of Energy, and two individuals on his staff upon whom he relied most heavily: William Wegner, deputy director for Naval Reactors, and David T. Leighton, associate director for surface ships and the light-water breeder reactor. The date was already a famous anniversary in the history of atomic energy: it was the thirty-fifth of the Fermi experiment and the twentieth of the first criticality of the Shippingport Atomic Power Station. The ceremony at the White House was to mark the beginning of routine operation of Shippingport with its light-water breeder core. A blackboard, prominently displayed so that everyone could see it, dominated the room. At 10:46 the flurry of newspapermen and photographers stilled as President Jimmy Carter, a proud alumnus of the Naval Reactors program, turned to Rickover with a broad grin and said: "You might tell us what to expect."

Electronics connected the blackboard to a screen in the control room at Shippingport. Words written on the board would appear upon the screen; in this way, Rickover explained, the men in the control room would receive the president's order. The president wrote: "Increase light-water breeder reactor power to 100%, Jimmy Carter." After pausing for a moment he underlined the word "breeder." At the power station Thomas D. Jones II, the plant superintendent, in the presence of Robert E. Kirby, chairman of the board of the Westinghouse Electric Corporation; John M. Arthur, chairman of the board of the Duquesne Light Company; and William H. Hamilton, general manager of the Bettis Atomic Power Laboratory, set about carrying out the instructions from the White House.

In the Oval Office Rickover spoke of the significance of the event. With its reactor core of uranium 233 and thorium, Shippingport would demonstrate the feasibility of breeding, a process in which the reactor produced more fuel than it consumed. Success would vastly increase the energy resources of the world. In addition, the goal could be achieved within the limits of existing reactor technology; indeed the majority of the nuclear power stations in operation or planned were the type that could be converted to breeders.[1]

The ceremony marked only the latest event in the existence of a facility that was already world-famous in the history of atomic energy. The Shippingport Atomic Power Station was the first large-scale nuclear power plant in the United States and the first plant of its size in the world operated for the sole purpose of producing electric power and advancing reactor technology for civilian application. Its technical contributions were too many to list, but many of the reactor components—main coolant pumps, valves, piping, and steam generators—were the first to be designed, developed, and fabricated for civilian nuclear-power application. The station was the first to have reactor containment, a structure that housed all parts of the plant containing the reactor and primary system in a series of large, interconnected vapor-tight vessels. Uranium dioxide fuel contained in zircaloy tubing developed for Shippingport was so successful that it was widely adopted by industry. Shippingport proved that an atomic power station could function on a utility network, either as a baseload plant meeting a steady demand for power or as a swing-load plant meeting the demand for power that fluctuated over a period of time. Standards for personnel training and procedures for safe operation and maintenance were developed to serve as models for the civilian power industry.[2]

Shippingport had another importance. The station was the sole responsibility that Rickover had in the civilian nuclear-power program. In the naval program he was responsible for the design, development, and safe operation of all the navy's nuclear propulsion reactors, and for the selection and training of the personnel who manned them. The civilian power program he could influence only by the work he did and by the examples he set at Shippingport. It was a responsibility he took seriously. No part of the station's design, development, construction, operation, or personnel escaped his vigilance. Although the origins, construction, and early operation of the Shippingport Atomic Power Station have been described elsewhere, the effect of Rickover and the station upon the development of civilian nuclear power cannot be understood without some repetition of key decisions and events.

Early Quest for Civilian Nuclear Power

Rickover's first contacts with civilian nuclear power were incidental.[3] In 1946 the Bureau of Ships sent him, four other officers, and three civilians to Oak Ridge to join engineers from industry in learning the fundamentals of nuclear technology. Although the interest of the naval group was on ship propulsion and that of the other engineers was on civilian power, all were to work on a reactor that Farrington Daniels, a chemist with the wartime program, had proposed. The project was to be little more than an experiment, but it was to show that the technology, as primitive as it was, could produce power.

Like most people during the war, Rickover had known nothing of the Manhattan project. He was awed by its achievement. Listening to scientists, some of them unbelievably young, explain abstruse concepts and scrawl complicated formulas on the blackboard was an exciting, if humbling, experience far from his own background as a practical naval engineer. In the light of the undeniable accomplishments of these men, he found their confidence and assurance impressive. But as work on the Daniels project began, he was startled to observe that beneath the glittering facade of articulate certainty was an almost total unawareness of the principles and standards of safety and reliability that the engineer had to meet in the real world. As it turned out, the Daniels reactor was never built because its concept was too naive. Realizing that the project held nothing of value for them, Rickover quickly imposed on the navy group an arduous program of study, listening, and questioning.

The Oak Ridge experience left Rickover a legacy of keen distrust of scientists, an attitude that marked all his future undertakings. He was not opposed to science or to scientists, but scientific truth was not engineering truth, nor was the mission of the scientist the same as the task of the engineer. The scientist in his quest had to exercise strict discipline to exclude human bias, preconception, and prejudice; the engineer in his job had to take these frailties into account, for his machines and devices would be operated by and in the midst of humans with all of their shortcomings. Both approaches were essential, but for practical application of nuclear technology the principles of engineering had to govern.

Not until 1949 did the commission establish the division of reactor development. By that time Rickover had the naval nuclear propulsion program well started. In addition to his small Washington office, he had the Bettis Atomic Power Laboratory, very recently acquired by the commission and operated under contract by the Westinghouse Electric Corporation. The sole mission of Bettis was to develop propulsion reactors for the navy. Rickover also had some work at the Knolls Atomic Power Laboratory, owned by the commission and operated by the General Electric Company at Schenectady, New York. In contrast to Bettis, at that time Knolls had many commission assignments. Rickover had already stamped his mark upon the program. His philosophy of engineering permeated and animated every aspect of it. He and his men directed the technical efforts and made the key decisions on reactor materials, fuel elements, control mechanisms, core design, steam characteristics, instrumentation, and plant layout. Professional engineers, they drove with almost single-minded zeal and determination toward nuclear propulsion. The naval nuclear propulsion program had strong leadership and a definite goal: a reactor plant that would operate safely and reliably in a combat ship. Finally, Rickover had narrowed the possible reactor types to two: pressurized water at Bettis and sodium cooled at Knolls.

The civilian nuclear-power program had a very different set of characteristics. Its objective was to develop a reactor to the stage where a utility, on economic grounds alone, could choose to buy an atomic power station from more than one manufacturer. That goal required the participation of the utilities, their associated industries, and several commission laboratories. Of the possible reactor types, no one could say which would be best for civilian power; perhaps one would be most suitable for one part of the country while another would be the most desirable elsewhere. In addition, the barriers of classification and secrecy remained high because the reactor technology for producing fissionable materials for military purposes overlapped the reactor technology for civilian power reactors.

The civilian power program faced an even more formidable obstacle in the shortage of uranium. The wartime program had been based largely on supplies from the Belgian Congo. That mine was near exhaustion, and prospecting had not yet revealed adequate new sources. A series of crises—the failure to gain international control of atomic energy in the United Nations, the fall of Czechoslovakia, the Berlin blockade, the collapse of China, and the Russian detonation of an atomic bomb—led the United States to accelerate its atomic-weapon production effort and to undertake the development of the hydrogen bomb. Defense requirements consumed almost all of the uranium, leaving little for the development of civilian power reactors.

The arcane complexities of nuclear physics contained a possible way out for civilian nuclear power. Theory and experiments indicated a reactor might be designed that could generate power and produce more fuel than it consumed. The mechanics of the breeding process appeared deceptively simple. Existing reactors were based on natural uranium, an element about 99.3 percent uranium 238 and 0.7 percent uranium 235. Of the two, it was the scarcer that was crucial to the production of energy. When struck by a neutron moderated—or slowed down—by collision with water, graphite, or some other suitable substance, uranium 235 gave off about two neutrons. That was not much. Calculations and experiments showed that one was likely to be absorbed in reactor materials or escape, but the other remained and, if moderated, continued the fission process. The reactors built by the Manhattan Engineer District during the war to produce plutonium for weapons used natural uranium for fuel. The reactors that Rickover was designing for propulsion were also based on uranium but highly enriched in uranium 235. As uranium 235 was the only naturally occurring isotope that could sustain a chain reaction, it was as much a resource to be hoarded as petroleum or natural gas.

However, uranium 238, by absorbing a neutron, decayed radioactively into plutonium 239, a fissionable material. When fissioned by fast neutrons, plutonium produced power and enough neutrons to create more plutonium. Over a period of time a reactor of this type could convert enough uranium 238 to plutonium to refuel itself and one other reactor. Plutonium was toxic and required stringent precautions in working with it. On the other hand, the Manhattan project, and later the commission, had gained considerable experience in producing and processing the element for weapons.

Thorium 232 was another element offering the possibility of breeding. More plentiful than uranium, thorium 232, by capturing a moderated neutron, became uranium 233, a fissionable material and, consequently, a potential reactor fuel. A reactor fueled with uranium 233 could breed more uranium 233 from thorium 232. The breeding gain would not be as much as in the uranium-plutonium approach, for calculations showed that a thorium 232-uranium 233 reactor would breed only enough fuel to replenish itself. Furthermore, because uranium 233 had some undesirable characteristics for weapon use, the wartime program had not put much effort into it. As a result the amount of practical experience with the element was very little.

In September 1950 Rickover assessed the prospects for breeding. He saw three major areas in which much work had to be done. Two dealt with reactor design: preventing the loss of neutrons and providing a core with a high neutron flux per unit volume. The third was fuel reprocessing. Unless this step was carried out with unparalleled efficiency, the additional fuel made in the reactor would be lost. He thought the naval propulsion reactors under design met many of the requirements to explore breeding. It might be possible to modify future propulsion reactors to obtain data on both the thorium and plutonium approaches. The breeder effort, he argued, might be more soundly based if carried out as part of the propulsion program. Possibly he was making a bid to have part of the breeder effort; in any case, he was pointing out some problems that had to be faced.[4]

Without question, to design and develop a breeder reactor was extremely challenging. In 1950 the commission cancelled the intermediate power-breeder reactor under development by General Electric at Knolls. Early assumptions based on incomplete plutonium nuclear data had proved wrong, and the project was redirected toward naval propulsion, becoming the prototype for the submarine *Seawolf*. In December 1951 a very small breeder-reactor experiment, developed at the Argonne National Laboratory, went into operation at the National Reactor Testing Station in Idaho. By no means could the experiment be considered a power producer, although it lit a few light bulbs. Its main purpose was to test a particular technical approach; whether it actually demonstrated practical breeding was a matter of some controversy.

By the end of 1951 the shortage of uranium was easing. The commission's vigorous prospecting program was turning up large supplies of the element in the West. Although the urgency of breeding sharply diminished, it did not vanish. Uranium 235 was still a limited natural resource. All that had been done was to push back the time when breeder reactors would be essential.[5]

Triumph on the Desert

Rickover had no part in the civilian nuclear power program, although he followed the technical developments closely. The burden that he placed upon himself and his people left little time for anything but nuclear propulsion. The first great triumph came on 31 May 1953 at the National Reactor Testing Station. Commissioner Thomas E. Murray, an engineer and a staunch ally of Rickover, opened the throttle of the Mark I, the prototype for the *Nautilus*. Steam from the reactor flowed to the turbine. Once sure that the plant was operating as desired, Rickover and Murray climbed out of the prototype down to the floor of the building. They walked to the stern. Before them a shaft rotated. Both men watched silently. For the first time atomic energy was producing a significant amount of power in a form and with the reliability needed to drive machinery. In June the Mark I reached full power and made a simulated run across the Atlantic.[6]

The Mark I was a superb achievement. Only seven years earlier Rickover had first arrived at Oak Ridge. He knew nothing about atomic energy save what he was able to pick up from the few sources available to him. He had no mandate from the navy nor the commission to develop a nuclear propulsion plant. He had no organization; indeed, the officers with him were not under his cognizance, and when they returned to Washington they were not kept together. He had no laboratories or trained men. The technology he needed did not exist. Theories were plentiful, but facts were scarce. No one knew the best design for a reactor that would generate the power needed to drive a submarine. No one was certain what would be the best medium to transfer heat from the core to the boilers. No one knew the best materials for fabricating the core or its fuel. No one knew how the materials would withstand the prolonged exposure to radiation. No one was certain of the best means for controlling the reactor. No one had fabricated pumps, valves, and steam generators to the standards that were required. No one had faced the problems of plant reliability and crew safety. Nor was it just the nuclear part of the propulsion plant about which so little was known. Placing a steam propulsion plant into the hull of a submarine raised difficult engineering problems, for the water surrounding a submarine compressed the hull—the greater the depth the greater the compression—while the heat expanded the components of a steam plant.

The success meant a sharp decrease in the importance of the sodium-cooled approach. Only two reactors of this type were to be completed for the propulsion program—one at West Milton, New York, and the other for the submarine *Seawolf*. All other nuclear-powered ships of the navy were to be propelled by pressurized-water reactors greatly advanced, of course, over the Mark I and the *Nautilus* plants.[7]

A Civilian Reactor Project

It was unfair to expect the civilian power reactor program to have a comparable success. Classification was still a barrier to dissemination of information, solutions to many technical problems were uncertain, and development and construction costs for civilian power plants, even if only necessarily rough estimates, were far too high for private industry to manage by itself. Within the commission and in Congress grew a recognition that some form of government-industry partnership was necessary and that the Atomic Energy Act had to be amended to make participation by industry easier.[8]

These factors the new Eisenhower administration recognized and added some of its own. To honor its pledge to cut government spending, the administration pruned several programs in early 1953. In the field of atomic energy, a proposed reactor for an aircraft carrier was a casualty. Eisenhower was willing to reconsider the decision if the project was reoriented to civilian application. Deeply and emotionally convinced that the future of mankind required that the atom be developed for peaceful uses, the president saw American construction of the world's first large-scale atomic power station as a prize worth seeking. The commission was willing to take the position that the pressurized-water reactor approach was promising for commercial application. The joint committee supported the project.

Opposition to Rickover and pressurized-water technology, however, was intense. Within the division of reactor development the argument ran that the technical approach, while suitable for naval propulsion, was too wasteful of uranium 235 for its use to be encouraged in civilian application. Moreover, the generating capacity, if based on the carrier project, would not be large enough to have any economic significance. By sponsoring a pressurized-water plant to gain international prestige, the commission risked distorting the development of nuclear technology. Finally, a reactor based on one designed for an aircraft carrier hardly seemed the best vehicle for developing reactor technology for civilian application. And there was Rickover himself. If the project was to be carried out as a cooperative venture with industry, he was not the man for the job. His hard-headed, hard-driving, personal, and direct leadership would leave little scope for industry. Rickover would dominate—and once he was in the civilian power program, it would be impossible to get him out.[9]

After a battle that split the staff, the commissioners, and the joint committee, the commissioners assigned the project to Rickover on 16 June 1953. Even then a last minute flurry of hurried intrigues among the staff, the General Advisory Committee, the commission, and the joint committee threatened to overturn the decision. The appointment of Lewis L. Strauss to replace Gordon Dean as commission chairman forced a review. On July 9 the commission reaffirmed its action.[10] Only the strong and vigorous support of Murray at the White House and in the commission made that outcome possible.

Rickover was well aware that his record of achievement had enabled Murray to back him. He knew that he was moving into new technical areas, even if propulsion technology offered a good foundation, and he was deeply conscious that his decisions would set a pattern for industry. Being first, if important for international prestige, was an evanescent prize. Constructing a nuclear power plant that could operate as an integral part of a utility network, and yet be flexible enough in its layout and sufficiently instrumented to advance civilian reactor technology—these were the real objectives.

Development and Construction

Three organizations dominated the history of Shippingport. The first was Naval Reactors and Rickover. The second was Bettis, by now comprising a group of highly skilled and experienced people in many technical disciplines. Under a contract supplement signed 9 October 1953, the laboratory was to design, fabricate, test, and assemble the reactor and its heat-transfer system. The third was the Duquesne Light Company. A privately owned utility that had served the Pittsburgh area for sixty years, Duquesne, under a contract with the commission dated 3 November 1954, agreed to provide the site, construct the turbine generator portion of the plant, operate and maintain the entire facility, and contribute $5 million to develop and build the reactor. Duquesne would buy the steam produced by the reactor.[11]

From the first, safety dominated the thinking of Rickover and his engineers. Careful and meticulous engineering went into all components, particularly those, such as pumps and valves, that came into contact with hot radioactive water. The pressure vessel containing the core was the largest that industry could fabricate. It dictated that the station capacity would be 60 net electrical megawatts. However, anticipating that advances in nuclear technology might eventually increase the power output of the core, Duquesne was to install a 100-megawatt electrical generator. The design of the radioactive-waste disposal system called for a great deal of thought, for it was to be the first to be built in a populated area. Instruments were to monitor every aspect of the plant, because in many instances operational data from Shippingport would be the first that could be checked against theory. Nowhere was the concern for safety more evident than in the establishment of four barriers between the radioactivity within the fuel and the environment: encapsulating the radioactive fuel in a highly corrosion-resistant cladding of a zirconium alloy; putting the seal-welded primary reactor coolant system behind pressure-containing walls; housing the reactor and its steam system in a series of interconnected containers; and, finally, placing the reactor plant underground.

The core design, originated by Alvin Radkowsky, Naval Reactors' chief physicist, was another unusual feature of Shippingport. The "seed-blanket" design that he proposed in September 1953 made use of the different properties of uranium 235 and uranium 238. The name came from the arrangement of two types of fuel elements. Those designated the "seed" were highly enriched uranium 235 and were surrounded by a "blanket" of elements made of natural uranium. The seed was the driving force, as it alone sustained fission. Neutrons from uranium 235 continued the fission process and converted the uranium 238 in the blanket to plutonium 239 for fissioning by fast neutrons. The design offered the advantage of simplified reactor control, but its chief beauty was its use of natural uranium. The blanket was planned to last the life of at least two seeds. Over time a considerable amount of the total power produced—perhaps half—would come from the far more plentiful uranium 238 than the scarce uranium 235.[12]

Fuel technology developed for the *Nautilus* gave fair assurance for the seed: it was the blanket elements that posed the most difficult problem. To last the life of more than one seed, they had to maintain their integrity and dimensional stability for a long time in an environment of intense radiation and in the presence of corrosive hot water. As uranium was neither corrosion resistant nor dimensionally stable, the fuel-development effort at Bettis was investigating various uranium alloys. Uranium-molybdenum looked most promising. Unfortunately, in the summer of 1954 samples exposed in a test reactor produced troubling data. Extrapolating them to the conditions expected in a power reactor revealed a major corrosion problem. The matter was extremely serious, for the coolant could deposit within the primary system the radioactive fission products released from the fuel, contaminating the plant to such an extent as to force its shutdown. More research might yield the solution, but the greater effort would require the construction of special facilities designed to produce an environment approximating that of a power reactor. Such facilities had never even been designed, let alone built or operated. In addition, their existence would be no guarantee of success.

As a secondary effort Bettis was developing uranium dioxide, a fundamentally different type of fuel. Although encouraging, the work was still at an early stage. No one could yet tell whether the promise was true, for possibly the laboratory had not gone far enough to uncover the real problems. Switching the effort to uranium dioxide meant a drastic revision of the Bettis program. Rickover hesitated. In neither approach could he see certainty, but the schedule was pressing him hard.

At Bettis on 26 April 1955, he weighed the pros and cons, studied the data, sounded opinions, and considered schedules. Remembering some work he had seen during a recent trip to England, he placed a transatlantic call. The British failed to clarify the problem: if anything, they strengthened the case for alloys. But one quality of uranium dioxide attracted him. Corrosion was oxidation: uranium dioxide was already oxidized and in a sense already "rusted." Insofar as contact with hot water was concerned, uranium dioxide should be able to maintain its dimensional stability.

His was the decision and he made it. Blanket assemblies were to be uranium dioxide contained in zircaloy tubing. His action had long-range significance, for the fuel proved excellent in operation and became widely adopted by the civilian power industry.[13]

By that time the site at Shippingport had begun its transformation. Although President Eisenhower had started the bulldozers by remote control from Denver, Colorado, on Labor Day, 6 September 1954, winter had prevented large-scale construction. November 1955 saw the beginning of the erection of the reactor container, the interconnected steel vessels housing the reactor and the primary system. For further protection

Rickover had called for a concrete wall around the container. The container was not finished until 1 September 1956. A month later the pressure vessel, manufactured by Combustion Engineering Incorporated, arrived. With some difficulty it was suspended by a framework until thermal insulation protected by a covering of thin stainless steel could be applied. In February 1957 it was cautiously lowered into position, and on October 6 came the installation of the core: for eight tense hours its 58 tons were gently lowered into the pressure vessel. On 2 December 1957 Shippingport reached criticality.[14]

Responsibility

As the construction of the Shippingport station neared completion, Naval Reactors, Westinghouse, and Duquesne prepared for the shift in responsibilities. Under its contract with the commission, Duquesne was to supervise, operate, and maintain the entire station. Article I of the contract stated that the company would assume its responsibility upon "completion of construction," a term defined as the delivery of sufficient steam to bring the turbine up to speed and to synchronize the generator.[15]

To operate Shippingport, Duquesne had chosen personnel, in so far as possible, from its own ranks. The engineers for the station had about ten years of experience with the company, but still had a good part of their professional careers before them and were young enough to have the flexibility and interest to learn the demands of a new technology. Very early in the project Rickover arranged for lectures on atomic energy for Duquesne executives, a technique he used with every new major contractor. As far as the station was concerned, far more important was the rigorous training he arranged for Duquesne operating personnel at Bettis and at the *Nautilus* prototype. The prototype experience was particularly valuable, since the men were actually learning on a reactor of the same general type as Shippingport. For a few special areas such as health physics (protection of personnel against radiation), chemistry, and instrumentation and control he called upon other commission facilities for assistance.[16]

In May 1957, Lawton D. Geiger, manager of the commission's Pittsburgh area office, began conversations with Westinghouse and Duquesne on the transfer. The area office, located on the same site as Bettis, handled the daily relations, especially financial and administrative, between Rickover and the laboratory. On September 20 Geiger wrote to Philip A. Fleger, chairman of the board and the chief executive of Duquesne, that bringing the turbine to speed and synchronizing the generator would occur at a stage when the reactor would not have been sufficiently tested at various power levels to determine its stability under different operating conditions. It was hardly in the interest of the commission or Duquesne, Geiger continued, for the company to accept responsibility for a nuclear plant that had not yet been proven safe or reliable.[17]

Fleger reacted vigorously. A strong-willed lawyer and executive prominent in Pittsburgh business circles, he sharply resented the imputation that his company could not be trusted to assume and exercise its responsibilities safely. He saw the proposal Geiger was transmitting as undermining the spirit of trust and cooperation with which Duquesne and the commission had entered the contract. For three years the commission had been training Duquesne personnel: recently the utility had requested proposals on how to improve the effort. It had received none. Consequently, Fleger could see no reason to depart from the contract: Duquesne was ready to operate the nuclear portion of the plant upon generator synchronization and with such assistance from Westinghouse as might be necessary.[18]

Rickover turned to W. Kenneth Davis, director of the division of reactor development, and to the commissioners. What he was asking, he pointed out, was not unusual, for it was customary and proper for the designer of any complex equipment to take responsibility for initial testing. The widespread public interest in Shippingport and the commercial future of the pressurized-water reactor required special care for the first stages of power operation. The recent accident in England on October 10 to the Windscale reactor No. 1, in which some radioactivity was released into the atmosphere, was an example of what could happen, for British investigation attributed the accident partly to errors of judgment on the part of the operating staff, and these in turn stemmed from weaknesses of the organization.[19]

He saw a way around the difficulty. Turn the station over to Duquesne in accordance with the contract as Fleger wished, but have government representatives present at all key stations to observe and advise the operators, with the understanding that Bettis personnel could act as government representatives. If a situation arose that was considered by either party to affect the safety and integrity of the plant, the two should confer and if failing to agree, shut down the plant or otherwise put it in a safe condition. Davis accepted the arrangement. Furthermore, he assured Fleger, close commission supervision would end when the operation tests were completed, estimated to last about two weeks. Then the commission would exercise normal supervision.[20]

Rejecting the commission proposal, Fleger countered on November 4 with one of his own. Duquesne would decide who should be present during power operation tests; he made no mention of the commission's authority in the reactor portion of the plant—which the commission owned. As Rickover interpreted the plan, commission personnel would be consulted only when Duquesne and Bettis disagreed, an arrangement that jeopardized the commission's statutory responsibility for the safe operation of the plant. The proposal hardly met the view of the advisory committee on reactor safeguards, an independent group of technical experts who, at a recent meeting with Bettis, commission, and Duquesne personnel, stressed the need for all available advice and counsel.[21]

On 9 December 1957, Rickover and Fleger agreed that Duquesne would assume responsibility for the plant at generator synchronization, that the company would man all operating positions, and that it would conduct the power operation tests in accordance with procedures drawn up by the company, Westinghouse, and the commission. Although the utility would arrange for Westinghouse assistance, the personnel would be chosen with the concurrence of the commission. Finally, if any question arose during power operation tests that in the opinion of either Duquesne or the commission involved safety, the company would shut down the plant.[22]

Summarized in a letter of December 12 from Davis to Fleger, this understanding appeared to overcome all obstacles. On December 16 Joseph C. Rengel, the Bettis project manager, informed Lieutenant Commander Donald G. Iselin, the commission's Pittsburgh area office project manager, that Westinghouse was ready to turn the plant over to Duquesne for synchronization of the generator and to assume the role of consultant to the company and technical advisor to the commission. To the Duquesne crew the moment was fast approaching for which they had been training and which they had helped bring about. In accordance with the agreed plan, George M. Oldham, the Duquesne plant superintendent, had Lee R. Love bring the turbine from slow roll up to the speed needed for synchronization. At this point progress stopped.[23]

Naval Reactors personnel had found some procedures incomplete and the plant deficient in some respects. Seven men from the Rickover organization—the Washington office, the Pittsburgh area office, and Shippingport—met in a stormy session with eight men from Westinghouse and seven from Duquesne. For most of that night the group worked to correct the deficiencies and complete the procedures.[24] The next day, December 17, Rickover flew in from Washington. He was disturbed by what he heard. He was no longer sure that the wording of the agreement with Duquesne was strong enough.

That night steam again flowed to the turbine and its speed built up to the point of synchronization. Rickover called a halt. Not until the wording of the agreement was strengthened to state that a government representative would be present at all times, and that he would have the authority to shut down the plant or otherwise place it in a safe condition, would Rickover agree to let the synchronization continue. The Duquesne personnel objected. No one denied that the reactor belonged to the commission and that the commission had certain statutory obligations. The heart of the matter was whether Rickover through his representative would exercise the authority without proper regard to the demands of the Duquesne network. The impasse was resolved by the selection of Iselin as the first government representative—a position that was inevitably to be abbreviated to "NR Rep." During his duty at the site, Iselin had won the confidence of Rickover, Duquesne, and Westinghouse. On 18 December 1957, Duquesne brought the turbine to synchronous speed and closed the main generator breaker. For the first time nuclear-generated power flowed over the Duquesne system. At 11:10 on the morning of December 23 the Shippingport Atomic Power Station reached its full power of 60 net electrical megawatts.[25]

True enough, reactor-produced power had flowed over transmission lines before. At the National Reactor Testing Station the experimental breeder reactor No. 1 produced token amounts of electricity in December 1951. The boiling-water reactor experiment No. 4, also at the station, produced enough electricity to light up the small town of Idaho Falls on 17 July 1955. The next day at West Milton, New York, the sodium-cooled submarine prototype reactor delivered a small amount of power for a very short time to the Niagara-Mohawk Company. However, these events were little more than stunts. In 1954 the Russians put into operation a small atomic power plant at Obninsk that produced electricity for civilian use. In October 1956, the British Calder Hall station supplied power to the national distribution system, but the reactor was also designed to produce plutonium for the British weapon program. Shippingport was the first full-scale plant designed and operated solely for the purpose of advancing civilian reactor technology.[26]

Much of the dispute about the government representative in the control room at Shippingport dealt only with the first power operation tests. Rickover was, of course, also concerned with later operations. He and Fleger soon agreed that the arrangement reached the night of generator synchronization would last for the duration of the contract—a length of time that was to span a quarter of a century. Rickover thought that having a technically trained and properly qualified man on watch, who was independent of the organization and men operating the station and was armed with the authority to shut down the reactor if he thought it necessary, an essential ingredient to safe operation. This representative would combine three fundamental attributes: competence, independence, and authority.[27]

Appraisal

From its first operation Shippingport proved a technological success and became an international showpiece, but its impact on the infant nuclear-power industry was difficult to assess. That subject was on the mind of John A. McCone, successor to Lewis L. Strauss as chairman of the commission, when he accepted an invitation from Rickover to get out of Washington and see the Naval Reactors installations where "he would learn something." Escorted by Rickover and some of his senior engineers, McCone visited several facilities, among them Knolls, Bettis, and Shippingport, on 10 and 11 September 1958.

An engineer as well as an industrialist, McCone could appreciate what had been accomplished and was both fascinated and troubled by his impressions. Without doubt Rickover and his team were doing a magnificent job, but the techniques they had developed for naval reactors were so elaborate and expensive as to make their adoption by a civilian power industry most unlikely. Nonetheless, Rickover, his engineers, and his contractors would admit no shortcuts: industry would have to reach these standards. From other sources outside the program McCone had heard otherwise. These views, however, lacked the concrete technical data he had learned to expect from engineers in the propulsion program. McCone thought many companies were making huge investments in plant, equipment, and personnel, entering a new field without understanding what they were getting into, and hoping that somehow advances in technology would bail them out. Rickover and his people were so highly critical of the commission's civilian power program that McCone felt certain that the knowledge and experience won by the Naval Reactors organization were not available to other parts of the division of reactor development.[28]

Unquestionably, relations between the naval propulsion program and the rest of the division were strained. In truth, Rickover had little respect for most people working on other projects. He believed they only administered, only read reports, and only worked—if then—during office hours. His own men he thought of as a special and exclusive team. He wanted them kept that way, free from the trappings and paraphernalia of bureaucracy. He would not, for example, allow other members of the division free access to the laboratories or prototypes. The workload of development and training was too heavy to permit interruptions without good reason.

The attitude in other branches of the division, at least in the lower echelons, was usually hostile. More than one engineer, perhaps knowing nothing from personal experience, expressed strong distaste for the Naval Reactors operation. Few questioned the excellence of the work: it was what they perceived as the atmosphere that they objected to. Very little chance existed to dispel this view because casual meetings between the members of Naval Reactors and the rest of the division seldom occurred. Occasions for informal contacts were even less after 1958 when the division moved to the commission's new headquarters in Germantown, Maryland, leaving Naval Reactors in its temporary buildings near Main Navy on Constitution Avenue.

Although the naval nuclear propulsion program was highly classified, Rickover was responsible for a number of technical manuals, among them volumes on shielding, zirconium, hafnium, and beryllium, as well as a handbook on reactor physics. These were part of the harvest of unclassified information winnowed from the mass of data and shared with others. Moreover, he was quick to answer requests for information and advice from senior members of the commission staff, the commissioners, and the chairman. As for Shippingport, periodic and topical reports kept the nascent civilian power industry up-to-date on both technical aspects of the plant and its operating experience. In 1958 at the Second International Conference on the Peaceful Uses of Atomic Energy held in Geneva, Switzerland, the United States offered a series of technical volumes. One contained essays on Shippingport written by Naval Reactors and contractor personnel. In February 1959 the commission set up a school for reactor operators at the plant, allowing foreign personnel to attend.[29]

At the end of 1961, Fleger of Duquesne, I. Harry Mandil, in charge of the reactor engineering branch of Naval Reactors, and Philip N. Ross, general manager of Bettis, summarized four years of plant operation at a conference in Tokyo. Shippingport had more than met its objectives. Two 1,000-hour full-power runs on seed 1 and three 1,300-hour full-power runs on seed 2 showed no unusual problems. The plant had operated with the reliability and continuity required by a baseload plant, and yet its response to rapidly changing power demands had shown it could handle swing loads. Under normal conditions shutdown and start-up were carried out faster than any modern conventional plant on the Duquesne system. Procedures devised to safeguard personnel and protect the environment were successful, and no operating hazards had occurred. The need for well-trained operators and maintenance personnel, and for detailed procedures was greater than for conventional power plants because of the overriding demands of safety, but Shippingport had shown it could be done. Of course there had been problems. In four years three coolant pumps had failed. Two were of the same design, and curiously all were in the same loop, but that appeared to be a coincidence. Furthermore, some of the steam generators had to be modified. Indeed, difficulty with the steam system was the principal cause of station downtime. Even as the three men were speaking in Tokyo, Shippingport had begun a 3,000-hour effective full-power run on seed 3 that was to be completed successfully in March 1962. All in all, the plant had proved well-suited for operation by a utility.

The seed-blanket core was working well. Operation on the first seed ended on 7 October 1959. Designed for a life of 3,000 effective full-power hours, it had actually reached 5,806. The second seed was depleted on 14 August 1961. Designed for 5,000 effective full-power hours, it had reached 7,900. The blanket elements—which had posed the greatest technical challenge—were far surpassing expectations. They had been designed to last 8,000 effective full-power hours or the life of the first two seeds. When the two seeds were replaced, careful examination showed the blanket in excellent condition. It would last through the life of the third seed and possibly through the fourth. Finally, calculations showed that the blanket furnished over 50 percent of the power.

So promising were the results that the design and fabrication of a second core had begun. It was to have a capacity of 150 electrical megawatts, and a life equivalent to 20,000 effective full-power hours. Because the turbine capacity was only 100 electrical megawatts, a heat sink was to absorb the extra power.[30]

The Civilian Nuclear-Power Program

The Tokyo conference was evidence that the civilian nuclear-power program had come a long way since the start-up of Shippingport. At the end of 1961 the commission listed two more large central station prototypes in operation, another ten being built or planned, and four small prototypes under construction. Of these, eleven were light-water reactors, a fundamental designation meaning that highly purified ordinary water was the heat-transfer medium. Into this category fell the pressurized- and boiling-water reactors—the latter a type in which boiling took place in the core. Capacity was another measure of progress, and here too the advance was startling, for one proposed station was to have a capacity of 355 net electrical megawatts.[31]

While Shippingport and the commission's civilian nuclear-power program were contributing to power reactor technology, other factors were at work. The Atomic Energy Act of 1954 eased legal obstacles by permitting private ownership of reactors under commission license, greater access to technical information, a more liberal patent policy, and certain services and materials. As additional incentive the commission announced on 10 January 1955 a power-reactor demonstration program that offered limited assistance to private and public utilities interested in building and operating nuclear power stations. Nonetheless, progress toward an independent self-sustaining nuclear power industry was slow.[32]

The commission turned to Frank K. Pittman, director of reactor development, for a study of the causes of industrial reluctance and the means to overcome them. In April 1961 he presented the preliminary results. They showed that high financial risks in plant construction, the lack of data from operating plants, and site selection were the major problems.

The best answer seemed to be another nuclear power station, constructed by the government and built on a utility grid with the premise that the utility purchase the station when it proved technically and economically sound.[33]

The proposal required careful thought. The reactor would have to be large enough—perhaps several hundred megawatts—to become economically competitive with fossil-fueled plants. Furthermore, no utility would be interested in ultimately purchasing and operating the station unless the technology was well developed: only the pressurized- and boiling-water reactors met that criterion, although that point was not mentioned in the paper. Moreover, the commission contribution, whatever its form, would be substantial, raising the issue of whether the expenditure was to go into a well-developed technology or would be better spent on other promising approaches.

Rickover followed the discussions carefully. Shippingport was near to fulfilling its original objective. If the new plant was to be pressurized water—or even some other type—and if he got the assignment, he could remain a part of the civilian nuclear-power program. To that effort he could bring some of the engineering direction and discipline he thought was sorely needed. On 27 February 1962 Mandil telephoned Bettis, asking the laboratory to evaluate several designs—the capacity of the largest was 750 electrical megawatts—and not to confine itself to the seed-blanket approach.[34]

Industry had not adopted the seed-blanket design, but had taken up the slightly enriched core. As the name of the latter implied, the core consisted of fuel elements slightly enriched in uranium 235. The seed-blanket design required two types of fuel elements, both expensive to manufacture; the slightly enriched core required only one. The seed-blanket approach aimed at long-lived cores (which added to their expense) in order to decrease the number of times the reactor would have to be refueled: with less expensive slightly enriched cores, more frequent refueling would have to be tolerated. Furthermore, power density in the slightly enriched cores was more uniform. The differences between the two types represented different philosophies: for the propulsion reactors, Rickover wanted cores that would last a long time without refueling—his ultimate goal was a core that would last the life of a ship. In the 1960s, to an industry no longer faced with a shortage of uranium, the goal of the naval nuclear propulsion program, however admirable technically, did not make sense economically.

Reshaping The Program

The consideration of the proposed nuclear-power plant was taking place against a complicated political background involving Congress and the

White House. On 15 March 1962, Glenn T. Seaborg, chairman of the commission, received a sharply worded letter from Chet Holifield, chairman of the Joint Committee on Atomic Energy. Declaring that never had the status of technology been brighter for civilian power, he warned that the technological potential and American leadership as well as investment would be lost unless a few large demonstration plants were built. To prevent that dismal prospect, he called for the committee and the commission to frame a new program that would have as its heart a new generation of power reactors, among which one of the Shippingport type should certainly receive serious consideration. Seaborg and his administrative assistant, Howard Brown, saw an opportunity. A letter from the president asking the commission to assess its civilian power program would give that effort added impetus and commit the administration to a more vigorous program. To Seaborg's delight, the White House accepted the idea as well as the drafts of letters between him and the president. On March 17 the commission chairman got the expected letter from President John F. Kennedy, asking the commission to measure its civilian reactor program in relation to the nation's future energy needs and resources, and to propose a schedule for developing and constructing nuclear power plants. In this effort the commission could call upon other government agencies for help. The schedule called for the completion of the study by September. In his reply Seaborg observed that the commission would coordinate the work with the joint committee, a necessary piece of diplomacy, for at best relations between the committee and the executive branch were sensitive.[35]

Holifield and his colleagues were fighting for a much larger civilian power program than the Kennedy administration wanted. Caught between the joint committee and the White House, the commission witnesses had to face a bipartisan attack in the hearings that began on March 20. To some committee members the president's request was a confession that the commission's nuclear power program had failed, a contention they buttressed by pointing out that the commission had not included requests for funds to start new prototypes or for the cooperative program with industry. The commission argued otherwise. Water reactors, it asserted, were near their goal of producing economically competitive power; all that was needed was the construction and operation of a few full-scale nuclear power stations to give the utility executives confidence. The commission hoped to work out cooperative ventures with industry for at least one station. To advance other reactor concepts that had promise for the longer term, the commission proposed to support and sponsor construction of small prototypes having a capacity of 100 to 200 electrical megawatts. Another project, although as yet only to be a study, was a seed-blanket reactor larger than the one at Shippingport.[36]

A study could be defined in many ways. On April 5 Holifield met with Seaborg and three other commissioners to discuss the entire civilian nuclear-power program. The congressman wanted no misunderstanding: the study of seed-blanket development and design should not be merely calculations and analyses summed up in a report, but should include enough engineering and development work upon which to base preliminary cost estimates. Rickover amplified the thought in his testimony before the committee on May 18. He would examine several concepts and undertake an intensive investigation of all phases of reactor technology: physics, heat transfer, hydraulics, and mechanical design. He did not know what the plant would be like nor could he predict a construction schedule. Certainly it would not generate economically competitive power, but it would be a major and necessary step toward that goal. Instead of getting bogged down with details at this stage, it was better to rely on a technically competent and well-led organization. From anyone else the argument might well have seemed too vague, open ended, and even egotistical. On the other hand, he and the group he was proposing to undertake the study had an unequaled record of achievement. And he stated flatly that if at some point success became doubtful, he would kill the project.[37]

For a short time in 1961 it seemed possible that the large power reactor—the proposed commission-industry project—and the large seed-blanket reactor might be one and the same. That possibility soon died. Explanations varied, but it seemed likely that forces within the commission and the division of reactor development were strong enough to keep the cooperative project away from Rickover. On 23 August 1962 the commission invited proposals from industry to participate in the design, construction, and operation of a nuclear power plant of proven design and of at least 400 electrical megawatts capacity. For its part the commission would provide limited financial assistance for nuclear research and development work, preliminary and detailed design, and other specified areas. The utility was to provide the site, construct the plant, assume all other costs, and operate the plant for five years after initial criticality. (Eventually a cooperative arrangement was made with the Connecticut Yankee Atomic Power Plant for a slightly enriched 580-electrical-megawatt pressurized-water reactor plant that began producing electricity in August 1967.) Rickover received money for a separate study of the seed-blanket reactor.[38]

He had already mobilized Bettis. Ross announced on 5 July 1962 that George W. Hardigg would manage the new, large power reactor project and would have reporting to him William C. Purcell, manager, power plant engineering; Harry F. Raab, Jr., manager, physics; and Frank Schwoerer, manager, reactor engineering. They would be supported by

John S. Buko and James J. Perhacs, responsible for production and technical support and drafting. All had strong backgrounds; many came from the D1W, an extremely ambitious and challenging project aimed at developing a very high-powered core for surface ships.[39]

Without question Rickover was embarking upon a controversial project. Elements within the division of reactor development thought a large seed-blanket project had little technical merit and would only soak up funds needed for other parts of the program. While industry believed its role would be too small, public power advocates claimed industry's role would be too large. Against these forces the very existence of the project was a tribute to the respect with which Congress held Rickover. That fact entailed a special responsibility: Rickover would not build the plant unless it was a major advance in reactor technology.

Report to the President

Whether a large seed-blanket nuclear power station would result from the study, even with its design and engineering work, was an open question. The report to the president that the commission sent to the White House on 20 November 1962 was not encouraging. As Kennedy had asked, the commission placed nuclear energy in the context of meeting the nation's total future energy requirements. Extrapolating from past consumption, estimates showed that perhaps in a few decades the need for power would outstrip the supply of fossil fuels. While other sources of energy could help fill the gap, none could make a greater contribution than nuclear power. Although pressurized- and boiling-water reactors were the types nearest to becoming economically competitive to fossil-fueled plants, they were inefficient in their use of uranium 235. Only breeder reactors could realize the full potential of atomic energy.

In its discussion of breeding, the commission emphasized the uranium 238-plutonium 239 approach. Even if it demanded very advanced and sophisticated technology based on fast neutrons, a fast reactor could produce enough fuel for itself and another reactor. A breeder based on thorium-uranium 233, although using slow neutrons, would produce only enough fuel for itself. Although light-water reactors—the pressurized- and boiling-water types—depended upon slow neutrons, for technical reasons the chances of breeding were very slim. The future of breeding with thorium-uranium 233 also required experimental reactors from which would come the data and experience required for operating prototypes.

In its discussion of reactor types, the commission gave the seed-blanket approach an unenthusiastic footnote. Studies and experiments were deemed worthwhile, and dropping for a moment into the Biblical philosophy of beating swords into plowshares, if large-scale nuclear disarmament ever came about, the highly enriched uranium 235 from weapons could be fabricated into seeds.[40]

The press gave the commission's report to the president a good reception. *Nucleonics,* a monthly periodical that followed atomic energy matters closely, found a healthy optimism coupled with sincere concern about the health of the nuclear power industry. To comments that the document contained nothing new, a newspaper quoted Pittman that because the commission program had been in existence for eight or ten years, there was no reason to expect any sudden revelations. Industry appeared to have no objection to the commission's constructing prototypes. Holifield stated that he was favorably impressed, but shrewdly remarked that the real test of the report would be what the administration did with it.[41]

The Atomic Industrial Forum, an organization of utilities, reactor designers and manufacturers, architect-engineers, consultants, and fuel producers, circulated a complicated questionnaire designed to give each category of membership a chance to express views on the report. In April 1963 the forum had its replies. Interpreting them was not easy, as the forum admitted, for no consensus emerged on what the future of the civilian nuclear power station should be. On the seed-blanket reactor, however, opinions were clear. The questionnaire asked for comments on the statement that developmental studies and experiments on the concept were worthwhile. Thirty-nine replied yes, but these answers were tempered with highly qualifying phrases. ". . . it is not obvious that the reactor concept is significantly different from other PWR or BWR's." "But not too many dollars!" "Its value is much less certain than other types." Thirty opposed the studies and experiments, declaring: "Expenditure of funds in this area is a diversion of necessary funding elsewhere." "Development of this concept appears to lack any technical or economical justification." "Government does not need to pursue." "No evidence that there is any technical or economic incentive for this type of core design. It could be utilized in almost any PWR when there were such incentives." "Reasons for building this type are not strong enough. It is probably included only because of its strong advocacy by a particular individual." "If industry sees no advantage for this reactor, it shouldn't be built. The AEC shouldn't spend the taxpayers' money on it."[42]

A Possibility At Bettis

To Rickover and others of his staff studying the report to the president as it circulated in draft, the message was clear: with emphasis on breeding, the commission was unlikely to support the large seed-blanket reactor. On the other hand, results of work at Bettis were showing a new possibility. The laboratory was working on various designs, one of which used uranium 233—not for breeding but for a fuel. On 19 November 1962, Hardigg reported that preliminary analysis showed a theoretical breeding ratio with a uranium 233 seed and a thorium blanket. It was not a breakthrough, but the report of measured and deliberate advances.[43] As could be the case with development, gains toward one objective brought another into range. While Radkowsky was enthusiastic, Rickover and Mandil were not. To them the data from Bettis was interesting and even promising, but far from providing the technology needed to fabricate a core. Their interest remained on the contribution that a large seed-blanket uranium reactor could make to civilian power.

In succeeding months the technical promise at Bettis grew, and the political current in the commission flowed more strongly toward breeders. Rickover, at the laboratory 18 March 1963, predicted a hard fight to get support for the large seed-blanket. On April 12 he forwarded an interim report to Pittman summarizing four designs, two based on uranium and two based on thorium. In one of the thorium designs, a seed of uranium 233 was surrounded by a thorium blanket and operated for the maximum formation of uranium 233. Calculations showed that after three years the blanket assemblies could be processed and the uranium 233 extracted. If fuel reprocessing losses could be kept low, it might be possible to reach a self-sustaining cycle.

> . . . . that is to say, using the thorium-uranium-233 cycle, *it may be feasible to breed in a light water cooled and moderated seed blanket core.*

In his transmittal memorandum Rickover noted that the report illustrated his philosophy: turn a technical program over to experienced personnel, and the results could far exceed those originally envisioned.[44]

Rickover briefed the commission on the study of the advanced seed-blanket 500-megawatt plant on May 13. The reactor core would be large, about fifteen feet in diameter and about eight feet high. The seed would be uranium 235 and the blanket uranium 238. But the center of the core could be used to demonstrate the feasibility of breeding. If the project were to be carried out, he believed it should be as a cooperative venture with industry but in the manner of Shippingport, in which the government built and owned the entire reactor portion of the plant. It would be expensive, he conceded, but the approach could be one answer to conserving resources. The problem, Seaborg observed, was expense: if it were too costly, the commission would not be able to get authorization for the complete reactor portion. Maybe the commission could assist in the breeder part.[45]

The reference to the Shippingport-type arrangement was revealing. For that project Rickover had exercised direct control over the reactor portion of the plant. In no other way would he be able to accomplish what he wanted to do and what he thought essential: set technical and personnel standards for large power plants.

Opposition

Seaborg's comment on cost was significant. If a tightening budget was forcing sacrifices, in the minds of many on the commission staff the seed-blanket reactor was a good candidate.

For an outside, yet informed, scrutiny of the reactor program, the commission turned to the General Advisory Committee, which set up a subcommittee. Its members were well qualified. Lawrence R. Hafstad, a physicist and former director of the Applied Physics Laboratory of the Johns Hopkins University, had been the first director of the commission's division of reactor development and knew Rickover well. Manson Benedict, professor of nuclear engineering at the Massachusetts Institute of Technology, had served in the wartime atomic energy program and had been a member of the reactor safeguards committee. Kenneth S. Pitzer had been a director of the commission's division of research, while William Webster was a utility executive, a former deputy secretary of defense, and had a deep, practical interest in civilian power.

After a briefing by the nuclear propulsion organization and the division of reactor development, the subcommittee made its report on 19 August 1963. It admitted that efficient utilization of thorium as a form of nuclear fuel conservation was as important as the uranium-plutonium cycle and should even be pushed. But the subcommittee recommended strongly against full funding by the commission of a 500-megawatt seed-blanket reactor. The commission should complete the development of new components, demonstrate the feasibility of breeding with the seed-blanket core at Shippingport, and let industry take over. Other reactor concepts were more worthy of commission support.[46]

Rickover replied that he had considered using Shippingport, but decided against it. Breeding with thorium depended upon using every neutron. The smaller the core volume, the greater the chance of neutrons escaping. The Shippingport pressure vessel limited the size of the core to such an extent that it would be impossible to demonstrate breeding. Moreover, the subcommittee had overlooked several other important lessons that would come from constructing, testing, and operating a large power reactor. Light-water reactor technology, he was convinced, was poised on the edge of a breakthrough.[47]

Opposition from the General Advisory Committee was more of an annoyance than anything else and never developed into a serious threat. The reason was simple. Rickover had found a potential partner who was interested in a large nuclear power plant.

The California Project

In 1960 the citizens of California voted a $1.75 billion bond issue for a huge system of dams, canals, and tunnels to transport water from the central to the southern part of the state. The rugged terrain separating the area required some powerful pumping stations. For one of these, located in the Tehachapi Mountains, the state was considering an atomic power plant. After talking with the commission in March 1963, state officials contracted for a study by industry of various reactor types.[48]

Neither memories nor records are clear how Rickover and the state officials came together. That they should do so was not unexpected, for Rickover followed developments in civilian power closely. On 23 September 1963 in Los Angeles he and Mandil described the large seed-blanket reactor to the state officials. Rickover emphasized that in the near future nuclear power would not be as economical as power from conventional sources, but that picture could change in the long run. He thought a reliable large nuclear power station was worth the state's consideration. The state's plans were still in the early stage: the final draft of the study on the type of reactor would not be ready for months, and a decision on the type of plant and its location might take another year. Without question the California officials were interested in the large seed-blanket reactor: William E. Warne, director of the state's department of water resources, made arrangements to visit Bettis. In the meantime he and his colleagues studied the interim report.[49]

Warne's visit of November 10 and 11 to the laboratory and to Shippingport went well. Not only was Rickover his host, but Holifield, Commissioner James T. Ramey, and Pittman were also on hand. The requirements for the water project demanded an extremely reliable plant operating with a minimum of shutdowns. From the presentations by Ross and other Bettis personnel and from his inspections of the laboratory and the power station, Warne was impressed with the technical excellence that could be brought to bear—a quality that he attributed directly to Rickover. With this background, the long time between refuelings—about ten years—seemed possible. Perhaps, too, it would be possible to work out an arrangement in which the power would also be used to convert salt water to fresh water. On November 18 Warne wrote Seaborg that California was interested in working out a cooperative arrangement with the commission for a 500-megawatt seed-blanket reactor. To apprise the commission of both the status of the conversations and the technical development of the reactor, Rickover, Mandil, Radkowsky, Rockwell, and Karl G. Scheetz, a young engineer following the project, along with a contingent from Bettis, briefed the commission on December 9. Two days later Seaborg replied to Warne that Pittman and Rickover would discuss an agreement.[50]

Warne responded on the last day of 1963 with a draft agreement as a basis for negotiations. California anticipated that it would ultimately need 1,200,000 kilowatts of pumping demand and 10 billion kilowatt-hours of electrical energy annually for the water project. The department wanted to secure the lowest-cost energy with which to pump water; the commission was interested in the development of a large power reactor to generate electricity. Turning to specifics, the state would provide the site, the turbine generator portion of the plant, and would also fund the engineering and construction cost of the nuclear reactor part of the plant. The commission would perform the research and development work necessary for the design, development, and construction of the nuclear portion of the reactor plant and would train the operating crews at no cost to the state. The commission would furnish the first reactor core, but the state would pay for the use of the core at a mutually agreed upon charge. Title to the entire power plant, except for the first core and those facilities needed for testing, would lie with the state. And it would be the state that would operate the plant.[51]

California would not pay more for the power from the commission-owned first core than the cost of power delivered to the station site from any other source—a logical enough stipulation. As the visit to Bettis indicated, Rickover was aiming at a core life of ten years. To the state officials that meant the station had to produce economically competitive power ten years after the beginning of operation. Considering that construction alone would require a few years, that risk did not seem too great. On the other hand, ten years was about three times the core life for commercial reactors, so the technical challenge was severe. Furthermore, building various parts of the water project that would rely on the Tehachapi pumping station meant that Rickover could not be late. Warne's draft did not mention a schedule for the station, but in Rickover's mind it was a heavy obligation he would have to meet.

On 16 January 1964, Governor Edmund G. Brown gave his approval for further negotiations. The next day Rickover, Pittman, and Mandil talked with state officials in Sacramento. For them the question was whether the station would be economical in ten years. Rickover responded frankly that he did not know: that was for the state to determine. Until a study comparing costs of purchasing power from other sources was completed, neither the state nor the commission could make any substantial move. September was the target date for the power-cost study; that did not leave much time, considering the steps that the commission had to go through to get congressional authorization. Furthermore the plant site was still to be selected.[52]

Of the state officials none was more enthusiastic about the nuclear power station than Brown. Contacts with Rickover stimulated the governor's imagination. He and his wife, on their way to a political rally on the afternoon of July 8, drove with Rickover to the Mare Island Naval Shipyard at Vallejo. Fascinated by the conversation and deeply impressed by the new Polaris submarine *Stonewall Jackson*, in dry dock after completing its initial sea trials, Brown was fired by the vision of a nuclear age.[53]

By now the site had been narrowed to an area south of Bakersfield or to a coastal location near Point Hueneme. With the project coming closer to reality, Rickover decided to strengthen the effort. On July 21 he told Bettis that Knolls, which had already done some calculations, was to provide additional support. Mandil listed specific areas; they included analytical and experimental physics, fuel element development, reactor mechanical and thermal design, reactor kinetics and control, and control rod drive mechanisms. Rickover stressed two things: the commission would not support the project unless it had a reasonable chance of breeding; for his part he would accept no technical compromises or short cuts.[54]

Preliminary discussions went well. On July 22 Brown authorized the state to enter detailed negotiations. The next day Rickover and his men briefed the commissioners. Seaborg, a Californian for some years, recognized that Brown faced a tough political battle, but that was not the commission's affair. Seaborg and his colleagues gave their approval for Rickover to negotiate.[55]

David T. Leighton, handling the project since Mandil's resignation, found negotiations straightforward. In August Warne accepted the financial arrangements—the state would fund $80 million of the estimated capital costs for the entire plant, and the commission would fund $20 million for the design and "first-time charges." On 22 October 1964, the state accepted the terms of a memorandum of understanding, a document setting forth the basic principles.[56]

Now came the mobilization of effort to get commission funds for the project into the president's budget. Seaborg wrote to President Johnson on November 18 that the seed-blanket reactor had one of the highest priorities among the nonmilitary items in the commission's program. The next day Holifield, not only a member of the joint committee but a congressman from California, added his support in a letter to Johnson. From Sacramento, Brown telegraphed the president, appealing for personal assistance in getting congressional approval. Even the Bureau of the Budget gave its endorsement with the understanding that, except for reasons of compelling national interest, commission support would not extend beyond the first ten years—the estimated life of the first core. And, added the bureau, the new project should lead to a sharp decrease in the cost of research and development at Shippingport.[57]

All went smoothly. Johnson included the large seed-blanket reactor in the budget and on 1 January 1965 the memorandum of understanding, signed by Robert E. Hollingsworth, general manager of the commission, went to Warne.[58]

Cancellation

There was every reason to think that the project was moving ahead smoothly. The political support it had mustered was impressive, and no one had better reputations in reactor technology than Rickover, Naval Reactors engineers, and Bettis and Knolls. On 21 January 1965, Philip R. Clark, responsible for core design, was at Bettis reviewing the fuel element program. The laboratory was proposing a number of changes in fuel irradiation testing, an effort in which sample elements were exposed to various conditions in a test reactor. With the ten-year core life that Rickover was striving for, considerable extrapolation of the data was necessary. But since the test program had begun, the laboratory and Washington had changed some of the core parameters; hence, the need for a new test effort. The laboratory believed that it was time to proof-test about four basic fuel types: the seed and blanket elements for the breeder section, and the seed and blanket elements for the rest of the core. Clark, while agreeing that a change in testing was necessary, asked for further review. He was worried that fabrication techniques for the samples might differ too much from those planned for the actual core.

That evening Rickover flew into Pittsburgh. Arriving at Bettis he listened to the conclusions of the meeting. He declared emphatically that development of the fuel elements was probably the most difficult task that the laboratory and Naval Reactors had yet undertaken. The best men had to be assigned to the effort. He expected that initial plans in a complicated project would have to change, but alterations had to be based on technical grounds alone. In a project so advanced, individuals were likely to take stands that were based on personal opinions and pride. He wanted none of that.[59]

On February 15 at Bettis, Leighton, Clark, and Radkowsky began a four-day review of the fuel element work. Rickover arrived on the evening of the last day. He heard that test results showed some anomalies, but nothing that could not be explained; some problems, but nothing that could not be solved. He listened with growing unease. Responses to his questions gave him no confidence; all his instincts and experience were warning him that something was very wrong. He grew angrier and angrier, accusing people of poor work. Finally, he called for a task force. Under the full-time direction of Ross, it was to assess all available data and make recommendations. Ross could call on anyone at Bettis, and he could get help from Knolls.[60]

On April 8 Leighton and several NR engineers—Clark, Scheetz, John

E. Mealia, Richard G. Scott, and Robert H. Steele—flew to Bettis. Ross reported that within the last few weeks the laboratory had gained a greater understanding of the troubling phenomenon and had made progress in developing an analytical model to predict and evaluate fuel element performance. However, the model had yet to receive experimental verification, and the task force found the need for much basic information on fuel element properties. It all added up to a new major research effort. Leighton, deeply disturbed, telephoned Rickover. He was already planning to fly to the laboratory, but under Leighton's urging advanced his schedule.[61]

On 9 April 1965, Rickover heard the data. They confirmed his worst fears. As bad as the technical uncertainties were, they were not his greatest worry: it was his premature commitment to the state of California. Its officials, knowing little about atomic energy, were depending upon him. They were making their plans for the water project on the assumption he could deliver a reactor with a ten-year core life which, at the end of that period, would deliver economically competitive power. They were fighting political battles for the plant and risking their careers. There was Congress, which had accepted his assurances and supported him, and there were his friends in the commission.

Yet nothing was clear cut. The problems were not insuperable: many of those men present—and he considered them, along with those at Knolls, as the best engineers in the country—assured him of that. He called Leighton aside and asked for his advice.

"Kill it," came the swift response.

The two men reentered the conference room. Rickover asked each man for his views. Nearly all recommended going ahead.[62]

He ended the meeting by asking Ross for a report on proposed future work. On the flight back to Washington, Rickover planned the next steps with Leighton. They followed quickly. Because the technical problems might bear upon other reactor projects, he had a report distributed in the commission. He talked to Holifield on April 12, telephoned Warne on April 13, and flew with Leighton to Los Angeles on April 14. He talked to the state officials, including Governor Brown. Rickover explained that he believed the technology of the project was sound; he still had confidence in oxide fuel and in the seed-blanket design. He still thought he could demonstrate breeding and he could construct a nuclear power plant that would meet the state's requirements. But it would take more time. That was a commodity the state did not have.[63]

Rickover was to look back on those months in 1965 as some of the most difficult in his career. He was astonished by the understanding with which those men who had backed him, from whatever organization, accepted the news. There were no recriminations. On his trip to California he visited the Holifields in their home, where they were having a birthday party for one of their daughters. He was warmly welcomed as a personal friend. These and other instances of thoughtful courtesy also became a part of his memory of this time. One reaction, manifested later, was unexpected. He found failure had not diminished his reputation: indeed, he gained increasing trust and the confidence of others by his decision. Without question his decision was correct. To have pushed ahead might have meant success, but it might also have meant a massive research and development effort that could have seriously diverted himself, his engineers, and the laboratories from their primary task of developing naval propulsion reactors. Fortunately, the difficulties with the fuel came at a time when neither the state nor the commission had committed sizable funds to the reactor. Relieved of the pressure of meeting a schedule, Bettis continued to study the fuel anomalies. Technically, the state and the commission were still partners, and all that had happened was a delay: in actuality, no one doubted that the project had received a lethal blow.

Reorientation

For the rest of the year Bettis and Knolls, using their own facilities along with the materials testing reactor at the National Reactor Testing Station and the NRX research reactor at Chalk River, Canada, worked on the fuel development. In essentials fuel elements were simple. They consisted of uranium fuel and a cladding. The cladding had to have certain characteristics: good heat transfer, high resistance to corrosion, and low rate of neutron absorption. The design for the California project called for four basic types of elements: seed and blanket for the major part of the core— that which would produce by far the greater amount of power—and the seed and blanket elements for the breeder-demonstration part of the core. The time between refuelings would be two years for the breeder demonstration but nine or ten years—almost double or treble the core life offered by commercial manufacturers—for the major part of the core. Original estimated values for such properties as cladding strength, fuel strength and growth rate, fuel thermal conductivity, and fuel stability, were incorrect. To be more specific, the oxide fuel material grew more than expected and was stronger than anticipated. Instead of molding itself plastically to fit into the provided space, the oxide pressed hard against the zircaloy cladding, which was weaker than expected.

Over the year a great deal had been learned. A seed-blanket appeared achievable but, thought Rickover, the breeder elements required more development effort than had been envisioned. The laboratories had gained a much better understanding of the basic properties of fuel element materials and of analytical and testing techniques. The analytical procedures had been developed into a computer code, CYGRO-I, to predict in detail stresses and temperatures inside the fuel and their effect upon cladding. Although more rigorous and detailed than any other known design procedures, many of the input values were still not well known.

Rickover outlined three options for the commission: continue with the research and development work on the California project core, seeking a new partner if the state could not accept the delay; continue the research and development work on a large seed-blanket-reactor nuclear central power station, but one that was redirected toward a breeder demonstration and a shorter-life core; and finally reorient the effort toward a research and development program to demonstrate breeder technology in the Shippingport reactor. On 21 December 1965, the commission selected the third choice.[64]

In September 1963 Rickover had rejected the General Advisory Committee's proposal to use Shippingport to demonstrate breeding, but in the following two years the data looked more promising. During the first months of 1966, he sent Mealia to Bettis to listen and observe. He found that the laboratory, in its struggle over fuel element development for the large seed-blanket reactor, had neglected many important areas. These had to be explored. On March 16 John E. Zerbe, the laboratory's light-water breeder project manager, requested approval of approaches toward a conceptual design; no feasibility problems had yet been uncovered to installing a light-water breeder core in Shippingport.[65]

The technical problems inherent to a breeder demonstration in Shippingport were formidable. It was not only necessary to acquire more data on the physical and nuclear characteristics and properties of thorium and uranium 233, but it was also essential to carry out design and testing of mechanical components, material tests, thermal and hydraulic studies of reactor fuel design, nuclear design critical experiments, and, of course, fuel irradiation. Although Bettis remained the lead laboratory, Knolls advised, checked calculations, and performed experiments. In general terms the technical problems could be divided into four categories: the reactor coolant and moderator, fuel, fuel cladding, and reactor control. So delicate was the relationship between these four areas that an advance in one often had a detrimental effect upon another.

The reactor coolant-moderator was an example of how a change in one factor influenced another. Water moderated the neutrons to thermal energies at which the fission process took place. However, water also absorbed neutrons. Reducing the amount of water in the core—an approach called "squeezing out some of the water" in the laboratory discussions—lessened the number of neutrons captured. But decreasing the water meant reducing the moderating effect, with a consequent increase in neutron energies.

Turning for a moment to numbers: at thermal energies uranium 233 gave off an average of 2.3 neutrons per neutron absorbed, although not all reactions took place at these energies. At intermediate energies that number appeared to decrease to 2.07, an almost impossibly slim margin for breeding. But through sophisticated experimental and analytical techniques, Bettis and Knolls discovered that the actual value was 2.13. Furthermore, at high-energy ranges fast fission produced additional neutrons in thorium, and in addition caused a reaction in which a neutron captured by thorium caused the emission of two neutrons. Putting the data together and considering all the various possibilities, the number of neutrons produced for each neutron absorbed in uranium 233 was found to be 2.26. At that ratio breeding again became a possibility.

The narrow margin of excess neutrons led to very tight specifications for the reactor fuel. Bettis had determined that the reactor fuel should be oxides of thorium and uranium 233. The characteristics looked good. Tests showed that the oxides behaved similarly to the uranium oxides in the first two seed-blanket cores, although with a higher melting point, greater dimensional stability at high temperatures, and better corrosion resistance. Final design required four types of pellets. The Oak Ridge National Laboratory produced the uranium 233 oxide, and Bettis had hoped that a contractor would manufacture the pellets. Because the stringent specifications were too deterring Bettis did the pellet manufacture on the laboratory site.

Plans called for zircaloy tubing to contain the pellets. The core design required four types of tubing. The Wolverine Tube Division of Union Oil Products undertook the assignment to fabricate the tubes, but found the specifications hard to meet; improved quality-control procedures proved the answer. The company received its first batch of ingots in March 1972 and sent the first tubes to Bettis in January 1973.

The tubes with their fuel had to be assembled in modules. Space between the tubes through which water would pass to remove the heat was only a few hundredths of an inch. In order to prevent the over ten-foot-long rods from bowing and touching each other—for that would interrupt the flow of the coolant-moderator and cause an increase in temperature in the immediate area—rod support grids were necessary. Commercially made grids for power reactors were available, but once again specifications were too demanding. Because no vendor would offer fixed-price bids, the laboratory ended up making them. As finally designed and fabricated, each grid was composed of several hundred stamped components of AM-350, a type of stainless steel. Wire pins, passing through a hinged joint, held the components together. Although not part of the plan, the grids and fuel rods were breathtaking in their beauty.

In most reactors, rods of neutron-absorbing material controlled the reactor. For the initial Shippingport reactor Rickover had selected hafnium as the control-rod material. In the light-water breeder, however, the presence of any material that would absorb neutrons was to be avoided as much as possible. The answer lay in the seed modules. They were the driving power of the reactor; moving them vertically changed their positions with relation to the fixed blanket modules and altered the core geometry to attain the required neutron balance. Bettis assembled the core modules. The task required a great deal of manual labor, a strange aspect to an outsider observing the creation of a highly advanced technical project. To carry out the massive job, the laboratory hired several hundred individuals, many just out of high school, who found themselves working regularly ten to twelve hours a day, six days a week. They did a good job, even though some of the work was relatively sophisticated. Each grid, for example, demanded over 2,000 precise measurements, and each usually had to be measured twice.

The constraint on core size imposed by the Shippingport pressure vessel was overcome by better physical data, and by a sophisticated core design that used three types of fuel modules. The three central modules were hexagonal, identical, and symmetrical, and made up of the movable seed and the stationary blanket. Seed and blanket contained a mixture of thorium and uranium 233, but in different proportions. As might be expected, the seed contained more uranium 233. These modules were designed as if they were to be used in a large central station reactor and indeed could be. The purpose of the other two types of modules was to provide the environment of a large central station reactor core in the three central modules. Nine hexagonal modules, each with seed and blanket rods, surrounded the central modules. The nine flattened the power distribution within the core. The fifteen modules on the circumference of the core contained only thorium; they captured neutrons that might otherwise have escaped to match the neutron leakage typical of a large core.[66]

No group of reactor engineers or reactor physicists had more skill or experience than those in the Naval Reactors organization at Washington or in its laboratories at Bettis and Knolls. Rickover gave all his projects intense personal attention, but those who participated with him sensed something different in his attitude toward the light-water breeder program. Doubtless, his original interest stemmed in large part from a desire to remain a vital part of the commission's civilian power program, but the possibility of breeding seized his imagination. The frequent trips he made to review the work on several projects at Bettis found him questioning in thorough detail the highest level of laboratory management directly concerned with the technical work. Again this was nothing new, but many individuals who were working with him on other projects were aware of a difference. Over and over he stressed the importance of simplicity—that the most important objective was to demonstrate breeding in a practical engineering design of a light-water reactor.[67]

Men in the effort found themselves caught up in a project that demanded the most from them. For some people the succession of seasons and the passage of the years blurred, and what remained were memories of experiments, of components being fabricated, of tense and stormy meetings, and of a growing feeling that the effort was sound. In so many technical ventures, initial ideas look good, only to collapse beneath the weight of stubborn and disappointing data. But the light-water breeder was different. Hard-won data eroded uncertainty and confusion and in their place erected exhilaration, confidence, and certainty.

Decontamination At Shippingport—Core One And Core Two

While the laboratory was working on the light-water breeder core, the Shippingport Atomic Power Station was continuing to generate power for Duquesne. Operation with the first core ended on 9 February 1964. The blanket had been designed to last for 8,000 hours, the life of two seeds. In actuality, the blanket accumulated 27,780 equivalent full-power hours and used up four seeds. To turn to another statistic, on its first core Shippingport had generated a total of 1,798,581,700 kilowatt hours (gross) electricity. The blanket provided more than half the total.[68]

During the life of core 1, radiation surveys of the primary system, around the reactor vessel, and other areas within the reactor plant containers, showed an increase in the average radiation level. The radioactivity of the primary coolant had not increased; that level had not changed significantly during the operation of core 1. Investigation showed that the increase came from minute particles resulting from corrosion. By passing through the core the particles became radioactive, and by coming to rest in certain parts of the cooling system, increased the level of radioactivity in those areas. Bettis had already begun to develop a second seed-blanket core. The new core was to have a capacity of 150 electrical megawatts, more than double that of the first core, yet fit within the same pressure vessel. Because the Duquesne turbogenerator was limited to 100 megawatts, the commission installed a heat sink to dissipate the remainder. Furthermore, the new capacity required new main coolant pumps and heat exchangers. Decontamination of the plant to reduce radiation levels would simplify the task of making the modifications as well as the subsequent plant testing and operations.

Using the decontamination process, system, and procedures developed by Bettis, Duquesne began the job on 29 February 1964 and finished a few weeks later on March 14. Chemical solutions removed the radio-active particles to an on-site decontamination facility for storage and processing. Measurements of radiation levels taken before and after de-contamination showed that the effort was successful. It was the first in-place decontamination of an entire nuclear power plant.[69]

With core 2 seed 1 the Shippingport station reached its design capacity on 25 September 1965. After operating for 13,652 equivalent full-power hours, and generating 1,953,000,000 gross kilowatt hours, the station was shut down to install seed 2. Replacing seed 1 began on 20 March 1969 and was completed in sixty-one working days. On core 2 seed 2 Ship-pingport reached full power on 23 August 1969.[70]

On 4 February 1974 the plant operators felt a severe turbine vibration and promptly shut down the plant. Investigation revealed severe damage to the turbine. No one was injured, and the accident did not involve the reactor portion of the plant.[71] As repairs were necessary, Rickover had a choice: he could wait for repair of the turbine and restart the plant, or he could end operation on core 2 and use the time to upgrade the station components and prepare for installing the light-water breeder core. He chose the latter course, a decision made easier because seed 2 had already exceeded its design goal.

Independent Assessments

The development of the light-water breeder reactor core was taking place against a background of growing public concern over the quality of the environment. The National Environmental Policy Act, becoming effective in 1970, required federal agencies to issue lengthy statements on the environmental impact of proposed major actions. On 23 July 1971 the Federal Court of Appeals found that in its licensing procedures for the Calvert Cliffs nuclear power plant in Calvert County, Maryland, the commission had not complied with the act in several respects. The court ruled that the commission itself had to make an independent review of all environmental effects at all decision points in the licensing process. The ruling had a major impact on the civilian power program, for it affected all nuclear power reactors in operation, under construction, or at the licensing stage. In June 1973 the United States Court of Appeals for the District of Columbia in the case of the *Scientists' Institute for Public Information Inc., v. The United States Atomic Energy Commission* signifi-cantly broadened even further the scope of the statement. Not only did it have to cover a particular installation, but it also had to include the environmental impact that the installation caused upon the industry that supported it. For the light-water breeder reactor, this meant not only an analysis of Shippingport with its new core but also of a hypothetical industry.[72]

After a public hearing in Pittsburgh and the release of a preliminary statement for comment by the public, the Energy Research and Development Administration (successor to the Atomic Energy Commission in 1975) issued a five-volume *Final Environmental Statement, Light-Water Breeder Reactor Program* in June 1976. In summary, the purpose of operating the light-water breeder reactor core was to develop and test the technical feasibility of a breeder core design and to confirm the workability of the individual systems and components as part of the overall reactor system. The technology was to be made available to industry for the design and building of cores that could be installed in existing plants. The principal benefit from the approach was the use of thorium, a large potential energy source. Successful application of the light-water breeder technology should lead to a short-term expansion of uranium mining and milling, for increased uranium 235 would be needed to build up an inventory of uranium 233 from thorium. Once that point had been reached, the need for uranium mining and milling should decrease, to the consequent advantage of the environment. The facilities associated with the two fuel cycles—the light-water reactors and the light-water breeder reactors—would be nearly the same. However, decay products of the byproduct isotope uranium 232 gave off a more penetrating radiation and therefore required some facility modifications. The Energy Research and Development Administration concluded that there was no reason to defer or alter the schedule for the operation of the light-water breeder reactor core.[73]

Because the Shippingport reactor was government-owned, it was not subject to licensing procedures. But as the goal of the program was the application of light-water breeder reactor technology to the nuclear power industry, Rickover chose to follow the licensing procedures required for a commercial nuclear power station. Working closely together, Bettis and Naval Reactors prepared a ten-volume safety analysis report for the Nuclear Regulatory Commission, the agency that took over the regulatory functions from the Atomic Energy Commission. The volumes were heavily technical, touching every aspect of core design and plant operation. Rickover sent the volumes to the regulatory commission on 30 June 1975. That organization began its evaluation and also sent copies to the advisory committee on reactor safeguards.[74]

On 22 July 1976 the Nuclear Regulatory Commission made its official determination. Subject to a few technical modifications, Shippingport, with its light-water breeder reactor core, could be operated without undue risk to the health and safety of the public—provided that Naval Reactors continued to exercise rigid control over design, construction, operator training and qualification, and reactor operation. The commission took a few months longer to consider a few technical matters, but on December 8 it issued a supplementary report confirming its earlier findings. Thereafter, the advisory committee concluded in August that the station could be operated as planned.[75]

The state of Pennsylvania, however, had yet to be heard from. Its interest in Shippingport went back to the early days of the project. In July 1954 the Atomic Energy Commission had informed the state of plans to build the station. The commission and its successor agencies continued to keep state officials informed. The state had its own agencies, among them an advisory committee on atomic-energy development and radiation control, to monitor atomic-energy activities within its boundaries. Its members had visited Shippingport and attended meetings of the advisory committee on reactor safeguards. On 23 December 1976, the state Department of Environmental Resources raised several technical issues. In brief, the state officials believed that the Nuclear Regulatory Commission and its advisory committee had focused too much on the reactor and the core—on the innovative features—and not enough on the rest of the plant.[76]

The Shippingport station was old, and in some respects later technology and standards had passed it by. On the other hand, Rickover replied on 23 March 1977, his philosophy on safety was extremely conservative. He had upgraded the station where necessary to ensure its safe operation and to conform with standards of the regulatory commission and the advisory committee on reactor safeguards. The specific questions he answered at length and in detail. Not completely satisfied, Pennsylvania turned to the commission and the advisory committee. The commission replied that it concurred with Rickover's reply, and the advisory committee, after reviewing the state's position, found no reason to change its earlier determination. On 12 August 1977 Pennsylvania declared that it had no further comments. At that point the date for criticality at Shippingport was about two weeks off.[77]

Criticality and Operation

The first module for the light-water breeder core arrived at Shippingport from Bettis in January 1976, the last in March 1977. Transfer took place without incident, for Bettis had met with the police of all nearby local jurisdictions to explain the project and answer questions.

On August 25 Rickover brought only three of his Washington personnel with him to Shippingport: James W. Vaughan, Jr., in charge of nuclear plant components and of producing the light-water breeder reactor core; Harry F. Raab, Jr., chief physicist; and Jack C. Grigg, director, division of instrumentation and control. Some measure of the continuity of the Naval Reactors program could be gained by observing that Rickover and Grigg had been present when Shippingport first reached criticality in 1957;

Vaughan came to work for Naval Reactors that year, while Raab began working as a Westinghouse employee at Bettis in 1951 and transferred to the Washington organization in 1972.

Bringing Shippingport to criticality took hours. Every step in the procedures had to be followed in proper sequence. Naval Reactors policy, which Rickover developed and insisted upon, was verbatim compliance with written procedures. Furthermore, completion of each step was a prerequisite for the next step. Under the strict instructions of Naval Reactors, only specific individuals had the authority to state from their own knowledge that the necessary action had been completed. They had to sign—legibly—a check-off list.[78]

At 12:30 on the morning of 26 August 1977, the Duquesne operators began the approach to criticality by lifting twelve seed assemblies into the blanket assemblies. The neutron flux increased as the bank entered the core to reach criticality. Based on theory and experiment that point had been calculated; just how close theory and actuality would come together was to be determined. The Duquesne operators raised the bank in small increments, lifting it for seven seconds and waiting for twenty-three seconds. First readings were slightly erratic, but the trend soon became clear. At 4:38 A.M. the light-water breeder reactor reached criticality: the bank was only 0.55 inch higher than calculated. It was amazingly close to prediction.[79]

Shippingport operated very well on its new core. After the planned operation of 18,000 equivalent full-power hours, the advisory committee on reactor safeguards on 6 May 1980 agreed it was acceptable to operate the reactor to 24,000 effective full-power hours. Rickover hoped to go to 32,500 hours, which forecasts plotted would fall about the end of 1984. He saw a unique opportunity to gain data on the maximum fuel life of the only power reactor ever to be operated using thorium-uranium 233 fuel. If light-water breeders were to take their place in industry, economics, conservation of resources, and management of nuclear wastes called for getting all possible data.[80]

Others disagreed. In March 1981 the General Accounting Office, which assisted Congress to meet its legislative and oversight responsibilities, recommended shutting down the plant in January 1982 and beginning proof-of-breeding experiments. These the office deemed more important than continued operation of the plant for technical data. Although the Science and Technology Committee of the House of Representatives accepted the reasoning, the Senate Energy Committee did not. Toward the end of 1981 Rickover, under tight budget restraints, decided that Shippingport would be shut down on 1 October 1982. Whether breeding had taken place would take years to determine, but at the time he made his decision every sign was favorable.[81]

The "NR Rep"

From the first start-up to the final step in unloading the fuel, nine men served as NR Rep. Only twice during a quarter of a century of plant operation did the on-watch representative have to shut down the plant. On 15 March 1958 he thought Duquesne was cooling down the reactor too quickly, and on 10 June 1958 he intervened until the company corrected deficiencies in nuclear instrumentation. That record, Rickover was convinced, showed that a government representative in the control room at all times was not an onerous burden to a properly run nuclear power station.

In 1982 the Naval Reactors office at Shippingport consisted of a manager, two assistants, and five duty representatives. The manager was an engineer from the Washington organization or a program field office. In a few instances, when the plant was inactive for a considerable period of time, perhaps for refueling or for installing or replacing major components, Rickover assigned a manager with a particular technical background. Of the two assistants, one watched over reactor services and maintenance work, while the other monitored radiological controls. In essence the two assistants were the manager's eyes for what went on in the nuclear part of the plant outside the control room. One of the five duty representatives was always on watch in the control room.

Rickover considered his representative—the manager of the Shippingport branch office—a key member of his organization. While the manager was a civilian engineer, the others were usually enlisted or formerly enlisted naval personnel. That background meant that these men had already been trained, first for six months in reactor theory at a naval nuclear-power school and then for another six months of practical experience at a Naval Reactors prototype. In addition each had compiled an excellent service record in a nuclear ship. Rickover personally interviewed these men for their jobs at Shippingport. They were the only enlisted men he interviewed except for the crew of the NR-1, a small nuclear-powered research submarine.

They were trained at Shippingport in a program that ended in an eight-hour written examination. If they passed this hurdle, they returned to Washington for an oral examination by senior engineers. Only then did they receive a formal letter signed by Rickover that they were qualified as duty representatives. Nor did their training stop there; at intervals they were checked to make sure that they maintained their proficiency. During the time at Shippingport they were under the direct and close observation of the Naval Reactors division in Washington; each representative was responsible for his own actions and could not expect to be shielded by the manager. Rickover was proud of them.

Discipline was strict. Under no circumstances could his man on watch leave the control room except as required by an approved emergency procedure. He had to focus his attention on all plant operations that could affect the reactor. He had to make certain that Duquesne correctly used the proper procedures for all reactor plant evolutions, and he had to follow them step by step. If more than one evolution was in process, he was to monitor the one having the greatest potential impact on safety. He had to attend briefings on operations that were to occur on his shift. He had to make sure that control room operators strictly complied with the manual, promptly bringing any instances of informality to the attention of the Duquesne nuclear shift supervisor. He had to tour the control room hourly, paying special attention to plant parameters and to the status of reactor plant controls, and he had to log the results of each tour. Under no circumstances could he perform any other task, such as updating a manual, while on watch.[82]

Rickover absolutely prohibited informality. First names, slang, skylarking, and horseplay were not permitted. Laxity in official relationships within the control room could lead to loose plant procedures and so to errors in plant operation. He ordered that watches be arranged so that the government duty representative and the Duquesne reactor operators were not always on the same shift. The ban on personal relationships carried over outside the plant. Under no circumstances were Rickover's men to have social contacts with either Duquesne or contractor personnel.

The system was not perfect and lapses did occur. On one occasion Rickover sent an engineer to Shippingport to strengthen the instructions governing the duty representatives. Before the instructions were put into effect, Wegner and Rickover made them even more stringent. Rickover insisted that the instructions be mounted so that the representative could see them at all times. Because the representative had to see all of the control room, working out the proper arrangement required some ingenuity. Placing the instructions on a tripod and angling them so as not to obscure the view was the solution.

Contributions

Rickover was inclined to give a great deal of credit to his representatives for the continued excellent record of the Shippingport Atomic Power Station. To congressmen and utilities officials he pointed again and again to the importance of having technically competent men on watch at all times—men who were independent of the organization. Some of Rickover's engineers, while not denigrating the importance of the representative, believed that occasionally Rickover overstressed that function. In their view the greatness of Shippingport was based on the imagination, vision, and foresight that went into the design, engineering, development, and construction of the station. Rickover's reply was that a single incompetent individual could wreck a plant—no matter how excellent the design, development, fabrication, and training.

Shippingport's record proved that the Rickover standards could be applied to civilian nuclear power. But the price was high. His man on watch, he used to observe, was no longer a human: he could not joke; he could not make idle conversation; he could not let his attention stray; he was accountable for every moment of his watch; and his work governed certain relationships off watch. In Rickover's view the problem with utilities was that they frequently had men of legal or financial backgrounds for their executives who did not have the understanding of the technical discipline required.

If the Shippingport Atomic Power Station showed how civilian nuclear plants could be operated safely, would the lessons be learned? On this question he had mixed opinions. It was not the technology that was the danger; it was human frailties. Even with men he had selected and trained and with facilities he had designed and developed, the demands upon him personally were tremendous. Perhaps some other way existed to achieve safety and reliability, but he knew of none.

Significance

The significance of the Shippingport Atomic Power Station has to be considered in two phases: demonstrating the feasibility of pressurized-water reactors for civilian power plants, and demonstrating the feasibility of light-water breeder reactors.

Contributions of Shippingport during the first phase were immense. When the project began, there was no question that power from the atom was possible. But whether that power could be produced safely, reliably, and in the amounts required for industrial needs was still in doubt. From the moment of start-up, Shippingport ended all uncertainty. Its record is more astonishing because for the first time many components—fuel, valves, pumps, piping, and heat exchangers—were designed, developed, and fabricated for a civilian nuclear power plant. Finally, basic problems of radiation safety and control were solved, and utility personnel were trained to operate a nuclear power station.

Once the nuclear power industry had widely adopted pressurized-water reactors, Shippingport's mission was accomplished, and its importance diminished. If Rickover and Naval Reactors were to stay in the civilian power program, they had to have a new goal. Light-water breeding was a good possibility, since it was based on pressurized-water technology. Although industry had little interest in the effort, Rickover saw that the successful development of light-water breeding would make available a new source of energy that could be obtained by adapting existing pressurized-water reactors. His hypothesis was never fully tested because opposition to nuclear power in the United States and the easing of the energy shortages of the early 1970s drastically reduced interest in all types of breeder reactors.

Perhaps Rickover was right when he speculated that the most lasting contribution of Shippingport was its demonstration that discipline could be maintained in a civilian nuclear power plant.

Admiral Rickover frequently ridiculed organization charts and management systems. He believed they almost always came to dominate. When that happened, the work existed to support the organization, instead of the organization existing to do the work. Nonetheless, for a technology as complicated as that developed by

CHAPTER NINE
"The Devil Is in the Details. . . ."

the naval nuclear propulsion program, he had to have an organization and a management philosophy. The following pages describe Naval Reactors around 1980, toward the end of Admiral Rickover's career.

The organization Rickover headed was unique in its structure, authority, and influence. The source of its strength appeared obvious. Its leader was in charge of the naval nuclear propulsion program virtually from its beginning. He had brought to the program over two decades of practical experience as a naval engineer. He made the first crucial decisions about the technology and the organization that would develop it. He had three points of support. He was responsible to both the Navy and the Atomic Energy Commission (and its successor agencies) and he was particularly close to Congress, especially the joint committee. He selected and trained his own personnel and insisted upon performance. Furthermore, the times were right for the program, a statement not meant to ignore the struggles that took place or the technical obstacles that had to be overcome. A list of the factors that made up the great competence of the organization he led can never be complete: the sum was always greater than its parts. Permeating the entire program was a spirit that repelled some, but attracted others to work hard, to sacrifice elements of their personal lives, and to remain proudly with the effort for years.

In 1980 Rickover held two titles. In the Department of Energy he was deputy assistant secretary for Naval Reactors and reported to the assistant secretary for nuclear energy. In the organization chart, that position was just below the secretary. In the navy Rickover was the deputy commander, nuclear propulsion directorate, a part of the Naval Sea Systems Command that was a component of the Naval Material Command. The chief of naval material reported to the chief of naval operations, who in procurement and training was responsible to the secretary of the navy.

Summarizing Rickover's responsibilities was difficult, for at times the line of definition was deliberately vague. In the Department of Energy he was responsible for research, design, and development for naval nuclear propulsion plants and civilian power reactor programs assigned to him. For the construction, testing, and operation of these reactors he established the necessary specifications, criteria, and procedures. He had primary responsibility within the department to ensure that appropriate consideration was given to protect military, government, contractor personnel, and the general public from radiation and all other health and safety hazards arising from carrying out the program. He certified to regulatory officials on the adequacy of safety procedures, facilities, and personnel for the naval nuclear program and its civilian responsibilities. As a department official he maintained a representative and staff at shipyards engaged in naval nuclear propulsion work.

In the navy he was in charge of the research and development pertaining to naval nuclear propulsion. He was responsible for the design, specifications, construction, certification, testing, refueling, overhaul, and conversion of naval nuclear propulsion plants and all aspects of safety relating to them. He gave technical assistance in the selection, training, and qualification of personnel for operating and maintaining the plants, and in operating and inspecting naval nuclear-powered ships insofar as the reactor plant was involved.[1]

His position was never completely secure and often under challenge. Every two years the secretary of the navy and the chairman of the Atomic Energy Commission or the chief executive of its successor agencies had to agree that he could serve an additional two years. The two-year period had evolved in 1962 and 1963. In 1962 he was a vice admiral and subject to retirement because he was 62 years old; however, the law permitted the president to defer an officer's retirement until the age of 64. Senator Henry M. Jackson, a close friend of Rickover's, a powerful member of the Senate, and a leader in the Democratic party, urged President John F. Kennedy to exercise the authority, stating that without Rickover's vigorous leadership it was doubtful if the United States could maintain its superiority over the Soviet Union in nuclear propulsion. On February 11

Secretary of the Navy John B. Connally deferred Rickover's retirement until 1 February 1964.[2] But after that date Rickover would have to leave.

Rickover did not want to retire. Not only was the technical work shifting to advanced and more sophisticated core design and development, but the nuclear fleet was growing rapidly and imposing new demands. Much work had to be done and he wanted the challenge.[3] Getting the commission's support would be no problem. Glenn T. Seaborg, the commission chairman, and his colleagues had several matters to worry about, but the Naval Reactors program was not one of them. It was the navy's position that was doubtful.

Complicated negotiations filled most of 1963. The navy was reluctantly willing to extend his tour of duty if some of his authority was clipped. Many of his superiors—officers and civilians alike—resented the influence he had with Congress. But perhaps the most serious issue was his method for selecting officers for the program. No officer could enter the nuclear propulsion program unless Rickover approved. The possibility that Rickover would retire from the navy and stay on to lead the program as a civilian was examined and discarded by him, his senior engineers, the commission, the navy, and the joint committee. The end of the year saw a compromise in which the influence of the committee played a great part. Rickover would remain for two more years, and at the end of that time the question would be reopened. What evolved was a pattern where every two years Rickover's term was renewed. It was never a matter that he could take for granted, and as time went by, each reappointment was more difficult to achieve.[4]

In the final analysis Rickover's tenure depended upon his technical achievements. They, in turn, were largely the result of the organization he had forged and led—Naval Reactors.

Naval Reactors

Rickover frequently declared that he had no organization, an assertion he backed up by pointing to his organization chart. Unlike most such diagrams, which were filled with rectangles and squares linked by solid and dotted lines to show the chain of authority, the flow of information, and the functions of coordination, his chart consisted of one square labeled "Deputy Commander SEA 08"—the letters and numerals standing for the nuclear propulsion directorate of the Naval Sea Systems Command.[5] In 1980, with a total of 359 engineering, financial, naval, and clerical personnel in his Washington office, he solemnly issued an extremely elaborate organization chart. Only the title, date, and signature were in English; the numerous squares bore Chinese characters.

Of course he had an organization. The development and application of pressurized-water technology was far too complex not to demand areas of specialization. His organization fell into roughly three major elements: technical engineers; project officers; and fiscal, organization, and logistical specialists.

SENIOR PERSONNEL 1980

Theron H. Bradley	Director, Submarine Systems (S8G) Division
Charles H. Brown, Jr.	Director, Instrumentation and Control Division
Walter P. Engel	Director, Reactor Safety and Computation Division
Alan G. Forssell	Director, Surface Ship Systems Division
Mark Forssell	Director, Submarine Systems Division
Thomas L. Foster	Program Manager for Fiscal, Acquisition and Logistics Management
Souren Hanessian	Program Manager for Trident and Advanced Submarine Projects
Paul W. Hayes	Director, Submarine Systems (S5W) Division
William M. Hewitt	Director, Secondary Components Division
William S. Humphrey	Director, Reactor Refueling Division
A. R. Newhouse	Program Manager for 688-Class Submarines
James A. Palmer	Program Manager for Surface Ships and Water-Cooled Breeders
David B. Pye	Director, Nuclear Components Division
Harry F. Raab, Jr.	Chief Physicist
Paul D. Rice	Director, Nuclear Technology Division
Thomas N. Rodeheaver	Director, Reactor Engineering Division
Gene L. Rogers	Program Manager for Commissioned Submarines
Carl H. Schmitt	Executive Assistant for Security, Public and Foreign Matters
David G. Scott	Program Manager for Shipyard Matters
Jean E. Scroggins	J-Item Engineer
Robert H. Steele	Director, Reactor Materials Division
F. Benjamin Stilmar	Program Manager for Prototype and Shippingport Atomic Power Station Operations
James W. Vaughan, Jr.	Deputy Director
Robert A. Woodberry	Director, Reactor-Plant Valve Division

The titles of the technical divisions showed the roles of the technical managers. The divisions were: engineering (reactor-plant design); nuclear components; instrumentation and control; surface-ship systems; submarine systems; S5W submarine systems; S8G submarine systems; refueling; nuclear technology (radiological and chemical control); materials; reactor safety and computation; reactor-plant valves; and secondary components (steam-plant equipment). In general, the men handling these branches focused on technical components or parts of propulsion systems. Although the section heads of the technical branches were deeply involved in development, performance, and deadlines, their responsibility—at least in theory—was confined to their area.

Seeing that the technical elements were pulled together for a specific enterprise was the job of the project officer. Again the names of the branches revealed the responsibilities: prototype and Shippingport operations; surface-ship and water-cooled breeders; commissioned submarines; Trident and advanced submarines; 688-class attack submarines; and manager for shipyard matters. Almost all project officers had served as a Rickover shipyard representative. The experience seasoned them and gave them the necessary perspective to see beyond components to an entire system.

One job did not fit easily into any category. The executive assistant for security, public, and foreign affairs took care of press relations, classification and protection of technical data, and monitoring the nuclear activities of other navies. His position was another example of Rickover's determination to have his own people handle every aspect of the program.

Another job perplexed outsiders. Jean E. Scroggins, one of the four women in his office, was J-item engineer, a position Rickover insisted be listed in the yellow pages of the Department of Defense telephone directory. As J-item engineer—the letter came from her first initial—she was charged with keeping track of all items upon which Rickover had questions. Each item was assigned a J-item slip and sent to the appropriate section for an answer. She ensured that each question was answered in a reasonable amount of time and that Rickover was kept informed. Her keen sense of humor and fine instinct for diplomacy served both Rickover and Naval Reactors well.[6]

At first glance the organization of the engineers at Naval Reactors seemed to belie Rickover's assertion that he had no organization. What he meant was that the job took precedence over hierarchy and organization and he would shift engineers as needed. He had seen too many instances in which organization was a barrier to creative solutions, a wall behind which individuals hid in anonymity, and a table of organization that marked vested interests and jurisdictional disputes. He watched constantly for any sign of a hierarchy with all of its burden of rigidity: that quality could be fatal in a complex and potentially dangerous technology.

The use of project officers and technical engineers plus the ability to move them from one assignment to another—which he did only after a great deal of thought—gave Rickover at least two perspectives and usually many more when he was confronted with difficult decisions.

Convinced that technical and fiscal discipline were inseparable, Rickover had each technical section responsible for all aspects of its operations—including placement of orders, cost estimates, equipment delivery, contract terms, and budgeting. But in addition, he had a section consisting of supply corps officers and civilians who gave yet another perspective, much as the project officers provided a different view from the engineers on technical issues. The section had an all-encompassing title: "Fiscal,

Acquisition, and Logistics Management." Because the activities were non-technical and nonengineering, but were directed to the business aspects of the program, the group was sometimes called the "business section." Although the term never became common currency, it served as a useful shorthand designation.

Supply corps officers in Naval Reactors played a far different part from the one they had had elsewhere in the navy. There they were often relegated to a secondary status, following through in the wake of decisions in which they had not participated. In Naval Reactors Rickover insisted that no technical decision be made without taking into account fiscal and contractual ramifications. Rickover also looked to these officers for budgeting and for carrying out the functions of a controller in private industry, a role that the supply corps had long ago relinquished in the navy. As part of fiscal, acquisition, and logistical management, the business section also oversaw the contracting, budgeting, logistical, and administrative activities of the navy and the Department of Energy that supported the naval nuclear propulsion program. The supply of spare parts for the nuclear propulsion plants was an area Rickover followed with particularly deep interest. He was intensely proud that over 90 percent of the requests could be filled off the shelf compared with 70 percent for the rest of the navy.

He believed it was part of his responsibility to highlight for Congress the problems he encountered in procurement. Because of his interest in the subject and his relationship with Congress, he played a major part in obtaining legislation establishing the cost-accounting standards board, strengthening the renegotiation board, and requiring contractor certification of claims against the government. In the mid-1960s Rickover became worried by the laxity with which private shipyards were handling ship construction, overhauls, and other matters under government contract. With the help of the business section, he uncovered and documented problems and launched a personal crusade against them, a struggle that became a never-ending series of battles. Throughout the 1970s he led a lonely but vigorous campaign against false and inflated claims. When Litton Industries (of which Ingalls Shipbuilding Division was a part), Newport News, and Electric Boat decided to follow nonnuclear shipbuilders by submitting large claims to recover overruns, he insisted that his people determine the facts and document cases where the claims were false, and follow prescribed agency procedures for referring instances of apparent fraud. At the time he left Naval Reactors his allegations of fraud were under government review.[7]

As in so many things, Rickover had taken a routine function—that of the supply officer—and transformed it into something greater. Of necessity, technical work had to come first, but he made sure that the men and women of fiscal, acquisition, and logistics management never became second-class citizens. Over the years he came to rely on these individuals in his struggle to reform such areas as contracts, shipbuilding claims, and a host of other subjects. His interest and enthusiasm created an exhilarating environment for the bright young officers and civilians who made up the nontechnical, nonengineering, nonmilitary part of Naval Reactors.

Rickover shaped Naval Reactors so that it was lean, flexible, and responsive. Through his technical, project, and fiscal people he could make decisions. Arriving at them was not always fast, or as quick as certain of his men wanted, but so many factors, some of them imponderable in technical development, had to be taken into account as well as the impact of a course of action on other activities. But with project, technical, and fiscal individuals he had three perspectives. Not all individuals consulted agreed with his decisions, although usually a broad consensus had been reached on most issues before they arrived at his desk. Through trust gained by years of training and experience with some of his senior people, he was sometimes content to glance at a recommendation to see if they had concurred. At other times he took the role of devil's advocate, pressing his people unmercifully on their reasons—the whys, hows, and wheres—to see if they actually knew what they were talking about.

PERSONNEL

Naval Reactors was composed of carefully chosen professionals. In the very early days of the program Rickover obtained his leading personnel from the navy, especially officers who had chosen to specialize in engineering. The weakness of this approach was that advancement in the navy depended in part upon rotation from one assignment to another every few years. Rickover asserted then and later that nuclear technology could not be mastered during a standard tour of duty. Two trends soon developed: officers resigned from the navy to stay with the program, and Rickover increasingly recruited civilians. In either case the goal was continuity. At first Rickover had selected his engineers largely by personal contacts with the Webb Institute of Naval Architecture, a few universities, and from the navy. As desperate as he was for personnel, he almost always sent them first to school, either at Oak Ridge or at the Massachusetts Institute of Technology. He personally made sure that the instruction met with the needs of the program, and when in the vicinity, he called upon students and instructors.

As the program expanded, he turned to the naval reserve officers training corps at the best universities. In 1957 he asked the professors of naval science to recommend their best students. The harvest was rich: of about two dozen he chose around nineteen or twenty. He continued to use this source, although the number of qualified candidates declined during those years in which the better universities dropped the naval reserve officers training corps. He also drew engineers from the nuclear-power officer candidate program, in which the best candidates from all colleges could apply for nuclear-power training. Candidates had to come from reputable schools and had to have taken their degrees in technical areas, usually a field of engineering, but occasionally in science or mathematics. Students with good records were invited to Washington. If they passed their interviews with the engineers and Rickover, and if they volunteered for the program, they were accepted.

Rickover refused to draft anyone. Those who were good but did not volunteer received a special briefing on the program and a chance to change their minds. All who accepted had to remain in the navy and in the program for four or five years. A man who worked out well might receive an offer to stay with the program after his term of service had expired. Although not everyone wished to do so, enough accepted to keep the organization going, but Rickover never had any surplus.

Most of the new engineers received their initial assignments from Rickover's deputy director, who did his best to match a junior officer's background and the needs of the division. He would not assign a new man to the office of a project officer because new engineers lacked the background to contribute anything. For the first six months or a year the new man received on-the-job training in Washington. During that time he took a ten-week course with a curriculum including nuclear reactions and reactor physics, reactor-plant operations, reactor core materials, reactor core design and construction, electrical power systems and instrumentation systems, primary and secondary fluid systems, water chemistry control, radiological control, and reactor protection and safety. The instructors were carefully chosen from the technical sections. Rickover allowed no one to teach who was not qualified—and the students had to pass examinations.

Six months at the Bettis reactor engineering school was the next step in training. The student took six weeks of applied nuclear physics as a prerequisite for reactor theory, reactor-plant dynamics control and safeguards, and radiological fundamentals and shielding design. He also took mathematics, heat transfer and fluid flow, engineering statistics, integrated reactor-plant development, applied structural mechanics, and reactor and power-plant design. Excluding conferences and final examinations, total school hours came to over 560. The average weekly total class contact was twenty-five hours. Courses usually met four to six hours a week, and individual class sessions were normally two hours. For each hour of lecture two hours of outside work were required. The pace was fast, the work tough, and progress measured by frequent tests. After passing a final examination, the student was awarded a certificate that some local universities accepted as credit toward a graduate degree.[8]

About halfway through the school, the student had a chance to state his preference for headquarters work. His assignment, however, depended on Rickover's assessment of the needs of the division. Technical chiefs received some of the students and project officers the others—this was the point at which the project officers got new people. A few would remain in the sections to which they were first assigned, but more often they moved about, for a change meant a chance to broaden experience and qualify for greater responsibility. James W. Vaughan, Jr., for example, sequentially headed four major sections—valves, chemistry and radiation control, fuels and materials, and then primary components, before becoming deputy director. He was determined to make a career in the program. His hard work and management performance were rewarded by more challenging assignments and increasing responsibility.

Rickover exercised the same care in selecting and training recruits for his business group. In the early days of the program, he selected only experienced supply corps officials with sea experience, usually of the rank of lieutenant and lieutenant commander. In later years he began recruiting young officers straight out of basic training at the Navy Supply Corps School in Athens, Georgia. Again emphasis was on quality, and those selected performed so well that in the ensuing years Athens became the principal recruiting source for his supply officers. The selection process was rigorous. After reviewing the academic and service records of the Athens students, an officer from Naval Reactors went to the school and interviewed perhaps eight or ten promising candidates. Those who evidenced a desire to join the program and commit themselves to stay for their entire four or five years of naval obligation, were called to Washington for more thorough interviews—a minimum of three with section heads prior to the final one with Rickover. For those accepted there were challenges, opportunities, and an environment conducive to getting the job done. Whatever the problem—budget, logistics, or contracting—they could count on Rickover's backing.

Rickover was adamant in his refusal to accept experienced people from the outside—from another part of the navy, the Department of Energy, university faculties, or private engineering companies. Once he accepted a physicist, but only because he had been deeply involved in the program for years and had held responsible positions as an employee of a contractor. Another exception was a lawyer who came to the division for a few years to fight a particularly complicated legal problem. A third was from the Department of State, a tough combat veteran who for some time handled aspects of the international activities of the program.

THE FIELD OFFICES

Rickover had seventeen field offices. The size, variety, and scope of the activities at Bettis and Knolls dictated that the field offices monitoring the laboratories were the largest in the program. Each was headed by a manager. The Pittsburgh office, with sixty-one civilians and seven officers, was slightly larger than the Schenectady office with its fifty-eight civilians and three officers. The laboratory field offices were divided into two main sections: administrative (including fiscal and contractual matters) and technical (which included all test procedures and similar matters). Both the administrative and technical representatives reported directly to Rickover. Most field offices were much smaller and were headed by a field representative known locally as the "NR Rep." At the Norfolk Naval Shipyard Rickover's representative had five assistants trained in naval reactor plant work as senior technicians.

Whether a field office manager or an "NR Rep," the job was difficult. To the contractor he was an extension of Rickover, snooping to uncover and report problems. To the Washington office he was also Rickover's man. Section heads had to deal with the field representative directly, for he needed their advice and they had to have his information. But both had to avoid the slightest suspicion that anyone stood between the head of a field office and Rickover.

The organization of a field office varied, but it usually had a section dealing with radiation safety and control and another covering quality control. One of the main responsibilities of the field representative and his people was to spot shipyard difficulties before they became major problems. Seemingly minor events and incidents could signal a deficiency in yard management, organization, or qualifications of workers. The field representative had a narrow line to walk: he was to judge performance on how nuclear work was done. He had to tell the contractor what was wrong, but he could not tell him what to do. If the representative did so, he was committing the grave sin of taking over the contractor's job and relieving him of his responsibility. On the other hand, a field representative could not just write reports: he had to make things happen. Rickover stated that to be a field representative took "God-like qualities." Admittedly, these were hard to achieve, but he expected them to try.

Without fail, the representative had to telephone Rickover on certain days of the week. Making the calls always held an element of uncertainty. He could not know Rickover's mood or the particular problem engaging him. He could not know if it was a good time to press forward with a recommendation or if it was better to wait. He could not, as if he were in Washington, walk down the corridor to ask advice from a colleague. Because Rickover reacted fast, the representative had to know his facts—insofar as they could be ascertained—and explain them carefully. If the representative had nothing to report, he still had to call in. Rickover might slam down the receiver and not say a word, but the record in the office would show that the representative had called and all was well. At other times the calls might be long and stormy.

Reports from the field offices were complicated and governed by precise rules aimed at making sure that as few people as possible stood between Rickover and the work. The basic document was the weekly letter from the field representative. Other reports written by the representative's assistants would be attached to it. These would detail problems found by firsthand examinations of the nuclear propulsion plant of a ship lying at a pier, fabrication work at a shop, and numerous other activities. That report went to Rickover. The head of the field office did not know the content or subject in advance—he did not see the report until after it was signed. He was forbidden to alter a word. He could comment and note certain actions. He could cross out a paragraph if he thought the subject was minor, but the words had to remain legible. Under certain circumstances three individuals might comment. Each had to be clearly identified and his signature clearly written. Rickover always read the letters, underscoring significant sections and scrawling his own comments before sending them on for action.[9] Those reports that had nothing to say roused his suspicions: maybe everything was going well, but on the other hand maybe the man was not looking. With his own experience with yards and contractors stretching back over decades and with his constant contacts from several sources, he could often sense when problems were building up beneath a calm surface.

The shipyard field representative had one of the toughest jobs in Naval Reactors. He faced heavy pressures from every direction. It was natural for him to become part of his surroundings; he could walk down to the waterfront to inspect a ship at the pier or over to the building ways to check the work on a ship. The yard officials could offer very reasonable explanations of difficulties and delays, observing that only the field representative and the yard understood the real causes holding up the work. By succumbing, the representative was assuming Rickover's responsibility for judging the situation. Rickover watched for the slightest sign that his men in the yard were stepping out of line, destroying unintentionally their usefulness by not reporting accurately or by encumbering themselves with relationships that destroyed their perspective. He did not allow the field office men and their families to have social relationships with the contractors.[10]

It was an important job. If the hours were long and the strain great, there were also compensations. Rickover backed his men. Finally, the field representative could see improvement in the yard's performance—noting that certain procedures had been changed and he had played a part in that process. He could see victories, but knew the campaign was never-ending. Significantly, most of the senior engineers at Naval Reactors had been field representatives.

THE RICKOVER ROLE

Rickover refused to be the captive of a single source of information. He ridiculed the managerial theory of "span of control," according to which "no supervisor can supervise directly the work of more than five, or at the most six, subordinates *whose work interlocks*."[11] Rickover had thirteen technical engineers and six project engineers reporting directly to him, and on special matters he did not hesitate to seek out an individual man in a branch. In the fiscal division he often dealt directly with men working on special assignments. From contractors and field installations he received telephone calls on Mondays and Fridays from sixteen individuals, and on Wednesdays the same men plus four more. On Tuesdays and Thursdays nineteen other people telephoned. These were scheduled calls; any of these people—and others—could call him during an emergency or on a particularly complex issue.

The same philosophy underlay the written sources of information. The "pinks" system (in which pink carbons of completed and uncompleted correspondence went to Rickover each working day) was another approach. Most of the correspondence was drafted by young engineers. Under no circumstances was a section chief or a project manager allowed to intercept or alter a pink. Not only were the pinks an excellent training device, but they kept Rickover informed of current and impending actions. As already noted, Rickover received several independent reports from every site, which frequently contained comments.

In his Washington office the overlapping responsibilities of the section chiefs and project managers gave him different perspectives. If the matter had fiscal or contractual implications, some of his business people had views for him to consider. Supposing that the problem was one in the field; he would have the thoughts of his own representative and those of the contractor. The technical engineers were interested in the origins and extent of a component failure and its implications for ships in commission and those under construction. A project manager was worried over the impact on a schedule. The individual from the fiscal section was concerned with financial aspects. Usually these three men, all of whom had served for years in the program and knew each other and Rickover well, could agree on a course of action. They presented the alternatives and pointed out the consequences to Rickover. But he decided.

In some instances the issue was such that it was possible to illustrate the problem by a diagram or a mock-up of a component. A few of his engineers took over the conference room just outside his office, and when all was ready he came in. At the slightest indication of vagueness or ambiguity he interrupted, demanding clarity and facts. Some meetings were brief, but others were long and stormy with arguments that could be heard some distance down the corridors. By holding all the reins, he could delay his decisions or carry them out quickly.

His system also entailed obligations. Some seemed trivial until it was realized they were part of his means of control. He kept track of the status of unanswered correspondence. Each morning he received a summary that showed him how many letters were unanswered, how long they had been in the division, and who was responsible for preparing replies. Furthermore, the summary showed the status of previous days so that he could see whether a branch was improving. A chief who accumulated a heavy backlog was liable to get a quick summons to Rickover's office to explain.

He never claimed his organization was perfect, that things did not go wrong, or that he and his engineers did not make mistakes. At his infrequent meetings with the section heads, he would catalog the errors. Too often young engineers were proposing changes, perhaps to technical specifications or procedures, without understanding why they had been established in the first place. Frequently, the younger men did not understand that the plants were to be run by sailors—not engineers. Too often, pressed by time, engineers were coming to a proposed agreement with a contractor before Rickover had a chance to consider the matter from all its aspects. Here, as in the case of the field representative, an improper assumption of responsibility was taking place. Rarely did Rickover let the multiplicity of reports reaching him obscure fundamental issues. In one instance a series of minor problems—of which everyone knew some—had been occurring. An investigation showed that a serious situation had developed because the manager was having trouble handling the work. Neither the site representatives nor the Washington engineers had analyzed the problems and realized their implication.

When his people had trouble with the system, Rickover would react quickly. On information he received, he might immediately call a contractor and set in motion a sequence of events for which it was hard to see an end.

Some men could not stand the pace. Exhausted and stripped of their resiliency, they left, some of them carrying bitter and angry thoughts. For some these would fade, to be succeeded by memories of being part of a major technical program that had achieved outstanding results and had contributed inestimably to national security. On that subject those who stayed with the program and those who left agreed: the results were outstanding and the program important.

The demands of his system upon himself were heavy. Every few hours a secretary placed a new stack of mail on his desk. Every day the pinks came in. He could not ignore or delay reading the mail or the pinks. He could never get too far away from them. Even at the end of a sea trial when a tug had nudged the submarine into dock and the crane had just swung across a gangplank to the ship, a messenger waited with a briefcase stuffed with documents from the office. Even in the rare times he was in the hospital he had the office mail delivered to him, sometimes working on it only hours after an operation. He never knew what the next telephone call might bring. He was not—could not be—away from his work for long.

He was proud of his system and convinced it was the best way to handle technical programs—or any important undertaking. With his several sources of information, many competing with each other and each with its own perspective, he was seldom caught totally unaware. The various facets, writing letters and reports, personally proposing and defending recommendations, were superb training devices. And he believed his system offered an unparalleled opportunity for men to grow into responsibility. The leanness and responsiveness of his organization, the training and competence of his men, his own multiple sources of information, allowed him to act fast. It was the technical competence and ability to move quickly that distinguished his program from those of other government organizations. Those he contemptuously dismissed: "They only administrate."

The Seagoing Navy—Officers

The description of Naval Reactors, the field offices, the recruiting and training of personnel, and Rickover's role belong to that part of the effort that dealt with reactor development, prototype construction and operation, commissioned ship problems, and ship construction. Another and more controversial aspect was the selection of officers who wished to serve in the nuclear-powered navy.

The origins of the issue went back to the selection of Eugene P. Wilkinson to command the *Nautilus*. Rickover was convinced that most of the submarine officers who had commanded the diesel-electric boats of World War II could not adapt to the demands of nuclear technology. The choice of Wilkinson did not cause much trouble because he was an experienced submariner who had served a tour of duty in the technical part of the naval nuclear propulsion program. But it was Rickover's contention that to meet his responsibility to the commission for the safe operation of the reactors he had to train the officers and men who would operate the propulsion plant. To see whether the officer was capable of receiving the training, he had to interview him personally.[12]

Eventually a compromise evolved. The Bureau of Naval Personnel, which handled officer assignments, nominated candidates for training. Rickover interviewed those approved by the bureau. Since the bureau had some idea of the qualifications for which Rickover was looking, the individuals were already highly selected. By 1980 by far the greater number of candidates were midshipmen from Annapolis and from different college programs: the Naval Reserve Officers Training Corps, the navy's Officer Candidate School, and the Nuclear-Power Officer Candidate program. All candidates had to meet certain requirements in mathematics and science.

The essential fact was that no one could hope to command a nuclear-powered ship unless Rickover had accepted him into the program. To many officers this was a good deal of authority to entrust to one man. On the other hand, the training program was recognized as tough and excellent. It was Rickover's interviews that drew the most criticism.

Each officer candidate had to undergo four interviews—three by senior engineers in the program, and the last by Rickover. The first three interviews each lasted about twenty minutes. To be sure the sessions were uninterrupted, Rickover insisted that the engineer conduct it in an office that was not his own; by doing so, he could talk to the candidate without the distraction of telephone calls or other claims on his attention. The engineer had records before him that showed the courses taken, grades achieved, and the man's class standing. The engineer's questions were aimed at determining the level of the man's knowledge, his willingness to work hard, and his ability to express himself. At the end of the interview the engineer wrote his evaluation of the candidate's potential, and gave a brief summary of the questions asked, the length of the interview, and his recommendation.

When the candidate, accompanied by an officer, entered Rickover's office, he already knew where the admiral and the officer would sit, the type of questions he was likely to encounter, and above all that he was to answer quickly and honestly. Rickover had before him the independent appraisals and recommendations of three of his leading engineers.

Predicting the path the questions would take was hard, but it usually depended upon the candidate's replies. Rickover was not interested in establishing academic qualifications; that was the purpose of the earlier interviews. His primary purpose was to assess the man's ability to grasp an unexpected situation, to think quickly, and to answer a question directly without qualification or evasion. These qualities he deemed essential to the operation of a nuclear propulsion plant. Rickover might ask about the man's class standing, what he gained from any extracurricular activities he had listed, how much time he spent in study, and a few basic questions about his academic major. Occasionally he might elicit a promise to study a certain number of hours a week in the future. In some instances the questions were personal: was he engaged, who had proposed?

In many instances Rickover made a decision in a single session. None of the interviews were easy; about half were rough. Sometimes the candidate claimed knowledge he did not have and should have known he could not finesse. A man who claimed he would use his leadership to fix a condenser pump was asking for trouble, and he should have known better. A reply of "No excuse, sir" to a question on the reason for low academic standing evoked an angry tirade—for the response was no answer. A frank admission of laziness would have been better. Equally bad was the man who, having put himself in an illogical and false position, "stuck to his guns," under the impression that he was showing firmness. This type was promptly removed from the office and placed in another room to reconsider the question and his answer. A few candidates might undergo three or four sessions with Rickover before he reached a decision.

Occasionally he accepted a man his engineers would have rejected, or refused a man they would have taken. Although he tried to keep the sessions uninterrupted, he could not avoid the telephone calls from the field, the laboratories, or members of Congress. On the days of interviews—particularly when several hundred midshipmen from the Academy were involved—Rickover might not leave the office until after midnight. And the next morning the sessions would begin again. Although the main purpose of the interviews was to get the best people he could, that was not the only reason for all the effort, trouble, and time. A born teacher, Rickover also hoped that the sessions taught lessons. For the first time in his career a young man might have discovered the emptiness of the rhetoric of leadership with its emphasis upon dedication and motivation. For the first time he might begin to exercise his own judgment instead of accepting that of others.[13]

After receiving their commissions as ensigns, the men he accepted went to nuclear power school in Orlando, Florida, for six months of academic training tailored to the needs of the nuclear operator program. The pressure was intense. For most students the nuclear power school was far more difficult than anything they had encountered before. Next came six months at a prototype either at Idaho Falls, Idaho, West Milton,

New York, or Windsor, Connecticut. Here the demands were even greater. A young officer standing a student watch was vividly aware that the dials he watched on the instrument panel were readings on a real reactor—not a simulator. He marked his progress by passing a series of examinations and by demonstrating his competence through actual performance.

Roughly 10 percent failed, mostly for academic reasons, although a few were dropped for disciplinary causes. Before an officer was dropped from the program, Rickover personally studied the record, noting the efforts to stave off failure by counseling and additional work. Often a man had received several hours of individual instruction each week in an effort to help him qualify. Usually the evidence was so plain that he gave his approval after a brief study of the records. No officer was dropped without Rickover's personal approval.

From the prototype, officers were usually assigned to a nuclear ship. Again came more study and more instruction. The new arrivals, already qualified on the prototype, had to requalify on the shipboard plant. After two or three years of sea duty as engineer officer of the watch, the man, now a lieutenant junior grade or a full lieutenant, should be ready to take the examinations to qualify him as an engineer officer, the officer who heads the engineering department of a ship. For this purpose, the man returned to the Naval Reactors office in Washington for an oral and written examination on the technical matters, and another interview with Rickover. Again the questioning was intense, and again the purpose was to ascertain if the man had the qualities to exercise the responsibility. If he failed, he went to another part of the navy.

After serving as engineer and as executive officer, the next step was command. For three months in Rickover's headquarters, prospective commanding officers underwent further study and examination. At the end Rickover talked to them briefly. The tone of the remarks was never congratulatory; instead, he bluntly spoke of his doubts that they really understood the nature of the responsibility they were assuming. Even after all the years of training they had undergone, he believed most of them would rely on leadership techniques. Many of them, he thought, were filled with their own importance, a feeling that "they knew better." Now he could do little more than warn them that the lessons they had been taught were based on almost three decades of safe operation of nuclear ships.

For nuclear submarines and cruisers this pattern was the same: after nuclear power school and prototype training the officer served as engineer officer of the watch, engineer officer, executive officer, and finally commanding officer. For nuclear aircraft carriers, however, the route was different. Because captains of these ships had to be aviators, they came into the program at a later stage in their careers. After passing through nuclear power school and prototype training they became executive officers and, if all went well, went on to become commanding officers. They were the sole exception to the rule Rickover had established that on nuclear ships all commanding officers had to have qualified as engineer officers. Reactor officers and engineer officers of the nuclear carriers came from nonaviator nuclear-trained surface officers. After duty on a carrier they could hope for command of a nuclear cruiser.[14]

The Seagoing Navy—Enlisted Personnel

Most enlisted men entered the nuclear program after going first through boot camp, and then to "A" school where they received their first training in a technical specialty. By doing well and meeting the requirements, a man could volunteer for nuclear power school. Most volunteers went directly from "A" school to a two- to six-week preparatory school for additional work in mathematics and physics. Next came six months at a nuclear power school followed by six months at a prototype. Again the hours were long and the work intense. The ratio of instructors to students was high; in the prototype, usually one instructor supervised one student. On the site were classrooms for additional work, for the officers and the men had to study several plant manuals and diagrams. Rickover, always anxious to improve conditions for studying, saw carrels—small spaces set aside for individual study—while visiting the Firestone Library in Princeton. He promptly adopted the idea. Furthermore, he insisted that study spaces be monitored to make sure that no noise—no radios, no skylarking—broke the silence.[15]

Rickover did not review the records of an enlisted man who was failing. Nevertheless, the man was not dropped without the approval of the Washington office. Rickover would not tolerate the use of drugs. An officer or man expelled from the program for any reason was off the site in a few hours.

On board ship enlisted personnel could advance through their rates, and as long as they stayed out of trouble, never hear of Rickover and the nuclear propulsion directorate. However, there were two exceptions that were significant and indicative of Rickover's approach to his responsibility. He interviewed enlisted men assigned to the NR-1, the nuclear-powered research submarine. The ship was so small that enlisted men found themselves assuming roles that officers would have taken in a larger submarine. He also interviewed enlisted men who, after satisfactory service at sea, volunteered to be part of his organization at Shippingport. He insisted upon talking to these men because the work at Shippingport would require not only initiative and strength of character, but also the technical knowledge needed to direct the shutdown of the plant when conditions were unsafe.

To handle the training of officers and men and some of his other relations with the operational navy, Rickover had a small staff of seagoing naval officers, headed by two captains assigned to him for a tour of duty as operational training assistants. One handled enlisted personnel and officers—the latter from the time they entered the program until they were qualified to become prospective commanding officers. The other was responsible for prospective commanding officers and for commanding officers. When reports from nuclear ships showed a possible area of trouble, the training officers frequently acted for Rickover in gaining more information or straightening matters out. Qualifications for both positions were, of course, to have gone through the nuclear program and to have had a successful command at sea.

Management, Responsibility, and Creativity

Rickover was thoroughly aware that the way he ran his job was contrary to the tenets of conventional management. Frequently the morning mail brought into Rickover's office advertisements for seminars, symposia, and short courses in management. For a few hundred dollars he and his engineers could learn the secrets of making decisions, motivating employees by valuable and practical techniques, coping with the information function, developing effectiveness in managers who managed other managers, and promoting the optimization of the science and art of program management by conceptualizing, structuring, testing, and coordinating improvements in management systems and functions. Usually he threw the announcements away, but sometimes, after scribbling brief and caustic comments, he routed them through the division. He was delighted when he discovered in *Webster's New World Dictionary of the American Language* that one definition of "symposium" was an "entertainment characterized by drinking, music, and intellectual discussion." The drinking and entertainment, he thought, were probably true.[16]

He found the qualifications of those who led ongoing problem-solving seminars and ongoing problem-solving workshops ridiculous and their claims preposterous. How, he wondered, did one become a professor of decision-making sciences? So many of these people, he observed, had engaged in training activities, written articles, contributed to books edited by other management specialists, and were members of consulting firms. But so few had any practical experience to offer. He was particularly incensed when brochures directed at government employees invited them to attend functions at personal or government expense when a government official was a principal speaker.

If it was simply a matter of quacks offering cures for snakebite to a gullible public, he would have had only the indignation of anyone encountering a sham. What he saw, however, was something far more serious. No longer could civilization depend upon easily available natural resources. Technologies should be developed to use those resources that are scarce and hard to work. New technologies, as they became more complex, pervasive, expensive, and dangerous, could lead to increasing social tension. To keep them under control demanded intense personal dedication and intellectual discipline as well as an understanding of human nature and society. To believe that any except the most minor and routine problems would yield to "management breakthroughs" was a perilous fraud.

He had not reached this conclusion idly. He had read the major texts on management during the late 1930s. When he was head of the electrical section in the Bureau of Ships, he had over his desk precepts of management in a neat gold-colored frame. Finding them impossible to use he returned to the principles he had developed during his career and built upon those. Through the years he continued to glance through some of the business journals and was disturbed by the growing emphasis upon theory. Since 1946 he had been in the forefront of a major technical development that had revolutionized sea power and found application in civilian life. As judged by the results, he believed his methods were worth study.

There was another aspect about which he spoke seldom but felt deeply. He was certain his approach to technical problems brought to fruition latent talent that otherwise would have remained unripened, smothered beneath layers of industrial or governmental bureaucracy. He watched his people closely. Those who showed intelligence, sensitivity, and an appetite for responsibility he moved into positions of greater importance. Those who failed were removed. Because he selected his people just out of college and drove them hard, they tended to be young in years but old in experience. On one rare occasion when he gathered the members of his Washington office in a large conference room, he remarked to a bystander that the sight of so many young and intelligent people was exciting, almost awe-inspiring. He could award no higher praise than to tell someone he had "grown." It was an accolade rarely bestowed and then only after years of assessment and evaluation. Not only had he achieved tangible results with his principles, but in the highest sense of human values they were also creative.

Hard work was sometimes tedious, often frustrating, always essential, and in the final analysis enriching. That was what he meant when he remarked: "The Devil is in the details but so is salvation."[17]

The first alarm sounded about 4:36 A.M. on 28 March 1979. The main feedwater pumps had shut down; the emergency feedwater system started up, but because of closed valves failed to supply the steam generator. Deprived of water, the steam generator went dry, and a relief valve lifted and did not reseat. Assurance soon gave

CHAPTER TEN
Independence and Control

way to desperation as plant personnel tried to find out what had happened, what was going on, and what should be done. Ominously the number of radiation alarms multiplied. At 6:56 A.M. the plant superintendent and the technical superintendent declared a site emergency. As the guards swung closed the access gates to the plant, steps were taken to notify officials of the state of Pennsylvania and the Federal Nuclear Regulatory Commission. Within hours the Three Mile Island nuclear power plant achieved a grim notoriety.[1]

The world watched, heard, and read of the struggle to regain control of the plant. One investigation followed another to uncover technical failures, human errors, and administrative weaknesses. Among the opinions sought by Congress and the president were those of Rickover. Letters reaching his office and comments in the press declared that the civilian nuclear power industry needed the same type of leadership, training, and discipline that characterized the navy's nuclear-propulsion program under Rickover.[2]

At the time of the Three Mile Island accident, Rickover was in charge of 152 reactors, including Shippingport. The Three Mile Island plant and all of Rickover's reactors were pressurized water, but the difference between the propulsion reactors and Shippingport on the one hand, and the commercial plants on the other, was substantial. It was not the technology for which Rickover's views were sought, but his methods for maintaining standards of work and proficiency of operation. His record bore testimony to their efficacy. He had been in charge of the joint navy-commission nuclear propulsion program since 1949. His first reactor, the Nautilus *prototype, had started up in 1953 and was still in operation. None of the reactors for which he was responsible had suffered a casualty even remotely as serious as the accident that had occurred at Three Mile Island.[3]*

One reason was his insistence upon maintaining standards and procedures and his refusal to permit any deviation from them without a technical review and without his permission. Although recognized for his role in the development of nuclear propulsion and civilian power, his means for ascertaining the performance and competence of the men routinely operating the plants and facilities for which he was responsible were less well known. They are illustrated in the following pages by examination of the techniques he devised for ensuring that standards were maintained at shipyards and in all operating nuclear ships, and for controlling radiation exposure and protecting the environment. He summarized his thoughts along these lines in his observations on the accident at Three Mile Island. Procedures, standards, and philosophy were permeated by a basic thought: the need to accept the discipline of technology.

In the initial phase of constructing the first nuclear ships, Rickover believed he could rely on existing technology. Experience soon disillusioned him. Standards that he had taken at face value proved to be goals, not specific requirements that had to be met. Procedures that he had assumed prescribed exact steps were treated only as useful guides. He and his engineers soon realized that the problems they faced were not only the development of the reactor, with all of its imperative demand for safety and reliability, but also the lack of a sound technical foundation upon which to build. This was the meaning of his speech, "The Never Ending-Challenge," which he delivered in 1962 to the 44th annual National Metals Congress; this was the warning he gave to the audience in the long and ominous list of failures of quality control and quality assurance in industry. Although the inquiry into the loss of the *Thresher* did not determine the immediate cause of the tragedy, it did at least uncover the compelling necessity for immediate upgrading of the work in all the yards.[4]

To a lay observer, major shipyards were unlike any other industrial institution. Huge, thick-walled cavernous brick buildings built decades ago were next to sterile modern structures run up recently. Whether new or old, the buildings had shops for an amazing variety of functions, all of which were aimed at building, maintaining, or repairing modern combat ships, themselves designed to withstand the massive stress and strain of the sea as well as to contain weapons, propulsion plants, and living quarters. The scope and variety of the work was bewildering. Huge cranes, towering against the sky, lowered huge and heavy components onto a ship in dry dock; nearby, small modern buildings housed delicate electronic equipment needed to provide exact measurements.

Rickover had several techniques for finding out how well a shipyard was maintaining the standards and keeping the procedures over the work for which he was responsible. His own man in each shipyard having nuclear work was an indispensable source of information. The shipyard representative reported at least twice a week by telephone and once a week in writing. But something else was needed—a project officer in Washington to follow all the yards in which Naval Reactors had work. In 1968 Rickover brought back Gene L. Rogers, his representative at Pearl Harbor, to handle shipyard matters. In the course of visiting several yards with William Wegner, Rogers began to realize the immensity of the task. The only way to upgrade a yard was to inspect and correct, building upon those practices that were proving sound and codifying them. Such practices were incorporated in a quality-control manual written by David G. Scott, an experienced engineer who had served as field representative in Idaho and later had become special assistant for quality assurance to the program manager for shipyard matters.

The shipyard audit was the technique that Rickover, Wegner, Rogers, and Scott devised over the years. By 1980 the general pattern had become well established. One point was fundamental: the audit was not a snap inspection to uncover shortcomings. The yard knew a month or two ahead of time that it was scheduled for a week-long investigation by competent and experienced personnel from Naval Reactors into the causes of deficiencies. Insofar as practicable, the audit was to measure performance against written instructions, not against the subjective judgment of an engineer. Examples were official documents covering various aspects of refueling, specifications for quality control, and procedures of inspecting government-furnished equipment. In some instances procedures and practices had to be traced step by step. In other cases spot checks were the only means of determining performance, for it was obviously impossible to examine all the documentation and all of the work on every ship in the yard.

A week was none too long. To make sure that assignments were clear, Rogers, the senior project officer, held a brief meeting in Washington with those men who would be making the audit. Each man was responsible for specific technical areas, and each had definite tasks. Each received a sample form to report his finding, and instructions that explained the rules and terms that would be used. Some of those at the meeting had taken part in as many as thirty audits, and a few were taking part for the first time; but all were technically trained and experienced and had been in the program for years. For special areas Rickover called upon a few men from other installations, perhaps from a prototype, a supply depot, or a laboratory. From the yard, however, he took only Naval Reactors representatives or their assistants—never an employee. Of the dozen members of the team, he had three that investigated compliance with radiation-control procedures. That was an area that he watched most carefully, recognizing that an inadvertent release of radioactivity could do tremendous harm.

At the Yard

Most members of the team flew to the city nearest the yard on Sunday evening. The next morning at 7:00 they assembled in the office of the field representative. He took them a short distance to a building that was old, large, and almost empty. For the team's purpose it was perfect: enough space to expand and yet maintain privacy; enough office furniture, even if grimy and dirty. For the first hour the representative, aware that his own performance was being assessed, described the background material he had gathered: records on radiological controls, schedules, quality control, testing, overtime, and several other areas. From his perspective the chief problem was the lack of test engineers. They were already spread very thinly over the waterfront, and the scheduled workload would make conditions worse. He saw evidence that the strain was beginning to tell.

His survey was barely completed when the shipyard commander and his staff of officers and civilians entered. With their explanation of how they saw their problems, the team gained one more viewpoint.

A contractor employee from Knolls who did not attend these initial meetings had already begun reviewing the yard's technique for inspecting welds by radiography. He first talked to the chief of the radiographic organization to see how its members fulfilled their responsibilities: how they chose techniques for radiographing various types of welds; how they were certain that the men performing the welds were qualified; and how they processed and examined the radiographic film. He also studied records for accuracy and completeness. A few minutes later, in a darkened room, he scanned the actual film. He did not expect to find gross errors, for the yard's film interpreters, reviewers, and test examiners had good reputations, but he might find trends that unchecked might lead to an erosion of specifications, or he might uncover a misinterpretation of official standards. After several hours he found but one discrepancy: one exposure had been misfiled. Even so, the labeling of the film was correct so that there was no possibility of confusion over the identification of the joint and the ship.

An expert from the Naval Reactors representative's office from another yard was examining procedures for carrying out and inspecting the results of ultrasonic tests of brazed joints. He did not check the test of every brazed joint the yard had performed since the last audit, but he did examine the test results of every joint that had been brazed on one ship in overhaul. Because the number of these joints under the cognizance of Rickover's organization was small and confined to systems that did not carry high pressure, the task did not take long. Later in the morning he was down at the waterfront, going through the engine room of a submarine that was in the final stages of overhaul. He scanned tags fastened to valves and components to see if they were accurately and properly filled out, and he examined measures taken to prevent dirt from getting into the reactor system.

The vertical audit was another major technique. Briefly, it was a detailed examination of a job from start to finish. To be a useful gauge of information, the task had to be of some complexity. Beginning with the first work order and the signature of the authorizing engineer, the audit traced every step, from the issuance of blue prints and technical manuals and tools, to the tracing of procedures by which materials were procured and quality control maintained. At times discussions ventured into English usage. Almost from the beginning of the program, Rickover refused to accept the permissive meaning of "should." In manuals and standards issued by headquarters "shall" and "should" were both mandatory. Some documents contained a phrase that Rickover had developed: the individual signing the paper had personally observed the work described above and certified that it had been done correctly. Once the auditor was puzzled because a job was marked satisfactorily completed before the component had been tested. The explanation was simple: the particular component could not be tested until the larger system of which it was a part, and which was also being worked upon, was back in operation.

The yard's own organization to check the quality of the work came under survey. One worry of the Washington engineer was whether the yard's quality-assurance group was falling into a routine that might leave unexamined some areas. He noticed that a preliminary report was submitted to the group that had just been audited; although the practice did allow explanation of alleged deficiencies, he warned that it could also open the way for pressure to change findings. He also thought using supply officers to check material received was not always sound; they usually did not have sufficient technical knowledge to know if the yard was actually getting the quality of material for which it was paying.

Investigating the means by which the yard qualified men for nuclear work was another part of the audit. Two Washington engineers sat in on an examination given by a three-man board of the yard to a young man who had studied for a higher-paying position in radiation control. The problem was simply stated. On a Sunday morning a hypothetical submarine was in dry dock, discharging some water containing low-level radioactivity into a tank. The hose had parted, spilling some of the water onto the dry-dock floor. The board told the young man the instrument readings, the time of day, the weather, and the wind direction. On a blackboard the candidate listed the actions he would take, dividing these into two categories: one for protecting personnel and the other for protecting the environment. From time to time the board interjected questions. At the conclusion, after the man had left the room, each member of the board wrote down his grade on a small slip of paper that he handed to the leader. (Later Rickover wanted to know how the audit team could tell that the shipyard had not tried to create a favorable impression by selecting its best men to be examined.)

The routine of the first days of the audit was much the same: early breakfast at the motel, a drive to the yard, and immediate dispersal to the assignments for the day. Lunch was grabbed as opportunity offered. A late afternoon meeting assessed preliminary findings: the yard's production group was being swamped by changes to technical work documents; coordination between nuclear and nonnuclear work on the ships was poor; one yard engineer was frequently down on the waterfront, but others were not; preparations for a refueling were behind schedule, and facilities and planning were inadequate; the shipyard examination that crane operators had to pass contained questions that had been used previously; a radiation drill found the yard response slow; and many of the best-qualified engineers were in offices instead of on the waterfront where they were needed.

Usually a brief meeting with the shipyard commander and his staff followed. The purpose was to get a specific response to a definite question. No attempts were made to probe the shipyard deeply on why the problems existed; that was Rickover's job, and no one could do it better.

Each day ended later and later, a reflection of the amount of work that had to be done before Rickover arrived on Friday. On Wednesday afternoon Wegner flew in. He heard some hurried preliminary evaluations, but spent most of his time on other matters. He was concerned about the ability of the yard to handle a projected heavier workload. He sounded out the relations between the captains of the nuclear ships and the yard. To gain insight he attended a meeting between the captains and the shipyard commander, sessions that owed their existence to a long struggle that Rickover had fought years ago to give the captains a forum to raise issues.

Thursday evening was rugged. For the audit to fulfill its function, the shipyard commander and his staff had to have a complete copy of the report to study on Friday morning before Rickover arrived. With several detailed forms to complete, the engineers spread out into the vacant spaces of the nearly abandoned building. As soon as one form was complete, it went to the team leader. Not one to mince words, Rogers shot it back if it was not clear or in the prescribed format. As the number of completed forms accumulated, the field office furnished secretaries to convert the penciled scrawls into neatly typed entries. As the hours wore on, navy yeomen from the ships took the place of the secretaries. By one o'clock Friday morning most of the work had been done, and all of the team, except for the leader and a few engineers, had left. A few troubling items remained; it was terribly important to be accurate. Rickover would no more tolerate sloppy work on the part of his own men than he would on the part of the yard. By 2:30 A.M. the last form had been edited and typed. One man from the field representative's office drew the assignment of reproducing the forms and collating and binding them, so that every member of the team, the shipyard commander and his leading staff, and Rickover, could have one.

Friday was busy. There was still information to be gathered, some records to be checked further, and other business to be discussed. In addition, the report itself had to be studied to answer Rickover's own questions. Late in the afternoon he swept in. He was tieless, dressed in khaki with no insignia. He turned at once to the report. Not every item would be discussed with the shipyard commander, just those that had been asterisked. Some things disturbed him. He wondered if the commander had been given sufficient time to study the items; if the data on overtime were accurate; and finally, he had to be realistic: how much improvement could he expect?

When he was ready, the shipyard commander and his staff, perhaps two dozen officers and civilians, crowded into the room. About the only open space was that separating the shipyard commander and Rickover. Rickover turned at once to business. Most of what he had to say, he declared, was aimed at the civilians: they and not transient officers were in charge and therefore were responsible. As the commander went down the list of items giving explanations, Rickover interrupted with questions. Once he asked for estimates of how long it would take to correct a situation; he did not want exact time, but he wanted an idea. On overtime, always a sore subject with him, he had found that in some yards individuals were working extra hours year in and year out, and the additional pay had become a significant fraction of their income. Theft of government property was another matter he watched closely—the loss of tools was far too high.

Occasionally he expanded a narrow fact to a matter of philosophy. So often he had heard pledges to do better; so often he had received written promises to take action; and so seldom had he seen results. Why should he believe them now? The yard had to recognize that management systems did not answer—and could not answer—problems of modern technology. Knowledge of the job—competence—was essential, and competence could not be achieved without continuity. Neither competence nor continuity in themselves were sufficient: inspection was an essential ingredient. The yard commander and his staff simply could not sit in their offices; they had to get down to the waterfront. They had to get personally involved.

The room was silent. Not even the noise of pulling a blind to shut off the rays of the late afternoon sun broke the spell. For many of these men—and those of Rickover's office as well—driven as they were by the bitterly conflicting imperatives of standards and schedules, the perspective of his philosophy revealed the discipline of technology. These were not the words of an unknown figure who had descended from a remote niche in the upper reaches of a bureaucratic hierarchy, but the thoughts of a man who lived by the words he was urging others to adopt. Some of these men had felt the lash of his anger, but they could neither deny his decades of experience nor doubt his own commitment.

The meeting was over. To the sounds of chairs pushed back against the wall and tables shoved aside, the commander and his staff filed out. The personnel of the yard and of the team did not mix.

That too was important. No fraternizing between the Naval Reactors organization and the yard; no getting together after work for a drink at the club; no going out to a restaurant for dinner; no visiting as a guest in someone's home; no easy terms of first-name familiarity; no feeling that the yard and Rickover's men were "in this job together." The members did not always eat as a group, but no one mingled with outsiders. No one knocked off work early to take in a movie or a play. Of course there were lighter moments, for these were intelligent men who had seen a great deal of life, who could recognize absurdities and capture them in raucous stories. But they kept to themselves.

Not all audits went smoothly. Rickover was very hard on his own men if he thought their assessments hurried or inaccurate. The yard was uneasy, for by the nature of the situation it was on the defensive. No matter how good its records, shortcomings and failures were bound to occur. Rickover could be devastating if he thought the yard was slacking off, growing careless, easing up on procedures, and undermining standards. At times he was doubtful that the audits did much good. Perhaps some improvement took place, but gains so painfully made could be lost so soon if one yard commander was succeeded by another who was less competent, or if a private yard brought in a manager whose loyalty was to the balance sheet rather than to the technical work. The point Rickover hammered home again and again was that nuclear technology was a jealous mistress, intolerant of failure.

It was dusk when Rickover left the building, but he still had work to do. A car took him along the side of a dry dock in which floodlights shone on submarines almost concealed by scaffolding, and out on a pier along which ships were silently moored. At the very end was a barge with living quarters. It was ugly but functional—affording austere housing for officers and men whose ships were undergoing repair.

A handful of officers commanding the nuclear ships in the yard were waiting for him in the wardroom; he took his place at the head of a table and they sat down. In a low conversational tone he spoke of the importance of the nuclear navy. It was nuclear submarines with missiles that made up a major element of the deterrent strength; it was nuclear submarines that could best defend the sea lanes upon which the nation depended; it was nuclear surface ships that could steam long distances at high speed to scenes of emergencies. The advantages conferred by nuclear propulsion entailed great responsibilities, just as greater gifts meant a greater obligation to serve. A job should be a calling; it should be a religion. Their duty to the United States was one of morality.

No moral obligation was easy to discharge. Formulas of leadership were worthless. Essays on leadership in the Naval Institute *Proceedings* did harm, for they were written by young officers without experience and read by young officers without experience. If a man knew his job, leadership would follow inevitably, but leadership without knowledge was an empty shell, liable to crack under the slightest pressure. Priorities had to be kept clear; all the tactics and strategy taught by the Naval War College were of little use if the ship could not operate properly. A commanding officer had only two duties: train his men and keep his ship ready to fight. A commanding officer who let his ship go downhill was a traitor to himself, his men, and his country.

Why didn't they get around their ships more? Why didn't they inspect more often? When their ships were in port, why didn't they go through them on weekends, particularly after midnight? That was the time to learn. Not too long ago an engineering officer of the watch of a ship in port decided on his own initiative to take a man off watch. His action was against procedures, but he was trying to be "nice" and a "good guy." Rickover's man discovered the breach, the commanding officer did not. How could men who had pride in their ship have someone outside learn about something wrong before they did? Why didn't the captains call for the important logs the first thing in the morning? In fifteen minutes they could read them and probably catch a glimpse of trouble before it started. Recently he had helped to establish the senior officers ships' material readiness course at the Idaho site to teach nonnuclear-trained officers how to inspect. An attitude that seemed ingrained in all of them was that their job was to command—someone else would take care of their ship.

Nothing was final—that was the hardest lesson to learn. Men do not stay trained. No matter how firm or how formally procedures were promulgated, the insidious and subtle process of erosion sets in at once. Only the commanding officer can stop the process. Take the matter of formality—giving and acknowledging commands and reporting data in exact prescribed terms. Inevitably, men became slack and took to slang or private jargon. Misunderstanding was bound to occur, and accidents had no better breeding ground than the haze of confusion.

Rickover turned briefly to some of the large issues confronting the navy and the nuclear propulsion program, but he came back again and again to the same theme. The commanding officers were well trained, and they had been given good ships. He was always accessible, day or night. His people were always available. But nothing could relieve the commanding officer of his responsibility.

His small audience seated around the table was intent. To many people in the navy Rickover was a legend, but to these officers he was not. They had been midshipmen when they first met him. All of them had gone through his schools and prototypes. All of them had been interviewed by him several times. All of them had been through the prospective commanding officers' course in his Washington office. Probably all had felt his fury over shortcomings. Doubtless some of them had reservations about his strictures on leadership and management—he suspected that they did. But they could not ignore the superiority of the nuclear navy to the nonnuclear navy. Better than most people they could evaluate the technical achievements and results.

Not until after the officers left did he have dinner. Usually he ate alone or with one or two of his people. Then he liked to talk about other issues. His thoughts turned to a recent speech of Chief Justice Warren E. Burger of the Supreme Court calling for a prolonged study of the three branches of government to see what revisions were necessary to make an eighteenth century heritage able to meet the demands of the twentieth century. Rickover, widely read and a close practical student of government, was intrigued by the idea. Certain fundamental changes were necessary, but he was not sure that study of the three branches would lead to anything except more studies. He was inclined to favor a constitutional convention. Although some people—press pundits and professors—were against the idea, he thought the natural good sense of the American people would prevent the establishment of any wild schemes. He did not think that Americans of today were less able than those of six generations ago. And nothing could do more to safeguard democracy and remove the alienation that so many people seemed to feel toward their government than their participation in restructuring it.

Reluctantly he dropped the topic. Tomorrow held more conferences with yard officials and the long flight back to Washington.

Whether a naval or a private yard, the audit technique was much the same. Differences between the two stemmed from the contractual nature of the arrangement with the private yard. Recommendations had to be couched more carefully; nothing must be proposed that might lead to a misinterpretation of a clause or an unwarranted conclusion that contract provisions were being modified. Nothing must be said that relieved a private company of its responsibility, or laid the foundation for financial claims to be levied later against the government. As far as technical matters were concerned—compliance with standards and procedures—the audit made no distinction between naval and private yards.

Operational Reactor Safeguards Examination

Formidable in the cool grey light of morning, the Polaris submarine steamed slowly up the harbor as a tug from the nearby naval yard closed the distance between them. As the two ships came together, a handful of officers from the tug leapt swiftly over to the submarine and were escorted below. As the tug went back toward the yard, the submarine turned toward the harbor mouth and the open sea.

The four visitors were to examine the material conditions of the propulsion plant and the ability of the nuclear-trained officers and men to meet their responsibilities. In the wardroom coffee cups and a huge tray of pastries lay on the green-covered table. The cups were filled immediately, but the pastries were waved aside. The captain, his executive officer, and his engineering officer talked with the four visitors about the schedule for the next few days.

Making sure that officers and men maintained their proficiency after completing their nuclear training was an old problem. In the early years of the program the Naval Reactors organization, chiefly under Theodore Rockwell, administered crew quizzes at different stages of a ship's career. The first was when construction of a ship was nearly completed; only when he was satisfied with the level of knowledge would Rickover give permission to bring the reactor to criticality. Another quiz was given after a ship was refueled; again Rickover had to be certain of the crew's competence before he would allow the plant to go critical. The third was a quiz of a crew of an operating ship. It was Rockwell's intent that the crew of every operational ship be examined every two years, but when he resigned in August of 1964, the number of ships was clearly becoming too great for Washington headquarters to maintain that schedule.

Something more had to be done if Rickover was to meet his responsibility of assuring safe operation of naval propulsion reactors. If his own organization could not do the job, another would have to take over. The logical solution was to use the officers of the nuclear fleet, for they had training and experience. Making the shift was not easy. Rickover, while recognizing that a change was needed, was reluctant to trust any other group on matters of safety. Naval organization was an obstacle. Rickover as an engineering duty officer had no naval authority over seagoing operational officers. On the other hand, as a commission official he had an obligation to ensure safe operators. By using the commission mandate, Wegner worked out a plan for transferring the task to the fleet while still maintaining Rickover's control. A board composed of nuclear-trained officers from the fleet would conduct the examinations. Rickover would select every member of the board and would receive a copy of the report. The increasing number of nuclear ships, and a schedule calling for an inspection of each one at least once a year, forced the establishment of a number of boards, three in the Atlantic and two in the Pacific. Most examinations were scheduled about six months in advance, although a ship with a poor record might be given only forty-eight hours' warning.

Four officers made up each board for submarines. A captain with at least one tour of duty as a commanding officer of a submarine was the senior member; the other three were lieutenant commanders who had been engineer officers. They graded the ship in six categories: operations; administration; radiation control and chemistry; material; cleanliness and stowage; and level of knowledge. On the basis of their findings in these areas they assigned an overall mark. Although the entire board had studied the results of earlier inspections of the ship, a junior member had drawn up the present examination. Because of his familiarity with the ship's record, he would act as the board's secretary. With the green baize cloth covering the wardroom table pushed aside and later removed, the team set to work.

Over the next four hours the wardroom table disappeared beneath files of reports, volumes of instructions, and technical manuals. Each team member, working with an officer or a leading petty officer, scanned the records. Certain phrases rose above the general hum of talk: "I want to see the long-range training plans." "The physical condition of the records ought to be better." "Show me the procedures you followed." "How did the problem manifest itself?" "Is this man's record incomplete?" "What did you do?" "Why?" "What do the instructions say?" The atmosphere was serious and businesslike, with no time for levity or jokes. When lunch interrupted work and ship's officers sat at the table, conversation turned to old friends and former duty stations; nothing was said about the course of the examination.

Immediately after the table was cleared, the senior board member and his colleagues took up the drill schedule with the commanding officer, the executive officer, and the engineer officer. The ground rules were firm. Nothing the board did relieved the commanding officer of his responsibility for the safety of his ship. If he and the two other officers saw an exercise going badly, they could stop it. If, for some valid reason, the commanding officer did not want to conduct a particular drill, he or the board could suggest another. Insofar as possible, the ship was to operate as if it were on a routine patrol. The board would not operate any equipment, answer any questions, nor issue any orders to any watchstander.

With a full understanding reached, the board went back to the propulsion-plant compartments. Although the pattern for each drill varied, one member was usually stationed in the reactor control area where the engineer officer of the watch was stationed; two others were assigned positions to observe activities; and the fourth was free to move about as necessary. Over the next several hours and into the night one drill followed another: a sudden reactor shutdown while the ship was submerged, a failure of some components, or a warning reading on some instrument. Every instance required a rapid analysis and a quick response on the part of the engine-room crew. The board members, having synchronized their watches, rushed from one place to another, noting times and actions.

Between drills the board members elaborated their notes. The senior member took intervals to conduct a material and cleanliness and stowage survey. On hands and knees, flashlight in hand, he crawled through bottom compartments, peering beneath bed plates, and getting into areas almost inaccessible. Accompanying him as best he could was a junior officer from the ship, jotting down notes. The inspection served two purposes: gaining information, and training a young officer.

With the drills completed, the board turned to assessing the training of the officers and crew. Each member was given an office or some secluded space where without distraction he could question selected personnel. The three junior members of the board examined enlisted men, usually one by one but occasionally taking two at a time if the subject and candidates under review were suitable. The officers told the men the ground rules, and warned them to answer questions without being influenced, for example, by the examiner making notes at one time and not another. Most of the enlisted men showed at least a trace of nervousness that the officer tried to dispel without, however, relaxing the businesslike atmosphere of the session. For the enlisted men the questions were practical: the plant was operating in a specified condition and some emergency occurred or some instrument gave an unusual reading—what would he do?

The senior member questioned separately two young officers who had qualified as engineer officers of the watch. In a formal atmosphere, they were asked questions that required a grasp of the theory behind the propulsion plant and an ability to derive mathematical answers.

To prepare its report, the board took over the ship's library, a long narrow compartment with a shelf-like table running along one bulkhead. Time pressed heavily, for the report had to be finished, even if only handwritten, before they left the ship. The senior member led the critique, but all four gave their assessments. Most of the time a combination of experience and technical knowledge made a prolonged discussion unnecessary and agreement on a grade came quickly, particularly on such matters as cleanliness and stowage. But disagreements had to be resolved. A member could not simply change his mind; he had to state the reasons for his position and either be persuaded by the others or persuade them. As was to be expected, differences were usually three to one. That, however, was not the important fact, for the one man might have been stationed in an area where he saw an action of particular significance that the others could not have seen.

Drills were the hardest to evaluate. With great care the members constructed from their notes a chronology of the steps the ship's company had taken for each evolution. The reason was simple. As one action followed another, the possibility of different interpretations increased. It was obviously unfair to mark a man down if what he was doing was correct on the basis of the information or command reaching him, even if it might not have been the best answer to the situation. As a consequence, the board called for volumes of manuals and instructions. As the hours went by, every flat surface in the library, including the deck, disappeared from sight. Eventually an enlisted man was stationed outside the door to bring the needed references. Even brief meals in the wardroom were discontinued; now trays were brought in as the work continued.

Well past midnight, hours after the ship had returned to port and moored alongside the tender, the board completed its report. The members and the ship's captain crossed over to the surface ship which, after the cramped quarters of the submarine, seemed huge and the passageways endless and deserted. The first of two conferences was held by the submarine squadron commander (to whom the submarine's commanding officer reported), the senior board member, and the commanding officer. In this group, matters as sensitive as personnel weaknesses and shortcomings could be discussed, and the captain had a chance to explain in private some of the problems from his perspective. In a larger meeting all the ship's nuclear-trained officers—the captain, executive officer, engineer, and engineer officers of the watch—met with the entire board. In more detail deficiencies were cited and the ship's officers given a chance to respond. Because Polaris submarines have two crews, the officers of the second crew were present to learn of the difficulties they might face on the next patrol. These men did not sit at the table and took no part in the proceedings.

In a few weeks Rickover got the formal report. As a rule summaries were enough for him, for he could not take the time to probe into details unless something unusual had been uncovered. A table divided into three columns listed the results of the previous examination, the present examination, and whether the ship had improved or not—the term for falling off was "degraded." On those rare occasions—and they existed—when a ship was above average in all categories, Rickover would offer congratulations along with a warning not to ease up and let things get slack. An above-average evaluation in all categories was proof to Rickover that the standards he levied could be met. Most often a ship had done well in some categories and not in others; in these instances he wanted to know the reasons for the degraded conditions. An attempt to answer on the telephone was never sufficient. He required the commanding officer to write him a special letter explaining the failures and detailing definite corrective actions. Promises to "do better" and "try harder" were never enough: Rickover wanted a specific written commitment. Knowing that Rickover would read the letter, the commanding officer had to analyze what had gone wrong.

Rickover was harshly critical of those men whose ships had fallen below average in several categories. Over the telephone he discharged a torrent of bitter language, casting doubts on the man's ability, intelligence, and strength of character. Two reasons lay behind the tirade. One was to pierce the man's defenses and to get him to think. The other was more personal. The officer had been given an opportunity and was failing to measure up; he had been given a responsibility and was falling short. To Rickover no greater crime existed than a betrayal of responsibility.

Radiation Control

From his first days at Oak Ridge in 1946, Rickover realized that the application of atomic energy to naval propulsion depended upon protecting the ships' personnel, the public, and the environment from radiation. Radiation was not an unknown danger. Soon after the discovery of X-rays in 1895, experience showed that large doses of ionizing radiation were harmful, and several scientific bodies had proposed limits to exposure. During World War II the atomic-energy program had created facilities and material that gave off radiation many orders of magnitude greater than X-ray sources. Rickover and the officers with him heard lectures describing types of survey instruments and personnel monitors and the need for trained, alert individuals capable of exercising initiative. Paul Hinshaw lectured on the pattern of irradiation injuries. Health physics, as protection of personnel against radiation had come to be called, was clearly a major discipline.[5]

Radiation affected not only the living but also the unborn. Rickover was particularly fascinated by the lectures of Hermann J. Muller. Before a public audience on 8 April 1947, the famous geneticist spoke of his experiments with the fruit fly, the slow course of evolution, and the harmful effects of the vast majority of mutations. Particularly applicable was Muller's observation: "We must, therefore, resolve not to let our birthright of human material, the product of countless past ages of striving, and beyond all things our most precious possession, be forfeited for immediate gains." In a smaller group the next day, Muller talked in a more technical vein of the genetic effects of radiation. To gain more knowledge Rickover visited Muller's laboratory at Indiana University at Bloomington, Indiana.[6]

Roughly speaking, protection against radiation from naval-reactor operation could be divided into three parts. One was the design and operation of the reactor to make sure that, insofar as humanly possible, no accident would cause a massive release of radiation. The second was the development of shielding to protect the ship's company, who had to live and work within a short distance of the reactor. The third was the prevention of contamination of the personnel and the environment of the shipyards, ports, and those facilities needed to support the naval nuclear propulsion program. All three areas were closely linked, but for the sake of simplicity, they are dealt with separately in the following paragraphs.

The importance of safe reactor design and operation was obvious, although the means for achieving these goals were not always clear and could never be taken for granted. To give advice on reactor design, operation, and site selection, the newly created Atomic Energy Commission in the fall of 1947 established a group of technical experts, first known as the Reactor Safeguards Committee, a decade later renamed the Advisory Committee on Reactor Safeguards and given statutory status. Over the years Naval Reactors and contractor engineers and physicists presented the details of the design and proposed operation of the land and shipboard reactors. Before each session Rickover and his men prepared meticulously, for nothing could have been more damaging than an adverse report. Although never as a routine matter, the committee found that the navy projects could be operated without undue risk and hazard, provided that in addition to meeting the technical standards, Naval Reactors continued to be responsible for the training of the operators.[7]

Shielding was an integral part of reactor design. At Oak Ridge Rickover and the men with him found that of all the elements of reactor technology, shielding had received the least analysis. Certainly the scientists and engineers of the Manhattan Project recognized the danger of radiation, but because they were not constrained by weight and space, they could reach empirical solutions and press on to more urgent tasks. For propulsion reactors, far more experimental data and material knowledge were necessary. Moreover, shielding design demanded a fundamental decision: how much radiation were the operators and associated personnel to receive? In the aircraft nuclear propulsion program, the air force decided that to decrease the weight of the proposed plane, the shielding would have to be cut and the crew would have to accept higher exposure. Rickover could have followed a similar course, for weight and space were serious concerns of marine engineers and naval architects. In a personal decision that marked the future of the naval nuclear propulsion program, Rickover determined that no one in the effort or associated with it would be exposed to radiation in excess of levels established by civilian authorities for civilian personnel.[8]

The decision was extremely important. It meant that the men in the nuclear ships would on the average receive only one-tenth the amount of radiation exposure they would average over their lives from natural background and medical X-rays. Had he decided otherwise—and in 1957 a chief of the Bureau of Ships proposed that he reduce the weight of the ships by decreasing the shielding—the outcry against the navy would doubtless have been so severe as to imperil the existence of the propulsion effort. He was very proud that the requirements he set for the Nautilus were so conservative that after a life of almost a quarter of a century, the ship could still meet radiation standards, even though these had become more stringent over the years. [9]

Rickover maintained his intense scrutiny of radiation exposure and in certain areas would delegate his responsibility to no one. A case in point were changes in the use of the space just outside the shielding, an area where men were not permitted to loiter, but which was suitable for certain uses such as storage. Occasionally a different use of this space was proposed. He insisted upon studying the plan, hearing the reasons for the change, and only when satisfied would he give his approval. He had, he once admitted, a subsidiary interest for investigating a proposal. Space on a ship was limited; change in one area had to be compensated for in another. As a rule, he remarked, it was the enlisted men who lost, and he would not permit that to happen without an excellent reason.

Radiation standards played an important part in the visits of nuclear-powered ships to ports. Nowhere was this role more evident than in the visit of the attack submarine Swordfish (SSN 579) to Sasebo, Japan. The ship entered the harbor on Thursday morning, 2 May 1968, and moored alongside the repair ship *Ajax* (AR 6). On Monday morning May 6, at 9:30, a small boat operated by the Japanese government, equipped with environmental monitoring instruments and manned by the Japanese Maritime Safety Agency, began circling the two ships, beginning at a distance of about thirty-five yards and spiraling outward. At 10:07 the instruments showed abnormally high readings—which were, however, a thousand times less than the radiation levels and radioactivity concentrations considered acceptable by the International Commission on Radiological Protection and the United States Federal Radiation Council. Ten minutes later the boat returned to the 10:07 A.M. position; readings were normal. Nonetheless, discharge of radioactive water from the ship into the harbor was a possible inference.[10]

The Japanese government promptly informed the American embassy, which immediately turned to Washington. The captain of the *Swordfish* stated on May 6 the ship had done nothing to cause the abnormal readings and on May 11 the ship departed to meet its operational commitments. U. Alexis Johnson, the American ambassador, asked for technical assistance on May 13. Three men from Naval Reactors arrived in Tokyo on May 15: William Wegner, deputy director; Murray E. Miles, chief, nuclear technology branch; and William L. Givens, special assistant to the deputy director. They were greeted by demonstrators.

For a week the three men, designated the technical review group, consulted with Japanese and American authorities and analyzed the data. As a base, they had a survey taken in April that showed no contamination. A careful analysis of water and bottom samples by the Japanese and Americans showed nothing abnormal. A board consisting of commission and navy personnel met the *Swordfish* at sea and examined records and questioned officers and crew. Everything confirmed the commanding officer's earlier statement and the conclusion of the technical groups: nothing the ship had done had caused the abnormal findings.

No satisfactory explanation was ever found for the event. Radar or welding could have caused spurious readings on the monitoring instruments; so could boat vibration, movement of the boat, or bumping by personnel. On the other hand the instruments might have picked up activity from radioisotopes discharged by a nearby hospital up the Sasebo River. Although the technical group could not eliminate these or other causes, they could conclude officially and without reservation that the *Swordfish* did not discharge radioactivity of any kind into the atmosphere or the surrounding waters. Political pressures, however, caused the Japanese government to suspend the visits of nuclear ships until October.

Americans, too, were deeply sensitive to the dangers of radiation. In September 1977 a former nuclear welder at the Portsmouth Naval Shipyard was admitted to the Veteran's Administration Hospital in Boston for diagnosis and treatment of possible aplastic anemia. Dr. Thomas Najarian, a hematologist, examined the man. The patient's records showed a radiation exposure during six years of work so low as to be a most unlikely cause of the illness. But because the patient remarked that so many of his coworkers had died at a comparably early age, Najarian decided to look into the matter. He faced certain handicaps. Under the regulations of the Veteran's Administration, a study, if he chose to do one, would have to be on his own time and with his own money. Najarian's first efforts led him to believe that the death rate was unusually high for men who had done nuclear work at the yard. Unable to carry on the study alone, he turned to the Boston *Globe* for assistance. Gaining his information mainly from death certificates, Najarian found ten definite leukemia deaths and reason to suspect an estimated additional twelve. That gave him a total of twenty-two deaths from leukemia where he expected the number would be five. On 19 February 1978, the Boston *Globe* broke the story.[11]

Congressman Paul G. Rogers, chairman of the subcommittee on health and environment of the House Committee on Interstate and Foreign Commerce, had already been holding hearings on the effects of low-level radiation on human health. The charges of the Boston *Globe* were clearly of interest. After Najarian, Rickover and Miles testified, explaining safety procedures and precautions, and showing that the records indicated that the radiation exposure a shipyard worker received was far below the national standard. Such was not to say that there were no problems, for radiation was always a problem. Triggered by a study of the effects of low-level radiation at Hanford, Washington, a Department of Energy nuclear facility, the navy had already begun a study of shipyard workers, but it would take time to complete. The Najarian effort would probably have had no impact because neither he nor the Boston *Globe* would release their data. At the end of the hearings Rogers and the subcommittee called for the Department of Health, Education and Welfare to investigate Portsmouth. The department turned to its Center for Disease Control and the National Institutes for Occupational Safety and Health.[12]

An unexpected development occurred near the end of the year. The Critical Mass Energy Project, an anti-nuclear group, got hold of an inspection report that Rickover had signed and that was highly critical of radiation control at Portsmouth. He had signed the report on 30 December 1977. On 28 February 1978 he had described to the Rogers subcommittee the strict shipyard controls that governed the exposure of Portsmouth and other shipyard personnel to radiation. Finding the report and the testimony difficult to reconcile, Rogers asked for an explanation. The cause of the contradiction was simple. As Rickover had testified, the yard was living up to the code of federal regulations governing the control of handling radioactive material. No matter how well any yard was doing, Rickover was certain it could do better.[13]

The Najarian-Boston *Globe* findings fell apart. In studying more complete data from navy records, Najarian, before a Senate subcommittee on 17 June 1979, testified he could not confirm his earlier findings; nonetheless, investigation of the effects of low-level radiation was important. In December 1980 the National Institute for Occupational Safety and Health and the Center for Disease Control completed its study. The study did not discover any relationship between exposure to radiation and mortality from any cause among the yard personnel when compared to the United States white male population. It did not observe any excess in leukemia mortality in radiation-exposed personnel when compared to non-radiation-exposed personnel of the yard.[14]

Frequently in his testimony before Congress, Rickover submitted two periodic reports: *Environmental Monitoring and Disposal of Radioactive Wastes from U.S. Naval Nuclear-Powered Ships and Their Support Facilities* and *Occupational Radiation Exposure from U.S. Naval Nuclear Propulsion Plants and Their Support Facilities*. The environmental report went back to 1959, although it only received wide distribution after 1965. The occupational radiation-exposure report first came out in 1978, partly to answer some of the questions raised by the Najarian allegations.

The environmental report of February 1982 showed that the navy had in operation 121 nuclear-powered submarines, twelve nuclear-powered surface ships, and support facilities consisting of eight shipyards, fifteen tenders, and three submarine bases. The total gamma radioactivity in liquids released in all ports and harbors from the program was less than 0.002 curies and less than 0.4 curies at sea in 1981, figures that had not changed in years despite the increasing number of ships. No increase of radioactivity above normal background levels had been detected in harbor or sea water anywhere, and while some radioactivity could be detected around a few operating bases and piers due to releases in the 1960s, the maximum activity observed was small compared to the naturally occurring radioactivity and was steadily declining. Conservative estimates of radioactive exposure to members of the public from sources within the program was a minute fraction of national and international standards and a minute fraction of the exposure from natural background radioactivity. The Environmental Protection Agency conducted independent surveys of American harbors to verify the navy's findings.[15]

Water samples, marine life, and debris had been collected from the two lost submarines, the *Thresher* and the *Scorpion*. The last survey of the *Thresher* in 1983 and the *Scorpion* in 1979 showed no evidence of release of radioactivity from the fuel elements; some radioactivity from other systems was detected in areas near the wreckage, but in small amounts compared to naturally occurring radioactivity.

Low-level solid radioactive waste materials—such as contaminated rags, plastic bags, and scrap material generated during ship maintenance—were packaged, shielded as necessary, and shipped to burial sites licensed by the Nuclear Regulatory Commission or a state. The 1982 report showed a five-fold reduction in the volume of these wastes produced each year since the late 1960s despite half again as many ships.

Data summarized by the occupational exposure report also set forth a notable record. From the beginning of the program about 118,000 shipyard workers and 54,000 naval officers and enlisted personnel had been monitored for radiation. None had exceeded the federal limit allowing five rem (roentgen equivalent man) exposure for each year beyond the age of eighteen. Since 1967 no person had exceeded the federal limit, which allowed up to three rem per quarter year, nor in that period had anyone exceeded the navy's self-imposed limit of five rem per year for radiation associated with naval nuclear propulsion plants.

Furthermore, the naval nuclear propulsion program had taken the lead in reducing the radiation exposure limits. Until 1965 the limits of external exposure in the United States and abroad were three rem per quarter year and five rem accumulated dose for each year beyond the age of eighteen. In that year the International Commission on Radiological Protection, while continuing to accept these standards, recommended that exposures exceeding five rem per year should be infrequent. Two years later the naval nuclear propulsion program accepted the recommendations as an upper limit. Over the years other bodies—the Atomic Energy Commission and its successor agencies, the Nuclear Regulatory Commission and the Environmental Protection Agency—either accepted that standard or recommended that it be followed.

The policy on exposure to internal radioactivity, from radioactive substances entering the body through air, water, or food and through surface contamination by the mouth, skin, or wound, was to reduce the amount as low as reasonably achievable. No civilian or military personnel in the naval nuclear propulsion program had ever received more than one-tenth the federal annual occupation exposure limit from internal radiation exposure caused by radioactivity associated with naval nuclear propulsion plants.[16]

Shippingport, an anomaly in the program in so far as its purpose was concerned, was scrutinized with equal thoroughness. Because the purpose of the station from its inception was to demonstrate the feasibility of nuclear power for civilian use, reports on the plant were handled under the procedures established by the Nuclear Regulatory Commission. The reports were made available to the public.[17]

Rickover could take personal credit for the record. The basic decisions that he had made at the beginning were crucial to protecting the personnel and the environment. He exerted continual pressure to reduce radiation exposure and to protect the environment. He assigned extremely

able people from his office to the effort: Theodore Rockwell, James W.
Vaughan, Jr., Murray E. Miles, and Paul D. Rice. He charged the field
office managers, laboratory directors, and shipyard commanders with a
special responsibility in radiation control. It was a record of which all
involved could be proud, but like so many aspects of nuclear technology,
the achievement was the consequence of constant and unremitting effort.

Three Mile Island

In the wake of the news from Three Mile Island, one of President Carter's
early actions was to establish a group to investigate and draw lessons
from the accident. Under its chairman, John Kemeny, the President's
Commission on the Accident at Three Mile Island heard, on 27 April
1979, the views of Dr. John Deutsch, director of energy research and
acting assistant secretary for energy technology for the Department of
Energy.

Deutsch had several points to make. The department's responsibility
for operational commercial nuclear power plants was very limited, for
regulation of design, construction, operation and maintenance, reliability
of quality assurance, and training were the functions of the Nuclear
Regulatory Commission. Nonetheless, because of its technical capabilities, the department had furnished emergency assistance, and because of
its responsibilities in developing nuclear reactors and managing nuclear
waste, the department had an obvious concern with the investigation of
Three Mile Island. Promising complete cooperation with the commission
and offering to do all he could to explain the department's activities at
the site of the accident, Deutsch had something else for the group to
consider—the outstanding record of the naval nuclear propulsion program under Rickover.

Deutsch had some firsthand acquaintance with the effort. A visit to
the Idaho site where he had observed the prototypes and schools had left
him with a vivid impression of the training Rickover insisted on for the
navy program. To the President's Commission on the Accident at Three
Mile Island he said of the naval nuclear propulsion program:

> It emphasizes training and education in a way that would be thoroughly
> astonishing to you if you were not already familiar to it. And I urge you, in the
> strongest possible terms, to take a look at that program. It is not enough to ask
> Admiral Rickover to come here and testify in front of you. Mr. Rickover is part
> of our organization but the Admiral will convey an incredible sense of what he
> does and how he does it, and the history that he brings with it. That will be
> important to you. I urge you to do it. But I also urge you to step beyond that
> and actually look and see what is involved in the technical depth of his
> organization, because it is there, in the training and education, continuity, and
> certification of operators, exercises, component testing, quality assurance, all
> of these items exist and I urge you to study that in some depth, which will give

you a contrast to the archetypal commercial power system where you have a utility working against regulation, or working with reference to regulation, to look at an organization which is built on integral engineering and technical competence throughout its whole pattern.

Kemeny soon came to the crucial question: Was it possible to apply the Rickover standards for naval operation to civilian power and still have a profitable industry? Admitting the different conditions, Deutsch believed it could be done.[18]

Kemeny and his commission met with Rickover and his senior engineers on 23 July 1979. Comparing commercial and naval reactor plants could yield useful lessons, Rickover thought, but great care had to be exercised in applying any specific methods or procedures from the naval program to civilian power. Furthermore, he warned against concentrating too much on technical detail and too little on broad causes. Again he stressed the need for understanding the technology of nuclear power by utility managers, plant designers, components designers and fabricators, architect-engineers, construction companies and their inspectors, and the engineers and technicians who assembled and tested the plant, as well as the people who maintained and calibrated the equipment and the operators. "Managers must get out of their offices and see what is really going on."

The design philosophy had to allow for operator errors. He had taken that aspect into account in the earliest days of his own program when he coined the phrase "sailor proof"—by which he meant that the plant had to be designed with the recognition that even well-trained sailors were not infallible. Emphasis in design should be on preventing accidents, not on coping with them after they occur.

At the Three Mile Island plant the number of alarms was far too great, and some sounded during routine operation; in this casual atmosphere plant operators lost the ability to recognize and respond to new problems or new conditions. In Rickover's plants he would not tolerate such conditions. It was not unusual for his reactors to operate for an extended period without any alarms, and to operate for an extended period with several alarms was unheard of. Formality and discipline had to be enforced. Only if they were upheld under routine conditions would they be present during an emergency. These qualities were difficult to achieve, especially when the plant was in steady operation and the operator had only to monitor what was going on and had little directly to do. At Three Mile Island boredom had set in, and without formality and discipline attention wandered, and the conditions were ripe for an accident.[19]

Aware that regaining public confidence would be difficult, Rickover turned to an idea he had proposed over the years: the best thing the utilities could do was to set up their own independent technical organization. They would still have to have their own technical competence; they could not abrogate that responsibility, but they would have a group to turn to for advice on the design, construction, and operation of nuclear plants and to enforce standards in training and operation. The new body could not be run by consensus nor by standards that were the lowest common denominator.[20] Although he did not say so, the philosophy of his proposal resembled closely the relations between his division and the yards, laboratories, and the nuclear fleet.

Rickover had already appeared before Congressman Mike Mc-Cormack's Subcommittee on Energy Research and Development of the House Committee on Science and Technology. On 24 May 1979, a crowded hearing room heard him describe his concept of total responsibility. He early recognized that the unique demands of nuclear power and its potential effect upon public safety meant that responsibility had to be unified. It could not be split between one man in the Atomic Energy Commission and another man in the navy. It would not work if one man in the commission was responsible for the program and another man in the commission responsible for the laboratories doing the research and development. It would not work, as was so often the case with the navy, if several admirals were in charge of different phases of the program. Compartmentalization of responsibility meant that no one was responsible. Turning to a sentence he had used often before, "Unless you can point your finger at the one person who is responsible when something goes wrong, then you have never had anyone really responsible."

From the beginning Rickover had recognized that nuclear propulsion demanded requirements and standards far more stringent than those then in use. He had to develop them in order to build propulsion plants that met the criteria of reliability, resistance to battle damage, high shock, and close proximity of the crew to the reactor plant. He had to be conservative. He listed several examples: simple system design with primary reliance on direct operator control instead of automatic control; land prototypes of the same design of the shipboard plant to test different operating conditions; extensive analyses, full-scale mockups, and tests; strict control of manufacture of all equipment, including extensive inspections by specially trained inspectors; detailed and extensive operating procedures and manuals prepared and approved by technically competent people knowledgeable of plant design; and frequent, thorough, and detailed audits of all aspects of the operation of naval nuclear-powered ships. Furthermore, aspects of the naval nuclear propulsion program were independently reviewed by the Nuclear Regulatory Commission and the Advisory Committee on Reactor Safeguards.

Training was at least as important as the other elements of his program. Mental abilities, qualities of judgment, and the level of training had to be commensurate with the responsibility of operating a nuclear reactor. He outlined briefly for the committee the main characteristics of his training program. Probably the best indication of the significance he gave to the subject was revealed in the division of his prepared statement; of 111 typewritten pages, 88 dealt with training.[21]

Testifying before the McCormack subcommittee and the Kemeny Commission he thought were useful steps and besides, with his prominence, he could not do otherwise. But something more direct was needed, and at his urging, Deutsch arranged a meeting between Rickover and a number of utilities executives from across the nation. For six hours on August 8 he sat across a table from them, explaining his philosophy and answering questions.

He thought the utilities had failed to give enough attention to technology. Although on the defensive now, they had to realize that nuclear power was an essential part of a complicated response to the energy crisis. But the utilities had to act fast to regain their credibility with the public.

Most of the executives agreed, but a few felt his approach could not be incorporated into their system. In the prevailing climate of criticism they had a tough time getting their story across. When applying for rate increases, they got publicity that made them seem as nothing but money grubbers, and attempts to break through this stereotype had usually been unsuccessful. Rickover was well aware of the problems. In the course of his career, Rickover had been the subject of much partisan and inaccurate reporting. Nonetheless, he thought that if stories clearly wrong in fact could be shown to newspaper executives, some results could be achieved. The utilities, he observed, were not without some political strength.

The best way to gain credibility was by achieving technical competence. He went back to the early days of the navy program when he set up a course that Westinghouse officials, including the chairman of the board, attended every Monday night for twenty weeks. He did the same for General Electric and his other major contractors, and he found the give and take good for them and for his own people. Of course, senior management could not have detailed technical knowledge, but they could acquire enough background to sense when they needed advice. (The lack of technical knowledge in senior management, he observed, was endemic throughout American senior management and a grave national weakness.)

Perhaps the utilities should establish a vice president who would have full responsibility for the nuclear plants of his company and for nothing else. He should have a staff technically competent in design and training and composed of men of high caliber with incentives to stay in the same job or area of specialization as long as possible. Without interrupting the meeting for lunch, Rickover went on to outline the way his office operated, how it depended upon reports, inspection, and training to gain and maintain technical competence, and he described the organization that he had outlined to the Kemeny Commission.

He spoke of several miscellaneous items: of the large size of the control room in commercial plants that made it impossible for any operator to know what was going on, of the number of alarms, of the dangers of relying on simulators for training. Of all the topics, none drew more attention than the plant representative he had stationed at Shippingport with authority to shut down the plant. One official did not like the idea of an outsider whose action could have so much effect upon other parts of the network. Rickover pointed out that since 1957 his representative had only had to shut down Shippingport twice. A Duquesne executive admitted that the requirement had not been onerous. Enforcing discipline upon a plant that was operating in steady state was hard, Rickover agreed, but it had to be done. His representative was on no account given any other job: nothing must distract him from his responsibility.

To see the training program in action, in October some of the executives visited the Naval Reactors facility in Idaho. The environment of single-minded dedication, arduous and exhausting as it was, gave at least some idea of Rickover's concept of what the utilities would have to do.[22]

In addition to appearing before the Kemeny Commission and Congress, Rickover received a private assignment directly from President Carter. Proud of his association with the early nuclear program, the president never concealed his admiration for Rickover. Since Carter had been in the White House, he and Rickover had occasionally exchanged views, usually in the Oval Office. On 31 May 1979, however, the president and his wife and daughter paid an unexpected visit to the Rickovers. During the conversation Carter asked Rickover to study the results of the investigation by the Kemeny Commission and summarize his own personal views. On December 1 Rickover sent his analysis to the president.

Studies of dam failures, industrial accidents, aircraft crashes, and shipwrecks often showed a pattern. A number of equipment failures and operator errors had preceded the event. Recognizing and correcting them could have prevented the accident. Three Mile Island showed the "classic" pattern. But the very nature of nuclear technology gave the added dimensions of exposure of people to radiation and its longtime consequences. The only solution was constant and unremitting discipline to keep the chain of events from forming that would lead inexorably to tragedy. That discipline should be exercised by an organization set up by the utilities and not by the government. Toward the end of his letter to Carter he wrote:

> Some have suggested that the success of naval nuclear power is a result of the discipline which can be enforced in a military environment, but which

cannot be achieved in a commercial nuclear environment. I do not agree. I believe that adequate discipline can be obtained in commercial nuclear power.

Discipline is an essential characteristic of any successful program and of any successful person. The discipline in the naval nuclear program has been successful not because this involves military applications, but because I have insisted upon staffing the program with intelligent, motivated people, whom I hold accountable. . . .

He was worried that the Three Mile Island accident would stimulate the government to spend vast sums of money on systems to prevent accidents. He warned Carter against such a false solution.

There has been too much emphasis on research and development in nuclear power and not enough on the daily drudgery of seeing that every aspect of nuclear power is in fact properly handled every day by each of the organizations involved. *That* is where the emphasis is needed.[23]

A Need for Spirit

He received a gracious letter from Kemeny, expressing appreciation for the time he had given them. Members of McCormack's subcommittee thanked him, and after his testimony, Rickover was surrounded by people who wanted to talk to him. Several utility executives thanked him by letters to him and to his superiors. President Carter, in a handwritten note, called Rickover's letter excellent, with many points that he would incorporate in a message to Congress and to the people.[24] But what influence did Rickover have?

He was frankly pessimistic. Even though he had shown that technical competence and discipline could be achieved, he did not think his example would be followed. Without his constant driving force, he did not think that the naval program would be successful; why should it be otherwise with civilian power? He did not mean that he himself was indispensable—but he was convinced that only technical competence and discipline could truly handle technology. The thought sounded like a cliche or truism, and yet anything less was shadow without substance, flesh without spirit.

No matter where an individual was in the naval nuclear
propulsion program—in Naval Reactors, the laboratories, the
contractor plants, the shipyards and the ships—the technology was
exacting. From one disgruntled commanding officer Admiral
Rickover received a letter stating that if nuclear propulsion was so

CHAPTER ELEVEN
Discipline of Technology

harsh in its demands, the navy would do well to find another
propulsion system. Rickover, tossing the letter aside for a moment,
remarked that technology brings its own discipline, a truth he was
not sure society understood.[1]

What he meant was quite simple: the stronger the forces of
nature harnessed by a technology, the more discipline was needed
by those who design, build, operate, and maintain the products of
that technology. Such discipline could only be exercised by a strong
technical group that was itself the product of that discipline. As
early as 1946, he realized that nuclear propulsion could not be
achieved by the usual navy or industrial organization. Accordingly,
he always took great care in recruiting, training, and creating the
conditions under which his people could work at their profession.

It would be possible to dismiss his philosophy as rationalization,
but the outstanding record of the program and the caliber of people
who remained with him for years suggests something else—the
discipline of technology was a vital force in the naval nuclear
propulsion program. More than once he observed that his was not
the only way of doing things; he was well aware that the program
was the product of unique circumstances. But if a technology was
one in which a failure could lead to catastrophe, following the
discipline of technology was crucial.

When the Bureau of Ships sent Rickover, four other officers, and three
civilians to join engineers from industry at Oak Ridge, it knew that its

ultimate goal was a propulsion reactor, one which would produce usable amounts of power reliably and safely and which could be operated by a navy crew. The question was not the goal, but how to achieve it. The main difference separating Rickover from the bureau was one of timing; Rickover believed the technology was sufficiently developed to embark upon a propulsion program, while the senior officers of the bureau were more cautious.

Through its production and research reactors brought into operation during the war, the Manhattan Project proved that a controlled chain reaction could be achieved and that the basic technology existed. But for ship propulsion the technology had to be developed for reactor fuel of long life and high integrity; materials that could withstand intense and prolonged radiation; a coolant that could remove heat expeditiously; and safe methods of reactor control. It was not a matter of meeting new technical requirements—these themselves had to be determined.

From his observations at Oak Ridge and from his own experience, Rickover was quickly convinced that nuclear propulsion demanded strong central control. Someone had to lay out the plant, set specifications and standards for materials and components, monitor tests, draw up schedules, and from all the diverse activities create a propulsion plant the likes of which had never been seen outside of fiction. Some legal problems had to be resolved. The Atomic Energy Act of 1946 had declared that research and development of atomic energy was the responsibility of the commission. On the other hand, the navy built ships. By adroit maneuvering, the help of others, and luck, Rickover was assigned to both agencies to develop naval nuclear propulsion. From that position he could follow one of two courses: either he or a contractor could run the program. He had no difficulty making that decision.

Obviously, he could not do the entire job himself. The organization he built was based, explicitly in parts and implicitly in others, on two premises. Reactor technology was complicated and intolerant of ignorance or error, and he had to have men around him to enable him to exercise the control he thought essential.

As a nucleus he sought those men whom he knew. The officers who were with him at Oak Ridge, Lieutenant Commander Louis H. Roddis, Jr., Lieutenant Commander James M. Dunford, Lieutenant Commander Miles A. Libbey, and Lieutenant Raymond H. Dick, were young, promising, and possessed technical backgrounds. He called back individuals, among them I. Harry Mandil and Robert Panoff, who had worked under him during the war when he ran the electrical section of the Bureau of Ships. He called back men with whom he had served who had the special abilities he was seeking: Paul E. Dignan, who as a chief petty officer had been under his command on the China Station; and John F. O'Grady, a former enlisted man whose unorthodox methods of operation had produced startling results in Okinawa during the war. Without hesitation Rickover interrupted careers: Dignan had won a commission and was about to crown his career by realizing the ambition of every officer—command of a ship. O'Grady had returned to civilian life and had before him a most promising business venture. He came to the program only because his mother was persuaded by Rickover of the importance of the effort. Both men performed Herculean tasks in seeing that components were produced and delivered on schedule. Rickover chose no man because of friendship, but because the individual would work hard and had the potential to grow.[2]

Dignan and O'Grady were examples of individuals selected to fulfill tasks to support the technical work, and for that same reason Rickover gradually established a group in Naval Reactors for contract and fiscal matters. The intent was control, not independence, although Naval Reactors exercised initiatives to a far greater degree and with far more speed than most government agencies. The commission furnished funds to develop the propulsion plant, but it had to fit into a ship the navy had authorized and had received appropriations to build. Other practical reasons dictated against independence—some household jobs Naval Reactors did not want to be bothered with, preferring to leave them to the navy or to the commission in order to concentrate on technical work. Reactor technology shaped Naval Reactors into a lean, flat, and flexible organization.

The Rickover Role

Rickover saw Naval Reactors as an extension of himself; there was never any doubt in his mind—nor in the minds of others—who was in charge. As his reputation and that of the naval nuclear propulsion program grew, he received requests from various sources—among them government officials, leaders of industry, and editors of business publications—to explain how he ran a large and successful enterprise. To those asking for articles he usually gave a contemptuous refusal, but once in a great while he would ask a member of his staff to draw up a brief piece, checking it over carefully, however, before it was released. Before congressional committees he was more expansive; he wanted them to understand how he worked because he frequently needed their help. He was at his best, however, in talking in his office to a few individuals about his job. All three sources are useful in revealing how he saw his role.

For the September 1979 issue of *Management Magazine* Rickover reluctantly provided an article, "Management in Government." Characteristically, he observed that he did not think the piece would do much good. Senior civilians in the government had been trained to believe that anyone well versed in a few rules for handling people and situations could administer any program, no matter how sophisticated the technology. Those individuals who survived and advanced were the ones most adroit in laying the blame for failure elsewhere. This was the type of management that caused citizens to lose faith in their government.

In a series of paragraphs, each with a heading in bold type, Rickover listed the qualities necessary for a leader of a technical program. He should feel that he personally owned the job, and he should accept responsibility—which meant a willingness to be personally identified when things went wrong. He had to know what was going on, to work out some simple and direct way of keeping informed, and to have the means for an independent review. He had to get into details, for when they were ignored a project could slide into failure so fast that no policy decisions, however astute, could resurrect it. He had to face facts—to recognize failure for what it was and not continue, hoping that somehow things would work out.[3]

The article was not inspiring. No one could doubt that following its precepts could lead to more effective management, for who could deny the value of working hard, accepting responsibility, establishing priorities, facing facts, and knowing what was going on? Even the injunction to get into details, while avoiding those that were trivial, was sound. But all the piece did was to tell a manager what he should do, not how he should do it. The article offered no blueprint, no formula, no organization chart. That was because Rickover believed such precepts were false and dangerous. By training men to know their jobs and to do them well, all else would fall into place.

He had tried to make that point years before when Americans, shocked by the Russian Sputnik and their own well-publicized failures in space, were seeking a way to catch up. Senator Lyndon B. Johnson, chairman of the preparedness investigating subcommittee of the Committee on Armed Services, had adopted the space program as his special interest. In late 1957 and early 1958 Johnson held hearings in which he sought the views of leaders in industry, universities, and government as to what should be done.

Eleven senators were present on 6 January 1958 when Rickover began his testimony in executive session. Following him, the schedule called for eight men from the army and navy who held jobs of importance in research and development. These men included Lieutenant General James M. Gavin, chief of the office of research and development, office of the chief of staff, U.S. Army; Major General John B. Medaris, commander, Army Ballistic-Missile Agency; and Assistant Secretary of the Navy (Air) Garrison Norton. All were men with distinguished records.

Rickover did not have a prepared statement. All he proposed to do was to explain how he ran the naval nuclear propulsion program and answer questions. He spoke of the need for the government to have people at least as capable as those in industry; never, he warned, should a contractor dominate a government project. In his view the subcommittee was preoccupied with organization. That was the easiest part of the program. The real difficulty was finding a good man, for perhaps only ten to fifteen people in the United States were qualified to run a major research and development program. Find the man, protect him from trivia, and judge him by the results he achieved. The key to success was finding potentially good people and training them. That was what he did.

His audience was somewhat dismayed and bewildered. Johnson wondered how good people were to be obtained if the committee did not study successful organizations and see how they were operated. Senator Prescott Bush pointed out that many competent witnesses had spoken of the need for new organization concepts. Johnson came back to the argument that troubled him. He had some sympathy with Rickover's view of the importance of people, but he did not agree that they could work effectively without good organization. He admitted that many reorganizations created entities more cumbersome than their predecessors. That, however, did not mean that reorganizing was wrong; just that it had not been done right.[4]

If Sputnik was a shock to the public, so was the Three Mile Island accident twenty-one years later. On 24 May 1979, Rickover testified on reactor power plant safety systems before the subcommittee on energy research and production of the House Committee on Science and Technology. For this hearing he had a lengthy prepared statement for the record, which set forth the basic principles of the Naval Reactors program. Again and again he came back to the imperative necessity of training people in their jobs.

> Properly running a sophisticated technical program requires a fundamental understanding of and commitment to the technical aspects of the job and a willingness to pay infinite attention to the technical details. I might add, infinite personal attention. This can only be done by one who understands the details and their implications. The phrase, "The devil is in the details" is especially true for technical work. If you ignore those details and attempt to rely on management techniques or gimmicks you will surely end up with a system that is unmanageable, and problems will be immensely more difficult to solve. At Naval Reactors, I take individuals who are good engineers and make them into managers. They do not manage by gimmicks but rather by knowledge, logic, common sense, and hard work and experience.[5]

While Rickover could be extremely eloquent in testimony on management, for it was a subject on which he had strong feelings, he was his most philosophic in the informality of his office, particularly at the end of the business day. In the early evening the telephone rang less often; all but one of the secretaries in the outer office had left; and none of his men were waiting to see him. Leaning back in his battered rocking chair, placing a foot on the desk, which even at this hour was still heaped high with papers he had yet to scan, he would speculate about the causes behind some event that had happened at one of the laboratories or at Naval Reactors.

His job was to find out what had to be done and sweep away as much of the intervening detail as possible. Neither task was simple. Rickover held a person responsible for his job and saw that he did it. But giving someone a task meant seeing that the man had the conditions in which to work and that he was protected from interference—particularly important in government service where procedures were so bureaucratic. Rickover's job was to force a man to think about his work; that was the reason for inspections and reports—to make a person assess where he was, where he had been, and where he was going. Rickover saw himself as a traffic cop directing the flow of work. Rickover described himself as a chief of a tribe, who had to see that the fires were never allowed to die. One of the hardest things anyone had to learn was that the job was never done. Every day the cave had to be swept.

On behalf of the program—and the stipulation is important—he demanded much from his people. He tried to focus all the activities of Naval Reactors on the work to be done, for work and nothing but work was the nexus. He had virtually no social relationships with anyone in the program, for he believed that they created false situations. Too many times he had seen a leader put a friend in a subordinate position only to find that both men were apt to let personal feelings warp technical judgments, often with the result that neither the technical work nor the friendship endured. On the other hand, he was always available on technical matters or when a person was in personal difficulties. Somewhat to his surprise, he found that wholehearted concentration on the work stimulated and challenged people. Many stayed in the program for years. When he left, the hundred most senior people had been with the program for an average of fifteen years, and the twenty division heads averaged twenty years. Because of continuity, training, and experience, Rickover saw Naval Reactors as an island of excellence in a sea of mediocrity.[6]

Factors for Success

Good people are attracted to a successful program and tend to remain with it for years. In the course of this study, a number of individuals were asked for their views on the factors that led to the program's success. The following paragraphs endeavor to summarize their opinions. None of those who voiced their thoughts are responsible for the interpretation placed upon them here. Furthermore, in a program and organization so complex, an attempt to list and sort out the factors inevitably fails, for all are woven together, and separating them can no more convey their spirit than plans or drawings can capture the power and beauty of a ship at sea.

The program had a strong leader. Rickover was not an individual who, in a routine move, had been assigned to take charge of a program already in existence. In contrast, he schemed and fought to bring the nuclear propulsion program into being, tying himself so closely to the effort that to many minds they became almost identical. Without doubt his personal determination was a leading factor in the success of the program. If it succeeded, he succeeded; if it failed, he failed.

He drove himself hard. At one time the General Accounting Office, unable to believe that he could have visited so many places in only a few days, thoroughly audited his travel records and found out that he was indeed attending the many meetings in the places and at the times he reported. Jimmy Carter never forgot the sight of Rickover constantly working during a long and weary flight to the National Reactor Testing Station. Without his personal commitment, Rickover could not have required so much from his people.

Leadership implies a goal, and a goal implies movement, resulting at times in failures and at times in successes. In human terms, some people can adapt to the demands of a certain type of leadership and others cannot. At best, Rickover was a difficult man to work for. He did not hesitate to require the sacrifice of personal and domestic plans that might have been made and approved long ago. In argument he could be loud, vociferous, and abusive. Not surprisingly, he lost some people. A few were simply bad choices, but others were not. Although excellent in their jobs, they left because of personal clashes with Rickover or perhaps because they were unwilling to accept the inroads on their personal lives. Others departed after years of hard and outstanding work because they wanted to try something different or something that might be more rewarding financially. None of the reasons for leaving were peculiar to the naval nuclear propulsion program, and not all of the departures were dramatic or stormy.

The spirit of Naval Reactors was another facet to the success of the program. This spirit was manifest from the first interview with Rickover and with the emphasis on training in the practical aspects of reactor technology. In the early years of the program, Rickover helped set up the Oak Ridge School of Reactor Technology. He visited the people he sent there to find out not only how they were doing, but if the instructors were good and the curriculum sound. He persuaded the Massachusetts Institute of Technology, which had long taught naval officers marine engineering and naval architecture, to begin a course on nuclear engineering. Again the emphasis had to be upon the practical. In later years when he sent his new engineers to the school he established at Bettis, he required them to write him a letter detailing what they had learned and giving their views on the quality of the courses and teachers. On the return of the students, he met and questioned them. Although a young engineer might not talk to Rickover again for several years, he was aware that he had entered a closely knit organization, one that had high spirit and morale.[7]

A new engineer was given a small area of responsibility and a chance to advance. Because Rickover insisted upon talking directly to the individual who knew the most about a problem, direct contact with him could be unexpected and sometimes bruising. As the individual's responsibility increased, however, the more contact he had with Rickover. Earning his confidence was a long, slow, and arduous affair. The quotation from Dante, "All hope abandon, ye who enter here" inscribed over his office door, and the portrait of St. Apollonia holding a freshly extracted tooth in pincers (she was the patron saint of dentists) while looking fixedly at the observer, were tokens that sessions with Rickover could be tough.

It was not always easy to understand what he was driving at because he himself might not know, only sensing that something was wrong. By probing deeply beneath appearances, he either confirmed his suspicions or allayed his fears. In these sessions Rickover drew a line between technical matters and those he called "political," the latter category dealing with schedule and budgetary considerations. He wanted technical recommendations unmuddied by other factors—they might be so important as to have to govern, but that was his responsibility. Insofar as possible, engineering came first.

For that reason those who accepted Rickover's method of operating found Naval Reactors an exhilarating place to work. He was accessible, but once into a problem it was hard to get him out. He was open to new ideas, but they had better be backed with technical justification. He could be convinced, although the struggle might be long. Rickover was always pressing for improvement and never content to just meet minimum standards—the lead that Naval Reactors took in radiation control was but one example. He would inspect, he would read reports, he would read letters. He was anything but a dictator who pontificated over technical matters. It was not that he would back a man he knew was right—valuable as that was—but he would back a man whose judgment he had learned to trust on an issue whose outcome could not be predicted.

Rickover's insistence upon the highest standards of engineering was a challenge many found hard to resist. Engineering is a difficult and demanding profession, a mixture of hard facts mixed with unknowns and uncertainties and leavened with all the inconsistencies of human nature. The chance to follow the profession to the extent it was practiced in the naval nuclear propulsion program was rare. It was easy enough to declare that nuclear technology demanded engineering integrity; living up to that principle required discipline.

Strong leadership, high morale, and stress on engineering led to lengthy terms of service in the program, a factor that Rickover and others in Naval Reactors considered cardinal to its success. Rickover, indeed, was convinced that continuity was an essential part of the discipline of technology. Yet that aspect was not part of the initial effort, but resulted from circumstances that could not have been predicted.

To turn to Rickover first, from the time he graduated from the Naval Academy in 1922 he had held increasingly responsible positions ashore and afloat, moving from one assignment to another every few years. That normal pattern was broken in the summer of 1953 when Congress saved him from retirement and forced the navy to promote him to rear admiral. It was Congress again that caused his promotion to vice admiral in 1958 and prevented the navy from retiring him as regulations required in January 1964. He had to be reappointed every two years after 1964; and although that action was never an absolute certainty, because of the political alliances he had built up and the undeniable achievements of the program he remained in charge for the next eighteen years.[8] In December 1973, Congress forced his final promotion to full admiral.

The length of service of his engineers evolved differently, however. With an expanding program Rickover could no longer be content with the number of naval officers he could obtain, nor could they risk their careers by serving too long in Naval Reactors. He also had to find some better way to recruit civilians than the informal method he had been following. In 1957 he began taking men from units of the Naval Reserve Officers Training Corps at the better engineering schools. These men had made a commitment to remain in the navy for four or five years and were willing to spend that period in Naval Reactors. During this time they not only got intensive training but a chance to participate in a program they thought was important. Most of the section heads in later years were men who had chosen to remain after their terms of naval service had expired. The long initial commitment had given them a chance to know the work thoroughly before they decided to stay. Long association with each other did not mean that strong disputes over technical recommendations did not take place, but the common training, the goal, and acceptance of engineering integrity meant that clashes did not have the petty bureaucratic features so often characteristic of other parts of the government.

Remaining with the program brought another satisfaction. Many people found a fascination in being part of a project at its inception—

Shippingport, for example—seeing it develop and operate, and knowing how the technical decisions and struggles that had taken place worked out in practice. Over the years their jobs might have changed, but their knowledge of the project remained.

One point has yet to be mentioned. The challenges and opportunities of engineering at the forefront of a technology were not enough in themselves to have held those who remained and found themselves working long hours and frequent weekends as well as having occasionally stormy sessions with Rickover. What wove all the strands together was the conviction that the naval nuclear propulsion program was important to the nation. To use a word that has become rusted and dulled through disuse, a strong element of patriotism ran through the length and breadth of the effort.

The Shield

In the abstract it seems obvious that in a technical program engineering should hold prime importance. In Naval Reactors engineering was more than an ideal, for in its name Rickover selected his own people, ran his own schools, shifted the work in the organization as he thought the situation demanded, and created and maintained an organization to handle fiscal, contractual, and logistic affairs. He had two laboratories that had no assignments save those received from Naval Reactors: the needs of the program did not have to vie for priorities and staff in a multipurpose installation. He was able to give life to his concept of total responsibility.

Again and again program personnel spoke of the shield he erected under which they could get quick decisions and fast action, and which protected them from the bureaucratic trivia that so often plague government enterprises. The first step in building that protection came from the initiative he seized at Oak Ridge in learning all that he could about reactor technology. His knowledge, his combative spirit, shrewdness, and record of accomplishment enabled him to gain control of the effort in the navy, while the confusion and uncertain organization in the early Atomic Energy Commission gave him opportunity. The brilliant way in which he and his advisors used their dual responsibility to the commission and its successor agencies and to the navy was an indispensable element. So, too, were his relations with Congress, with the joint committee and its successor bodies, as well as with the authorization and appropriations committees.

The shield evolved as the program evolved, but the principle remained the same. To protect the naval nuclear propulsion program from the military, Rickover called upon his allies in Congress for help. When the Atomic Energy Commission was abolished and many of its functions transferred first to the Energy Research and Development Administration and later to the Department of Energy, the legislation creating both agencies specifically provided that the naval nuclear propulsion program remain under civilian control. In the apparently mundane task of drawing up position descriptions, Rickover's authority was carefully scrutinized to prevent any erosion of his responsibilities. Honed by abrasive struggles dating back to the first efforts to get the program established, Naval Reactors had the experience to foresee bureaucratic and organizational stratagems as they arose and the adeptness to forestall them.[9]

Protection was far more than marking off areas of responsibility in official documents; the effort also took care and diplomacy on the part of all members of Naval Reactors. Once the program had garnered its first successes and gathered momentum, Rickover and those associated with him gained tremendous influence. Individuals representing the program had to exercise caution so as not to make any commitments they could not carry through. For his part Rickover and his advisors were wary of taking on an issue they could not win. Nevertheless, their call for an investigation of possible fraudulent claims of shipbuilders against the government was one instance where they embarked upon a major fight, the outcome of which they could not foresee.[10]

If it was the shield that allowed the excellence of engineering to flourish, it was the excellence of engineering that justified the shield. Neither could exist without the other.

Criticism

Conceivably, the factors that led to the success of the program and to the existence of the shield could also have produced stagnation and sterility. Other programs that originally flourished have met such a fate when that which produced success was allowed to become "law." Rickover and Naval Reactors, with their grip on naval nuclear propulsion development, have been accused of blocking improvements, most particularly in failing to produce a small, light, cheap reactor. To many individuals in the navy, the civilian secretariat, and the defense establishment, it seems most implausible that some other type than pressurized water has not evolved that would be better for ship propulsion.

The candidates usually proposed—sometimes with considerable influence behind them—are gas-cooled, liquid metal-cooled, and organic-moderated approaches. Each concept was considered extensively by Naval Reactors and the laboratories and found unsuitable for naval ship propulsion. Studies and reactor experiments in non-navy development programs showed the gas-cooled reactor required an impossibly high degree of fuel integrity. For the *Seawolf,* Naval Reactors had developed and operated a liquid-metal land prototype and a shipboard plant, recognizing that the system was corrosive and its coolant highly radioactive. Although the reactors worked, pressurized water was far better suited for ship propulsion. After extensive evaluation, Naval Reactors found that the predicted advantages of the organic concept were illusory, and under radiation the coolant broke down into a tar-like substance that fouled heat-transfer surfaces.

Even if one believes that Naval Reactors was governed by self-interest in continuing to find pressurized-water reactors superior for naval combatant ships, it is hard to overlook the use of this type, not only in other navies, but in civilian power programs worldwide. Although there can be no certainty that a new approach will not appear, its advantages would have to be very significant to overcome the demonstrated reliability of pressurized-water reactors and the investment in development, production, maintenance, processing, and training facilities.

An alternative to small, light, cheap reactors—smaller, lighter, and cheaper nuclear-powered ships—could be built, but at the sacrifice of such items as habitability, shielding, and spare components.

As of 31 January 1982, the naval nuclear program had accumulated over 2,300 reactor years of operation. Since the *Nautilus* first went to sea in January 1955, nuclear ships had steamed over 49 million miles. The ballistic missile submarines had completed 2,000 patrols since the *George Washington*, the first Polaris submarine, went to sea at the end of 1960. About 40 percent of the navy's major combatant ships were nuclear powered. Over 8,400 officers and 44,500 enlisted men had been trained in the nuclear program. And since the beginning of the program, there had never been an accident involving a naval reactor nor a release of radioactivity to the environment that had adversely affected public health or safety.[11]

A Question of Personality

Individuals who knew Rickover well over the years might question whether the discipline of technology—not yet defined—or simply his own personal way of running things shaped the naval nuclear propulsion program. Every job he had held since he graduated in 1922 from the Naval Academy he had handled the same way, involving himself directly in the work, driving his men hard, training them, and giving them responsibility as soon as they could absorb it. He had achieved results. He was the youngest engineer officer in his destroyer squadron of eighteen ships— a duty he was given when he was about a year out of the Academy. He raised the battleship *New Mexico* from near the bottom in engineering efficiency to first place. He made an outstanding record as head of the electrical section of the Bureau of Ships during World War II. He had circumvented hierarchy and ignored protocol and etiquette to get the job done and, in the process, risked his career. Without doubt, his direction of the naval nuclear propulsion program showed these same traits.

The similarity between the pre-nuclear and nuclear phases of Rickover's career suggests that his approach had produced results in different environments. If that were the case, it gave grounds for thinking his principles could be effective elsewhere.

Application

Although Rickover acknowledged that the development of nuclear propulsion was inevitable and that his was not the only way to run a program, he believed that his management principles could be applied elsewhere. What he and Naval Reactors pointed to with pride as their special contribution was the superb record of operation and safety. That record he considered the true measure of the effectiveness of the principles he and Naval Reactors brought to the naval nuclear propulsion program.

Primacy of engineering and total responsibility were absent when three men were killed in a nuclear accident occurring in a small army power reactor; at the core meltdown at Three Mile Island; and in the construction and operating flaws that sapped public confidence in the civilian nuclear-power program. As in other areas of life, accidents happen and people die or the environment suffers grievous damage. The possibility of casualties increases as the population grows, gathers in greater density, and demands more and more from diminishing resources. If the risks to humanity and to the quality of life is to decline, the discipline of technology must govern.

Institutionalization

To many people it seemed as if Naval Reactors, the naval nuclear propulsion program, and Rickover were identical. Implicit in this assumption was doubt that the principles that had created the discipline of technology could be transferred from one leader to another. Rickover himself was not certain.

At the end of 1981 John H. Lehman, secretary of the navy, abruptly announced that Rickover would not be reappointed for "actuarial" reasons, a reference to the fact that 27 January 1982 would see Rickover's eighty-second birthday. By agreement, the navy and the Department of Energy selected Admiral Kinnaird R. McKee to lead the program. An Academy graduate of the class of 1951, McKee served in eight diesel-electric submarines and commanded a small experimental craft before he was interviewed and selected by Rickover for the nuclear program. In 1958 McKee completed his nuclear-power training and helped place the *Skipjack* in commission. After serving in her, he became executive officer of the *Nautilus* in 1961 and a year later of the Polaris submarine *Sam*

Houston. He spent 1964 to 1966 in Naval Reactors before his assignment to command the submarine *Dace.* During his three years in the *Dace,* the ship was twice awarded the Naval Unit Commendation. He served in increasingly responsible positions, becoming a vice admiral in 1978. McKee was an officer experienced in nuclear-submarine operations and in high command when he succeeded Rickover on 1 February 1982.

Some codification and definition of the program was essential. President Ronald Reagan signed executive order 12344, effective 1 February 1982, which spelled out the organization of the nuclear propulsion program. Its dual nature continued: McKee was responsible to the Department of Energy and to the navy. He was to serve eight years, although the secretary of energy and the secretary of the navy by mutual agreement could terminate or extend the appointment. He was advanced to the grade of full admiral. (Congress confirmed this action in March.) He was to supervise directly Bettis and Knolls, the prototypes, and other facilities. He was to be responsible for the safe operation of the nuclear propulsion plants. He was to report to the commander, Naval Sea Systems Command under the chief of Naval Material Command as the deputy commander, nuclear propulsion directorate; to the assistant secretary for nuclear energy in the Department of Energy as the deputy assistant secretary for naval reactors with direct access to the secretary of energy; and to the chief of naval operations as the director, naval nuclear propulsion program. He was to have direct access to the secretary of the navy and other senior officials in the department concerning matters relating to the program, and to all government officials who supervised, operated, or maintained naval nuclear propulsion plants.[12]

To the Senate and House Armed Services Committees McKee pledged his commitment:

> There will be no reductions in standards, or changes in the proven practices that have been instrumental in achieving the level of competence and technical integrity we currently enjoy in every aspect of the program.[13]

Pragmatic evidence that the discipline of technology continued can be found in two crucial facts: two years after McKee made this statement, nearly all of the senior men Rickover had selected and trained were remaining, and younger men who had spent years attaining mastery of technical subjects were staying with the program. Perhaps more than Rickover himself realized, he had institutionalized the principles that had governed the nuclear propulsion program.

The Discipline of Technology

Technology is the means of applying the resources of nature to the uses of man. The catalysts are the men and women who in ages past first brought a cutting edge to a stone, and their descendants who design homes, automobiles, aircraft, communications satellites, and nuclear propulsion plants. By their actions they assume a responsibility. In a primitive society a technological failure may have grave but limited consequences. In a modern society consequences can be catastrophic.

Only by adopting the discipline of technology did Rickover see a way to minimize the possibility of disaster. Many times he tried to express this thought: "Technology knows no rank"; "Technology will not yield to leadership"; "Technology will not obey an order"; and "You can't argue with technology."

The aphorisms might have little direct meaning for a manufacturer of many everyday products, or for most people doing paperwork in offices, but to men developing products at the forefront of an advanced technology they cannot be so easily set aside. The success of the naval nuclear propulsion program cannot be readily dismissed. The discipline of technology means that the organization must adapt to the technology, and not the technology to the organization. For advanced development, data are never complete, particularly if the product of a complex technology is to operate at high standards for years. The discipline of technology requires exhaustive testing of materials and components to determine the laws of nature. If these are not absolute in the sequestered atmosphere of scientific laboratories or research centers, there is no reason to expect they are better known on the shop floor. The discipline of technology requires thorough and deep consideration of the match between the product and its use, and intense analysis of the present and anticipated future conditions of operation.

The discipline of technology raises moral and ethical questions. Technological development undertaken as a profit-making venture can bring about circumstances involving ethical considerations when goals slip far beyond their schedules and when cost estimates soar far over budget. The operation of highly complex machinery without proper maintenance and training can also raise similar questions. The discipline of technology can make sad reading in the balance sheet and in the annual report to the stockholders. But so can newspaper headlines about accidents caused by the poor design of a component or the faulty training of an operator.

Rickover was convinced that the discipline of technology was essential to the survival of society. He thought it unfortunate that those who benefited most from technology usually accepted its benefits without question, indeed almost as a right. No force penetrated more deeply into a society than technology nor was more active in transforming it. Yet the dangers of technology and its flawed products raised serious questions. A society based on technology but alienated from it was dangerously divided.

Rickover did not see the discipline of technology as a denial of human nature. He did not care what a person did off duty so long as the activity did not interfere with the performance of his work or bring the program into disrepute. But more important, the discipline of technology conferred upon an individual the greatest challenge of all—acceptance of responsibility.

> Responsibility is a unique concept: it can only reside and inhere in a single individual. You may share it with others, but your portion is not diminished. You may delegate it, but it is still with you. Even if you do not recognize it or admit its presence, you cannot escape it. If responsibility is rightfully yours, no evasion, or ignorance or passing the blame can shift the burden to someone else. Unless you can point your finger at the man who is responsible when something goes wrong, then you have never had anyone really responsible.[14]

APPENDIX ONE
Design and Engineering Principles

The following paragraphs are excerpted from Joint Economic Committee, *Economics of Defense Policy,* Adm. H. G. Rickover, Part 1, 97th Congress, 2d Sess. (Washington, G.P.O, 1982), p. 74.

Because a warship must be able to perform its mission and return under combat conditions, the nuclear propulsion plant therefore must be engineered to survive battle damage and severe shock; to operate reliably and safely in close proximity to the crew; and to be repaired at sea by the crew if necessary. Standards for materials and systems are rigorous and only premium products with a proven pedigree are used in the reactor to minimize maintenance and take maximum advantage of long core lives.

Building and operating effective naval nuclear propulsion plants involves many engineering and design considerations. The following are important tenets of the program's engineering philosophy:

Avoid committing ships and crews to highly developmental and untried systems and concepts.

Ensure adequate redundancy in design so that the plant can accommodate, without damage to ship or crew, equipment or system failures that inevitably will occur.

Minimize the need for operator action to accommodate expected transients. If the plant is inherently stable, the operator is better able to respond to unusual transients.

Simplify system design so as to be able to rely primarily on direct operator control rather than on automatic control.

Select only materials proven by experience for the type of application intended and insofar as practicable, those that provide the best margin for error in procurement, fabrication, and maintenance.

Require suppliers to conduct extensive accelerated life testing of critical reactor systems components to ensure design adequacy prior to operational use.

Test new reactor designs by use of a land-based prototype of the same design as the shipboard plant. Prototype plants can be subjected to the potential transients a shipboard plant will experience, so problems can be identified and resolved prior to operation of the shipboard plant.

Train operators on actual operating reactors at the prototypes. Simulators are not an acceptable training device for naval operators.

Confirm reactor and equipment design through extensive analyses, full-scale mockups, and tests.

Use specially trained inspectors and extensive inspections during manufacture; accept only equipment that meets specification requirements.

Concentrate on designing, building and operating the plants so as to prevent accidents, not just cope with accidents that could occur.

APPENDIX TWO
Naval Reactors
Organization as of 1982

SECTION HEADS	SECTION NAME	YEAR ENTERED PROGRAM
Charles H. Brown, Jr.	Director, Instrumentation & Control Division	1965
Walter P. Engel	Director, Reactor Safety & Computation Division	1958
Alan G. Forssell	Director, Surface Ship Systems Division	1956
Mark Forssell	Director, Submarine Systems Division	1955
Thomas L. Foster	Director for Fiscal, Acquisition & Logistics Management	1963
Souren Hanessian	Program Manager for Trident & Advanced Submarine Projects	1957
Paul W. Hayes	Director, Submarine Systems (S5W & S8G) Division	1954
William M. Hewitt	Director, Secondary Components Division	1958
Wiliam S. Humphrey	Director, Reactor Refueling Division	1954
James A. Palmer	Program Manager for Surface Ships & Water Cooled Breeder	1962
Gerald H. Prudom	Program Manager for Prototype & Shippingport Atomic Power Station Operations	1969

SECTION HEADS	SECTION NAME	YEAR ENTERED PROGRAM
David B. Pye	Director, Reactor Engineering Division	1963
Harry F Raab	Chief Physicist	1951
Paul D. Rice	Director, Nuclear Technology Division	1966
Gene L. Rogers	Program Manager for Commissioned Submarines	1954
John W. Sadler	Director, Nuclear Components Division	1962
Carl H. Schmitt	Executive Assistant for Security, Public & Foreign Matters	1965
David G. Scott	Program Manager for Shipyard Matters	1958
Robert H. Steele	Director, Reactor Materials Division	1958
John W. Vaughan, Jr.	Deputy Director	1957
Robert A. Woodberry	Director, Reactor Plant Valve Division	1970

APPENDIX THREE
Executive Branch Organization

Chief Executive—1958–1982

PRESIDENTS

Dwight D. Eisenhower	Jan. 1953–Jan. 1961
John F. Kennedy	Jan. 1961–Nov. 1963
Lyndon B. Johnson	Nov. 1963–Jan. 1969
Richard M. Nixon	Jan. 1969–Aug. 1974
Gerald R. Ford	Aug. 1974–Jan. 1977
Jimmy Carter	Jan. 1977–Jan. 1981
Ronald Reagan	Jan. 1981–

Department of Defense—1957–1982

SECRETARIES

Neil H. McElroy	Oct. 1957–Dec. 1959
Thomas S. Gates, Jr.	Dec. 1959–Jan. 1961
Robert S. McNamara	Jan. 1961–Feb. 1968
Clark M. Clifford	Mar. 1968–Jan. 1969
Melvin R. Laird	Jan. 1969–Jan. 1973
Elliott L. Richardson	Jan. 1973–May 1973
James R. Schlesinger	July 1973–Nov. 1975
Donald H. Rumsfeld	Nov. 1975–Jan. 1977
Harold Brown	Jan. 1977–Jan. 1981
Casper Weinberger	Jan. 1981–

Department of the Navy—1957–1982
SECRETARIES

Thomas S. Gates, Jr.	April 1957–June 1959
William B. Franke	June 1959–Jan. 1961
John B. Connally, Jr.	Jan. 1961–Dec. 1961
Fred Korth	Jan. 1962–Nov. 1963
Paul H. Nitze	Nov. 1963–June 1967
Paul R. Ignatius	Sept. 1967–Jan. 1969
John H. Chafee	Jan. 1969–May 1972
John W. Warner	May 1972–April 1974
J. William Middendorf III	June 1974–Jan. 1977
W. Graham Claytor, Jr.	Feb. 1977–July 1979
Edward Hidalgo	July 1979–Jan. 1981
John F. Lehman	Feb. 1981–

Naval Operations—1955–1982
CHIEFS

Admiral Arleigh A. Burke	Aug. 1955–Aug. 1961
Admiral George W. Anderson, Jr.	Aug. 1961–Aug. 1963
Admiral David L. McDonald	Aug. 1963–Aug. 1967
Admiral Thomas H. Moorer	Aug. 1967–Aug. 1970
Admiral Elmo R. Zumwalt, Jr.	Aug. 1970–June 1974
Admiral James L. Holloway III	June 1974–July 1978
Admiral Thomas B. Hayward	July 1978–July 1982
Admiral James D. Watkins	July 1982–

Bureau of Ships—1955–1966
CHIEFS

Rear Admiral Albert G. Mumma	April 1955–April 1959
Rear Admiral Ralph K. James	April 1959–April 1963
Rear Admiral William A. Brockett	April 1963–Jan. 1966
Rear Admiral Edward J. Fahy	Feb. 1966–May 1966

Naval Ship Systems Command—1966–1974
COMMANDERS

Rear Admiral Edward J. Fahy	May 1966–July 1969
Rear Admiral Nathan Sonenshein	July 1969–July 1972
Vice Admiral Robert C. Gooding	Aug. 1972–June 1974

Naval Sea Systems Command—1974–1982
COMMANDERS

Vice Admiral Robert C. Gooding	June 1974–Aug. 1976
Vice Admiral Clarence R. Bryan	Aug. 1976–March 1980
Vice Admiral Eugene B. Fowler	March 1980–

Atomic Energy Commission—1958–1975
CHAIRMEN

John A. McCone	July 1958–Jan. 1961
Glenn T. Seaborg	March 1961–Aug. 1971
James R. Schlesinger	Aug. 1971–Jan. 1973
Dixy Lee Ray	Feb. 1973–Jan. 1975

Energy Research and Development Administration—1974–1977
DIRECTOR

Robert C. Seamans	Dec. 1974–Jan. 1977

Department of Energy—1977–1982
SECRETARIES

James R. Schlesinger	Aug. 1977–Aug. 1979
Charles W. Duncan, Jr.	Aug. 1979–Jan. 1981
James B. Edwards	Jan. 1981–Nov. 1982

APPENDIX FOUR
Reactor Plant Designations, Prototypes, and Shipboard Plants (August 1985)

[*Note: Reactor plant designations usually consist of two letters and an intervening numeral. The first letter indicates purpose:*
    A = Aircraft carrier
    C = Cruiser
    D = Destroyer (Frigate)
    S = Submarine

The numeral indicates the model of that type of plant by the designer. The second letter indicates designer.
    W = Westinghouse (Bettis)
. G = General Electric (Knolls)
    C = Combustion Engineering

There are some exceptions.
    NR-1 = Naval Reactors 1, a research vehicle
    PWR = Pressurized-Water Reactor at Shippingport, Pennsylvania
    LWBR = Light-Water Breeder Reactor at Shippingport, Pennsylvania

Prototypes are located at one of three sites: National Engineering Station, Idaho Falls, Idaho; West Milton, New York; and Windsor, Connecticut.]

Land Prototypes

DESIGNATION	SHIP DEVELOPED FOR	LOCATION	DATE INITIAL CRITICALITY
A1W (2 reactors)	*Enterprise*	Idaho	(1) 21 Oct. 1958 (2) 10 July 1959
D1G	*Bainbridge*	West Milton	28 March 1962
S1C	*Tullibee*	Windsor	16 Dec. 1959
S1G	*Seawolf*	West Milton	20 March 1955
S1W	*Nautilus*	Idaho	30 March 1953
S3G	*Triton*	West Milton	18 Aug. 1958
S5G	*Narwhal*	Idaho	12 Sept. 1965
Modifications & Additions to Reactor Facilities (MARF)		West Milton	9 Oct. 1976
S8G	*Ohio*	West Milton	12 Dec. 1978

Shipboard Plants

DESIGNATION	# REACTORS PER PLANT	LEAD SHIP OF CLASS	SHIPS APPROPRIATED
A2W	8	*Enterprise*	1
A4W/A1G	2	*Nimitz*	6
C1W	2	*Long Beach*	1
D2G	2	*Bainbridge*	1
		Truxtun	1
		California	2
		Virginia	4
S2C	1	*Tullibee*	1
S2G	1	*Seawolf*	1
S4G	2	*Triton*	1
S5G	1	*Narwhal*	1
S6G	1	*Los Angeles*	48
S8G	1	*Ohio*	12
S2W	1	*Nautilus*	1
S3W	1	*Skate*	2
		Halibut	1
S4W	1	*Swordfish*	2

Shipboard Plants

DESIGNATION	# REACTORS PER PLANT	LEAD SHIP OF CLASS	SHIPS APPROPRIATED
S5W	1	*Skipjack*	5[1]
		Thresher	13[2]
		Sturgeon	37
		Glenard P. Lipscomb	1
		George Washington	5
		Ethan Allen	5
		Benjamin Franklin/ Lafayette	31

1. Does not include the *Scorpion*, lost May 1968.
2. Does not include the *Thresher*, lost April 1963.

Nuclear-Powered Ships Authorized Construction by Yard as of June 1985

General Dynamics (Electric Boat Division) (1952–Present)[1]

SUBMARINES

Attack	37[2]
Polaris	17[3]
Trident	5
Radar Picket	1[4]
Hunter-Killer	1
Research Vehicle	1

General Dynamics (Quincy) (1961–68)

SUBMARINES

Attack	4

SURFACE SHIPS

Cruisers	2

Newport News Shipbuilding & Dry Dock Co. (1958–Present)

SUBMARINES

Attack	22
Polaris	14[3]

SURFACE SHIPS

Carriers	4
Cruisers	6

Mare Island Naval Shipyard (1956–1972)

SUBMARINES

Attack	9
Polaris	7
Regulus	1[4]

Ingalls Shipbuilding Corp. (1958–1973)

SUBMARINES

Attack	12[5]

Portsmouth Naval Shipyard (1956–1971)

SUBMARINES

Attack	7[6]
Polaris	3[7]

New York Shipbuilding Corp. (1960–1967)

SUBMARINES

Attack	4[5]

SURFACE SHIPS

Cruisers	1

Total Commissioned Nuclear Ships as of June, 1985

SUBMARINES

Attack	95[8]
Polaris	32
Trident	5
Research Vehicle	1

SURFACE SHIPS

Cruisers	9
Carriers	4

Notes:
1. First year after the yard's name is when keel of first ship laid; second year is when last ship was commissioned.
2. Includes *Scorpion,* lost May 1968.
3. Includes four decommissioned.
4. Decommissioned.
5. Includes one laid down at New York Shipbuilding but completed at Ingalls.
6. Includes *Thresher,* lost April 1963.
7. Includes one decommissioned.
8. Includes one hunter-killer.

Source:
Data from "A Review of the United States Naval Nuclear Propulsion Program—June 1985," NRD.

Important Dates In Shippingport Atomic Power Station History

9 July 1953	AEC assigned civilian power project to Admiral H. G. Rickover and naval nuclear propulsion program.
September 1953	Alvin Radkowsky, chief physicist of Naval Reactors, proposed "seed-blanket" reactor core design for civilian power project.
9 October 1953	Westinghouse Corporation contracted with AEC to design, fabricate, assemble, and test reactor and primary heat system.
18 March 1954	Effective date of Duquesne Light Company contract with which it agreed to provide site, construct turbine-generator portion of plant, and operate and maintain entire facility.
6 September 1954	President Eisenhower initiated ground breaking for Shippingport Atomic Power Station.
26 April 1955	Admiral Rickover decided on uranium dioxide clad with zircaloy for blanket elements—a decision influencing civilian reactor development.
6 October 1957	Reactor core installed and construction of plant essentially complete.
2 December 1957	Shippingport Atomic Power Station reached criticality for first time.

18 December 1957	The first electricity generated by Shippingport transmitted through Duquesne Light Company's system to consumers.
23 December 1957	Shippingport reached net capacity of 60 electrical megawatts.
20 November 1962	AEC sent to President John F. Kennedy its *Civilian Nuclear Power . . . a Report to the President—1962*, which emphasized breeder reactors for commercial usage.
19 March 1963	Bettis Atomic Power Laboratory (Westinghouse) forwarded to Washington interim report stating breeding might be feasible in light-water moderated and cooled reactor.
1 January 1965	AEC and state of California reached general understanding on large seed-blanket reactor, with a central core to investigate possibility of breeding, to produce power for irrigation system in California.
25 September 1965	Shippingport reached full power of 150 electrical megawatts on core 2 seed 1.
20 December 1965	Admiral Rickover recommended to AEC that California drop the project because of anomalies in fuel testing, and instead use Shippingport for breeder experiment.
4 February 1974	Shippingport shut down on core 2 seed 2 due to extensive turbine vibration; steps begun for upgrading plant in preparation for LWBR.
26 August 1977	Shippingport reached criticality with breeder reactor for first time.
2 December 1977	Shippingport went to routine full power on 60 electrical megawatt light-water breeder reactor. (*Note:* See 2 Dec. 1957.)
20 May 1980	American Society of Mechanical Engineers recognized Shippingport Atomic Power Station as National Historical Engineering Landmark.
1 October 1982	Shippingport Atomic Power Station shut down for last time.

Abbreviations of Sources Cited in Notes

AEC	Records of the Atomic Energy Commission, Department of Energy, Washington, D.C.
BAPL	Bettis Atomic Power Laboratory, West Mifflin, Pennsylvania
CNO	Records of the Chief of Naval Operations, Department of Navy, Washington, D.C.
DDE	Dwight David Eisenhower Library, Abilene, Kansas
DLC	Duquesne Light Company, Pittsburgh, Pennsylvania
DOS	Department of State, Washington, D.C.
JFK	John Fitzgerald Kennedy Library, Boston, Massachusetts
LBJ	Lyndon Baines Johnson Library, Austin, Texas
NARA	National Archives and Records Administration, Washington, D.C.
NAVORD	Records of the Naval Ordnance Command, now part of Naval Sea Systems Command, Arlington, Virginia
NAVSEA	Records of the Naval Sea Systems Command, Arlington, Virginia
NAVSHIPS	Records of the Naval Ship Systems Command, now part of Naval Sea Systems Command, Arlington, Virginia
NHC	Records of the Naval Historical Center, Department of the Navy, Washington, D.C.
NRD	Records of the Naval Reactors Division, Department of Energy, Washington, D.C.

Notes

Chapter 1. Common Denominators

1. Quincy *Patriot Ledger*, 2 Dec. 1957; Boston *Daily Globe*, 2 Dec. 1957; *New York Times*, 3 Dec. 1957; Pittsburgh *Sun-Telegraph*, 2 Dec. 1957; *New York Times*, 3 Dec. 1957; Pittsburgh *Post Gazette*, 3 Dec. 1957; AEC Press Release No. 1228, 2 Dec. 1957, AEC; Shippingport Atomic Power Station, Graph Indicating "Initial Approach to Criticality," 2 Dec. 1957, DLC; Richard G. Hewlett and Francis Duncan, *Nuclear Navy: 1946–1962* (Chicago: University of Chicago Press, 1974), p. 254.
2. Richard G. Hewlett and Oscar E. Anderson, Jr., *The New World, 1939–1946*, vol. 1 of *A History of the U.S. Atomic Energy Commission* (University Park: Pennsylvania State University Press, 1962), pp. 111–12.
3. Lewis L. Strauss to president, 2 Dec. 1957, DDE.
4. Deck Log of the USS *Nautilus* (SS(N) 571), 2 Dec. 1957, CNO; William R. Anderson with Clay Blair, Jr., *Nautilus 90 North* (New York: World, 1959), pp. 62, 69, 85–86, 94–97.
5. Probably the best date for the inception of the naval nuclear propulsion program is June 1946 when the navy's Bureau of Ships arranged for contracts to study heat-transfer characteristics of sodium-potassium alloys and sodium-potassium, and sent five officers—including Rickover—and three civilians to study reactor technology at Oak Ridge. However, the joint program was not effective until early 1949. See Hewlett and Duncan, *Nuclear Navy*, pp. 28–35.
6. Ibid., pp. 132–34.
7. For a useful summary of the relationship see: Navy-AEC Relationships in the Naval Reactors Program, Oct. 1961, pp. 1–2, NRD.
8. The History Division of the U.S. Department of Energy has many publications available upon the history of the Atomic Energy Commission and its successor agencies. Three helpful for our purposes are: Alice L. Buck, *A History of the Atomic Energy Commission*, July 1983, DOE/ES-0003/1; Alice L. Buck, *A History of the Energy Research and Development Administration*, March 1982, DOE/ES-0001; and Jack M. Holl, *The United States Department of Energy: A History*, November 1982, DOE/ES-0004. For a history of the Navy Department reorganizations, see: Edwin B. Hooper, *The Navy Department: Evolution and Fragmentation* (Washington: Naval Historical Foundation, 1978); The Evolution of the Naval Sea Systems

Command, 1842 to Present, *NAVSEA*; Hewlett and Duncan, *Nuclear Navy*, pp. 362–66.

9. Hewlett and Duncan, *Nuclear Navy*, pp. 39–40, 98, 234, 239, 282–87, 352–56. For the status of the program at the end of 1957, see AEC, *Progress in Peaceful Uses of Atomic Energy, July–Dec. 1957* (Washington: Government Printing Office [hereafter cited as G.P.O.], Jan. 1958), pp. 293–95 and Appendix 8, *Nuclear Reactors Built, Building or Planned*, pp. 358–59. At the testing station the S1W prototype for the *Nautilus* was in operation and the A1W prototype for an aircraft carrier and cruiser was under construction. At West Milton the S1G prototype for the *Seawolf* was being dismantled and the D1G prototype for a destroyer was under design and would be built in the same structure. The S3G prototype for a submarine was under construction. The prototype being built at Windsor was the S1C, for a small submarine.

10. The number of personnel is from AEC Telephone Directory, Sept. 1957, AEC.

11. AEC Telephone Directory, Sept. 1957, AEC; Hewlett and Duncan, *Nuclear Navy*, pp. 397–98; AEC, *Progress in Peaceful Uses of Atomic Energy, July–December 1957*, pp. 315–16; document, "Admiral Rickover's Responsibilities," undated but typed 24 Jan. 1964; chief of naval personnel to Rickover, 14 Nov. 1955, NRD.

12. Hermann Bauer, *Das Unterseeboot* (Berlin, Germany: Verlag Von E. S. Mittler & Sohn, 1931). The book, translated by Rickover in 1936, is still on the shelves of the Naval Sea Systems Command Technical Library in an unpublished form. The biographical information in this section is based upon conversations with Admiral Rickover and upon his personal papers. Norman Polmar and Thomas B. Allen, *Rickover: Controversy and Genius, A Biography* (New York: Simon and Schuster, 1982), must be used with great caution.

13. For engineering standing, see Office of Chief of Naval Operations (Division of Fleet Training), *Report of Engineering Performance 1934–1935, United States Navy F.T.P. 153* (Washington: G.P.O., 1935), Table 4, Analysis of Performance; and the *Report of Engineering Performance 1935–36*, p. 3 and *1936–37*, p. 3.

14. For Engineering Duty Only, see Julius A. Furer, *Administration of the Navy Department in World War II* (Washington: G.P.O., 1959), pp. 236–37.

15. For ship overhaul, see "Reminiscences of Vice Admiral William P. Mack, USN (Ret.), Interviews Conducted by the U.S. Naval Institute," vol. 3, p. 115, NHC. For an account of their travels, see Ruth Masters Rickover, *Pepper, Rice, and Elephants* (Annapolis: Naval Institute Press, 1975).

16. For a very useful history of the section, see *Electrical Section History*, NAVSHIPS 250-660-24 (Washington: Navy Department, Bureau of Ships, undated but 1946), pp. 38–42.

17. The activities are well described in *Electrical Section History*. For Pearl Harbor, see Homer N. Wallin, *Pearl Harbor: Why, How, Fleet Salvage and Final Appraisal* (Washington: Naval History Division, 1968), pp. 230–31.

18. W. P. Welch, *Mechanical Shock on Naval Vessels*, NAVSHIPS 250-660-26 (Washington: G.P.O., 1946), pp. v–vi. The introduction refers to the shock resistance program energetically prosecuted by the Bureau of Ships, especially the electrical section. Rickover is given special acknowledgment for his constant interest in promoting the program.

19. *Electrical Section History*, pp. 38, 43–52.

20. Hewlett and Duncan, *Nuclear Navy*, pp. 28–33, 35–38, 52–58, 60–67, 74–76, 86–87; Clay Blair, Jr., *The Atomic Submarine and Admiral Rickover* (New York: Holt, Rinehart & Winston, 1954), pp. 19–22.

21. The early stages of the program are covered in the first chapters of *Nuclear Navy*. On the crucial nature of Rickover's principles, see Captain John W. Crawford, Jr.,

USN (Ret.), "Get 'em Young and Train 'em Right," U.S. Naval Institute, *Proceedings* (Oct. 1987): 103–8.

22. For the promotion struggle, see Hewlett and Duncan, *Nuclear Navy*, pp. 186–93. Admiral Elmo R. Zumwalt, Jr., chief of naval operations 1970–74 in his *On Watch: A Memoir* (New York: Quadrangle/Times Books, 1976), p. 98, writes that many middle-grade officers did not think Rickover's career should end in 1953.

23. This is a very brief and incomplete summary of a very complex process. Helpful accounts are: Subcommittee of the House Committee on Government Operations, *The Budget Process in the Federal Government*, 85th Cong., 1st sess. (Washington: G.P.O., 1957), pp. 5–8; Aaron Wildavsky, *The Politics of the Budgeting Process* (Boston: Little, Brown, 1979), Appendix, "Procedures," pp. 181–99; Alain C. Enthoven and K. Wayne Smith, *How Much is Enough?* (New York: Harper & Row, 1971), pp. 76–77; Carl W. Borklund, *The Department of Defense* (New York: Praeger, 1968), pp. 78–88. For a brief and helpful description of the congressional process, see John R. Blandford, "Testifying Before Congressional Committees," U.S. Naval Institute *Proceedings* 81 (March 1955): pp. 295–99.

24. Navy-AEC Relationships in the Naval Reactors Program, Oct. 1961, pp. 4–5, NRD.

Chapter 2. Submarines

Two useful books on submarine development are: Norman Friedman, *Submarine Design and Development* (Annapolis, MD: Naval Institute Press, 1984), and Norman Polmar, *Atomic Submarines* (New York: D. Van Nostrand, 1963). The end papers of the latter illustrate very well the relationship of one type to another.

1. H. G. Rickover to Jean (Scroggins), 10 March 1959, NRD. For press coverage, see as examples the *New London Day*, 10 March 1959; the *Washington Post* and *Times Herald*, 11 March 1959, the *New York Times*, 11 March 1959.

2. For *Skipjack*, see Norman Polmar, *Atomic Submarines* (New York: D. Van Nostrand, 1963), pp. 142–44; Norman Friedman, *Submarine Design and Development* (Annapolis, Md.: Naval Institute Press, 1984), p. 12

3. Richard G. Hewlett and Francis Duncan, *Nuclear Navy: 1946–1962* (Chicago: University of Chicago Press, 1974), pp. 281–87. The number of S5W submarines is from John E. Moore, ed., *Jane's Fighting Ships: 1977–78* (New York: Franklin Watts, 1977), pp. 551, 553–54, 557, and 559–60, and includes two lost at sea.

4. Hewlett and Duncan, *Nuclear Navy*, Appendix 2, "Construction of the Nuclear Navy, 1952–1962," p. 399; Polmar, *Atomic Submarines*, p. 153.

5. Harvey Brooks to G. W. Anderson, Jr., USN, 10 July 1962, NRD.

6. For a discussion on noise and a reactor, see Norman Friedman, *Submarine Design,* pp. 81–82, 136. For a discussion of the importance of acoustics, see Lt. P. Kevin Peppe, USN, "Acoustic Showdown for the SSN's," U.S. Naval Institute *Proceedings* 113 (July 1987), 33–37. Peppe received second honorable mention in the Arleigh Burke Essay Contest.

7. The Naval Nuclear Propulsion Program—A Joint AEC–Department of the Navy Program, March 1967, pp. 17–18, NRD.

8. Polmar, *Atomic Submarines*, pp. 151–53; Friedman, *Submarine Design*, pp. 73–74.

9. Subcommittee of the House Committee on Appropriations, *Atomic Energy Commission Appropriations for 1960*, 86th Cong., 1st sess. (Washington: G.P.O., 1959), p. 173; The Naval Nuclear Propulsion Program—A Joint AEC–Department of the Navy Program, March 1967, p. 23, NRD.

10. For reference to the Department of Defense letter, see H. G. Rickover to Frank K. Pittman, 25 Feb. 1959; The Naval Nuclear Propulsion Program—A Joint AEC–Department of the Navy Program, March 1967, p. 23, NRD.

11. H. G. Rickover to Frank K. Pittman, 25 Feb. 1959; F. K. Pittman to A. R. Luedecke, 26 Feb. 1959; The Naval Nuclear Propulsion Program—A Joint AEC–Department of the Navy Program, March 1967, p. 23, all in NRD.

12. W. C. Barnes, Report of Conference, Natural Circulation Reactor (NCR) Project [on] 11 May 1959, NRD.

13. The issue is summed up in John F. Floberg, Memorandum for the File, 3 Sept. 1959, AEC.

14. Natural Circulation Reactor Test Plant Progress Report, Oct. 1959–Jan. 1960, KAPL 3000-1, p. v; S5G Project Progress Report No. 1, Aug.–Sept. 1960, p. 1; The Naval Nuclear Propulsion Program—A Joint AEC–Department of the Navy Program, March 1967, p. 23, NRD.

15. For reference to the prototype schedule see the following AEC documents: *Annual Report to Congress of the AEC for 1960* (Washington: G.P.O., Jan. 1961), p. 146; *Major Activities in the Atomic Energy Programs Jan.–Dec. 1961* (Washington: G.P.O., Jan. 1962), p. 152; and *Annual Report to Congress of the AEC for 1962* (Washington: G.P.O., Jan. 1963), p. 188.

16. Hewlett and Duncan, *Nuclear Navy*, p. 173.

17. William M. Hewitt, notes entitled "8/25/71 NARWHAL info mtg.," NRD.

18. S5G Progress Report, 16 Dec. 1962–15 Feb. 1963, KAPL-3001-11, p. VI.3; S5G Progress Report, 16 Feb.–15 April 1963, KAPL-3001-12, p. VI.3; S5G Progress Report, 16 April–15 June 1963, KAPL-3001-13, p. VI.3. The Electric Boat Division, General Dynamics Corp. reports are: S5G Project Progress Report No. 18, Oct.–Nov. 1962, p. 42; S5G Project Progress Report No. 19, Dec. 1962–Jan. 1963, pp. 41–42; S5G Project Progress Report No. 20, Feb.–March 1963, pp. 46–47; S5G Project Progress Report No. 21, April–May 1963, pp. 44–45, NRD. Hewitt, notes entitled "8/25/71 NARWHAL info mtg.," NRD. For reference to the schedule, see AEC, *Major Activities in the Atomic Energy Programs, Jan.–Dec. 1961* (Washington: G.P.O., Jan. 1962), p. 152.

19. General Dynamics Electric Boat Division, S5G Project Progress Report No. 29, Nov., Dec. 1964 and Jan. 1965, pp. 3–5, 25, 42; S5G/S5G-2 Progress Report No. 30, Feb., March, and April 1965, pp. 3, 21, 42; S5G/S5G-2 Progress Report No. 31, May, June, and July 1965, pp. 1–2, 21; S5G/SSN671 Progress Report No. 32, Aug., Sept., and Oct. 1965, p. 1; S5G Progress Report, 16 Dec. 1964–15 March 1965, KAPL 3001-21, p. ix; S5G Progress Report, 16 March–15 June 1965, KAPL 3001-22, pp. ix, xi; S5G Progress Report, 16 June–15 Sept. 1965, KAPL-3001-23, p. ix; S5G Progress Report, 16 June–7 Dec. 1966, KAPL-3001-27, p. ix; S5G Progress Report, 8 March–7 June 1967, KAPL-3001-29, pp. ix-x; The Naval Nuclear Propulsion Program—A Joint AEC–Department of the Navy Program, March 1967, p. 23, NRD.

20. Moore, *Jane's Fighting Ships: 1984–85*, p. 652.

21. For Rickover's testimony, see Subcommittee of the House Committee on Appropriations, *Department of Defense Appropriations for 1965 Part 5*, 88th Cong., 2d sess. (Washington: G.P.O., 1964), pp. 454–56. For McNamara's views, see David L. McDonald, Memorandum for the Vice Chief et al., 27 April 1964, NRD. After the Bettis visit, Rickover prepared a letter for McNamara to sign which among other things asked the commission to emphasize the development of a fast escort submarine. See draft of a letter from: Robert S. McNamara to Glenn T. Seaborg, transmitted by letter from Glenn T. Seaborg to Robert S. McNamara, 29 April 1964, NRD. In his letter to Seaborg on 1 May 1964, NRD, McNamara stated that he found the visit most informative and that he supported enthusiastically the development work of the commission on surface ships and submarines. Joint

mittee on Atomic Energy (hereafter cited as JCAE), *Nuclear Submarines of Advanced Design*, 90th Cong., 2d sess. (Washington: G.P.O., 1968), Appendix 1, "High Speed Submarine Chronology," p. 42. See also undated Chronology—Fast Escort Submarine, NRD. Copies of all documents cited in the chronologies are in NRD.

22. Joint Committee, *Nuclear Submarines of Advanced Design*, Appendix 2, "Turbine Electric Drive Chronology," p. 69; undated chronology, Fast Escort Submarine, NRD.

23. JCAE, *Nuclear Submarines of Advanced Design*, Appendix 1, pp. 42–43; T. A. Hendrickson to manager, Schenectady Naval Reactors Office, 16 March 1965, and encl., "Report of Conference [held] March 9 and 10, 1965 — C-015," NRD.

24. Chief, Bureau of Ships to chief of naval operations, 17 March 1965; undated Chronology, Turbine Electric Drive Submarine, NRD.

25. Paul H. Nitze, Memorandum for the Chief of Naval Operations, 28 Jan. 1966, NRD.

26. David L. McDonald, Memorandum for the Secretary of the Navy, 4 April 1966; Chief, Bureau of Ships to Chief of Naval Operations, 7 April 1966; Chief of Naval Material to Chief of Naval Operations, 8 April 1966, NRD. See also: JCAE, *Nuclear Submarines of Advanced Design*, Appendix 2, "Turbine Electric Drive Chronology," p. 70.

27. H. G. Rickover, Memorandum for the Chief of Naval Operations, 6 May 1966, NRD.

28. John S. Foster, Jr., Memorandum for the Secretary of the Navy, 10 May 1966, NRD.

29. David L. McDonald, Memorandum for the Secretary of the Navy, 19 May 1966; Paul H. Nitze, Memorandum for the Chief of Naval Material, 14 June 1966; I. J. Galantin, Memorandum for the Secretary of the Navy, 20 June 1960, NRD; JCAE, *Nuclear Submarines of Advanced Design*, Appendix 2, p. 72.

30. Paul H. Nitze, Memorandum for the Secretary of Defense, 23 Aug. 1966, NRD. JCAE, *Nuclear Submarines of Advanced Design*, Appendix 2, p. 73; JCAE, *Naval Nuclear Propulsion Program—1970*, 91st Cong., 2d sess. (Washington: G.P.O., 1970), Appendix 9, "New Construction Major Surface Warships and Submarines Authorized Since World War II," pp. 232–33.

31. Chronology, Fast Escort Submarine, NRD. For an unclassified version, see JCAE, *Nuclear Submarines of Advanced Design*, Appendix 1, pp. 42–69.

32. 08 to 00, 19 Oct. 1966; H. G. Rickover, Memorandum for the Commander, Naval Ship Systems Command, 17 Dec. 1966; T. A. Hendrickson to File, 9 Feb. 1967, all in NRD.

33. For concept formulation, see C. B. Martell, Memorandum for the Chief of Naval Operations, 9 Sept. 1967; Charles Martell, Memorandum for the Vice Chief of Naval Operations, 29 Aug. 1967, NRD.

34. Several papers gathered under the general heading, "Points for Meeting with COMSUBLANT, COMSUBPAC, and CNO (OP-31)," NRD. Some are undated, but all pertain to the March 7 meeting.

35. Unsigned document, Notes for Meeting with CNO on 30 March 1967, NRD.

36. T. H. Moorer to Hyman G. Rickover, 11 Aug. 1967, NRD.

37. H. G. Rickover, Memorandum for the Chief of Naval Operations, 24 Aug. 1967, NRD. For a brief summary of congressional action for the 1969 and 1970 programs, see JCAE, *Naval Nuclear Propulsion Program—1970*, Appendix 9, pp. 232–34.

38. J. K. Nunan, Memorandum for Dr. John S. Foster, Jr., 18 Dec. 1967, NRD.

39. The following paragraphs on procurement are based on: JCAE, *Nuclear Propulsion*

Program—1967–68, 90th Cong., 1st and 2d sess. (Washington: G.P.O., 1968), pp. 18–28 and Chronology, Procurement of Main Propulsion Equipment for the [classified matter deleted] Submarine, pp. 477–95. Documents are in NRD.

40. The contract was signed much later. See Definitive Subcontract No. C-615-393(D) Between General Dynamics Corporation, Electric Boat Division and General Electric Company, . . . 4 June 1971, NRD. For reference to Naval Reactors' understanding of General Electric's reluctance, see T. A. Hendrickson and J. W. Whitney, Memorandum to File, Briefing for the Secretary of the Navy Concerning the Turbine Electric Drive Submarine April 15, 1968, NRD. See also JCAE, *Naval Nuclear Propulsion Program—1967–68*, pp. 478–95.

41. JCAE, *Nuclear Submarines of Advanced Design*, Appendix 1, p. 52.

42. House Armed Services Committee, *Hearings on Military Posture and An Act (S. 3293)*, . . . 90th Cong., 2d sess. (Washington: G.P.O., 1968), "ASW Study Chronology," pp. 8896–97 (hereafter cited as HASC for the House Armed Services Committee and SASC for the Senate Armed Services Committee).

43. HASC, *Naval Nuclear Propulsion Program—1980*, 96th Cong., 2d sess. (Washington: G.P.O., 1980), pp. 13, 84.

44. Figures on proposed submarine strength and stopping construction after 1970 are referred to in SASC, *Authorizing Appropriations for Military Procurement, Research and Development Fiscal Year 1969*, . . . 10 April 1968, 90th Cong., 2d sess., S. Report No. 1087, p. 5. Strength as of 1 Jan. 1968 is derived from Moore, ed., *Jane's Fighting Ships, 1984–1985*, pp. 653–58.

45. For a dramatic account of the *November* submarine and the *Enterprise*, see Patrick Tyler, *Running Critical: The Silent War, Rickover, and General Dynamics* (New York: Harper & Rowe, 1986), pp. 34–45. For the *November* class, see Norman Polmar, *Guide to the Soviet Navy* 3rd ed. (Annapolis, MD: Naval Institute Press, 1983), p. 110.

46. H. G. Rickover, Memorandum for the Secretary of the Navy, 15 Jan. 1968, NRD.

47. JCAE, *Nuclear Submarines of Advanced Design*, Appendix 1, p. 52.

48. Notes for Discussion with RADM Adair—Subject: NAVSHIPS Draft Report on SSN Concept Formulation (CONFORM) unsigned and hand-dated 1/27/69, NRD. Tyler *Running Critical*, pp. 52–53, 59–61, 64, 70, 72.

49. For *Jack*, see Moore, ed., *Jane's Fighting Ships 1984–85*, p. 655. Two sharply opposed and well-informed views on the Conform and the *688* origins are in the Comment and Discussion department of the U.S. Naval Institute *Proceedings* 113 (March 1987): 27 and (August, 1987): 23, 27. The first is by Norman Friedman, the second by Captain M. Eckhart, Jr., USN (Ret.).

50. For a reference to the Jan. 23 and Feb. 6 briefings, see JCAE, *Nuclear Submarines of Advanced Design*, Appendix 1, p. 52, 54–56. For Rickover's testimony, see JCAE, *Naval Nuclear Propulsion Program—1967–68*, pp. viii, 155–58, 164–68; Subcommittee of the SASC, *U.S. Submarine Program*, 90th Cong., 2d sess. (Washington: G.P.O., 1968), pp. 5–61. Tyler, *Running Critical*, pp. 45–50.

51. JCAE, *Nuclear Submarines of Advanced Design*, Appendix 1, p. 56.

52. JCAE, *Nuclear Submarines of Advanced Design*, Appendix 1, p. 56, 29 Feb 1986.

53. Tyler, *Running Critical*, pp. 65–67. Beshany recounted his role in "As I Recall . . . Selling the *Los Angeles*," U.S. Naval Institute *Proceedings* 113 (October 1987): 109–10.

54. Reference to Foster's testimony is JCAE, *Nuclear Submarines of Advanced Design*, Appendix 1, pp. 55–56, 59–61, under the dates 15 Feb., 19 March 1968. Foster's March 19th testimony can be found in Subcommittee of the SASC, *U.S. Submarine Program*, pp. 185–235. See also JCAE, *Nuclear Submarines of Advanced Design*, Appendix 1, pp. 56, 63–64.

55. Chairman, CNO Ad Hoc SSN Panel to Chief of Naval Operations, 30 April 1986, NRD.
56. Joint Committee, *Nuclear Submarines of Advanced Design*, Appendix 1, p. 66.
57. John S. Foster, Jr., Memorandum for the Secretary of the Navy, 28 May 1968, NRD.
58. U.S. Cong., Senate Committee *Authorizing Appropriations for Military Procurement, Research, and Development, Fiscal Year 1969, . . .* 10 April 1968, 90th Cong., 2d sess., S. Report No. 1087, pp. 5, 15. For the views of the House committee, see U.S. Cong., House Committee *Authorizing Appropriations for Military Procurement, Research, and Development, Fiscal Year 1969, . . .* 5 July 1968, 90th Cong., 2d sess., H. Report No. 1645, pp. 43-44.
59. For a summary of the Foster testimony, see JCAE, *Nuclear Submarines of Advanced Design*, Appendix 1, pp. 60-61; John S. Foster, Jr., Memorandum for the Secretary of the Navy, 25, 28 June 1968; Paul H. Nitze, Memorandum for the Secretary of the Navy, 1 July 1968, NRD. For the subsequent actions, see JCAE, *Naval Nuclear Propulsion Program—1970*, Appendix 9, pp. 232-34; force level is from Moore, ed., *Jane's Fighting Ships, 1984-85*, p. 650.
60. John S. Foster, Jr., Memorandum for the Secretary of the Navy, 28 May 1968; Robert A. Frosch, Memorandum for the Director, Defense Research and Engineering, 6 June 1968, NRD. For a summary, see JCAE, *Nuclear Submarines of Advanced Design*, Appendix 2, p. 74.
61. John T. Conway to Thomas H. Moorer, 18 July 1968 and attach., Summary of Pros and Cons, NRD.
62. H. G. Rickover to John T. Conway, 18 July 1968 and attach. For Foster's views, see John S. Foster, Jr., Memorandum for the Secretary of the Navy, 10 May 1966, NRD. For congressional interest, see H. G. Rickover to L. Mendel Rivers, 13 June 1968; William H. Bates to John O. Pastore, 21 June 1968; John T. Conway to John S. Foster, Jr., 24 June 1968; John Stennis to Clark M. Clifford, 25 June 1968; John O. Pastore to Paul H. Nitze, 8 July 1968; L. Mendel Rivers and William H. Bates to Clark M. Clifford, 26 July 1968; Joint Committee Press Release No. 587: Nuclear Submarine Hearing Released by the Joint Committee on Atomic Energy, 28 July 1968; Craig Hosmer to Clark M. Clifford, 29 July 1968; L. Mendel Rivers to Clark M. Clifford, 27 Aug. 1968; John O. Pastore to Clark M. Clifford, 14 Sept. 1968; John Stennis to Clark M. Clifford, 3 Oct. 1968; Strom Thurmond to Clark M. Clifford, 11 Oct. 1968; L. Mendel Rivers to Clark M. Clifford, 24 Oct. 1968, NRD.
63. Transcripts of News Conferences by Secretary of Defense Clark M. Clifford, 11 July, 15 Aug., and 25 Oct. 1968
64. This and much of the following information is based upon a research paper by Dana M. Wegner, "The NR-1"; R. M. Forssell to K. A. Kesselring, 23 Dec. 1964, NRD.
65. L. M. Schlanger, Report of Conference (C-076), Small Nuclear Propulsion Plant for A Deep Diving, Research Submarine: Review of Status of KAPL Preliminary Design Study, [on] 15 Jan. 1965, NRD.
66. Levering Smith, E. P. Wilkinson, H. G. Rickover, and William A. Brockett, Memorandum of Conference held in the office of Admiral McDonald, Chief of Naval Operations, [on] 28 Jan. 1965; Robert W. Morse, Memorandum for the Director, Special Projects, 12 Feb. 1965, NRD. JCAE, *Loss of the U.S.S. "Thresher,"* 88th Cong., 1st and 2d sess. (Washington: G.P.O., 1965), pp. 94-105.
67. Robert W. Morse to Dr. Glenn T. Seaborg, 12 Feb. 1965; H. G. Rickover and Levering Smith, Report of Conference (C-0127) [on] 24 Feb. 1965. Admiral Rickover and others remember his naming the ship, although the date is obscure. The first document with the name NR-1 is T. A. Hendrickson and E. R. Lacey,

Report of a Meeting Among Representatives of KAPL. . . . NR-1 Project. . . . [held] 31 March 1965 (C-021), NRD. For responsibilities, see Division of Responsibility in NR for NR-1 Project, hand-dated 5-1-65, all in NRD.

68. The *Washington Post*, 19 April 1965; The Naval Nuclear Propulsion Program—A Joint AEC–Department of the Navy Program, March 1967, pp. 23–24, NRD; Subcommittee of the House Committee on Appropriations, *Public Works Appropriations for 1966 Part 3*, 89th Cong., 1st sess. (Washington: G.P.O., 1965), pp. 162, 341–42; Code 1500 to Code 400, 4 Oct. 1965 and encl.; Chief, Bureau of Ships to General Manager, Electric Boat Division et al., 21 Sept. 1965; E. C. Brolin to H. G. Rickover, 9 Dec. 1965 and encl., NRD.

69. JCAE, *Naval Nuclear Propulsion Program—1967-68*, p. 31.

70. Moore, ed., *Jane's Fighting Ships, 1977-78*, p. 651; United States Department of Energy-United States Department of Defense, A Review of the United States Naval Nuclear Propulsion Program, June 1984, p. 19, NRD.

71. Moore, ed., *Jane's Fighting Ships, 1977-78*, pp. 551–54.

72. Hewlett and Duncan, *Nuclear Navy*, pp. 307–15. For an interesting account of Polaris development, see Harvey M. Sapolsky, *The Polaris System Development: Bureaucratic and Programmatic Success in Government* (Cambridge, MA: Harvard University Press, 1972).

73. Moore, ed., *Jane's Fighting Ships, 1977-78*, pp. 51–54; Ronald T. Pretty, ed., *Jane's Weapon Systems, 1981-82* (New York: Jane's, 1981), pp. 15–16; *Jane's Fighting Ships, 1977-78*, pp. 553–54.

74. Unpublished manuscript, Chronology of ULMS/Trident, December 1971, NRD. See also Norman Polmar and D. A. Paolucci, "Sea-Based 'Strategic' Weapons for the 1980s And Beyond," U.S. Naval Institute *Proceedings* 104 (May 1978): 100–101, and D. Douglas Dalgleish and Larry Schweikart, *Trident* (Carbondale, IL: Southern University Press, 1984), pp. 14–15, 41–42.

75. H. G. Rickover, J. Adair, L. Smith, Memorandum of Conference, [on] 12 May 1969; quote is from unpublished manuscript, Chronology of ULMS/Trident, December 1971, NRD.

76. H. E. Shear, Memorandum for Vice Admiral H. G. Rickover, USN, 12 Oct. 1970. Reference to the Oct. 28 decision is in R. W. Cousins, Memorandum for the Chief of Naval Material, 10 Nov. 1970; and Director, Strategic Systems Projects, to Commander, Naval Ship Systems Command (PMS-396), 27 Nov. 1970, NRD. In their case study, Barry E. Carter and John D. Steinbruner, "Trident," in *Commission on the Organization of the Government for the Conduct of Foreign Policy 4 Appendix K Adequacy of Current Organization: Defense and Arms Control* (Washington: G.P.O., 1975), pp. 175–82, conclude that in the Trident decision, the importance of obsolescence, speed, and silence were given undue emphasis. For a comment on the value of speed and silence for missile submarines, see Friedman, *Submarine Design*, pp. 77, 79. For concern over obsolescence of the Polaris ships and the relation of power to safety, see Zumwalt, *On Watch: A Memoir* (New York: Quadrangle/Times Books, 1976), pp. 154–57.

77. R. Y. Kaufman, Memorandum for the Distribution List, 29 Dec. 1970; unsigned document, Status of ULMS Program, 19 Jan. 1971; H. E. Shear, Memorandum for the Chief of Naval Operations, 16 Jan 1971; H. G. Rickover, Remarks on the ULMS Program . . . at meeting held . . . 19 January 1971; unpublished manuscript, Chronology of ULMS/TRIDENT, December 1971, NRD. Zumwalt, *On Watch*, p. 152 is in error in implying that the Trident submarine is powered by "a huge 60,000 horse power reactor."

78. For SALT, see Zumwalt, *On Watch*, pp. 152–57. SALT was also an element consid-

ered in the Jan. 19 meeting. See Development Concept Paper, Undersea Long-Range Missile System (ULMS), DCP No. 67, 6 Jan. 1971, NRD.

79. Vice Admiral Rickover's Notes for Discussion with Admiral Zumwalt on 10 June 1971 Concerning ULMS; unpublished manuscript, Chronology of ULMS/TRIDENT, December 1971, NRD. For a description of the missile, see Dalgleish and Schweikart, *Trident*, pp. 26–37.

80. Dalgleish and Schweikart, *Trident*, pp. 44–46; Polmar and Paolucci, "Sea-Based 'Strategic' Weapons," p. 103.

81. Zumwalt, *On Watch*, pp. 152–54; Dalgleish and Schweikart, *Trident*, p. 344. For Bentsen, see *Congressional Record* 92d Cong., 2d sess., vol. 118, pt. 20, pp. S 25650-1. For inflation, see James L. Buckley, *Congressional Record*, 92d Cong., 2d sess., vol. 118, pt. 20, pp. S 25662-3.

82. *Congressional Record*, 92d Cong., 2d sess., vol. 118, pt. 20, pp. S 25650-1, S 25687. Dalgleish and Schweikart, *Trident*, pp. 50–51, 56–57.

83. *Congressional Record*, 92d Cong., 2d sess., vol. 118, pt. 20. For Thurmond quote, see p. S 25659. For Rickover letter, see pp. S 25669-70. For the vote, see p. S 25702.

84. U.S. Cong., SASC, *Report Together with Separate and Individual Views on Authorizing Appropriations for Fiscal Year 1974. . .*, 93rd Cong., 1st sess. S. Report No. 385, pp. 39–40, 181–83, 194–97. For the Rickover to Pastore letter, see *Congressional Record*, 93rd Cong., 2d sess., vol. 119, pt. 24, pp. S 31542-44; Zumwalt, *On Watch*, pp. 157–63; Dalgleish and Schweikart, *Trident*, pp. 63–65.

85. *Ohio* Sea Trials Letter, 22 June 1981, NRD; Dalgleish and Schweikart, *Trident*, pp. 65–73.

86. Dalgleish and Schweikart, *Trident*, pp. 65–73.

87. Rickover, Memorandum for General Counsel of the Navy, 10 May 1971, in Joint Economic Committee, *Economics of Defense Policy: Admiral H. G. Rickover, Part 4*, 97th Cong., 2d sess. (Washington: G.P.O., 1982), pp. 3–7. The quote is on pp. 3–4.

88. Zumwalt, *On Watch*, p. 158.

89. For status of ships, see Moore, ed., *Jane's Fighting Ships, 1977–78*, pp. 649–52; *Ohio* Sea Trials Letter, 22 June 1981, NRD.

Chapter 3. *Thresher*

Two useful books on the *Thresher* are: John Bentley, *The Thresher Disaster: The Most Tragic Dive in Submarine History* (Garden City, NY: Doubleday, 1975); and Norman Polmar, *Death of the Thresher* (New York: Chilton Books, 1964). Of the two, Polmar has the greater command of submarine technology.

1. Admiral Rickover at one time gave plaques with this inscription to submarine commanding officers. He also gave one to President Kennedy and President Carter.

2. E. S. Arentzen and Philip Mandel, "Naval Architectural Aspects of Submarine Design," Society of Naval Architects and Marine Engineers, *Transactions* 68 (1960): 622–76; Andrew I. McKee, "Recent Submarine Design Practices and Problems," Society of Naval Architects and Marine Engineers, *Transactions* 67 (1959): 623–36; W. D. Roseborough, Jr., "The Evolution of the Attack Submarine," reprinted from *Sperryscope* in *Naval Engineers Journal* 74 (Aug. 1962): 425–29; Harry Jackson, "USS Albacore: The 'New Look' in Submarine Design," *Bureau of Ships Journal* 2 (March 1954): 2–4; R. P. Metzger, Rough Draft Memorandum to W. C. Barnes, Summary of Informal Discussion by Commander F. A.

Andrews . . . On 28 June 1955, 11 July 1955, NRD; Public Law 639, 84th Cong., Chapter 488, 2 July 1956, pp. 516–32.

3. Denys W. Knoll, Ship Characteristics Board Memo No. 129–57, 14 June 1957 with encl.; H. G. Hopwood, OPNAV Instruction 09010.119, 26 July 1957 with encl., all in NRD.

4. On the development and introduction of HY-80, see S. R. Heller, Jr., Ivo Fioriti, and John Vasta, "An Evaluation of HY-80 Steel as a Structural Material for Submarines," two parts, Naval Engineers Journal 77 (Feb. and April 1965): 29–44, 193–200; T. B. Cox and A. H. Rosenstein, A Review of Modern Naval Steels, Naval Ship Research and Development Center, Nov. 1969, MATLAB 420; Peter M. Palermo, A Summary of Submarine Structural Research, part 1: Conventional Hull Configurations, chapter 3: Fatigue of Submarine Hull Structures, Sept. 1964, David Taylor Model Basin Structural Mechanics Laboratory, Report C-1569-3.

5. Richard G. Hewlett and Francis Duncan, Nuclear Navy, 1946–1962 (Chicago: University of Chicago Press, 1974), Appendix 2, "Construction of the Nuclear Navy 1952–1962," p. 399.

6. Record of Proceedings of a Court of Inquiry Convened at U.S. Naval Submarine Base New London, Groton, Connecticut, and Portsmouth Naval Shipyard, Portsmouth, New Hampshire by Order of Commander in Chief, U.S. Atlantic Fleet, To Inquire into the Circumstances of the Loss at Sea of USS Thresher (SS(N)593), Which Occurred on 10 April 1963, Ordered on 10 April 1963, twelve volumes, testimony of Vice Admiral Hyman G. Rickover, vol. 3, p. 690. Hereafter these twelve volumes will be cited as Court of Inquiry. Rickover to Code 420, 14 June 1957; Rickover to Code 300, 6 Nov. 1957; all in NRD.

7. Joint Committee on Atomic Energy (hereafter cited as JCAE), The Loss of the U.S.S. "Thresher" (Washington: G.P.O., 1965), p. 79. H. K. Marks, Notes on Meeting, 9 Dec. 1957, NRD. Panoff continued to express his doubts about resilient mounting during another meeting with Morgan on Nov. 29. See Panoff, Memorandum to File, 2 Dec. 1957, NRD. On sound mounting, see Norman Friedman, Submarine Design and Development (Annapolis, MD: Naval Institute Press, 1984), pp. 81–82.

8. John Alden, "Portsmouth Naval Shipyard," U.S. Naval Institute Proceedings 90 (Nov. 1964): 89–105; John G. Tawresey, "The Portsmouth, N.H., Navy Yard," Society of Naval Architects and Marine Engineers, Historical Transactions, 1893–1943 (New York: Society of Naval Architects and Marine Engineers, 1945), pp. 28–30; Hewlett and Duncan, Nuclear Navy, pp. 159–61 and Appendix 2, p. 399, NRD.

9. Panoff to Rickover, undated but with handwritten notation, "HGR agreed on 12/7/57. . . ."; Panoff to file, 21 Jan. 1958; Chief, Bureau of Ships to Commander, Portsmouth Naval Shipyard, 23 Jan. 1958; Department of the Navy, Bureau of Ships, Contract for Design and Engineering Studies and Preparation of Working Plans for . . . SSN 593, . . . NObs-3994, all in NRD.

10. Naval message 282151Z, NAVSHIPYD PTSMH to BUSHIPS, 29 May 1958, NRD; Hewlett and Duncan, Nuclear Navy, p. 124.

11. Knoll, Memorandum for Admiral Burke, 13 Jan. 1959, NRD.

12. Transcript of a Special Meeting of the Ship Characteristics Board, Fleet and Submarine Force Commanders, and Representatives of the Shipbuilding Industry to Review the Building Program of USS Thresher (SSN 593), 27 Jan. 1959; J. B. Osborn, Memorandum to Rickover, 28 Jan. 1959; Knoll, Memorandum for Admiral Burke, 18 Feb. 1959, all in NRD.

13. JCAE, Loss of the U.S.S. Thresher, p. 76.

14. Heller, et al., "An Evaluation of HY-80 Steel as Structural Material for Submarines," part 2, *Naval Engineers Journal* 77 (April 1965): 195; JCAE, *Loss of the U.S.S. Thresher*, p. 81.
15. Testimony of Commander Clarence R. Bryan, Court of Inquiry, vol. 4, pp. 1045–49; Heller et al., "An Evaluation of HY-80 Steel as a Structural Material for Submarines," part 2, *Naval Engineers Journal* 77 (April 1965): 195–96.
16. Burke, Memorandum for the Record, 2 April 1960 in Burke Papers, NHC; President, Board of Inspection and Survey to Chief of Naval Operations, 22 April 1960 with encl., NRD; Burke, Memorandum for the Record, 25 April 1960, Burke Papers, NHC.
17. H. P. Rumble, memorandum, 7 April 1960; H. P. Rumble, Information Bulletin No. 30–60, 9 May 1960, NRD.
18. Harrison S. Sayre's report is published in JCAE, *Loss of the U.S.S. Thresher*, Appendix 15, "Review of Inspection Procedures for HY-80 Submarine Hull Welds," pp. 183–86.
19. Portsmouth Periscope, 8 July 1960; Axene to Rickover, 15 July 1960, NRD.
20. Testimony of Commander Dean L. Axene, Court of Inquiry, vol. 1, p. 18, NRD. Axene wrote of his training in " 'School of the Boat' for the *Nautilus*," U.S. Naval Institute *Proceedings* 81 (Nov. 1955): 1229–35.
21. Axene to Rickover, 1 July, 12 Aug., 9 Sept., 7 Oct., 4 Nov. 1960; Panoff, Memorandum to File, 6 July 1960, all in NRD.
22. Raymond V. B. Blackman, ed., *Jane's Fighting Ships: 1961–62* (New York: McGraw-Hill, 1962), p. 363. Description of the *Barbel* flooding is from a partial transcript of a board of inquiry convened 30 March 1961 to investigate the incident. Meyer's statement on casualties is on p. 11. Partial transcript in NRD.
23. Franklin D. Jones, ed., *Engineering Encyclopedia, 2nd ed.*, (New York: Industrial Press, 1954), vol. 1, pp. 173–74, vol. 2, pp. 1384–85; P. R. Clark, draft, Comparison of Brazed to Welded Joints, 26 June 1963, NRD. Brazing and welding techniques have been greatly simplified here for clarity.
24. USS *Thresher* (SS(N)593), Chronology of Silbraze Problem and Actions Taken in Connection Therewith, Court of Inquiry, vol. 11, Exhibit 226.
25. Naval message 031916Z, DEPCOMSUBLANT to BUSHIPS, 3 Feb. 1961, vol. 10, Exhibit 204; reference to bureau message 242339Z is in Portsmouth Memorandum, Production Officer to Head, Inspection Branch et al., 5 April 1961, vol. 11, Exhibit 209; Memorandum from E. M. O'Brien, Associate Supervisory Inspector to E. M. Henry, 23 May 1961, vol. 11, Exhibit 211, all in Court of Inquiry.
26. Prospective Commanding Officer, USS SNOOK (SS(N)592) to Chief of Naval Operations, 15 Feb. 1961; D. A. Scherer, FIRST ENDORSEMENT on PCO SNOOK . . . ltr, . . . 17 Feb 1961; Bucknell to Daspit, 4 March 1961, all in NRD.
27. USS *Thresher* (SS(N)593), Chronology of Silbraze Problem and Actions Taken in Connection Therewith, vol. 11, Exhibit 226; Portsmouth Naval Shipyard, Silver Brazed Sea Water Systems in Submarines, 1 March 1961, vol. 11, Exhibit 233, both in Court of Inquiry.
28. Commissioned Submarine Construction History as of 3/15/65; naval message 132307Z, NAVSHIPYD PTSMH to BUSHIPS, 13 April 1961; Axene to Chief of Naval Operations, 28 April 1961, all in NRD.
29. Testimony of Captain John J. Hinchey, Court of Inquiry, vol. 3, pp. 559–60.
30. James Jackson III, head of the shipboard and development test section of the industrial design division of Portsmouth, testified that the yard submitted a trial agenda to the bureau about two months before the trial, and that approximately a week before the trial the bureau changed the agenda to require diving in hundred-foot increments and the cycling of valves. See Court of Inquiry, vol. 2,

p. 501. However, Commander Axene in vol. 1, p. 265, and Captain Clarence J. Zurcher, assistant chief of staff for logistics, DEPCOMSUBLANT, in vol. 6, p. 1524, Court of Inquiry, refer to Rickover's intervention. Moreover, many individuals interviewed vividly remember this meeting. See also testimony of Captain William D. Roseborough, vol. 3, p. 616. For first test dive, see testimony of Commander Clarence R. Bryan, vol. 4, p. 1055, all in Court of Inquiry.

31. Rickover to A. R. Luedecke, 4 May 1961, AEC; Rickover to Chief of Naval Operations, 4 May 1961; James, Memorandum to Rickover, 4 May 1961, NRD.

32. Naval message 252316Z, USS THRESHER to COMSUBLANT, 25 May 1961; Axene to Rickover, 29 May 1961, both in NRD.

33. Naval message 312211Z, DEPCOMSUBLANT to COMNAVSHIPYD PTSMH, 31 May 1961, NRD.

34. The bureau steps are listed in USS *Thresher* (SS(N)593), Chronology of Silbraze Problem and Actions Taken in Connection Therewith, Court of Inquiry, vol. 11, Exhibit 226; typed note to Panoff, initialed by "R," 5 June 1961; Rickover to Deputy Commander, Submarine Force et al., SHIPALT SS(N)67, 7 Sept. 1961, NRD.

35. Officer in Charge, USS SNOOK to Chief of Naval Operations, 11 Sept. 1961, NRD.

36. Naval message DEPCOMSUBLANT to BUSHIPS, received 13 Sept. 1961, in JCAE, *Loss of the U.S.S. Thresher*, Appendix 1, "Navy Memorandum Concerning Submarine Salt Water Piping Systems," pp. 133–34.

37. Naval message 152242Z, BUSHIPS to DEPCOMSUBLANT, 15 Sept. 1961, Court of Inquiry, vol. 10, Exhibit 172.

38. Commander, Portsmouth Naval Shipyard to Chief, Bureau of Ships, 16 Jan. 1962; Rickover to Commander, Portsmouth Naval Shipyard, 28 Dec. 1961 with encl., Report of Evaluation of Reactor Plant Welding at Portsmouth Naval Shipyard, both in NRD.

39. Commander, Portsmouth Naval Shipyard to Chief, Bureau of Ships, 16 Jan. 1962; Commander, Portsmouth Naval Shipyard to Chief, Bureau of Ships, 18 Jan. 1962, NRD.

40. The text of the memorandum is in JCAE, *Loss of the U.S.S. Thresher*, pp. 73–74.

41. Axene to Rickover, 28 July 1961, NRD; Testimony of Commander Dean L. Axene, Court of Inquiry, vol. 1, p. 18. The *Thresher* participated in major tactical exercises 18–28 Sept. 1961 and 27–30 March 1962. See Commander Submarine Development Group TWO to Commander Submarine Force, U.S. Atlantic Fleet, 6 July 1962 with encl. titled Analysis Report of Exercise NUSUBEX 2-62, NRD.

42. Testimony of Captain John J. Hinchey, Court of Inquiry, vol. 3, pp. 560–61; JCAE, *Loss of the U.S.S. Thresher*, Appendix 17, " 'Thresher' (SS(N)593) Chronology," p. 189.

43. A. H. Keil, "The Response of Ships to Underwater Explosions," Society of Naval Architects and Marine Engineers, *Transactions* 69, 1961 (New York: Society of Naval Architects and Marine Engineers, 1962), pp. 366–410; William A. Shurcliff, *Bombs at Bikini, The Official Report of Operation Crossroads* (New York: Wm. H. Wise, 1947), Appendix 11, Section II: "Observations on Test 'B'," pp. 196–99; Samuel Glasstone, ed., *The Effects of Nuclear Weapons*, rev. ed., Feb. 1964 (Washington: Atomic Energy Commission, 1962), pp. 61–63. The vulnerability of submarines to nuclear weapons was described by Secretary of Defense Gates in January 1958. See Subcommittee of the House Committee on Appropriations, *Supplemental Defense Appropriations for 1958*, 85th Cong., 2d sess. (Washington: G.P.O., 1958), pp. 225–26. On 23 July 1958 Burke issued OPNAV Instruction 09110.2 authorizing shock tests against seven first-line combat ships. See Chief, Bureau of Ships to Chief of Naval Operations, undated but

about April 1961 with encl., NRD. Code 423, Bureau of Ships, First Draft, General Instructions for the Development of Submarine Shock Test Inspection Procedures, 25 May 1964, Table 1.1, Summary of Shock Tests on Operating Submarines and *Ulua*, NRD.

44. The careful preparations are seen in Report of Conference (C#027), USS *Thresher* (SS(N)593)—Proposed Full Scale Shock Tests, [on] 7 Feb. 1962; K. E. Swenson and R. A. Claytor to Rickover, 5 March 1962 with encl.; Chief, Bureau of Ships to Assistant Industrial Manager, THIRD Naval District, Groton, Conn., 4 April 1962 with encl. The post-testing studies are illustrated in Ronald E. Baker and Natalie T. Goldberg, Starshine Program for Storage, Retrieval, and Analysis of Shock-Damage Information, Dec. 1963, David Taylor Model Basin Structural Mechanics and Applied Mathematics Laboratories, Research and Development Report 1782; S5W-HLFE-4970, Report on Inspections and Measurements of SS(N)593 *Thresher* Reactor Plant After Shock Tests, 8 Oct. 1962; all in NRD. The last two detonations were more powerful than any used against the other submarines but were less powerful than scheduled.

45. JCAE, *Loss of the U.S.S. Thresher*, Appendix 17, " 'Thresher' (SS(N)593) Chronology," p. 189; testimony of Commander Dean L. Axene, Court of Inquiry, vol. 1, p. 26; Norman Polmar, *Death of the Thresher*, p. 20.

46. Chief, Bureau of Ships to Commander, Portsmouth Naval Shipyard, 11 July 1962, both in NRD; testimony of Captain Richard Riley, Court of Inquiry, vol. 2, pp. 529–39.

47. Testimony of Commander Dean L. Axene, Court of Inquiry, vol. 1, pp. 27–28, naval message 022021Z, DEPCOMSUBLANT to NAVSHIPYD PTSMH, 2 July 1962, NRD.

48. Testimony of Commander Dean L. Axene, Court of Inquiry, vol. 1, p. 27; Hewlett and Duncan, *Nuclear Navy*, Appendix 2, "Construction of the Nuclear Navy, 1952–1962," pp. 399–401.

49. For yard organization, see Court of Inquiry, testimony of Rear Admiral Charles J. Palmer, vol. 2, pp. 325–27; testimony of Captain John G. Guerry, Jr., vol. 5, pp. 1355–56; testimony of Captain William E. Heronemus, vol. 1, p. 124 and vol. 3, pp. 636–37; production department organization chart, 1 May 1963, vol. 10, Exhibit 193.

50. Testimony of Captain John J. Hinchey, vol. 3, pp. 559–60, in Court of Inquiry.

51. Testimony of Commander Dean L. Axene, Captain William D. Roseborough, Captain William E. Heronemus, USS *Thresher* (SS(N)593) Key Events PSA, all from Court of Inquiry, vol. 1, pp. 23, 27–29, vol. 3, pp. 589–94, 637–39, and vol. 10, Exhibit 192.

52. Testimony of RADM Charles J. Palmer, Court of Inquiry, vol. 2, pp. 329–33.

53. Reactor and ship data is from Hewlett and Duncan, *Nuclear Navy*, Appendix 2, pp. 399–401.

54. JCAE, *Loss of the U.S.S. Thresher*, Appendix 3, "The Never-Ending Challenge (By Vice Adm. H. G. Rickover, . . . October 29, 1962)," pp. 136–44.

55. *New York Times*, 30 Oct., 4 Nov. 1962; St. Louis *Post-Dispatch*, 7 Nov. 1962; *Washington Post*, 30 Oct. 1962; *Christian Science Monitor*, 30 Oct. 1962; *Business Week*, 3 Nov. 1962; *Time*, 9 Nov. 1962.

56. J. W. Vaughan to Rickover, 11 Oct. 1968, NRD; JCAE, *Naval Nuclear Propulsion Program—1970: Testimony of Vice Admiral H. G. Rickover* (Washington: G.P.O., 1970), Appendix 12, "Who Protects the Public? (By Vice Adm. H. G. Rickover, . . . 14 October 1962)," pp. 260–70.

57. Chief, Bureau of Ships to Distribution List, 13 Feb. 1962, Court of Inquiry, vol. 9, Exhibit 158.

58. In Court of Inquiry, Commander, Portsmouth Naval Shipyard to Chief, Bureau

of Ships, 9 May 1962, Exhibit 156; Chief, Bureau of Ships to Commander, Portsmouth Naval Shipyard, 29 May 1962, Exhibit 157, vol. 9; Findings of Fact, para. 97, vol. 1.

59. Chief, Bureau of Ships to Commander, Portsmouth Naval Shipyard, 28 Aug. 1962, Court of Inquiry, vol. 9, Exhibit 115.

60. 303B-2, Memorandum to 213X, 29 Nov. 1962, vol. 9, Exhibit 116. The actual figures in the Nov. 29 memorandum differ somewhat from those cited in the text, which are from vol. 1, Findings of Fact, paras. 102, and 105–8, all in Court of Inquiry.

61. Commanding Officer, U.S.S. *Thresher* to Chief, Bureau of Ships, 16 Nov. 1962, Court of Inquiry, vol. 9, Exhibit 111.

62. Testimony of Commander Dean L. Axene, p. 30; Findings of Fact, para. 166, both in Court of Inquiry, vol. 1.

63. Polmar, *Death of the Thresher*, pp. 26–28.

64. Naval message 191750Z, DEPCOMSUBLANT to CINCLANTFLT, BUSHIPS, 19 Jan. 1963, Court of Inquiry, vol. 7, Exhibit 46.

65. Harvey to Newton, stamped "Feb. 14 Rec'd"; Newton to Harvey, date illegible, but probably a few days after Harvey's letter, vol. 11, Exhibits 222, 223, both in Court of Inquiry.

66. USS *Thresher* (SS(N)593) Key Events–Building Period, vol. 10, Exhibit 192; testimony of Commander H. N. Larcombe, Jr., vol. 1, pp. 116–17; testimony of Lieutenant Raymond A. McCoole, vol. 1, pp. 166–67; Commanding Officer, USS *Thresher* (SSN 593) to Commander Portsmouth Naval Shipyard, 26 March 1963, vol. 9, Exhibit 96, all in Court of Inquiry.

67. Testimony of Captain William E. Heronemus, Court of Inquiry, vol. 3, pp. 641, 645.

68. USS *Thresher* (SS(N)593) Key Events–Building Period, Exhibit 192, vol. 10; testimony of Lieutenant Raymond A. McCoole, vol. 1, pp. 171, 259; testimony of Frank DeStefano, Chief Machinists Mate, vol. 1, p. 188; testimony of Captain William E. Heronemus, vol. 3, pp. 645–46, all in Court of Inquiry.

69. USS *Thresher* (SS(N)593) Key Events–Building Period, vol. 10, Exhibit 192; the sea-trial agenda is in Commanding Officer, USS *Thresher* (SSN 593) to Distribution, 2 April 1963, vol. 7, Exhibit 4, both in Court of Inquiry.

70. R. A. Claytor, Memorandum to File, 11 April 1963, NRD.

71. USS *Thresher* (SS(N)593) Key Events–Building Period, vol. 10, Exhibit 192; testimony of Captain William E. Heronemus, vol. 1, p. 128; testimony of LCDR Stanley Hecker, vol. 1, pp. 89–90, all in Court of Inquiry.

72. The sailing list is Exhibit 2; tracking charts of the *Thresher* and *Skylark*, Exhibits 35 and 36, all in Court of Inquiry, vol. 7.

73. Testimony of LCDR Stanley Hecker, Court of Inquiry, vol. 1, pp. 91, 110; Raymond V. B. Blackman, ed., *Jane's Fighting Ships: 1962–63* (New York: McGraw-Hill, 1962), p. 384; Court of Inquiry, Findings of Fact, vol. 1, paras. 12, 13.

74. Hewlett and Duncan, *Nuclear Navy*, p. 217; Polmar, *Death of the Thresher*, pp. 32–33; Findings of Fact, Court of Inquiry, vol. 1, para. 13.

75. Testimony of LCDR Stanley Hecker, vol. 1, pp. 89, 93, 110; Commander, Destroyer Development Group TWO to Commander, Submarine Squadron TEN, 27 March 1963, vol. 10, Exhibit 200; Commander Submarine Flotilla SIX to Commander Submarine Force, U.S. Atlantic Fleet, 18 April 1963, vol. 10, Exhibit 202; Findings of Fact, vol. 1, paras. 10, 18, all in Court of Inquiry.

76. Testimony of CDR H. N. Larcombe, Jr., p. 115; testimony of LCDR Stanley Hecker, pp. 91–92, both in vol. 1; tracking charts of the *Thresher* and *Skylark*,

vol. 7, Exhibits 35 and 36, all in Court of Inquiry; Polmar, *Death of the Thresher*, p. 34.

77. Testimony of LCDR Stanley Hecker, vol. 1, pp. 93–95; *Skylark* radio log, Exhibit 38; *Skylark* weather log, Exhibit 39, both in vol. 7; testimony of LT (jg.) James D. Watson, vol. 1, pp. 37–38; *Skylark* UQC (underwater telephone) log, vol. 7, Exhibit 16, all in Court of Inquiry.

78. *Skylark* UQC log, Court of Inquiry, vol. 7, Exhibit 16. The log is not easy to use. In some instances the names of the sender and receiver are reversed, and the times of the messages are transposed.

79. Testimony of LCDR Stanley Hecker, p. 96; testimony of Wayne H. Martin, RM3, pp. 63–65, both in vol. 1; *Skylark* UQC log, vol. 7, Exhibit 16, all in Court of Inquiry.

80. *Skylark* UQC log, Court of Inquiry, vol. 7, Exhibit 16. Since the log was marked in only whole minutes, the court was unable to determine the precise time of the critical message. It occurred sometime between 9:12 and 9:13. Hecker described the activity on the bridge at the time of the 9:13 message on p. 96 in Court of Inquiry, vol. 1. The exact wording of the last several messages sent by the *Thresher* was investigated in great detail by the court. See the testimony of Roy S. Mowen, Jr., BM3, pp. 57–61; Wayne H. Martin, RM3, pp. 64–66; LT (j.g.) James D. Watson, pp. 42–43, and Hecker, pp. 95–96, all in Court of Inquiry, vol. 1.

81. Testimony of LCdr. Stanley Hecker, vol. 1, p. 96–99. Hecker, Watson, and Mowen attested to the lack of alarm in the 9:13 message. See vol. 1, pp. 50, 61, and 105. Hecker's subsequent actions are described by Watson, vol. 1, pp. 43–46. The existence of one or more garbled messages which were not entered into the UQC log is confirmed by the testimony of Martin, vol. 1, pp. 66–67, all in Court of Inquiry; Polmar, *Death of the Thresher*, pp. 105–16. On blowing, see Friedman, *Submarine Design*, pp. 120–21

82. Testimony of LCdr. Stanley Hecker, p. 100; Findings of Fact, para. 23, both in vol. 1, Court of Inquiry.

83. Testimony of LCdr. Stanley Hecker, p. 110; testimony of LT (j.g.) James D. Watson, pp. 48–54, vol. 1, Court of Inquiry, Polmar, *Death of the Thresher*, pp. 51–55; Department of Defense News Release No. 509-63, 10 April 1963.

84. Naval message 110448Z, CINCLANTFLT to NAVWARCOLLEGE et al., 11 April 1963, Court of Inquiry, vol. 1, pp. "A"3-5. The biographical information comes from the Naval History Division.

85. *Congressional Record*, 88th Cong., 1st sess., vol. 109, pt. 5, 22 April 1963, pp. S 6697-S 6699.

86. The text of the memorandum is in JCAE, *Loss of the U.S.S. Thresher*, pp. 73–74.

87. Unsigned but by Rickover, Memorandum of Telecon Between Adm. Austin and Adm. Rickover, 17 April 1963; Rickover, Memorandum of Conversation with the Secretary of the Navy, . . . 24 April 1963, NRD.

88. H. G. Rickover, Remarks Concerning Court of Inquiry Convening on the USS *Thresher*, 30 April 1963, NRD; Rickover's testimony appears in the Court of Inquiry, vol. 3, pp. 690–709. The quote appears on p. 698.

89. Testimony of RAdm. Ralph K. James, vol. 5, pp. 1272–73; see also testimony on personnel of Capt. William D. Roseborough, vol. 3, pp. 614–15; testimony of RAdm. William A. Brockett, vol. 5, pp. 1253–59; testimony of Capt. John G. Guerry, vol. 5, pp. 1366–67, all in Court of Inquiry.

90. Testimony of VAdm. William R. Smedberg III, Court of Inquiry, vol. 6, pp. 1605–9.

91. The differences between Rickover and Smedberg are in Smedberg, Memoran-

dum for Vice Admiral Rickover, 14 Dec. 1961 with encl., Officer Manning Capability for Nuclear Powered Submarines for Period January Thru June 1962; Rickover, Memorandum for Admiral G. W. Anderson, Jr., 21 Dec. 1961; Commander Submarine Force, U.S. Atlantic Fleet to Chief of Naval Personnel, 26 Dec. 1961; Smedberg, Memorandum for Admiral Anderson, 23 Feb. 1962; Smedberg to Rickover, 10 April 1962 with encl., Statement of the Problem, dated 5 April 1962; unsigned, Memorandum of Meeting, 21 April 1962; Rickover, Memorandum for VADM W. R. Smedberg III, Chief of Naval Personnel, 19 June 1962; Smedberg, Memorandum for Vice Admiral H. G. Rickover, 21 June 1962, all in NRD.

92. The Findings of Fact, Opinions, and Recommendations are in unnumbered pages in Court of Inquiry, vol. 1, and vol. 6, pp. 1679–1718.

93. This reconstruction is drawn from Court of Inquiry, vol. 1, Findings of Fact, paras. 11–19.

94. Opinions, Court of Inquiry, vol. 1, paras. 1–6, 45.

95. JCAE, *Loss of the U.S.S. Thresher*, pp. 34–39; Operational Test of Tinosa's MBT Blow System: on 19 April 1963, vol. 8, Exhibit 76; testimony of Capt. Samuel R. Heller, Jr., vol. 5, pp. 1239–42; Opinions, vol. 1, para. 8, all in Court of Inquiry.

96. Findings of Fact, vol. 1, paras. 48 and 49, Court of Inquiry.

97. For the air system, see Court of Inquiry, Findings of Fact, vol. 1, paras. 48–50; for shock tests, see paras. 84, 86, and 96; the bureau directive is para. 98; the sentences quoted are in paras. 109 and 151.

98. Opinions, Court of Inquiry, vol. 1, paras. 1 and 55.

99. Recommendations, Court of Inquiry, vol. 1, paras. 1–20.

100. JCAE, *Loss of the U.S.S. Thresher* has unclassified versions of the hearings of 26, 27 June, 23 July 1963 and 1 July 1964. This paragraph is based largely on: Joint Committee on Atomic Energy, *Hearing to Receive Report on the Navy's Investigation of the Loss of the Thresher, 27 June 1963*, NRD. Maurer's testimony on June 27 is on pp. 135–48, 155–60, 166–96. The quotation is on p. 172.

101. For general reference to acoustical data, see two articles by Larry L. Booda in *Sea Technology*, "ASW—Challenges and Bold Solutions," vol. 14 (Nov. 1973): 24–27, and "Inflation And In-House Competition Squeeze Navy ASW Programs," vol. 15 (Nov. 1974): 22–30. Rickover referred to acoustical data and the *Thresher* in JCAE, *Loss of the U.S.S. Thresher*, pp. 60–61. That the reactor slowed or shut down is in Court of Inquiry, Findings of Fact, vol. 1, para. 18. For a summary of the three computer cases, see Opinions, vol. 1, para. 45.

102. Rickover et al., "Results of a discussion concerning the April 10 lofargrams. . . .," 9 July 1963, NRD.

103. H. G. Rickover et al., Report of Conference [on] 19 July 1963, undated, NRD. For the introduction of computer studies in court, see the testimony of Capt. Samuel R. Heller, Jr., vol. 1, pp. 241–49; vol. 2, pp. 556–58; vol. 5, pp. 1234–38; vol. 6, p. 1625; vol. 8, Exhibits 56, 87, 88; vol. 10, Exhibit 174; vol. 11, Exhibits 226A, 225. For computer cases, see Opinions, Court of Inquiry, vol. 1, para. 5.

104. Rickover et al., Report of Conference [on] 19 July 1963, undated; JCAE, Executive Session, Meeting No. 88-1-47, 23 July 1963, pp. 8–16, both in NRD.

105. JCAE, Executive Session, Meeting No. 88-1-47, 23 July 1963, pp. 5–8, NRD. The quote is on page 6.

106. Ibid. The first quote appears on p. 17; the second on p. 19.

107. Ibid., p. 19, 24–25.

108. Ibid., pp. 27–28.

109. Ibid., pp. 33–38, 44, 95–97. Rickover's complete testimony is in Ibid. For an unclassified version, see JCAE, *Loss of the U.S.S. Thresher*, pp. 59–90.

110. For a description of the *Robert D. Conrad* and the *Atlantis II*, see Robert L. Trillo, ed., *Jane's Ocean Technology: 1976–77* (New York: Franklin Watts, 1976), pp. 307, 318. For accounts of the search for the *Thresher*, see Polmar, *Death of the Thresher*, pp. 48–85; E. W. Grenfell, "USS Thresher (SSN-593), 3 August 1961–10 April 1963," U.S. Naval Institute *Proceedings* 90 (March 1964): 36–47; John Bentley, *The Thresher Disaster: The Most Tragic Dive in Submarine History* (Garden City, New York: Doubleday, 1974), pp. 231–82. Based heavily upon conjecture, the remainder of the Bentley book should be used with caution.

111. For a description of the *Trieste*, see Trillo, *Jane's Ocean Technology: 1976–77*, p. 20. A firsthand account of the 1963 attempts is Kenneth V. MacKenzie, "Search for the 'Thresher'," in James Dugan and Richard Vahan, eds., *Men Under Water* (Philadelphia: Chilton Books, 1965), pp. 31–36. Press Briefing, The Pentagon, Sept. 5, 1963, NRD.

112. Rickover to Brockett, 20 Feb. 1964, NRD. On the *Trieste II* and *Mizar*, see Trillo, *Jane's Ocean Technology: 1976–77*, pp. 96–98, 302–3. Message from CTG 168.2 to various addressees, 20 Aug. 1964; H. R. Heimholtz, Radioactivity Analysis on Mud and Water Samples Obtained by *Trieste II* During the 1964 Deep Search and Inspection Operation, 8 Sept. 1964, all in NRD.

113. For the position of Korth and Nitze on declassification of the joint committee transcripts, see JCAE, *Loss of the U.S.S. Thresher*, Appendix 8, "Correspondence Concerning Classification of Information Relating to the Loss of the Thresher," pp. 159–66; and Appendix 7, "Correspondence Concerning Delay in Schedule and Loss of Radiographs of USS *Tinosa*," pp. 155–58; Spencer E. Robbins, Memorandum for the Assistant Secretary of the Navy (Installations & Logistics), 2 Oct. 1963, NRD.

114. JCAE, *Loss of the U.S.S. Thresher*, pp. 93–95.

115. Chief, Bureau of Ships to Vice Admiral A. I. McKee, USN, Ret., undated, but 25 April 1963; Rickover, Memorandum of Conversation with Admiral James, 12 April 1963; James to Rickover, 19 April 1963 with attachs.; Code 1500 to Code 100, 22 April 1963; Code 100 Memorandum to [Code] 200 et al., 3 June 1963, all in NRD.

116. Chief, Bureau of Ships to Chief of Naval Operations, 20 Dec. 1963, NRD; JCAE, *Loss of the U.S.S. Thresher*, pp. 92–118.

117. Commander, Naval Ship Systems Command to Distribution List, 10 Oct. 1969 with attach. titled Submarine Safety Program, Report, dated December 1968, NRD. For reference to costs, see JCAE, *Loss of the U.S.S. Thresher*, pp. 108–9.

118. JCAE, *Loss of the U.S.S. Thresher*, pp. 124–28.

119. Ibid., pp. 117–20, 128–31.

120. Proposed *Scorpion* Press Release, 3 Feb. 1969; Summary of Findings of Court of Inquiry Convened to Inquire into the Loss of the USS *Scorpion* (SSN 589) Between 21–27 May 1968, undated, both in NRD. Adm. Austin, also president of the *Scorpion* court, requested information from Rickover about the safety of the ship's reactor. See Rickover, Memorandum for the President, Court of Inquiry Investigating the Loss of the *Scorpion*, 1 July 1968, NRD. It was anticipated that the Joint Committee on Atomic Energy would convene hearings on the loss of the *Scorpion*, but they were not held. See Naval Ship Systems Command to Chief of Naval Material, undated, but late 1968 with encls.; W. Wegner to H. G. Rickover, 21 Jan. 1969, NRD. In March 1973 a faulty depth gauge nearly caused the loss of the submarine *Greenling*. See Orr Kelly, "A Thresher-type Sub Tragedy Averted: Hush Hush Seaman-Officer Confrontation," *Washington Star*, 3 May 1973.

Chapter 4. Surface Ships—First Battles

Three good books by Norman Friedman trace the complicated development of destroyers, cruisers, and aircraft carriers. The Naval Institute Press at Annapolis, Maryland, published *U.S. Destroyers, An Illustrated Design History* in 1982, *U.S. Aircraft Carriers, An Illustrated Design History* in 1983, and *U.S. Cruisers, An Illustrated Design History* in 1984.

1. Secretary of Defense, Memorandum for Secretaries of the Military Departments, . . . 6 May 1969; SecNav Instruction 7043.2A 12 Dec. 1969; Department of Defense Directive 7200.4 6 Sept. 1983, NRD.

2. Richard G. Hewlett and Francis Duncan, *Nuclear Navy: 1946–1962* (Chicago: University of Chicago Press, 1974), Appendix 2, "Construction of the Nuclear Navy," pp. 399–401; Joint Committee on Atomic Energy (hereafter cited as JCAE), *Naval Nuclear Propulsion Program—1970* (Washington: G.P.O., 1970), Appendix 9, "New Construction Major Warships and Submarines Authorized Since World War II," p. 228.

3. For the evolution of the fast attack carriers, see M. St. Denis, "The Strike Aircraft Carrier: Considerations in the Selection of Her Size and Principal Design Characteristics," The Society of Naval Architects and Marine Engineers, *Transactions* 74 (1966): 260–94; Nathan Sonenshein, "Aircraft Carrier Design," in Frank Uhlig, Jr., ed., *Naval Review 1965* (Annapolis: U.S. Naval Institute, 1965), pp. 64–97; Desmond P. Wilson, "Evolution of the Attack Carriers: A Case Study in Technology and Strategy," in Joint Hearings Before the Joint Senate-House Subcommittee of the Senate and House Armed Services Committees (hereafter cited as SASC for the Senate committee and HASC for the House), *CVAN-70 Aircraft Carrier*, 91st Cong., 2d sess. (Washington: G.P.O., 1970), pp. 398–608. See also: Raymond V. B. Blackman, ed., *Jane's Fighting Ships: 1958–59* (New York: McGraw-Hill, 1958), pp. 337–38.

4. Raymond V. B. Blackman, ed., *Jane's Fighting Ships: 1959–60* (New York: McGraw-Hill, 1959), p. 377.

5. Ibid., pp. 389–91.

6. Dating from 1940, subsection 7295 of Title 10—Armed Forces, *United States Code*, states that battleships are considered aged after 26 years, carriers and cruisers after 20, submarines after 13, and other surface combat vessels after 16 years. See also Adm. Burke's testimony on 10 Feb. 1958 in Subcommittee of the House Committee on Appropriations, *Department of Defense Appropriations for 1959—Overall Policy Statements*, pp. 542–43; and VAdm., Combs, deputy chief of naval operations (fleet operations and readiness) on 19 Feb. 1958, in the hearing volume *Department of the Navy*, pp. 384–85; D. D. Lewis, "The Problems of Obsolescence," U.S. Naval Institute *Proceedings* 85 (Oct. 1959): 27–31.

7. Chief of Naval Operations to Distribution List, 13 Jan. 1958 and encl., The Navy Of The 1970 Era, NRD.

8. Hewlett and Duncan, *Nuclear Navy: 1946–1962*, Appendix 2, "Construction of the Nuclear Navy, 1956–1962," pp. 399–401. For status and background of the A1W, C1W, and D1G, see pp. 274, 280–81, 311–12, 355. U.S. AEC *Twenty-Fourth Semiannual Report of the AEC* (Washington: G.P.O., July 1958), p. 109; The Naval Nuclear Propulsion Program—A Joint AEC-Department of the Navy Program, July 1973, pp. 26–27, 30–31, NRD. The enlargement in the Newport News Dry Dock is from R. Broad to author, 23 Nov. 1977, NRD.

9. Figures are from a series of briefing aids, shipbuilding costs, undated but probably used toward the end of 1957, NRD.

10. Subcommittee of the Senate Committee on Appropriations, *Department of De-*

fense Appropriations for 1960, 86th Cong., 1st sess. (Washington: G.P.O., 1959), pp. 172, 1017–43, 1552–59.

11. JCAE, *Naval Nuclear Propulsion Program—1970*, Appendix 9, p. 228. For costs see: Blackman, ed., *Jane's Fighting Ships: 1958–59*, pp. 337–38.
12. JCAE, *Naval Nuclear Propulsion Program—1970*, Appendix 9, p. 228.
13. R. K. James, Memorandum Report of Meeting With Admiral Burke, 2 June 1959; Ralph E. Wilson, Memorandum to Op-03 and Chairman, Ship Characteristics Board (Op-43), 2 June 1959; Dunford to Rickover, 2 June 1959, NRD.
14. Rickover to Code 100, 19 Aug. 1959, NRD; Denys W. Knoll, Director, Ship Characteristics Division to Op-04B, 27 July 1959; Record Group 38 (hereafter cited as RG and numbers), Records of the CNO, E1288, NARA contains views of the office of the CNO.
15. Strictly speaking, the Russians had a civilian power plant before the Americans. However their plant at Obninsk had a capacity of only 5 mwe compared with 60 mwe for Shippingport.
16. Memorandum from Op-04 to Op-00, undated but probably 17 July 1959; Burke to McCone, 18 July 1959; Burke, Memorandum for the Secretary of the Navy, 18 July 1959; Burke, Memorandum for the Record, 22 July 1959, all in Burke Papers, NHC.
17. Rickover, Memorandum for the Secretary of the Navy, 2 Nov. 1959, and encls.; Rickover to Homer, 16 Oct. 1959, NRD.
18. Panoff, Review of Nuclear Propulsion Work at the Quincy Yard of the Bethlehem Steel Company, 9 Dec. 1959, NRD.
19. Rickover refers to the meeting in Rickover to Burke, 8 June 1960 and attachs., NRD.
20. Chief of Naval Operations to Hubbard, 7 Dec. 1959; Appendix 1 of encl. 1 to Miles H. Hubbard to Chief of Naval Operations, 25 Feb. 1960; Report of Ad Hoc Committee for the Examination of Costs of Nuclear Powered Surface Ships, Part 1 of encl. 1 to Hubbard to Chief of Naval Operations, 25 Feb. 1960, NRD. (Hereafter cited as Hubbard Report.)
21. Hubbard Report, p. 1-1, NRD.
22. Percentages are calculated from Hubbard Report, Appendix 3, "CG(N)9 Cost History," and "CVA(N)65 Cost History," NRD.
23. Hubbard Report, pp. 1-1–1-5, 1-9, NRD. Quotation is from p. 1-5.
24. Hubbard Report, pp. 1-12, 1-13, NRD.
25. Rickover to Burke, 8 June 1960 and attachs.; Rickover to File, 9 Jan. 1960, NRD.
26. Howard C. Brown, Jr., Memorandum for Files, 9 Feb. 1960; W. B. Franke to John A. McCone, Chairman, AEC, 2 Dec. 1959, in AEC 47/35, 4 Aug. 1960, AEC.
27. For Gates, see Subcommittee of the House Appropriations Committee, *Department of Defense Appropriations for 1961, Part 1*, 86th Cong., 2d sess. (Washington: G.P.O., 1960), pp. 61–62. For Franke, see *Part 2*, pp. 85–86; for Burke, *Part 2*, pp. 84–86; for Beakley *Part 5*, pp. 267, 275, 296–97.
28. JCAE, *Naval Nuclear Propulsion Program—1970*, Appendix 9, pp. 228–30.
29. Burke to secretary of the navy, with handwritten note "typed 6/18/60," NRD. James A. Douglas to McCone, 1 Aug. 1960 in AEC 47/35, 4 Aug. 1960; McCone to Douglas, 26 Aug. 1960, AEC.
30. For catapult development, see Sonenshein, "Aircraft Carrier Design," *Naval Review 1965*, p. 91, and Robert A. Bird, "Catapult Developments," *Bureau of Ships Journal* (Oct. 1958): 11–13, 20; "Story of ICCP: Big V, Little g," *Naval Aviation News* (April 1958): 10–11. For carriers with steam catapults, see Blackman, ed., *Jane's Fighting Ships: 1959–60*, pp. 360–3. See Norman Friedman, *U.S. Aircraft*

Carriers, An Illustrated Design History (Annapolis, MD: Naval Institute Press, 1983), Appendix B, "Catapults," pp. 377–80.

31. The correspondence and actions of the bureaus and Rickover are in CVA(N)65 Catapult Significant History, a chronology in NRD. See also Rickover's later recapitulations of the struggle in Unsigned Memorandum of Discussion . . . in VADM Rickover's Office on 13 Dec. 1967, . . . encl. 1 from Rickover to Commander, Naval Air Systems Command, 5 Jan. 1968, NRD.

32. Unsigned but written by Shaw, undated Memorandum to File, titled, Telephone Conversation 7/2/59—1430; Chief, Bureau of Ships to Chief, Bureau of Weapons, 25 July 1960; unsigned Memorandum of Discussion . . . in VADM Rickover's Office on 13 Dec. 1967, . . . encl. 1 from Rickover to Commander, Naval Air Systems Command, 5 Jan. 1968, NRD. Bureau of Naval Weapons, Research, Development, Test and Evaluation Quarterly Progress Report, July–Sept. 1960 and for Period Ending 30 Dec. 1960

33. Rickover to Commander, Naval Air Systems Command, 5 Jan. 1968; Shaw, Report of Conference [on] 10 Nov. 1960, Steam Catapulting Capability of the Nuclear Propulsion Plant Installed in ENTERPRISE (CVA(N)65), Rough Draft, NRD.

34. Op-04, Memorandum to Op-00, 27 Oct. 1960 and encl.; Cost Comparison DLG(N) vs. DLG, encl. 1 to Op-04, Memorandum to Op-00, 27 Oct. 1960, RG38, Records of the CNO, E1288, NARA. See also unsigned document, rough draft, 19 Nov. 1960, NRD.

35. The reasons are stated in an unsigned document, rough draft, 19 Nov. 1960, NRD.

36. Burke, Memorandum for the Record, 13 Nov. 1960, NRD.

37. Unsigned, undated document titled Naval Nuclear Ship Propulsion Program, with handwritten notation, "Developed for Burke on 11/26/60. . . ."; Rickover to Burke, 1 Dec. 1960 and encl., both NRD.

38. Rickover to Burke, 1 Dec. 1960 and encl.; Douglas to McCone, 5 Dec. 1960, NRD. For a reference to numbers of ships, see Op-42, Memorandum to Op-00, 16 Dec. 1960, RG38, Records of the CNO, E1288, NARA.

39. Burke, Memorandum for RADM Speck, 28 Nov. 1960, NRD.

40. The text of the treatise appears in several congressional hearings. See, for example: Subcommittee of the House Committee on Appropriations, *Department of Defense Appropriations for 1962, Part 6*, 87th Cong., 1st sess. (Washington: G.P.O., 1961), pp. 8–12.

Chapter 5. Surface Ships—the Alliance with Congress

Three good books by Norman Friedman trace the complicated development of destroyers, cruisers, and aircraft carriers. The Naval Institute Press at Annapolis, MD, published *U.S. Destroyers, An Illustrated Design History* in 1982, *U.S. Aircraft Carriers, An Illustrated Design History* in 1983, and *U.S. Cruisers, An Illustrated Design History* in 1984.

1. Henry L. Trewhitt, *McNamara* (New York: Harper & Row, 1971), pp. 1–2, 26–56; David Halberstam, *The Reckoning* (New York: Avon Books, 1986), pp. 204–10, 234–38.

2. Connally's biographical data is from the Naval History Division, NHC.

3. *Who's Who in America, 1984–1985* 2 (Chicago: Marquis Who's Who, 1984): 2935; Richard G. Hewlett and Oscar E. Anderson, Jr., *The New World, 1939/1946*, vol. 1 of *A History of the U.S. Atomic Energy Commission* (University Park: Pennsylvania State University Press, 1962), pp. 90, 109, 175, 182–84, 204–5, 251.

4. Richard G. Hewlett and Francis Duncan, *Atomic Shield, 1947/1952*, vol. 2 of *A History of the U.S. Atomic Energy Commission* (University Park: Pennsylvania State

University Press, 1969), p. 190; Richard G. Hewlett and Francis Duncan, *Nuclear Navy: 1946–1962* (Chicago: University of Chicago Press, 1974), pp. 53, 55–56, 70–71.

5. "Special Message to the Congress on the Defense Budget," 28 March 1961 in *Public Papers of the Presidents: John F. Kennedy, 1961* (Washington: G.P.O., 1962), pp. 229–40. Information provided by James in House Committee on Armed Services (hereafter cited as HASC for the House and SASC for the Senate Committee), *Hearings . . . Pursuant to H.R. 6151, To Authorize Appropriations for Aircraft, Missiles, and Naval Vessels. . . .* (hereafter cited as *Hearings Pursuant to H.R. 6151*), 87th Cong., 1st sess. (Washington: G.P.O., 1961), pp. 1471–72.

6. HASC, *Hearings Pursuant to H.R. 6151*, pp. 1462–63; SASC, *Authorizing Appropriations for Aircraft, Missiles, and Naval Vessels*, April 1961, p. 534.

7. Rickover, Memorandum of Telephone Conversation, 19 March 1961, NRD.

8. Unsigned document titled, Points to Cover with Sec Nav, 7 March 1961; unsigned document titled, Points to Cover with SECNAV, 17 April 1961; Rickover, Inclusion of two nuclear frigates in the Nuclear Surface Shipbuilding Program for FY 62, 18 April 1961, NRD.

9. Rickover, Inclusion of two nuclear frigates in the Nuclear Surface Shipbuilding Program for FY 62, 18 April 1961, NRD.

10. HASC, *Hearings Pursuant to H.R. 6151*, p. 1599.

11. Rickover's testimony is in HASC, *Hearings Pursuant to H.R. 6151*, pp. 1599–1618, 1607, 1614. Earlier bureau studies were reaching the same conclusion. See Norman Friedman, *U.S. Destroyers, An Illustrated Design History* (Annapolis, Md.: Naval Institute Press, 1982), pp. 330–32.

12. McNamara, Memorandum for the President, 28 April 1961, JFK. For McNamara's position, see Vinson's remarks in *Congressional Record*, 87th Cong., 1st sess., 24 May 1961, vol. 107, part 7, pp. 8813–14.

13. Shaw, Repeat DLG(N)'s Problems, with typed notation at top of page, "Discussed with Adm. Schultz and Capt. McQuilkin by HGR and M. Shaw on 4/24/61," 24 April 1961; unsigned untitled document, 29 April 1961, with handwritten label "Sec Nav," NRD; Friedman, *U.S. Destroyers*, pp. 336–39.

14. James, Memorandum for the Secretary of the Navy, 4 May 1961, NRD.

15. U.S. Cong., House Committee *Authorizing Appropriations for Aircraft, Missiles, and Naval Vessels*, 10 May 1961, 87th Cong., 1st sess., H. Report No. 380, pp. 41–43; *Congressional Record*, 87th Cong., 1st sess., 24 May 1961, vol. 107, part 7, pp. 8813–14, 8823.

16. U.S. Cong., Senate Committee *Authorizing Appropriations for Aircraft, Missiles, and Naval Vessels for the Armed Forces for Fiscal Year 1962*, 11 May 1962, 87th Cong., 1st sess., S. Report No. 253, p. 7; *Congressional Record*, 87th Cong., 1st sess., 15 May 1961, vol. 107, part 6, p. 7939, and 12 June 1961, vol. 107, part 8, pp. 10061–62; U.S. Cong., House Committee on *Authorization for Aircraft, Missiles, and Naval Vessels, Fiscal Year 1962*, 8 June 1961, 87th Cong., 1st sess., H. Report No. 462; Public Law 53, 87th Cong., S. 1852, 75 Stat. 94, 21 June 1961; Public Law 144, 87th Cong., H.R. 7851, 75 Stat. 365, 17 Aug. 1961; Rickover, Memorandum of a Conference among the Secretary of the Navy, Admiral James and Admiral Rickover, 13 June 1961 and attachs.; The Naval Nuclear Propulsion Program—A Joint AEC–Department of the Navy Program, March 1967, both in NRD.

17. Members of Surface Ship Reactor Engineering with contributions from Reactor Metallurgy, A1W Core Three Summary Design Report, Part I: Mechanical Design, WAPD-V-785, 23 March 1961, NRD.

18. Hewlett and Duncan, *Nuclear Navy*, p. 279; Newport News Shipbuilding and Dry

Dock Co. (hereafter cited as NNS&DDCo.), D1W Propulsion Plant Progress Report, 15 Jan.–31 March 1961, NRD.

19. P. A. Rude, Surface Ship Reliability, WAPD-V(3EC)-10, June 1962, NRD.

20. NNS&DDCo., D1W Propulsion Plant Progress Report, 1–31 Dec. 1961, NRD. The *Bainbridge* displaced 6,500 tons light, 7,600 tons standard, and 8,430 tons fully loaded, measured 564 feet overall, 57-7/8 feet in beam and drew 20 feet. See Raymond V. B. Blackman, ed., *Jane's Fighting Ships, 1962–63* (New York: McGraw-Hill, 1962), p. 325; Technical Progress Report, D1W Project, WAPD-MRR-10, Dec. 1961, BAPL.

21. Deputy chief of naval operations (development) to chief of naval operations, 27 Jan. 1961. Shaw and Rickover participated in the drafting of this document. See undated, unsigned Rough Draft #2 written by Shaw, typed 25 Jan. 1961, NRD. Connally, Memorandum for Chief, Bureau of Ships, Chief, Bureau of Naval Weapons, 1 May 1961, NRD.

22. Bethlehem Steel Co., Shipbuilding Division, USS Long Beach—Bethlehem Hull 1669, Report of Builder's Sea Trials and Preliminary Acceptance Trials on 5, 6, and 7 July 1961, 18 and 19 July 1961, 28 and 29 Aug. 1961, NRD; Quincy (Mass.) *Patriot Ledger*, 6 July 1961.

23. de Poix to Chief of Naval Operations, July 3, 1961, NRD.

24. For *Enterprise* organization, see Vincent P. de Poix, "Nuclear Aircraft Carrier Operations," *Naval Engineers Journal* 76 (June 1964): 387–96.

25. NNS&DDCo., Program of Events, Preliminary Acceptance Trials, Enterprise—CVA(N)65, Builders Hull No. 546, undated, encl. 1 to NNS&DDCo. to Supervisor of Shipbuilding, Newport News, Virginia, 27 Sept. 1961, NRD.

26. Newport News (VA) *Times-Herald,* 31 Oct. 1961; Department of Defense News Release No. 1232–61, 31 Oct. 1961, NRD.

27. *USS Enterprise News*, 1 Nov. 1961, NRD. "Briny" is misspelled in the source. For *Laffey,* see Department of the Navy, Office of the Chief of Naval Operations, Naval History Division, *Dictionary of American Naval Fighting Ships, Vol. IV* (Washington: Navy Department, 1969), pp. 17–19.

28. *USS Enterprise News*, 1 Nov. 1961, NRD.

29. Rickover to Luedecke, 2 Nov. 1961, NRD; *New York Times,* 4 Nov. 1961; CNO Letter to Flag Officers, Oct. 1961, NRD.

30. McNamara to Secretary of the Army et al., 22 Sept. 1961, JFK.

31. HASC, *Hearings on Military Posture and H.R. 9751, . . .* 87th Cong., 2d sess. (Washington: G.P.O., 1962), p. 3261. Description of TYPHON is based on George D. Lukes, Memorandum for Members, Panel on Naval Warfare et al., 27 Oct. 1960, with attach.; Harvey Brooks, Draft Memorandum for Dr. G. B. Kistiakowsky, 9 Dec. 1960, DDE; Applied Physics Laboratory, The Johns Hopkins University, Progress Report, Long Range TYPHON Missile, 31 Aug. 1961, NAVORD.

32. Robert E. Wilson, Memorandum for Chairman Seaborg, 26 Oct. 1961; unsent letter, Glenn T. Seaborg to McNamara, 15 Nov. 1961, AEC.

33. Howard C. Brown, Jr., Memorandum for File, 6 Nov. 1961; Seaborg, Memorandum for Dr. Frank K. Pittman, Director, Division of Reactor Development, 30 Nov. 1961; Dwight A. Ink, Memorandum to File, 16 Jan. 1962, AEC.

34. ADM George W. Anderson, Memorandum for VADM Rickover, 18 Jan. 1962; Rickover, Memorandum for ADM Anderson, 3 Feb. 1962, both in NRD. Although Rickover used the *Ranger* to illustrate some of the technical factors in conversion, the total cost of the *Ranger* is from Raymond V. B. Blackman, ed., *Jane's Fighting Ships: 1963–1964* (New York: McGraw-Hill, 1963), p. 313, which states that the Ranger's cost was $182,000,000.

Characteristics

Displacement	
Standard	60,000 tons
Full Load	76,000 tons
Dimensions	
Length	1,047 (o.a.)
Beam (extreme width of flight deck)	252 feet
Waterline	129½ feet
Draught	37 feet (max.)
Area of Flight Deck	4.1 acres
Guns	4 5 inch, 54 cal. dual-purpose
Guided Missiles	Regulus capability
Aircraft	80 to 60 (according to size and type)
Catapults	4 steam

The time from keel laying to commissioning of the *Enterprise* is derived from Hewlett and Duncan, *Nuclear Navy*, Appendix 2, "Construction of the Nuclear Navy, 1952–1962," p. 401.

35. Chief, Bureau of Ships to Chief of Naval Operations, 17 Jan. 1962; Webber, Draft 4, CNO Presentation Outline, 2 Feb. 1962, with handwritten notation, "2/3/62 MTG"; Manager, Naval Reactors to Distribution List, 3 March 1962, with encl., Report of Conference, Naval Nuclear Propulsion Plant Development, . . . 3 Feb. 1962, NRD.

36. For Korth's testimony, see SASC, *Military Procurement Authorization, Fiscal Year 1963*, 87th Cong., 2d sess. (Washington: G.P.O., 1962), pp. 402, 405. For Anderson, see p. 427.

37. Roswell Gilpatric, Memorandum for the Secretary of the Navy, 27 Feb. 1962; Korth, Memorandum for the Deputy Secretary of Defense, 8 March 1962; Korth, Memorandum for Deputy Secretary of Defense, 30 March 1962, with encl., (1), Review of the Navy's Nuclear Propulsion Development Program, March 1962, NRD.

38. The hearing on the *Nautilus* remains classified; a copy is in NRD. For an unclassified version of the *Skipjack* hearings, see Joint Committee on Atomic Energy (hereafter cited as JCAE), *Review of Naval Reactors Program and Admiral Rickover Award*, 86th Cong., 1st sess. (Washington: G.P.O., 1959), pp. 1–46. For the *George Washington,* see JCAE, *Naval Reactor Program and Polaris Missile System*, 86th Cong., 2d sess. (Washington: G.P.O., 1961).

39. The following paragraphs are based upon JCAE, *Tour of the U.S.S. "Enterprise" and Report on Joint AEC–Naval Reactor Program* (hereafter cited as *Tour of the U.S.S. "Enterprise"*), 87th Cong., 2d sess. (Washington: G.P.O., 1962). Leighton drafted ahead of time the points he thought should be made. See Leighton, Notes Relative to Enterprise, 26 March 1962, NRD.

40. JCAE, *Tour of the U.S.S. "Enterprise,"* pp. 1–4, 8–10, 12–13, 19–21, 23.

41. JCAE, Press Release #251, 1 April 1962, NRD.

42. For photographs of the ship, see *Enterprise Cruise Book, 1962* (Westbury, New York: Howard Wohl, n.d. but probably 1963), pp. 128–35, 156–95.

43. The Naval Nuclear Propulsion Program—A Joint AEC–Department of the Navy Program, May 1974, p. 27, NRD. This account of operations off Cuba relies heavily on The Atlantic Command CINCLANT Historical Account of Cuban Crisis—1963, NHC; Deck Log of the *U.S.S. Enterprise* CVA(N) 65, CNO; and Hayward's testimony before the JCAE on 30 October 1963. His unclassified

testimony is in JCAE, *Nuclear Propulsion for Naval Surface Vessels,*, 88th Cong., 1st sess. (Washington: G.P.O., 1964), pp. 49–68.

44. Chief of Naval Operations to Chief, Bureau of Naval Weapons, et al., 18 June 1962, NRD; Secretary of Defense, Preliminary Draft Memorandum for the President, 31 Oct. 1962, JFK.
45. McNamara, Memorandum for the Secretary of the Navy, 26 Nov. 1962, NRD.
46. Leighton, Memorandum to Rickover, 23 Nov. 1962, NRD.
47. Code 1500, Memorandum to Code 400, 8 Dec. 1962; Chief, Bureau of Ships to Chief of Naval Operations, 31 Dec. 1962, NRD.
48. JCAE, *Tour of the U.S.S. "Enterprise,"* pp. iii–iv.
49. RAdm John T. Hayward to Korth, 2 Jan. 1963, NRD.
50. Commission meeting 1902, 18 Dec. 1962, AEC.
51. Seaborg to McNamara, 7 Jan. 1963, AEC.
52. Chief of Naval Operations to Secretary of the Navy, 10 Jan. 1963, with attach. titled, Memorandum for the Secretary of Defense, unsigned and undated but originated on 10 Jan. 1963; OP-34 to OP-03, 12 Jan. 1963, NRD.
53. For Anderson's views, see Chronology of Four Reactor Carrier, undated but probably 17 Sept. 1963, NRD.
54. Unsigned and undated document, Major Points to be Made in Meeting with Secretary of the Navy on 11 Jan. 1963; Chronology of Four Reactor Carrier; Notes for Meeting with Admiral Anderson on 16 January 1963, NRD.
55. Anderson, Memorandum for the Chief, Bureau of Ships, 17 Jan. 1963; James, Memorandum for the Chief of Naval Operations, 21 Jan. 1963; NRD.
56. Korth, Memorandum for the Secretary of Defense, 23 Jan. 1963 in JCAE, *Nuclear Propulsion for Naval Surface Vessels,* pp. 229–30.
57. McNamara to Seaborg, 2 Feb. 1963; McNamara, Memorandum for the Secretary of the Navy, 22 Feb. 1963, both in Ibid., pp. 81, 230–31.
58. McNamara, Memorandum for the Secretary of the Navy, 22 Feb. 1963, also in Ibid., pp. 230–31. For an interesting description of a study in Ford, see Halberstam, *The Reckoning,* pp. 234–37.
59. The literature on systems analysis is extensive. I have relied heavily on: Alain C. Enthoven and Wayne K. Smith, *How Much is Enough* (New York: Harper & Row, 1971), and by the same authors, "Systems Analysis and the Navy," in Frank Uhlig, Jr., ed., *Naval Review 1965,* pp. 99–117, and "Systems Analysis–Ground Rules for Constructive Debate" in *Air Force Magazine* (Jan. 1968): 33–40; William W. Kauffmann, *The McNamara Strategy* (New York: Harper & Row, 1964); Klaus Knorr, "Cost-Effectiveness and Research," *Bulletin of Atomic Scientists* 22 (Nov. 1966): 83–86, 101; James R. Schlesinger, "Quantitative Analysis and National Security," *World Politics XV* (Jan. 1963): 295–315; Ralph Sanders, *The Politics of Defense Analysis* (New York: Dunellen, 1973), is very useful. The quote is from the *Naval Review* article, p. 99.
60. CNO msg 251619Z to COMCARDIV TWO, 25 Jan. 1963; Hayward to Rickover, Sunday, undated but 17 Feb. 1963, NRD.
61. The Naval Nuclear Propulsion Program—A Joint AEC–Department of the Navy Program, Sept. 1966, p. 30; Hayward to Rickover, undated but in March 1963; Peet to Rickover, 8 March 1963, NRD.
62. J. D. Parker, Ship Characteristics Board Memo No. 23-63, 5 March 1963, with encl. titled, Subject Characteristics; CNO to Chief, Bureau of Ships, 7 March 1963; Code 400, Memorandum to Code 100, 12 March 1963; Rickover, Memorandum for Chief of Naval Operations, 14 March 1963; Claude Ricketts, Memorandum for the Ship Characteristics Board, 15 March 1963, all in NRD.

63. Korth, Memorandum for the Secretary of Defense, 4 April 1963, and CNO to Distribution List, 28 March 1963, both in JCAE, *Nuclear Propulsion for Naval Surface Vessels*, pp. 231–39.
64. Leighton, route slip and office memo, 8 April 1963; Leighton to Rickover, 9 April 1963, NRD.
65. McNamara, Memorandum for the Secretary of the Navy, 20 April 1963, NRD. For an unclassified version see: JCAE, *Nuclear Propulsion for Naval Surface Vessels*, pp. 240–44.
66. Korth, Memorandum for the Secretary of Defense, 26 Sept. 1963, AEC; an unclassified version can be found in JCAE, *Nuclear Propulsion for Naval Surface Vessels*, pp. 104–7.
67. McNamara, Memorandum for the Secretary of the Navy, 9 Oct. 1963, AEC. For an unclassified version, see ibid., pp. 244–45.
68. Pastore to McNamara, 9 Oct. 1963, and Korth, Memorandum for the Secretary of Defense, 10 Oct. 1963, are in ibid., pp. 4, 245–46.
69. Both the letter (Gilpatric to Pastore, 11 Oct. 1963) and the press release are in ibid., pp. 4–6.
70. Vincent P. de Poix, Memorandum for File, 12 Oct. 1963; paper with penciled title, "McNamara Gave This to HGR in Mtg on 10/15/63," NRD. McNamara referred to the meetings in JCAE, *Nuclear Propulsion for Naval Surface Vessels*, pp. 164–65.
71. Point Paper on CVAN 67 with penciled note, "Given to VADM Schoech on 10/21/63," NRD.
72. For text of documents, see JCAE, *Nuclear Propulsion for Naval Surface Vessels*, pp. 2–7, 25–26, 118–19.
73. Ibid., pp. 17, 23, 51, 61–62, 70, 131, 144.
74. *Public Papers of the Presidents of the United States: John F. Kennedy, 1963* (Washington: G.P.O., 1964), p. 831.
75. JCAE, *Nuclear Propulsion for Naval Surface Vessels*, pp. 151–96, but especially, pp. 152–55, 163, 167, 179, 180, 196.
76. Ibid., pp. iii–v.
77. Pastore to President, 21 Dec. 1963, in JCAE, *Naval Nuclear Propulsion Program—1967–68*, 90th Cong., 1st & 2d sess. (Washington: G.P.O., 1968), p. 262; McNamara to Pastore, 15 Jan. 1964; Jackson to RAdm T. F. Connolly, 26 Feb. 1964; Connolly to Jackson, 5 March 1964, NRD; Rickover to Nitze, 3 April 1964; Howard Brown, Memorandum for the Chairman, 9 April 1964, *AEC*.
78. Paul Schratz, "The Nuclear Carrier and Modern War," U.S. Naval Institute *Proceedings* 98 (Aug. 1972): 19–25. JCAE, *Nuclear Propulsion for Naval Surface Vessels*, pp. 170–73 and notes; Knorr, "Cost-Effectiveness and Research," *Bulletin of Atomic Scientists* 22 (Nov. 1966): 85.
79. JCAE, *Nuclear Propulsion for Naval Surface Vessels*, p. 196.
80. *Daily News* (McKeesport, PA), 25 April 1964; Pittsburgh *Post Gazette*, 25 April 1964. The terms of the understanding with McNamara are in Seaborg to McNamara, 29 April 1964, with encl., AEC. Rickover described the tour briefly in JCAE, *Nuclear Propulsion for Naval Warships*, 92d Cong., 1st and 2d sess. (Washington: G.P.O., 1972), p. 145.
81. McNamara Memorandum for the Secretary of the Navy, 25 April 1964, JFK; McDonald, Memorandum for the Vice Chief, OPs-01 et al., 27 April 1964; Paul H. Nitze, Memorandum for the Assistant Chief of the Bureau of Ships for Nuclear Propulsion, undated but received in NR on 1 May 1964, NRD.
82. Rickover to Nitze, 6 May 1964, NRD.

83. OP-090C6 to OP-090, 5 June 1964, NRD. See testimony of McNamara in Subcommittee of the Senate Committee on Appropriations and SASC, *Department of Defense Appropriations, 1965*, pp. 79, 125; and McDonald, HASC, *Hearings on Military Posture and H.R. 9637*, 86th Cong., 2d sess. (Washington: G.P.O., 1964), pp. 7234–35.

84. H. G. Rickover to File, 19 May 1964; D. T. Leighton to Rickover, 19 May 1964, NRD. For comparison of *Enterprise* and *Midway,* see Raymond V. B. Blackman, ed., *Jane's Fighting Ships: 1964–1965* (New York: McGraw-Hill, 1964), pp. 318, 321.

85. For reference to the study, see Chief, Bureau of Ships to Chief of Naval Operations (Chairman, Ship Characteristics Board), 17 June 1964. For summary of the weaknesses of the smaller two-reactor carriers, see Paul H. Nitze, Memorandum for the Secretary of Defense, 16 July 1964, encl. 3 titled, Alternate Two-Reactor Propulsion Plant, *NRD.*

86. *Pittsburgh Press,* 5 June 1964, in *NRD* files. A reference to the June 8 briefing is in David L. McDonald, Memorandum for the Secretary of the Navy, 7 July 1964; Paul H. Nitze, Memorandum for the Secretary of Defense, 16 July 1964, both in *NRD.* Handwritten note, Connolly to VAdm. Rickover, undated but on or shortly after 16 July 1964; Office of the Secretary of the Navy, Memorandum for the Secretary of Defense, undated but after 16 July 1964, *NRD.*

87. Unsigned Memorandum to File, but probably written by Leighton, 6 Aug. 1964, NRD. Price's recollection is in Melvin Price to Harold Brown, 24 Jan. 1977, NRD. Rickover refers to the statement in JCAE, *Nuclear Propulsion for Naval Warships,* pp. 145–46. The Memorandum to File, 6 Aug. 1964, does not mention Brown's statement. D. T. Leighton, Memorandum to File, 30 July 1964, *NRD,* refers to another meeting in which Brown was reported to have said words to the effect that "Let's face it, the boss is in the bite now."

88. McNamara to Seaborg, 7 Aug. 1964; unsigned Memorandum for the Secretary of the Navy, hand-dated 7 Aug. 1964, *NRD. Public Papers of the Presidents of the United States: Lyndon B. Johnson 1963-1964, Book II* (Washington: G.P.O., 1965), p. 1042. News Conference of Honorable Robert S. McNamara, Secretary of Defense, The Pentagon, 22 Oct. 1964, NRD. JCAE, *Nuclear Propulsion for Naval Warships,* p. 149.

89. An unpublished research paper by Annette D. Barnes, "Operation Sea Orbit," is on file in NRD.

90. NAVWAG 33 has two titles: Interim Report, Nuclear Propulsion for Carrier Task Forces, 17 Sept. 1964; and Interim Report, Nuclear Power for Surface Warships, 26 Sept. 1964, NRD. The reports are identical. For the purpose of the report and its delay, see pp. 1, 6.

91. McDonald, Memorandum for the Secretary of the Navy, 26 Oct. 1964; Interim Report: Nuclear Propulsion for Carrier Task Forces, NAVWAG 33, 17 Sept. 1964, pp. ii–iii, 2–16, NRD.

92. McDonald, Memorandum for the Secretary of the Navy, 26 Oct. 1964, NRD. Center for Naval Analyses of The Franklin Institute, Nuclear Power For Surface Warships—Naval Warfare Analysis Group Study 33—Final Report, 22 Feb. 1965, pp. 1–3a, 35–36, NRD.

93. McDonald, Memorandum for the Secretary of the Navy, 6 May 1965; Nitze, Memorandum for the Secretary of Defense, 26 May 1965, NRD.

94. G.T.S., telephone call: From Harold Brown to Dr. Seaborg, 11 Aug. 1965, AEC; Charles J. Hitch, Memorandum for the Secretary of Defense, 26 Aug. 1965, LBJ.

Chapter 6. Legislating Nuclear Power into the Fleet

For additional background and technical information, see Norman Friedman, *U.S. Destroyers, An Illustrated Design History* and *U.S. Aircraft Carriers, An Illustrated Design History* published at Annapolis, Maryland, by the Naval Institute Press in 1982 and 1983.

1. For status, see John Moore, ed., *Jane's Fighting Ships: 1984–1985* (New York: Jane's, 1984), pp. 663, 676–77.
2. Center for Naval Analysis, NAVWAG Study 33, Interim Report. Nuclear Propulsion for Carrier Task Forces, 17 Sept. 1964, pp. 2–3, 21, 46, NRD.
3. Excerpts from Nitze to McNamara, 13, 18 Nov. 1964 are in Joint Committee on Atomic Energy (hereafter cited as JCAE), *Nuclear Propulsion for Naval Warships,* 92nd Cong., 1st and 2d sess. (Washington: G.P.O., 1972), pp. 150–52. McNamara, Memorandum for the President, 10 Dec. 1964, LBJ; JCAE, *Nuclear Propulsion for Naval Warships,* pp. 151–52.
4. For Holifield's speech, see JCAE, *Nuclear Propulsion for Naval Warships,* p. 152. For reference to Rivers's statement and speech, see Holifield to Rivers, 19 Feb. 1965, NRD.
5. House Committee on Armed Services, *Hearings on Military Posture and H.R. 4016...,* 89th Cong., 1st sess. (Washington: G.P.O., 1965), pp. 323, 331.
6. U.S. Cong., House Committee *Authorizing Defense Procurement ... ,* 29 April 1965, 89th Cong., 1st sess., H. Report 271, p. 7.
7. House Subcommittee on Defense Appropriations, *Department of Defense Appropriations for 1966: Testimony of Vice Adm. Hyman G. Rickover, U.S. Navy,* 89th Cong., 1st sess. (Washington: G.P.O., 1965), pp. 5–7.
8. U.S. Cong., House Committee *Authorizing Defense Procurement ... ,* 29 April 1965, 89th Cong., 1st sess., H. Report 271; U.S. Cong., Senate Committee *Authorizing Appropriations During Fiscal Year 1966 ... ,* 2 April 1965, 89th Cong., 1st sess., S. Report 144, pp. 8–14; U.S. Cong., Conference Committee *Authorizing Appropriations for Aircraft, Missiles, and Naval Vessels, 1966,* 25 May 1965, 89th Cong., 1st sess., H. Report 374, p. 2. U.S. Cong., House Committee *Department of Defense Appropriation Bill, 1966,* 17 June 1965, 89th Cong., 1st sess., H. Report 528, pp. 40–41; U.S. Cong., Senate Committee, *Department of the Navy Appropriations Bill, 1966,* 18 Aug. 1965, 89th Cong., 1st sess., S. Report 625, p. 36; Public Law 213, 89th Cong., 29 Sept. 1965, 79 Stat., p. 7; JCAE, *Naval Nuclear Propulsion Program—1970,* 91st Cong., 2d sess. (Washington: G.P.O., 1970), Appendix 9, "New Construction Major Surface Warships and Submarines Authorized Since World War II," pp. 230–31.
9. U.S. Cong., House Committee *Department of Defense Appropriation Bill, 1966,* 89th Cong., 1st sess. H. Report 528, pp. 40–41; U.S. Cong., Senate Committee *Department of Defense Appropriation Bill, 1966,* 89th Cong., 1st sess., S. Report 625, p. 36.
10. Unsigned Memorandum to File, but probably written by D. T. Leighton, 28 Dec. 1965, NRD.
11. The following correspondence or excerpts are in JCAE, *Naval Nuclear Propulsion Program—1967–68,* 90th Cong., 1st and 2d sess. (Washington: G.P.O., 1968), pp. 280–98; L. Mendel Rivers to Robert S. McNamara, 18 Oct. 1965; Robert S. McNamara to L. Mendel Rivers, 2 Nov. 1965; Blandford for L. Mendel Rivers to David L. McDonald, 5 Nov. 1965; L. Mendel Rivers to Lyndon B. Johnson, 10 Nov. 1965; L. Mendel Rivers to McNamara, 10 Nov. 1965; Chet Holifield to Robert S. McNamara, 14 Nov. 1965; Robert S. McNamara to L. Mendel Rivers, 1 Dec. 1965; Robert S. McNamara to Chet Holifield, 1 Dec. 1965; David L.

McDonald to L. Mendel Rivers, 1 Dec. 1965. Address by Congressman Chet Holifield . . . , 17 Jan. 1966.

12. McDonald's long-range program is in Memorandum to File, unsigned but probably by D. T. Leighton, 28 Dec. 1965, NRD. For McNamara's views, see his Memorandum for the President, 9 Dec. 1965, LBJ. For the visit to Texas, see McDonald, Memorandum for Secretary McNamara, 9 Dec. 1965, LBJ. McDonald and other members of the joint chiefs of staff saw Johnson on 10 Dec. 1965. See President's Daily Diary, 10 Dec. 1965, LBJ. For the administration's request, see JCAE, *Naval Nuclear Propulsion Program—1970,* Appendix 9, pp. 228–31.

13. House Committee on Armed Services (hereafter cited as HASC for the House and SASC for the Senate committee), *Hearings on Military Posture and H.R. 13456 . . . ,* 89th Cong., 2d sess. (Washington: G.P.O., 1966), pp. 7287, 7409–12, 7573–77, 8034, 8105–13. The quotation is on p. 7577.

14. H. G. Rickover to Vice Adm. John Hayward, 20 April 1966, NRD. HASC, *Hearings on Military Posture and H.R. 13456 . . . ,* p. 7577.

15. For Nitze's Memorandum for the Secretary of Defense, 22 April 1966 and Rivers's views, see HASC, *Hearings on Military Posture and H.R. 13456 . . . ,* pp. 8034, 8106–8.

16. HASC, *Hearings on Military Posture and H.R. 13456 . . . ,* pp. 8124–28, 8135–36, 8144–45, 8160.

17. U.S. Cong., House Committee *Authorizing Defense Procurement and Research and Development and Military Pay,* 16 May 1966, 89th Cong., 2d sess., H. Report 1536, pp. 6–14, 17–18, 24.

18. U.S. Cong., Senate Committee *Authorizing Appropriations During Fiscal Year 1967 for Procurement of Aircraft, Missiles, Naval Vessels . . . ,* 89th Cong., 2d sess., S. Report 1136, pp. 5–6, 10; U.S. Cong, House Committee *Authorizing Defense Procurement and Research and Development, and Military Pay,* 16 May 1966, 89th Cong., 2d sess., H. Report 1536, p. 2; U.S. Cong., House Committee *Authorizing Appropriations for Defense . . . ,* 30 June 1966, 89th Cong., 2d sess. H. Report 1679, p. 2; Public Law 501, 89th Cong., S. 2950, 80 Stat., 13 July 1966; JCAE, *Naval Nuclear Propulsion Program—1970,* Appendix 9, pp. 230–31. U.S. Cong., House Committee *Department of Defense Appropriation Bill, 1967,* 24 June 1966, 89th Cong., 2d sess., H. Report 1652, pp. 3, 8, 24; U.S. Cong., Senate Committee, *Department of the Navy Appropriation Bill, 1967,* 12 Aug. 1966, 89th Cong., 2d sess., S. Report 1458, p. 35; Public Law 687, 89th Cong., 15 Oct. 1966, 80 Stat., pp. 7–9.

19. JCAE, *Naval Nuclear Propulsion Program—1970,* Appendix 9, pp. 230–31. The Rivers and Holifield correspondence is in JCAE, *Naval Nuclear Propulsion Program—1967-68,* pp. 301–9.

20. JCAE, *Naval Nuclear Propulsion Program—1970,* Appendix 9, pp. 230–31; HASC and Subcommittee of the Committee on Appropriations, *Military Procurement Authorizations for Fiscal Year 1968,* 90th Cong., 1st sess. (Washington: G.P.O., 1967), pp. 96–97, 409. For a discussion of the DX, DXG, and DLON, see Norman Friedman, *U.S. Destroyers, An Illustrated Design History* (Annapolis, MD: Naval Institute Press, 1982), pp. 369–77.

21. SASC, *Military Procurement Authorizations for Fiscal Year 1968,* p. 641. For an idea of the response time, see John E. Moore, ed., *Jane's Fighting Ships: 1975-76,* p. 457.

22. Horacio Rivero, "As I Recall . . . ," *U.S. Naval Institute Proceedings* 105 (July 1979): 122–23; Nitze refers to the studies and the gas turbine ships in HASC, *Hearings on Military Posture and A Bill (H.R. 9240) To Authorize Appropriations During the Fiscal Year 1968 . . . ,* 90th Cong., 1st sess. (Washington: G.P.O., 1967), p. 718.

23. H. G. Rickover, Memorandum for the Secretary of the Navy, 3 Feb. 1967 and

encl., Comparison of Advantages and Costs of Nuclear Frigates and Destroyers to Their Conventional Counterparts, NRD. For an unclassified version of the memorandum and study, see HASC, *Hearings on Military Posture and A Bill (H.R. 9240)* . . . , pp. 1804–48. The quote is on p. 1805.

24. HASC, *Hearings on Military Posture and A Bill (H.R. 9240)* . . . , pp. 1848–49.
25. Ibid., pp. 1849–50.
26. Rickover, Memorandum for the Chief of Naval Operations, 9 March 1967, NRD.
27. U.S. Cong., Senate Committee, *Authorizing Appropriations During Fiscal Year 1968 for Procurement of . . . Naval Vessels* . . . , 20 March 1967, 90th Cong., 1st sess., S. Report 76, p. 19.
28. HASC, *Hearings on Military Posture . . . to Authorize Appropriations* . . . , 90th Cong., 1st sess. (Washington: G.P.O., 1967), pp. 1751–55.
29. U.S. Cong., House Committee *Authorizing Defense Procurement and Research and Development*, 2 May 1967, 90th Cong., 1st sess., H. Report 221, pp. 5–8. Quote is on p. 8. For the provisions of the Act, see Title I, Public Law 22, 90th Cong., S. 666, 5 June 1967, 8 Stat. 52.
30. Horacio Rivero, Memorandum for the Secretary of the Navy, 5 Aug. 1967; Office of the Chief of Naval Operations, Major Fleet Escort Force Level Study, vols. 1, 2, and 3, NRD. See especially vol. 1, pp. 11 and 23 for the ship characteristics; Elmo R. Zumwalt, *On Watch, A Memoir* (New York: Quadrangle/Times Books, 1976), pp. 100–104.
31. Rivero, Memorandum for the Secretary of the Navy, 5 Aug. 1967; Major Fleet Escort Force Level Study, vol. 1, pp. vii–viii, 11, 23; Major Fleet Escort Force Level Study, Supplement on Endurance, 15 Sept. 1967, NRD. For the origin of the supplement, see Zumwalt, *On Watch*, pp. 101–3.
32. Moorer, Memorandum for the Secretary of the Navy, 15 Sept. 1967, NRD. Supplement on Endurance, pp. 57–58. Zumwalt, *On Watch*, p. 103 states that sixteen to nineteen frigates could be justified with questionable assumptions.
33. Unsigned Memorandum for the Record, 7 Sept. 1967; unsigned Notes for Luncheon Meeting with Dr. Frosch on 12 September 1967; T. H. Moorer, Memorandum for the Secretary of the Navy, 15 Sept. 1967, NRD. Much of the Moorer Memorandum can be found in JCAE, *Nuclear Propulsion for Naval Warships*, pp. 194–97.
34. Leighton to Distribution, 22 Sept. 1967, NRD.
35. For excerpts from the correspondence, see JCAE, *Nuclear Propulsion for Naval Warships*, pp. 197–98; Public Law 96, 90th Cong., H.R. 10738, was signed 29 Sept. 1967.
36. JCAE, *Nuclear Propulsion for Naval Warships*, p. 202.
37. Rickover, Memorandum for the Chief of Naval Operations, 8 Nov. 1967, NRD; Nathan Sonenshein, "A New Approach to Navy Ship Procurement," U.S. Naval Institute *Proceedings* 95 (Jan. 1969): 135–40; Friedman, *U.S. Destroyers*, pp. 369–72.
38. Rickover, Memorandum for the Chief of Naval Operations, 8 Nov. 1967, NRD.
39. For excerpts of the letter, see JCAE, *Nuclear Propulsion for Naval Warships*, pp. 202–3.
40. For announcement of 29 Nov. 1967, see *Public Papers of the Presidents of the United States: Lyndon B. Johnson, 1967* (Washington: G.P.O., 1968), pp. 1077–78.
41. For a perceptive analysis of naval organization, see Vice Adm. Edwin B. Hooper's *The Navy Department: Evolution and Fragmentation* (Washington: Naval Historical Foundation, 1978), pp. 27–46.
42. JCAE, *Nuclear Propulsion for Naval Warships*, pp. 203–5. In 1985 the Naval Material Command was disbanded and its functions distributed to various other organizations.
43. JCAE, *Nuclear Propulsion for Naval Warships*, p. 205.

44. McNamara, Memorandum for the President, 20 Jan. 1968, LBJ.
45. SASC, *Authorization for Military Procurement . . . Fiscal Year 1969, and Reserve Strength,* 90th Cong., 2d sess. (Washington: G.P.O., 1968), pp. 199–201, 285; JCAE, *Naval Nuclear Propulsion Program—1967–68,* pp. 99–155; Chet Holifield to the President, 9 Feb. 1968, NRD.
46. McNamara, Memorandum for the President, 27 Feb. 1968, LBJ; H.G.R., Memorandum of Telephone Conversation with Congressman Holifield, 27 Feb. 1968, NRD. Without question Rivers had a great deal to do with the solution, but documentary evidence on his role is lacking. See the reference in JCAE, *Nuclear Propulsion for Naval Warships,* p. 208.
47. Clark M. Clifford, Memorandum for the President, 25 March 1968, NRD. The presidential memorandum is in JCAE, *Nuclear Propulsion for Naval Warships,* p. 210. See also JCAE, *Naval Nuclear Propulsion Program—1970,* Appendix 9, pp. 230–31; U.S. Cong., HASC, *Authorizing Appropriations for Military Procurement . . . ,* 90th Cong., 2d sess., 5 July 1968, H. Report 1645, p. 5.
48. Major Fleet Escort Force Level Study, vol. 1, p. 11–13; John Moore, ed., *Jane's Fighting Ships: 1984–1985* (New York: Jane's, 1984), p. 674.
49. For a very useful summary, see JCAE, *Naval Nuclear Propulsion Program—1970,* Appendix 9, pp. 228–29.
50. For the importance of the fiscal year 1970 program, see the Rickover and Leighton testimony in Subcommittee of the House Committee on Appropriations, *Department of Defense Appropriations for 1970: Part 6,* 91st Cong., 1st sess. (Washington: G.P.O., 1969), pp. 669–70.
51. U.S. Cong., Senate Committee *Authorizing Appropriations for Fiscal Year 1970 for Military Procurement . . . ,* 3 July 1969, 91st Cong., 1st sess., H. Report 290, pp. 32–35. *Congressional Record,* 91st Cong., 1st sess., vol. 15, part 17, S 23531-2; Press Release, From the Offices of Senator Clifford P. Case and Senator Walter F. Mondale, 12 Aug. 1969, NRD.
52. James D. Hittle, Memorandum for the Vice Chief of Naval Operations, 14 Aug. 1969, NRD. For the reference to the Hatfield report, see Subcommittee of the House Committee on Appropriations, *Department of Defense Appropriations for 1970 Part 6,* pp. 670–92, and unpublished paper about 15 July 1969 entitled "Impact of Recommendation of Hatfield Report," NRD; unsigned point paper dated 15 Aug. 1969 with handwritten note: "HGR gave this info to Chief of Naval Operations in telecon this date. L." And unsigned point paper entitled, "The Navy's Attack Carriers," hand dated 8-15-69 with note, "Given to Laird for luncheon mtg with Sen. Stennis," NRD. H. G. Rickover to John Stennis, 5 Sept. 1969, NRD. *Congressional Record,* 91st Cong., 1st sess., vol. 115, part 18, S 25070-25071.
53. *Congressional Record,* 91st Cong., 1st sess., vol. 115, part 18, pp. S 24779-80; and vol. 115, part 19, S 25291-25327. For authorization, see Public Law 121, 83 STAT 204, 91st Cong., 19 Nov. 1969, p. 3.
54. Senate-House Armed Services Subcommittee, *CVAN-70 Aircraft Carrier,* 91st Cong., 2d sess. (Washington: G.P.O., 1970), p. 2.
55. For Rickover's testimony, see ibid., pp. 634–742. For administration and congressional quotations referring to the NSC study, see JCAE, *Nuclear Propulsion for Naval Warships,* pp. 223–30. For Stennis's and Thurmond's efforts to get a decision from Nixon, see pp. 232–35. For Rivers's actions, see U.S. Cong., House Committee *Authorizing Appropriations, Fiscal Year 1971 . . . ,* 24 April 1970, 91st Cong., 2d sess., H. Report 1022, pp. 1–3; JCAE, *Naval Nuclear Propulsion Program—1971,* pp. 134–38, 143–47.
56. U.S. Cong., House Committee *Authorizing Appropriations for Fiscal Year 1971 . . . ,*

91st Cong., 2d sess., H. Report 1473, pp. 1–2. See also JCAE, *Naval Nuclear Propulsion Program—1971*, p. 146.

57. Subcommittee No. 3 (Seapower) of the HASC, *Hearings on Military Posture and H.R., 12564 . . . , part 2*, 93d Cong., 2d sess. (Washington: G.P.O., 1974), p. 940.

58. Ibid., pp. 1004–7, 1026–27, 1036–37. Quotation is from JCAE, *Naval Nuclear Propulsion Program—1974*, 93rd Cong., 2d sess., (Washington: G.P.O., 1974), p. 16.

59. Subcommittee of the HASC, *Hearings on Military Posture and H.R. 12564 . . . , Part 2*, pp. 1435–36.

60. U.S. Cong., House Committee *Authorizing Appropriations, Fiscal Year 1975, For Military Procurement . . .* , 10 May, 93d Cong., 2d sess., H. Report 1035, pp. 6–8.

61. For the text of Title VIII and Rickover's views, see H. G. Rickover, "Nuclear Warships and the Navy's Future," U.S. Naval Institute *Proceedings* 101 (Jan. 1975): 19–24.

62. *Congressional Record*, 93d Cong., 2d sess., vol. 120, pt. 12, pp. H 15495, H 15497–98, H 15508–10, H 16166–70, H 16183.

63. U.S. Cong., Committee *Authorizing Appropriations for Fiscal Year 1975 for Military Procurement . . .* , 30 July 1974, 93d Cong., 2d sess., H. Conference Report 1038, p. 51; Public Law 365, 88 STAT 399, 93d Cong.; *Congressional Record*, 93d Cong., 2d sess., vol. 120, pt. 19, pp. H 25503–4, H 25817; *Public Papers, 1974, Nixon* (Washington: G.P.O., 1975), p. 620.

64. For Bennett's views, see *The U.S. Navy: What Is Its Future?* (Washington: American Enterprise Institute for Public Policy Research, 1977), pp. 7, 35. Zumwalt to Hebert, 16 May 1974, NRD; see also Rickover's testimony in HASC, *Hearings on Military Posture and H.R. 11500 . . . Part 4*, 94th Cong., 2d sess. (Washington: G.P.O., 1976), pp. 529–94, and his article, "Nuclear Warships and the Navy's Future," U.S. Naval Institute *Proceedings* 101 (Jan. 1975): pp. 18–24; Moore, ed., *Jane's Fighting Ships: 1984–85*, pp. 636, 679.

65. U.S. Cong., Senate Committee *Department of Defense Authorization Act, 1978*, 21 June 1977, 95th Cong., 1st sess., S. Conference Report 282, p. 27; U.S. Cong., House Committee *Department of Defense Appropriation Authorization Act, 1979*, 95th Cong., 2d sess., H. Report 1402, pp. 13–14; U.S. Cong., House Committee *Department of Defense Appropriation Authorization Act, 1979*, 15 Sept. 1978, 95th Cong., 2d sess, H. Report 1573, pp. 14–15, 35–36; Public Law 485, 95th Cong., 92 Stat., 20 Oct. 1978.

66. John Moore, ed., *Jane's Fighting Ships: 1984–85*, pp. 661, 674–78.

67. HASC, *Hearings on Military Posture and H.R. 12564 . . . , Part 2*, pp. 1391–96, and conversations with Rickover.

Chapter 7. Technology and Diplomacy: The Multilateral Force

Two outstanding books on the MLF are: Henry A. Kissinger, *The Troubled Partnership: A Re-appraisal of the Atlantic Alliance* (New York: McGraw-Hill, 1965); and Glenn T. Seaborg with Benjamin S. Loeb, *Stemming the Tide: Arms Control in the Johnson Years* (Lexington, MA: D.C. Heath, 1987). In pp. 84–130, the commission chairman gives his unique perspective.

1. Notes for Briefing the Congressional Leaders at the White House, 3 Dec. 1957, AEC; Report of Bipartisan Congressional Meeting, 3 Dec. 1957, DDE.

2. Dwight D. Eisenhower, *Waging Peace, 1956–1961* (New York: Doubleday, 1965), pp. 229–32; James R. Killian, Jr., *Sputnik, Scientists, and Eisenhower: A Memoir of the First Special Assistant to the President for Science and Technology* (Cambridge:

MIT Press, 1977), pp. 230–33; "Statements at the Opening Session of the NATO Council Meeting, 16 Dec. 1957," in Department of State, *North Atlantic Treaty Organization: Meeting of Heads of Government, Paris, December 1957: Texts of Statements* (Washington: Department of State, 1958), pp. 35–41.

3. "Statements at the Opening Session of the NATO Council Meeting, Dec. 16, 1957," "Statements at the First Business Session of the NATO Council Meeting, Dec. 16, 1957," in Department of State, *North Atlantic Treaty Organization: Meeting of Heads of Government . . .* , pp. 35–41, 61–71.

4. "Annual Message to the Congress on the State of the Union," 9 Jan. 1958, *Public Papers of the Presidents of the United States: Dwight D. Eisenhower, 1958* (Washington: G.P.O., 1959), p. 11.

5. For the background and legislative package, see Strauss to Carl T. Durham, 27 Jan. 1958, and encl. in Joint Committee on Atomic Energy (hereafter cited as JCAE), *Amending the Atomic Energy Act of 1954*, 85th Cong., 2d sess. (Washington: G.P.O., 1958), pp. 2–11. For exchanges between Strauss and Clinton P. Anderson, see pp. 16–17, 40–41, 64.

6. H. G. Rickover, Naval Reactor Work in the United Kingdom, 20 Aug. to 31 Aug. 1956, in W. Kenneth Davis, Memorandum to K. E. Fields, 21 Sept. 1956, NRD. For an unclassified version of Rickover's testimony, see JCAE, *Amending the Atomic Energy Act of 1954*, 161–74.

7. JCAE, *Atomic Energy Legislation Through 87th Congress, 1st Session*, part I, The Atomic Energy Act of 1954, sections 91, 123, and 144, on pp. 28–30, 35–37, 39–41. For legislative history, see p. 154.

8. Foy D. Kohler to the Acting Secretary, 2 June 1959; Kohler to the Secretary, 20 June 1959; Robert Murphy, Memorandum for the President, 26 June 1959, DOS; Richard M. Nixon, *Six Crises* (Garden City, New York: Doubleday, 1962), p. 237.

9. J. M. McSweeney, Memorandum of Conversation [on] Kozlov Visit, 13 July 1959, DOS; *New York Times,* 12 July 1959; J. M. McSweeney, Memorandum of Conversation [on] Kozlov visit, 11 July 1959, DOS; Pittsburgh *Sun-Telegraph,* 12 July 1959. Rickover scrapbooks contain clippings from newspapers published throughout the country.

10. Memorandum for the Files of John A. McCone, 15 July 1959, AEC.

11. Unsigned, Memorandum of Conversation, 25 July 1959, DOS; Rickover, Visit of Vice President Nixon and Admiral Rickover with Mr. Kozlov, Deputy Foreign Minister Kumaza, and Ambassador Thompson At The Kremlin, Saturday, 25 July 1959, NRD.

12. For the agreement for cooperation, see AEC, *Major Activities in the Atomic Energy Programs, Jan.–Dec. 1959* (Washington: AEC, Jan. 1960), pp. 97–98.

13. Unsigned Memorandum by Rickover, Report of Visit to Nuclear Icebreaker Lenin by Vice Admiral H. G. Rickover, USN, at the Admiralty Shipyard, Leningrad, on 27 July 1959, dated 20 Nov. 1959, NRD. A Russian version of the visit is in *Komsomolskaya Pravda*, Moscow, 20 Dec. 1961. See also Washington *Daily News*, 27 July 1959.

14. JCAE, Executive Session, Meeting #86-1-39, 9 Aug. 1959; Rickover to McCone, 20 Aug. 1959; AEC.

15. Alastair Buchan, "The Multilateral Force: An Historical Perspective," *Adelphi Papers*, no. 13 (London: The Institute for Strategic Studies, Oct. 1964), pp. 4–5.

16. Robert R. Bowie, The North Atlantic Nations: Tasks for the 1960's. A Report to the Secretary of State, Aug. 1960, DOS. Robert R. Bowie, "Strategy And The Atlantic Alliance" in Francis O. Wilcox and H. Field Haviland, Jr., eds., *The Atlantic Community: Progress and Prospects* (New York: Frederick A. Praeger, 1963), pp. 191–214.

17. Clinton P. Anderson to Kennedy, 16 Nov. 1960, AEC.
18. Arthur M. Schlesinger, Jr., *A Thousand Days: John F. Kennedy in the White House* (Boston: Houghton Mifflin, 1965), pp. 851–55; "Address Before the Canadian Parliament in Ottawa, May 17, 1961," *Public Papers of the Presidents of the United States: John F. Kennedy, 1961* (Washington: G.P.O., 1962), p. 385.
19. James A. Dewar, "Britain and the Skybolt Affair," *Aerospace Historian* 18 (Sept. 1971): 129–34; William P. Snyder, *The Politics of British Defense Policy, 1945–1962* (Columbus: Ohio State University Press, 1964), pp. 24–28; George W. Ball, *The Discipline of Power: Essentials of a Modern World Structure* (Boston: Little, Brown, 1968), pp. 99–100. Harold Macmillan, *At The End Of The Day, 1961–1963* (New York: Harper & Row, 1973), pp. 341–43; Schlesinger, *A Thousand Days,* pp. 856–62; Andrew J. Pierre, *Nuclear Politics: The British Experience With An Independent Strategic Force, 1939–1970* (New York: Oxford University Press, 1972), pp. 224–26.
20. Unclassified transcript of telegram from Mr. Pierre Salinger, Nassau, to State Department . . . under date of 21 Dec. 1962, setting forth . . . "non-attributable" press conference, NRD; Schlesinger, *A Thousand Days,* pp. 862–65; Theodore C. Sorensen, *Kennedy* (New York: Harper & Row, 1965), pp. 564–68; Henry A. Kissinger, *The Troubled Partnership: A Re-appraisal of the Atlantic Alliance* (New York: McGraw-Hill, 1965), pp. 85–86.
21. Macmillan, *At The End of The Day,* p. 365; Brian Crozier, *de Gaulle* (New York: Scribners, 1973), p. 559.
22. George W. Ball, *The Discipline of Power,* pp. 102–6; Maxwell D. Taylor, *Swords and Plowshares* (New York: W. W. Norton, 1972), p. 283.
23. NATO Polaris Force, 17 Jan. 1963, AEC.
24. Seaborg, The President's Meeting with the JCAE, 18 Jan. 1963, AEC.
25. Rickover, Memorandum for the Chief of Naval Operations, 17 Jan. 1963, with encl., NRD.
26. "Statement by the President on the Proposed Multilateral NATO Nuclear Force, Jan. 24, 1963," *Public Papers of the President of the United States: John F. Kennedy, 1963* (Washington: G.P.O., 1964), p. 100.
27. Rickover, Memorandum Concerning Meeting Held in Admiral Anderson's Office Today, 2 Feb. 1963, NRD.
28. George W. Anderson, Memorandum for the Assistant Secretary of Defense (ISA), 5 Feb. 1963, NRD.
29. H. C. to O'Donnell, 7 Feb. 1963, JFK; The President's News Conference of 7 Feb. 1963, *Public Papers, 1963, Kennedy,* pp. 152–53.
30. Rickover, Comments on Multi-National Manning of Submarines, 9 Feb. 1963; "Points for Monday (President), Feb. 9, 1963," NRD; The President's Appointment Book, 11 February 1963, Jan.–June, 1963; Arthur M. Schlesinger, Jr., Oral History Interview with Vice Admiral H. G. Rickover, 17 Aug. 1964, JFK; Seaborg, Telephone call . . . from Adm Rickover, 11 Feb. 1963; Seaborg, Telephone Call to Bundy's Secretary, 14 Feb. 1963, AEC; MZ to Bundy, 14 Feb. 1963, JFK; Schlesinger, *A Thousand Days,* p. 874; Glenn T. Seaborg with Benjamin S. Loeb, *Stemming the Tide: Arms Control in the Johnson Years* (Lexington, MA.: D.C. Heath, 1987) pp. 86–87.
31. Schlesinger, Oral History Interview with Vice Admiral H. G. Rickover, 17 Aug. 1964, AEC; Rickover, Memorandum of Telephone Conversation with Admiral Sharp, 13 Feb. 1963, NRD; Schlesinger, *A Thousand Days,* p. 874. Rickover, in his oral history, dates the NSC meeting as Feb. 11 and refers to a memorandum from the Navy Department. The memorandum, however, is actually signed by Rickover and records the telephone conversation with Sharp on Feb. 13. The President's

Appointment Book, Jan.–June 1963, JFK, shows no meeting for Feb. 11, but does show one for Feb. 12. A. A. Wells, Memorandum for Chairman Seaborg et al., Presidential Instruction to Ambassador Merchant on MLF, 15 Feb. 1963 with attachment: John Lloyd III, Steering Group on Implementing the Nassau Decisions, Memorandum No. 17, "Instruction from The President to the MLF Negotiating Team," 14 Feb. 1963, AEC. The date of February 13 for presidential approval of the instructions comes from the attachment.

32. David Klein, Memorandum of Conversation in the President's Office, Monday, 18 Feb. 1963, 4:00 P.M., JFK.

33. Unsigned, Memorandum for the Record, Meeting in the Cabinet Room, 12:20 P.M., Thursday, 21 Feb. 1963; President, Memorandum for the Secretary of Defense, the Secretary of State, 20 Feb. 1963, both in JFK. Unsigned, Report of Conference, 1:30 P.M., 22 Feb. 1963 (In all probability the report was written by Rockwell. Rickover sent a copy to Seaborg.); Robert S. McNamara, Memorandum for the President, 27 Feb. 1963, both in NRD.

34. Livingston T. Merchant, Memorandum for the Secretary of State, 20 March 1963, DOS; Reinhardt, Incoming Department of State Telegram No. 1752 to Secretary of State, 5 March 1963, AEC; Furnas, William R. Tyler, Jeffrey C. Kitchen, Memorandum to the Secretary of State, 8 March 1963, DOS; unsigned (but probably by Rickover), Memorandum of Telephone Conversation with Colonel Crowson of the MAD of the AEC on 15 March 1963, 19 March 1963, NRD; Furnas to the Secretary, 12 March 1963, DOS.

35. Rockwell to File, Meeting with Gerard Smith, State Department, 21 March 1963, NRD.

36. Office of MLF Affairs, Office of the Assistant Secretary of Defense, International Security Affairs, Status Report on the Multilateral Force, 19 Aug. 1964; Paris Working Group, Report on Progress of the Mixed-Manning Demonstration, 30 Oct. 1965; Paris Working Group, Final Report on the Mixed-Manning Demonstration, 1 Feb. 1966, NHC.

Chapter 8. Shippingport

1. *Public Papers of the President of the United States: James Earl Carter 1977*, vol. 2 (Washington: G.P.O., 1978), pp. 2068–71.

2. For the early history of Shippingport, see Richard G. Hewlett and Francis Duncan, *Nuclear Navy, 1946–1962* (Chicago: University of Chicago Press, 1974), pp. 225–57 and *The Shippingport Pressurized Water Reactor* (Reading, MA: Addison-Wesley, 1958), a volume of technical essays written by participants in the project.

3. This section is based largely upon Richard G. Hewlett and Oscar E. Anderson, *The New World, 1939/1946*, and *Atomic Shield, 1947/1952* by Richard G. Hewlett and Francis Duncan, vols. 1 and 2 of *A History of the Atomic Energy Commission* (University Park: Pennsylvania State University Press, 1962 and 1969), and Hewlett and Duncan, *Nuclear Navy*. A lucid explanation of the nuclear processes described can be found in John F. Hogerton, *The Atomic Energy Deskbook* (New York: Reinhold, 1963), pp. 80–81, 321–26, 402–4, 557, and 578–79.

4. Rickover,"The Current Outlook for Breeding" (unpublished ms., 7 Sept. 1950), NRD.

5. Hewlett and Duncan, *Nuclear Navy*, pp. 194–96; Hewlett and Duncan, *Atomic Shield*, p. 498, 546, 551–52.

6. Hewlett and Duncan, *Nuclear Navy*, pp. 184–86.

7. Ibid., pp. 194–96.

8. Wendy Allen, "Nuclear Reactors for Generating Electricity: U.S. Development from 1946 to 1963," June 1977, RAND Report R-2116-NSF, pp. 20–27.
9. Hewlett and Duncan, *Nuclear Navy*, pp. 228–30; Allen, "Nuclear Reactors for Generating Electricity," pp. 28–32.
10. Hewlett and Duncan, *Nuclear Navy*, pp. 231–33.
11. Hewlett and Duncan, *Nuclear Navy*, pp. 235, 238; Contract Between the Duquesne Light Company and the U.S. AEC, Contract No. AT(11-1)-292, 3 Nov. 1954, NRD.
12. *The Shippingport Pressurized Water Reactor*, pp. 7–24, 43–55.
13. For the blanket fuel, see *The Shippingport Pressurized Water Reactor*, pp. 121–58; Hewlett and Duncan, *Nuclear Navy*, p. 246.
14. *The Shippingport Pressurized Water Reactor*, pp. 503–21; Hewlett and Duncan, *Nuclear Navy*, pp. 247–54. A very nice historical summary of the plant is in a pamphlet published in 1980 by the American Society of Mechanical Engineers, "Historic Achievement Recognized: Shippingport Atomic Power Station: A National Historic Mechanical Engineering Landmark."
15. Contract Between The Duquesne Light Company and the U.S. AEC, No. AT(11-1)-292, 3 Nov. 1954, NRD.
16. *The Shippingport Pressurized Water Reactor*, pp. 567–70.
17. Geiger to Donworth, 8 July 1957; Geiger to Fleger, 20 Sept. 1957, in AEC 649/34, 7 Nov. 1957, AEC.
18. Fleger to Geiger, 14 Oct. 1957, in AEC 649/34, 7 Nov. 1957, AEC.
19. Rickover to Davis, 25 Oct. 1957, in AEC 649/34, 7 Nov. 1957, AEC. For Windscale, see Atomic Energy Office, *Accident at Windscale No. 1 Pile on 10th October, 1957* (London: Her Majesty's Stationery Office, Nov. 1957). The reference to organizational weakness that Rickover mentioned in his memorandum is on p. 4.
20. Rickover to Davis, 25 Oct. 1957; and cable, Davis to Saxe, 28 Oct. 1957, in AEC 649/34, 7 Nov. 1957, AEC.
21. Rickover to Davis, 7 Nov. 1957, and encl., NRD. In his memorandum Rickover refers to Fleger's Nov. 4 proposal and quotes a small portion of it in the enclosure.
22. Message, Davis to Dunbar, info copy to Geiger, 13 Dec. 1957, NRD.
23. Rengel to Iselin, 16 Dec. 1957, NRD; "Shippingport Operations: From Start-up to First Refueling, 18 December 1957 to 7 October 1959," Duquesne Report DLCS-364, p. I-36–I-37, NRD, (hereafter cited as "Shippingport Operations," Duquesne Report and number).
24. Memorandum of Conference, 16 Dec. 1957, NRD.
25. "Shippingport Operations," Duquesne Report DLCS-364, pp. I-37–I-38, NRD.
26. Department of Energy, *Nuclear Reactors Built, Being Built, or Planned*, DOE/T1C-8200-R49 (DE85008063) PB85-703001, p. 34. AEC, *Major Activities in the Atomic Energy Programs, July–Dec. 1954* (Washington: G.P.O., Jan. 1955), pp. 44–45; Hewlett and Duncan, *Nuclear Navy*, p. 251.
27. Rickover to Fleger, 21 Dec. 1957; Fleger to Rickover, 24 Jan. 1958; Rickover to Fleger, 6 Feb. 1958, all in NRD.
28. McCone, Memorandum for the Files of John A. McCone, 24 July 1959; Memorandum for the Files of John A. McCone, undated but around 10 Sept. 1959, AEC. Although two of the above memos are undated, the paragraphs refer to the dates of the visit.
29. Annette D. Barnes, "Shippingport Atomic Power Station and Reactor Technology Dissemination" (unpublished ms., n.d.), NRD; for the essays written by Naval Reactors personnel, see *The Shippingport Pressurized Water Reactor;* AEC, *Major Activities in the Atomic Energy Programs, 1959* (Washington: G.P.O., 1960), pp. 113, 144; B. Lustman and Frank Kerze, Jr., *The Metallurgy of Zirconium* (New York:

McGraw-Hill, 1955); D. E. Thomas and Earl T. Hayes, *The Metallurgy of Hafnium* (Washington: G.P.O., n.d.); Theodore Rockwell, ed., *Reactor Shielding Design Manual*, 1956, AEC Report TID-7004; "Shippingport Operations," Duquesne Report DLCS-364, p. I-22.

30. P. A. Fleger, I. Harry Mandil, Philip N. Ross, "Shippingport Atomic Power Station Operating Experience, Developments and Future Plans, A Paper Presented at the U.S.-Japan Atomic Industrial Forum, Tokyo, Japan, 5–8 Dec. 1961," AEC IN-281; Shippingport Atomic Power Station Chronology (unpublished ms., n.d.), NRD.

31. AEC, *Major Activities in the Atomic Energy Programs, Jan.–Dec. 1961*, Appendix 10, "Nuclear Reactors Built, Being Built, or Planned in the United States as of 31 Dec. 1961" (Washington: G.P.O., 1962), pp. 461–62. The three central stations were Shippingport, Dresden Nuclear Power Station, and the Yankee Nuclear Power Station. The 355-megawatt plant was the Coast Nuclear Station of Southern California Edison.

32. Atomic Energy Act of 1954, P.L. 703, 83 Cong., 68 *Stat.* 919, Sects. 53, 103, 107, 153 in Joint Committee on Atomic Energy (hereafter cited as JCAE), *Atomic Energy Legislation Through 92d Cong, 1st sess.* (Washington: G.P.O., 1972); Wendy Allen, "Nuclear Reactors for Generating Electricity: U.S. Development From 1946 to 1963," RAND Report R-2116-NSF, pp. 36–39; AEC, *Major Activities in the Atomic Energy Program, July–Dec. 1954*, pp. vii–x; Hogerton, *The Atomic Energy Deskbook*, pp. 274–75.

33. Director of Division of Reactor Development, Civilian Nuclear Power Cooperative Program, undated document attached to Summary Notes of Informal Commission Meeting, 25 April 1961, AEC. The attached paper has a notation that it was discussed by the commissioners on 24 and 25 April 1961.

34. J. A. Hinds to File, 27 Feb. 1962, NRD.

35. Holifield to Seaborg, 15 March 1962; Kennedy to chairman, 17 March 1962; Seaborg to president, 17 March 1962, all in JCAE, *Development, Growth, and State of the Atomic Energy Industry, 1962*, 87th Cong., 2d sess. (Washington: G.P.O., 1962), pp. 4–8.

36. JCAE, *Development, Growth, and State of the Atomic Energy Industry*, 87th Cong., 2d sess. (Washington: G.P.O., 1962), pp. 8–58; *Nucleonics* 20 (May 1962): 20–21. For background and summary of the hearings and study, see George T. Mazuzan and J. Samuel Walker, *Controlling the Atom: The Beginning of Nuclear Regulation, 1946–1962* (Berkeley, CA: University of California Press, 1984), pp. 406–17.

37. Unsigned draft dated 9 April 1962 and titled: Notes of Discussion Held 5 April 1962 Between Chairman Holifield, Joint Committee on Atomic Energy and Chairman Glenn Seaborg. . . , NRD. The other projects were: an organic prototype, a design study on sodium graphite reactor, design assistance for large scale reactor, and policy on construction of advanced prototypes. For Rickover's testimony, see JCAE, *AEC Authorizing Legislation Fiscal Year 1963*, 87th Cong., 2d sess. (Washington: G.P.O., 1962), pp. 291–313.

38. AEC, *Annual Report to Congress of the AEC for 1962* (Washington: G.P.O., Jan. 1963), p. 153; Allen, "Nuclear Reactors for Generating Electricity: U.S. Development From 1946 to 1963," pp. 73–75; Assistant Secretary for Nuclear Energy, U.S. Central Station Nuclear Electric Generating Units: Significant Milestones (Status as of 1 July 1981), Sept. 1981, DOE Report DOE/NE-0030/3 (81) UC-2, p. 3.

39. Philip N. Ross, To All Members of Management, 5 July 1962, AL 62-37, AL 62-38, NRD.

40. AEC, *Civilian Nuclear Power . . . A Report To The President—1962*, pp. 3, 8–9, 12, 23, 35–36, 39–41, 50–52.
41. *Nucleonics* 21 (Jan. 1963): 20–22. For other and similar views, see Seaborg to Wiesner, 31 Jan. 1963 and attach., AEC.
42. Forum Staff, A Summary of Forum Member Views on the AEC Report. . . , April 1963, pp. 2, 75–78, 81–84, NRD.
43. Report of Conference Between Bettis and Naval Reactors Personnel by K. G. Scheetz (C#193), [on] 19 Nov. 1962, NRD.
44. Rickover to Frank K. Pittman, 12 April 1963, NRD. Bettis submitted its interim report in July. See Bettis Atomic Power Laboratory, Large Power Reactor Program, Interim Report, July 1963, Bettis Report WAPD-LPR-141, pp. 2–5, and Supplement, WAPD-LPR-154; Scheetz, untitled draft, 19 March 1963, all in NRD.
45. Commission meeting 1930, 13 May 1963, AEC.
46. Mandil, notes for Admiral Rickover, 13 Aug. 1963; General Advisory Committee to the AEC, Report of the Reactors Subcommittee on Seed-and-Blanket and Heavy Water Reactor Concepts, 19 Aug. 1963, NRD.
47. Rickover to Pittman, 20 Sept. 1963 and encl., Test of the Seed-Blanket Thorium Breeder Concept in the Shippingport Plant, NRD.
48. Reference to March 1963 conversations with Seaborg and the commission staff are in Warne to Seaborg, 18 Nov. 1963 in AEC 649/51, 25 Feb. 1964, AEC.
49. Mandil to file, hand-dated 24 Sept. 1963, NRD.
50. Warne to Seaborg, 18 Nov. 1963, in AEC 649/51, 25 Feb. 1964, AEC; Rickover to Pittman, 21 Nov. 1963; Summary Notes of Briefing by Naval Reactors Branch, Monday, 9 Dec. 1963, NRD; Seaborg to Warne, 11 Dec. 1963, in AEC 649/51, 25 Feb. 1964, AEC.
51. Warne to Seaborg, 31 Dec. 1963, and encl., Suggested Principles for Cooperative Financing Development, Design, Construction, and Operation of a Large Power Reactor, in AEC 649/51, 25 Feb. 1964, AEC.
52. Brown to Seaborg, 16 Jan. 1964 in AEC 649/51, 25 Feb. 1964, AEC; Mandil, Report of Trip by I. H. Mandil, 23 Jan. 1964, NRD.
53. Brown to Rickover, 13 July 1964, NRD. Data on the *Jackson* is from Commissioned Submarine Construction History as of 15 March 1965, NRD; Vallejo *Times-Herald*, 7, 8 July 1964, NRD.
54. Mandil, memo to file, 27 July 1964, NRD.
55. Summary Notes of Briefing by Naval Reactors . . . 23 July 1964. . . , NRD. Rickover was authorized to carry out negotiations in Seaborg to Brown, 24 July 1964, AEC. References to the Brown letter of 22 July are also in the 24 July 1964 letter, AEC.
56. Reference to Warne's acceptance is in CM 2040, 25 Aug. 1964; reference to the 22 Oct. 1964 acceptance is in Seaborg to Warne, 31 Dec. 1964, in AEC 1161/2, 5 Feb. 1965, AEC.
57. Seaborg to president, 18 Nov. 1964, AEC. The other civilian reactor projects for which Seaborg asked consideration were the high-temperature gas-cooled and heavy-water organic moderated reactors. Chet Holifield to the president, 19 Nov. 1964, NRD. Brown, telegram to the president, 21 Nov. 1964, NRD; Kermit Gordon to Seaborg, 17 Dec. 1964, NRD.
58. U.S. Bureau of the Budget, Appendix, *The Budget of the United States Governing for the Fiscal Year Ending June 30, 1966*, 89th Cong., 1st sess., House Doc. No. 16 (Washington: G.P.O., 1966), p. 742; Seaborg to Warne, 1 Jan. 1965, AEC. AEC files contain a letter from Seaborg to Warne with a handwritten date of 31 Dec. 1964. From other evidence, the 1 Jan. 1965 date is correct.
59. Clark to file, hand-dated, 9 Feb. 1965, NRD.

60. Clark to file, 3 March 1965, NRD.
61. Large Seed-Blanket Reactor Fuel Element Development Problems, NRD—dated only as May 1965. The Bettis meeting has been reconstructed from interviews. Clark to file, 28 April 1965, NRD.
62. Clark to file, 28 April 1965, NRD, refers to the meeting of April 8–9. Reconstruction of the meeting comes from interviews.
63. Rickover to Hollingsworth, 12 April 1965, NRD. Reference to the conversations and meetings is in Seaborg to Holifield, 19 April 1965; and Warne to Golze, 16 April 1965, attach. to Warne to Rickover, 16 April 1965, all in NRD.
64. Rickover to Hollingsworth, 20 Dec. 1965, and encl., NRD; CM 2166, [on] 21 Dec. 1965, AEC.
65. Report of a Conference Between Naval Reactors and Bettis Representatives (C#5) [on] 7 Jan. 1966, NRD; Report of a Meeting Among NR, Bettis and KAPL Representatives (JEM-C-10) [on] 24 Jan. 1966; Zerbe to Manager, Pittsburgh Naval Reactors Office, 16 March 1966, all in NRD.
66. There are several excellent publications describing the light-water breeder program. The least technical, and written before the station became operational, is *Light Water Breeder Reactor (LWBR) Division of Naval Reactors*, AEC; U.S. Department of Energy, *Light Water Breeder Reactor (LWBR)*, 1979; and *Design of The Shippingport Light Water Breeder Reactor (LWBR Development Program)*, Bettis Laboratory Report WAPD-TM-1208. Fuel rod dimensions are from the latter: see pp. 19, 24. Schedules are from an unpublished paper: Significant Dates for Fuel Rod Fabrication, 29 Sept. 1976, BAPL.
67. Rickover stated his principles in Mealia, Report of a Meeting Between Bettis and NR [on] (JEM-C-20), 18 May 1966, encl. to Clark to Manager, Pittsburgh Naval Reactors Office, 7 June 1966, NRD.
68. Shippingport Atomic Power Station, LWBR Core Highlights/PWR Project Highlights (unpublished ms., n.d.), NRD.
69. Decontamination of the Shippingport Atomic Power Station, Jan. 1966, Bettis Report WAPD-299; Shippingport Atomic Power Station Chronology (unpublished ms., n.d.), NRD.
70. Shippingport Atomic Power Station, LWBR Core Highlights/PWR Project Highlights (unpublished ms., n.d.), NRD.
71. Ibid.
72. Elizabeth Rolph, "Regulation of Nuclear Power: The Case of the Light Water Reactor," June 1977, RAND Report R-2104-NSF, pp. 42–47; Energy Research and Development Administration, *Final Environmental Statement: Light Water Breeder Reactor Program: Summary and Background*, vol. 1 of 5 volumes (Springfield: National Technical Information Service, Department of Commerce, June 1976), vol. 1, pp. II-52–II-53, NRD. For Calvert Cliffs decision, see U.S. AEC, *1974 Annual Report to Congress, Part One, Operating and Development Functions* (Washington: U.S. AEC, 1975), pp. 31–32; and Alice L. Buck, *A History of the AEC, Aug. 1982*, DOE/ES-003 (Washington: U.S. Department of Energy, 1982), p. 7.
73. Energy Research and Development Administration, *Public Hearing Record for the Public Hearing held December 4, 1975 on the Draft Environmental Statement ERDA-1541 (August 1975) for the Light Water Breeder Reactor Program*, Feb. 1976; Energy Research and Development Administration, *Final Environmental Statement, Light Water Breeder Reactor Program*, vols. 1–5. See especially vol. 1: I-1–I-5, NRD.
74. Shippingport Atomic Power Station, Safety Analysis Report for LWBR, vols. 1–10, NRD; *Federal Register*, vol. 40, no. 158, 14 Aug. 1975; Karl Kniel to Rickover, 22 July 1976, all NRD.

75. Kniel to Rickover, 22 July 1976; Kniel to Rickover, 8 Dec. 1976; and Moeller to Rowden, 19 Aug. 1976, NRD.
76. Early History of the Pressurized Water Reactor (PWR). . . , an unpublished document in NRD; Goddard to Rickover, 23 Dec. 1976, and encl.; reference to the 23 Dec. 1976 letter is in Rickover to Goddard, 23 March 1977, all in NRD.
77. Rickover to Goddard, 23 March 1977; Case to Gerusky, 25 April 1977; Fraley to Gerusky, 17 June 1977; Goddard to Rickover, 12 Aug. 1977, NRD.
78. The information for this paragraph was obtained through interviews with various Naval Reactors personnel.
79. A technical summary is in Results of Initial Nuclear Tests on LWBR (LWBR Development Program), June 1979, Bettis Report WAPD-TM-1336. See especially pp. 19–20 and p. 120.
80. Notes for Adm. Rickover for Meeting with Dr. Palmieri, OMB, Regarding Water Cooled Breeder Program, 10 July 1981, Background Information for Meeting with Dr. Palmieri, Office of Management and Budget, Concerning the Water Cooled Breeder Program, 10 July 1981, NRD.
81. The Department of Energy's Water-Cooled Breeder Program—Should It Continue?, Comptroller General of the United States Report EMD-81-46, p. viii; Background Information for Meeting With Dr. Palmieri, Office of Management and Budget, Concerning the Water Cooled Breeder Program, 10 July 1981; Rickover to Denton, 7 Dec. 1981, NRD.

    Analyses completed in 1987 of 524 randomly selected fuel rods concluded that the end-of-life fuel content of the core was 507.98 kg. The fuel content at the beginning-of-life core determined during core manufacture was 501.02 kg. The increase in fissile fuels was 1.39 percent plus or minus 0.14 percent. See Abstract in W. C. Schick, Jr., et al., "Proof of Breeding in the Light Water Breeder Reactor (LWBR Development Program) WAPD-TM-1612.
82. H. G. Rickover, Duties of the DOE Duty Representative, hand dated 5/14/79, NRD.

Chapter 9. "The Devil Is in the Details. . . ."

1. Quotation is from Derivation and Execution of Responsibilities of the Director, Naval Nuclear Propulsion Program, 24 May 1979, NRD; for the origins of the dual system, see Richard G. Hewlett and Francis Duncan, *Atomic Shield, 1947/1952*, vol. 2 of *A History of the United States Atomic Energy Commission* (University Park: Pennsylvania State University Press, 1969), pp. 189–93 and by the same authors, *Nuclear Navy, 1946-1962* (Chicago: University of Chicago Press, 1974), pp. 60–76. For the references in the text to NR in the legislation of ERDA, see Sec. 104(d), Public Law 438, 93d Cong., H.R. 11510, 88 Stat, 11 Oct. 1974, p. 4. For DOE, see Sec. 309(a), Public Law 91, S. 826, 4 Aug. 1973, 91 Stat 581.
2. Hewlett and Duncan, *Nuclear Navy*, 186–93. See Section 9, Public Law 305, 79th Cong., 2d sess., 21 Feb. 1946, pp. 3–4. Jackson to the president, 7 Feb. 1961, JFK; *New York Herald Tribune*, and *Washington Evening Star*, 13 Feb. 1961; *Washington Post*, 14 Feb. 1961. A search of the records at the John F. Kennedy Library did not disclose any evidence to substantiate direct and personal intervention by the president. Rickover referred to mandatory retirement and the joint committee discussed the matter, partly off the record in Joint Committee on Atomic Energy (hereafter cited as JCAE), *Tour of the U.S.S. "Enterprise" and Report on the Joint AEC-Naval Reactor Program* (hereafter cited as *Tour of the U.S.S. "Enterprise"*) (Washington: G.P.O., 1962), p. 44.

3. JCAE, *Tour of the U.S.S. "Enterprise,"* pp. 44–45.
4. Unpublished hearing, JCAE, "Management of the Naval Reactor Program, 15 August 1963," 88th Cong., 1st sess. (Washington: G.P.O., 1964). Because the entire hearing is only 29 pages long, no effort has been made to footnote the pages on which these paragraphs are based. For a brief account of the 1964 reappointment and for the reappointment process, see Elmo R. Zumwalt, Jr., *On Watch, A Memoir* (New York: Quadrangle/Times Books, 1976), pp. 98–100.
5. Naval Sea Systems Command and Naval Engineering Center, Organization and Functional Index (Washington: Department of the Navy, Feb. 1978), p. 94.
6. May 1980 NR Directory, NRD.
7. A complete list of Rickover's testimony on these subjects would cover many pages. Only a few are listed below. Joint Economic Committee, *Economics of Military Procurement, Part 2*, 90th Cong., 2d sess. (Washington: G.P.O., 1968), pp. 1–98. Senate Committee on Armed Services, *Weapon System Acquisition Process*, 92d Cong., 1st sess. (Washington: G.P.O., 1972), pp. 291–510; Subcommittee on General Oversight and Renegotiation of the House Committee on Banking, Finance, and Urban Affairs, *The Renegotiation Reform Act of 1977*, 95th Cong., 1st sess. (Washington: G.P.O., 1977), pp. 364–80. In 1968 the Joint Economic Committee published five volumes on Rickover's testimony, exhibits, and appendices under the title *Economics of Defense Policy: Adm. H. G. Rickover*. Part 1 has no specific subtitle but contains Rickover's testimony. The subtitles of the others are: *Part 2: Appendices*; *Part 3: Navy Contracts and Government Policies*; *Part 4: Shipbuilding Claims*; and *Part 5: Lawyers and Legal Ethics*. All were published by the Government Printing Office, 1982. For an account of disputes with the Electric Boat Division of General Dynamics, see Patrick Tyler, *Running Critical: The Silent War, Rickover and General Dynamics* (New York: Harper & Row, 1986).
8. Staff of Bettis Reactor Engineering School, Bettis Reactor Engineering School Curriculum Book, 1978, NRD; Capt. John W. Crawford, Jr., USN(ret.), " 'Get 'em Young and Train 'em Right,' " U.S. Naval Institute *Proceedings* 113 (Oct. 1987): 103–5.
9. Rickover to Naval Reactors Field Representatives at Shipyards, 8 Nov. 1976, NRD.
10. Rickover to Distribution List, Responsibilities of NR Representatives at Field Offices, Reissued 27 March 1962, NRD.
11. Quotation is from: Lyndall F. Urwick, "The Manager's Span of Control," in Harold Koontz and Cyril O'Donnell, eds., *Management: A Book of Readings*, 2nd ed., (New York: McGraw-Hill, 1968), pp. 176–79. See also Alice Buck, A History of Management Philosophy, unpublished document in the History Division, DOE.
12. For the origins of the interview program, see Hewlett and Duncan, *Nuclear Navy*, pp. 345–49.
13. Crawford, " 'Get 'em Young and Train 'em Right.' "
14. For an excellent summary of Rickover's training program for officers and enlisted men, see Statement of Admiral H. G. Rickover, USN, Director of Naval Nuclear Propulsion Program Before the Subcommittee on Energy Research and Production of the Committee on Science and Technology, United States House of Representatives, 24 May 1979, NRD.
15. For a far more detailed account of the training program for enlisted men, see Statement of Admiral H. G. Rickover, USN, Director Naval Nuclear Propulsion Program before the Subcommittee on Energy Research and Production of the Committee on Science and Technology, United States House of Representatives, 24 May 1979, NRD.
16. Rickover to Smith, 17 Sept. 1969, NRD; *Webster's New World Dictionary of the American Language*, College Edition (New York: World, 1968), p. 1478.

17. H. G. Rickover, "The Decision to Use Zirconium in Nuclear Reactors," in H. G. Rickover, L. D. Geiger, B. Lustman, *History of the Development of Zirconium Alloys for Use in Nuclear Reactors.* . . . (Washington: United States Energy Research and Development Administration, Division of Naval Reactors, 1975), p. 13.

Chapter 10. Independence and Control

1. Subcommittee of the Senate Committee on Environment and Public Works, *Nuclear Accident and Recovery at Three Mile Island*, Serial 96–14, 96th Cong., 2d sess. (Washington: G.P.O., 1980), pp. 35–40, 93–94, 241–44.

2. Ibid., pp. 3–4. A Subcommittee of the House Committee on Science and Technology held hearings on Three Mile Island. See *Nuclear Powerplant Safety Systems*, 96th Cong., 1st sess. (Washington: G.P.O., 1979). See also *Report of the President's Commission on the Accident at Three Mile Island. The Need for Change: The Legacy of TMI* (Washington, D.C.: October 1979). (Hereafter cited as the *Kemeny Commission Report.*) Rickover sent his own appraisal to President Carter in Rickover to the President, 1 Dec. 1979, NRD. For letters and press notices, see letters to the editor in the *New York Times*, 6 April 1980, and *Barron's National Business and Financial Weekly*, 13 Oct. 1980; and stories in the Albany *Times-Union*, 2 April 1979, and the *San Diego Union*, 30 Aug. 1980.

3. For number of reactors, see Rickover's statement in Subcommittee on House Committee on Appropriations, *Energy and Water Development Appropriations for 1980, Part 7*, 96th Cong., 1st sess. (Washington: G.P.O., 1980), p. 1924. For the *Nautilus*, see Richard G. Hewlett and Francis Duncan, *Nuclear Navy, 1946–1962* (Chicago: University of Chicago Press, 1974), pp. 328–29.

4. Joint Committee on Atomic Energy (hereafter cited as JCAE), *Loss Of The U.S.S. "Thresher,"* 88th Cong., 1st and 2d sess. (Washington, G.P.O.: 1965), Appendix 3, "The Never Ending Challenge (By Vice Adm. H. G. Rickover, USN, at the 44th annual National Metal Congress, New York, NY, 29 Oct. 1962)," pp. 136–44.

5. See Samuel Glasstone, *Sourcebook on Atomic Energy*, 2d ed. (New York: D. Van Nostrand, 1958), pp. 48–49, 588. See also Richard G. Hewlett and Oscar E. Anderson, Jr., *The New World*, vol. 1 of *A History of the United States Atomic Energy Commission* (University Park: Pennsylvania State University Press, 1962), pp. 206–7; handwritten notes and ditto sheets of lectures given by Morgan on 21 Oct. 1946, Ray on 2 Dec. 1946, and Hinshaw on 17 Feb. 1947 in binder titled Proj. Survey and Biology, NRD.

6. Notes on Muller lecture, Mutation & Genetic Effects, 9 April 1947, and two mimeographed papers: Mutational Prophyllaxis [sic] and Changing Genes in binder titled Proj. Survey and Biology, NRD. Quotation is from Changing Genes, p. 2. See also Rickover's recollections in Subcommittee of the House Committee on Interstate and Foreign Commerce, *Effect of Radiation on Human Health, Health Effects of Ionizing Radiation*, vol. 1, serial no. 95–179, 95th Cong., 2d sess. (Washington: G.P.O., 1979), pp. 1270–73; and Richard G. Hewlett and Francis Duncan, *Nuclear Navy*, p. 137.

7. For a description of the activities of the ACRS, see JCAE, *Radiation Safety and Regulation*, 87th Cong., 1st sess. (Washington: G.P.O., 1961), pp. 21–29. Rickover described program relations with the ACRS in the same hearing, pp. 363–64. For excerpts from the ACRS report of the commission, see JCAE, *Tour of the U.S.S. "Enterprise" and Report on Joint AEC-Naval Reactor Program*, 87th Cong., 2d sess. (Washington: G.P.O., 1962), pp. 40–43. For the establishment of the reactor safeguard committee, see Richard G. Hewlett and Francis Duncan, *Atomic Shield, 1946–1952*, vol. 2 of *A History of the United States Atomic Energy Commission*

(University Park: Pennsylvania State University Press, 1969), pp. 186–87; 196, 201–4.

8. For the status of shielding, see Rickover, The Shielding of Power Piles, M-3216, 14 Aug. 1946; Naval Group, Fundamentals of the Shielding Problem, M-3551, 2 April 1947, NRD.

9. Subcommittee of the Committee on Interstate and Foreign Commerce, Effect of Radiation on Human Health, pp. 1271–73; T. Rockwell to Files, 26 March 1957, NRD.

10. This and the following paragraphs are based primarily on Wegner to U. Alexis Johnson, 25 May 1968 and attach.: Report of Findings of the AEC's Technical Review Group, NRD. For political implications, see The Washington Post, 14, 15, 26 May 1968; the Washington Star, 17 May, 26 Oct. 1968; the New York Times, 17, 26 May 1968.

11. For Najarian's testimony, see Subcommittee of the House Committee on Interstate and Foreign Commerce, Effects of Radiation on Human Health, vol. 1, pp. 1234–42. For the Boston Globe, see pp. 1226–28.

12. For testimony by Rickover and Miles, see Subcommittee of the House Committee on Interstate and Foreign Commerce, Effects of Radiation on Human Health, vol. 1, pp. 1270–1326. For reference to the Hanford study, see p. 1298.

13. P. G. Rogers, T. L. Carter, and E. J. Markey to Rickover, 19 Dec. 1978; Rickover to Chairman, Subcommittee on Health and Environment, Committee on Interstate and Foreign Commerce, House of Representatives, 8 Jan. 1979, NRD; Subcommittees of the House Armed Services Committee, Naval Nuclear Propulsion Program—1979, 96th Cong., 1st sess. (Washington: G.P.O., 1979), pp. 9–13.

14. Manchester (New Hampshire) Union Leader, 3 July 1979; Division of Surveillance, Hazards Evaluations, and Field Studies, National Institute for Occupational Safety and Health, Centers for Disease Control, Public Health Service, U.S. Department of Health and Human Services, "Epidemiologic Study of Civilian Employees at The Portsmouth Naval Shipyard, Kittery, Maine," Dec. 1980, pp. 31–32.

15. These paragraphs attempt to summarize a complicated technical subject. For details see P. D. Rice, G. L. Sjoblom, J. M. Steele, B. F. Harvey, Environmental Monitoring and Disposal of Radioactive Wastes From U.S. Naval Nuclear-Powered Ships and Their Support Facilities, 1981, Feb. 1982, Naval Nuclear Propulsion Program Report NT-82-1, pp. 1–2, 8–10, 15–17, 31. The number of shipyards is eight, however, and not nine.

16. These paragraphs also attempt to summarize a complicated technical subject. For further details, see P. D. Rice and J. F. Brice, Occupational Radiation Exposure from U.S. Nuclear Propulsion Plants and Their Support Facilities 1981, Feb. 1982, Naval Nuclear Propulsion Program Report NT-82-2, pp. 1–3, 25, 33–34. For a definition of rem, see Samuel Glasstone, Sourcebook on Atomic Energy, pp. 594–95.

17. For an example, see 1981 Annual Environmental Report: Radiological—Vol. #2, Duquesne Light Company, Beaver Valley Power Station and Shippingport Atomic Power Station.

18. For Deutsch's views, see Transcript of Proceedings, President's Commission on the Accident at Three Mile Island, Hearing at Washington, D. C., 27 April 1979, pp. 2, 4, 6–7, 12–14, 24, NRD. See also Crisis Contained: The Department of Energy at Three Mile Island, A History, December 1980, DOE/EV/10278-T1, UC-41, 80, prepared by Philip L. Cantelon and Robert C. Williams of C&W Associates/Historical Consultants.

19. Comments by Admiral H. G. Rickover, USN, Director, Naval Nuclear Propulsion

Program, In Meeting With Members of The President's Commission on the Accident at Three Mile Island, 23 July 1979, NRD.

20. "Rickover Urges Electric Utility Firms To Form Nuclear Power Monitor Unit," The *Washington Post*, 22 Jan. 1977.

21. Statement of Admiral H. G. Rickover, USN, Director of Naval Nuclear Propulsion Program Before the Subcommittee on Energy Research and Production of the Committee on Science and Technology, United States House of Representatives, 24 May 1979, NRD.

22. Notes by author, ". . . on Utility Executive Conference, Aug. 8, 1979, . . . ," NRD. *Nucleonics Week*, 11 Oct. 1979.

23. The *Washington Star*, 1 June 1979. Much of the preceding paragraphs and quotations are based on Rickover to the President, 1 Dec. 1979, NRD.

24. John G. Kemeny to Rickover, 30 July 1979. The president's comment was handwritten on the margin of a letter from Rickover to Clough, 3 Dec. 1979, NRD.

Chapter 11. Discipline of Technology

1. Conversation with Rickover.

2. For selection of officers for Oak Ridge, see Richard G. Hewlett and Francis Duncan, *Nuclear Navy, 1946–1962* (Chicago: University of Chicago Press, 1974), pp. 31–32.

3. Rickover, "Management in Government," *Government Magazine* 1 (Sept. 1979): 16–19.

4. Subcommittee of the Senate Committee on Armed Services, *Inquiry Into Satellite and Missile Programs Part 2*, 85th Cong., 1st and 2d sess. (Washington: G.P.O., 1958), pp. 1379–1445. For remarks on organization, see pp. 1419–24.

5. Subcommittee of the House Committee on Science and Technology, *Nuclear Powerplant Safety Systems*, 96th Cong., 1st sess. (Washington: G.P.O., 1979). For the prepared statement, see pp. 888–917. For the quotation, see p. 1039.

6. Years of service are from: A Description of the Naval Nuclear Propulsion Program, 31 Jan. 1982, A Joint Program of the Department of the Navy and the Department of Energy in: Joint Economic Committee, *Economics of Defense Policy: Adm. H. G. Rickover, Part 1*, 97th Cong., 2d sess. (Washington: G.P.O., 1982), p. 73.

7. For Oak Ridge and MIT, see Hewlett and Duncan, *Nuclear Navy*, pp. 123–24.

8. For the promotion struggle of 1953, see Hewlett and Duncan, *Nuclear Navy*, pp. 186–93.

9. The legislation covers two successor agencies to the Atomic Energy Commission. For the Energy Research and Development Administration, see Sec. 104(d), Public Law 438, 93d Cong., H.R. 11510, 88 Stat, 11 Oct. 1974, p. 4; and for the Department of Energy, see Sec. 309(a) Public Law 91, 95th Cong., S. 826, 4 Aug. 1977, 91 Stat 581.

10. These paragraphs are based on conversations with Charles H. Brown, Jr.; Alan G. Forssell; Mark Forssell; Thomas L. Foster; Souren Hanessian; William M. Hewitt; William S. Humphrey; James J. Mangeno; John E. Mealia; David B. Pye; Gene L. Rogers; Karl G. Scheetz; Robert H. Steele; Luther I. Tatum; and James W. Vaughan, Jr.

11. For Rickover's testimony, see Joint Economic Committee, *Economics of Defense Policy: Adm. H. G. Rickover, Part 1*, pp. 57–58; and in the same document, A Description of the Naval Nuclear Propulsion Program, 31 Jan. 1982, A Joint Program of the Department of the Navy and the Department of Energy, p. 73.

12. For the Executive Order, see Subcommittee of the House Committee on Armed Services, *Naval Nuclear Propulsion Program—1982*, 95th Cong., 2d sess. (Washington: G.P.O., 1982), pp. 10–12.
13. Ibid., p. 5.
14. Joint Committee on Atomic Energy, *Radiation Safety and Regulation*, 87th Cong., 1st sess. (Washington: G.P.O., 1961), p. 366.

Sources

General

Writing a study of the naval nuclear propulsion program was an extraordinarily difficult task, in part because of the vast amount of records that exist. These include memoranda, correspondence, reports of many kinds—some of which were required twice a week, others monthly and quarterly—minutes of meetings, and notes of conversations and telephone calls. It would have been impossible to extract from documentary sources alone the circumstances of crucial decisions—perhaps even the existence of a turning point or the timing of significant events, without guidance. Only through interviews was it possible to find a way through the massive documentation that is an inherent part of any major contemporary effort. For that reason, this note on sources is arranged in the following order: interviews, primary sources, secondary sources, and physical evidence. Students of the nuclear propulsion program will also want to consult the essays on sources in: Richard G. Hewlett and Oscar E. Anderson, Jr., *The New World, 1939–1946* (University Park, Pennsylvania State University Press, 1962), Richard G. Hewlett and Francis Duncan, *Atomic Shield, 1947–1952* (University Park: Pennsylvania State University Press, 1969), and Richard G. Hewlett and Jack M. Holl, *Atoms For Peace And War, 1953–1960* (Berkeley: The University of California Press, 1989), the first three published volumes of the Atomic Energy Commission, and Richard G. Hewlett and Francis Duncan, *Nuclear Navy, 1946–1962* (Chicago: University of Chicago Press, 1974).

Interviews

With very few exceptions, all the individuals I wished to talk to granted interviews. Those who gave me the opportunity expressed themselves with a vigor, freedom, and candor that stemmed from a conviction that the nuclear propulsion program was important and that as much of its recent history as possible be recorded. Admiral Rickover helped arrange some of the interviews, but most I carried out without his prior knowledge, and I did not discuss the results with him.

Because the time under consideration was so recent and because some aspects of the program—and its leader—were controversial, I seldom recorded interviews. My technique was to read pertinent documents on the subject about which I needed information and prepare detailed questions. In this way an interview often became an informal conversation and at times flowed into areas that I had not anticipated. Furthermore, some interviews took place in circumstances in which it was impossible to record. I cannot express the debt I owe to those who talked to me, not only for answering questions but for proposing different explanations of events and motives, and correcting often simplistic views.

Former Presidents Richard Nixon and Jimmy Carter gave far more time in their interviews than they had first allotted: President Nixon to explain why he chose Admiral Rickover to accompany him to Moscow in 1959, and President Carter to speak of his admiration of Admiral Rickover's mastery of technology and the need for society to profit from his example.

Without doubt nuclear propulsion has transformed the navy. Those who endeavored to make clear its benefits and drawbacks, as well as some of the disputes, were: Secretaries of the Navy Fred Korth, Paul R. Ignatius, and J. William Middendorf II; Chiefs of Naval Operations: Admirals George W. Anderson, Jr., David L. McDonald, Thomas H. Moorer, Elmo R. Zumwalt, Jr., James L. Holloway III; Admirals I. J. Galantin, and Horacio Rivero; Vice Admirals Bernard L. Austin, John T. Hayward, Edwin B. Hooper, Raymond Peet, William F. Raborn, and Bernard M. Strean; Rear Admirals Dean L. Axene, Willis C. Barnes, Edgar Batcheller, William A. Brockett, John D. Bulkeley, Lawrence C. Daspit, Peter M. Hekman, Ralph K. James, Robert L. Moore, James B. Osborne, and Tazewell T. Shepard; Captains William R. Anderson, Edward L. Beach, Richard L. Cochrane, Harry A. Jackson, Saul Katz, and Norman C. Nash.

Nuclear propulsion was, for most of the period under consideration, a joint effort between the navy and the Atomic Energy Commission. Those who explained the commission's role were: former AEC Chairmen John A. McCone and Glenn T. Seaborg, and former Commissioner James T. Ramey; Director of Reactor Development Frank K. Pittman; James A. Dewar and John L. McGruder.

Admiral Rickover frequently expressed the debt of the naval nuclear propulsion program to Congress. Those who presented the congressional perspective were: Representatives Charles E. Bennett, Chet Holifield, Craig Hosmer, and Melvin Price. In addition, the following former members of the staffs of the House Armed Services Committee and the Joint Committee on Atomic Energy expressed their views: Edward J. Bauser, John R. Blandford, John T. Conway, and George Norris.

Members of Naval Reactors gave indispensable help. Those who spoke to me, often several times, to explain technical issues, the part technical developments played in far-reaching decisions, and the relations between Naval Reactors and other parts of the government and industry were: Anthony J. Baratta, Richard W. Bass, Robert S. Brodsky, Charles H. Brown, Jr., Philip R. Clark, John W. Crawford, Jr., Paul E. Dignan, Donald E. Fry, Alan G. Forssell, Mark Forssell, Thomas L. Foster, Jack C. Grigg, Souren Hanessian, Paul W. Hayes, William M. Hewitt, John J. Hinchey, William S. Humphrey, Darold L. Johnson, Robert L. Kingsberry, David T. Leighton, Kenneth A. MacGowan, I. Harry Mandil, James J. Mangeno, Howard K. Marks, John E. Mealia, Murray E. Miles, Robert E. Murphy, John F. O'Grady, James A. Palmer, Robert Panoff, David S. Pikul, David B. Pye, Harry F. Raab, Paul D. Rice, James B. Risser, Theodore Rockwell, Louis H. Roddis, Jr., Gene L. Rogers, Denis H. Rushworth, Karl G. Scheetz, David G. Scott, Milton Shaw, Glenn L. Sjoblom, Robert H. Steele, Karl E. Swenson, Luther I. Tatum, Donleroy Tilseth, Arthur E. Tryon, James W. Vaughan, Jr., William Wegner, and Joseph P. Zimmer.

Those from Naval Reactors' field offices who explained their jobs and their part in the program were: Barry M. Erickson, Arthur E. Francis, Carl K. Gaddis, Lawton D. Geiger, Charles A. Hansen, Thomas J. McGrath, and Edward J. Siskin.

For the perspective of Bettis Atomic Power Laboratory: Ellis T. Cox, Alan C. Davis, William H. Hamilton, and William R. Harris.

From the Knolls Atomic Power Laboratory: Adelaide B. Oppenheim, Carl R. Stahl, Terence O'Regan, and Harry E. Stevens, Jr.

The brief biographical account of Admiral Rickover is based on many talks with him. Others who contributed their reminiscences are: Rear Admiral Benton W.

Decker and Mrs. Decker, Captain Theodore J. Shultz, Captain Frederic S. Steinke, Dause L. Bibby, Mr. and Mrs. Crawford Coyner, William H. Fifer, Clayton B. Garvey, Chancy Whitney, and Swan Weber.

Several individuals from other government agencies and industry were generous with their time and thoughts. Their names and the organizations to which they belong or were formerly affiliated are: Robert R. Bowie, Department of State; Alain C. Enthoven, Department of Defense; Chase R. Stephens, Nuclear Regulatory Commission; Kenneth E. Doolan, former master, *Byron Darnton*, Merchant Marine; Lord Solly Zuckerman, former Chief Scientific Advisor to the British Government; Richard Broad, Newport News Shipbuilding and Dry Dock Company; Donald E. Craig, General Electric Company; William G. Atkinson and John S. Leonard, General Dynamics Corporation; and Joseph Zagorski, Duquesne Light Company.

Unpublished Sources

No account could be written of the naval nuclear propulsion program without access to Naval Reactors files. Personnel of the Naval Reactors program opened their files to us, in some instances consulting us before retiring material to storage or marking it for destruction. We are especially grateful to Jean E. Scroggins, Martha E. Claussen, and Beth J. Granger for their assistance, as well as to Chiefs Rose M. Brooks, Barbara J. Whitlark, Eric E. Bishop, James Bryan, W. Al Grimes, Frank Oldenberg, and John Ottery.

Frequently, technical reports are needed to trace the progress of a project. Sharon McKinstry Custer, Vicky Lubonski, and Shirley Jessup of the Naval Reactors library gave us free access to their holdings. For laboratory documents, reports, and other archival material we depended upon Raymond E. Denne at Bettis and upon Madeline T. Barringer, Stuart Sturges, and Helyn Walton at Knolls.

Other collections of unpublished material threw light on different aspects of the naval nuclear propulsion program. Under Dr. Dean C. Allard, Jr., the operational archives of the Naval Historical Center have valuable holdings that we consulted on such activities as Operation Sea Orbit, the voyage of the *Triton*, and the multilateral force. In addition, the archives have many oral histories recorded at the U.S. Naval Institute at Annapolis, Maryland, by the former director of oral history, Dr. John T. Mason, and the present director, Paul Stillwell. These offer valuable insights into controversies and personalities. Under Dr. David K. Allison, the David W. Taylor Research and Development Center has opened a valuable collection of documentary material and oral histories relating to the center's interest. For special problems we have also drawn upon the resources of the libraries and records of the Department of State and the Department of Defense.

The presidential libraries gave some insight into the views held by the chief executive and his secretary of defense of the nuclear propulsion program and its leader. The Dwight D. Eisenhower Library at Abilene, Kansas, documented the waning enthusiasm for nuclear propulsion for surface ships. The John F. Kennedy Library at Boston, Massachusetts, contains rich material revealing the adamant stand that Secretary McNamara took on building a nuclear-powered surface fleet and his concern over the introduction of new classes of submarines. Perhaps because of the scope of this study, the holdings of the Lyndon Baines Johnson Library at Austin, Texas, were of somewhat less help. All the libraries have oral histories and private collections of documents that occasionally provided a sudden insight into a difficult problem or personality.

Published Sources

The general political background of the Eisenhower, Kennedy, Johnson, Nixon, Ford, and Carter administrations can be gathered from memoirs, biographies, and studies of their administrations. Although helpful in conveying atmosphere and giving an occasional anecdote about Admiral Rickover, they contain little about the naval nuclear propulsion program. In recognition of this lack, Admiral Rickover and his staff incorporated an extensive bibliography in Joint Economic Committee, *Economics of Defense Policy: Adm. H. G. Rickover, Part 1* 97th Cong., 2d sess. (Washington: G.P.O., 1982), A Description of the Naval Nuclear Propulsion Program January 31, 1982, A Joint Program of the Department of the Navy and the Department of Energy, Appendix 1, Official Published Sources of Information on the Naval Nuclear Propulsion Program, pp. 94–103.

Of the 147 entries all but 6 are congressional hearings; even so, the list is not exhaustive. The most valuable hearings are those held by the Joint Committee on Atomic Energy which, until it was abolished in 1977, covered all aspects of the atomic energy program. Because many of the members served on the committee continuously for many years, they were very familiar with the nuclear propulsion effort, including the Shippingport Atomic Power Station and the light-water breeder project. From 1959 until 1981 Admiral Rickover testified annually on the status of the program. These hearings (not all, of course, before the joint committee) are listed in the bibliography noted above, and all have similar but not identical titles that indicate the nature of their subject. Frequently, the hearings contain chronologies drawn up from Naval Reactors files and also the text of documents and correspondence.

Admiral Rickover and his staff also appeared before the Senate and House Armed Services Committees and the Senate and House Appropriations Committees. Often the committees printed his testimony as a separately bound part of the hearings. For the views of other officials—the secretary of defense, the secretary of the navy, and the chief of naval operations, among others—it is necessary to go to other parts of the hearing.

Without question the hearings are valuable—often containing material not readily available elsewhere—but they must be used with caution. The hearings themselves are not completely accurate transcripts. Every witness has an opportunity to edit his remarks to expunge poor grammar and to make sure that the technical information in his testimony is recorded correctly. A witness cannot, of course, change his views. With the permission of the committee chairman, Admiral Rickover added to his testimony what he called "philosophy," often some historical anecdote to illustrate a point he had made in the hearing. By and large congressional committees welcomed Admiral Rickover and were courteous and friendly audiences. Most decisions, however, had been made before or after a hearing, sometimes by only a few individuals. Nonetheless, Admiral Rickover and his staff considered his testimony before congressional committees an important opportunity to get their views in the record. Exhibits, appendices, and usually testimony (always in the latter years) were all carefully prepared.

Students interested in tracing the technical evolution of ships will find that four books by Norman Friedman contain a wealth of information. The Naval Institute Press at Annapolis, MD, published *U.S. Destroyers, An Illustrated Design History* in 1982, *U.S. Aircraft Carriers: An Illustrated Design History* in 1983, *U.S. Cruisers: An Illustrated Design History* in 1984, and *Submarine Design and Development* in 1984. Norman Polmar's *The American Submarine* (Annapolis, MD, Nautical and Aviation Publishing Company, 1983) is also very useful. Polmar's book, *The Death of the Thresher* (New York: Chilton Books, 1964) still remains one of the best accounts of the loss of that ship. D. Douglas Dalgleish and Larry Schweikart in *Trident* (Carbondale, Illinois: Southern Illinois University Press, 1954) has a great deal of information on the Trident submarine and missile systems gleaned from unclassified sources and interviews. Some conclusions must be viewed with caution.

Three periodicals are of interest to the student of naval affairs. *Jane's Fighting Ships*, edited by John Moore and published by Jane's Publishing, New York, NY, is very useful, but some of its data must be used with care. The U.S. Naval Institute of Annapolis, MD, publishes its *Proceedings* monthly. Occasionally, praise and criticism of the naval nuclear propulsion program and Admiral Rickover are found in its pages. Readers with more technical interest will look to the *Naval Engineers Journal*, published in Washington, DC, by the American Society of Naval Engineers.

Two biographical works must be considered. In *On Watch, A Memoir* (New York: Quadrangle/Times Books, 1976), Elmo R. Zumwalt, Jr., former chief of naval operations, devotes several pages to an attack on Admiral Rickover. Flawed by a few errors, the book nonetheless is important evidence of the strong feeling that in some quarters existed against Admiral Rickover. Norman Polmar and Thomas B. Allen, *Rickover, Controversy and Genius, A Biography* (New York: Simon and Schuster, 1982), is disappointing and far below the standard that Polmar set in his other books. Patrick Tyler, *Running Critical: The Silent War, Rickover and General Dynamics* (New York: Harper & Row, 1986), has much of interest in the origins of the 688-class attack submarine and contract disputes with General Dynamics.

Controversy still lingers over the years during which Robert S. McNamara was secretary of defense. A good biography is sorely needed. His management techniques have received considerable attention. A small but very perceptive study of the decision on the *John F. Kennedy* (CVA 67) is to be found in James M. Roherty, *Decisions of Robert S. McNamara, A Study of the Role of the Secretary of Defense* (Coral Gables, Florida: University of Miami, 1970). Roherty supplements his essay with a chronology. Alain C. Enthoven, *How Much Is Enough?* (New York: Harper & Row, 1971), explains his application of systems analysis. Ralph Sanders, *The Politics of Defense Analysis* (New York: Dunellen, 1973), is a very useful effort to place systems analysis in context. David Halberstam's *The Reckoning* (New York: Avon Books, 1986) contains a fascinating account of the management philosophy typified by McNamara as applied to the American automobile industry.

The multilateral force remains an intriguing concept; to some individuals, more vigorous American leadership might have changed the world immensely for the better; to others it was a quixotic venture. On background, Henry A. Kissinger, *The Troubled Partnership: A Re-Appraisal of the Atlantic Alliance* (New York: McGraw-Hill, 1965), remains basic. Two more recent books by officials in the Kennedy administration catch some of the complications of the approach and how it became a casualty of the Nassau conference between President Kennedy and Prime Minister Macmillan in December 1962. These are: George W. Ball, *The Past Has Another Pattern* (New York: W. W. Norton, 1982), and Walt W. Rostow, *The Diffusion of Power, An Essay on Recent History* (New York: Macmillan, 1972).

George T. Mazuzan and J. Samuel Walker, *Controlling the Atom, The Beginning of Nuclear Regulation, 1946-1962* (Berkeley, CA: University of California Press, 1984), is an excellent account of the beginnings and early years of the civilian nuclear power industry. For a brief history of Shippingport, see a pamphlet by Francis Duncan and Jack M. Holl, "Shippingport, The Nation's First Atomic Power Station," put out by the History Division, Department of Energy in 1983. The pamphlet also has a bibliography.

The naval nuclear propulsion program began as a joint effort of the navy and the

Atomic Energy Commission. Both organizations changed over the years. *The Navy Department: Evolution and Fragmentation* (Washington: Washington Navy Yard, Naval Historical Foundation, 1979), by Vice Admiral Edwin B. Hooper is a brief account of the various reorganizations of the Navy Department. Admiral Hooper's survey of the post–World War II Navy Department is perceptive and thought-provoking. Under the leadership of Dr. Jack M. Holl, chief historian, Department of Energy, the History Division has written a number of pamphlets on federal energy agencies. Those of particular interest are: *A History of the Atomic Energy Commission*, Aug. 1982, DOE/ES-0003, and *A History of the Energy Research and Development Administration*, March 1982, DOE/ES-0001, both by Alice L. Buck; and *The United States Department of Energy: A History*, Nov. 1982, DOE/ES-0004, by Dr. Jack M. Holl.

Physical Evidence

No number of documents—no matter how highly classified—can begin to convey the complexities and accomplishments of Naval Reactors or the naval nuclear propulsion program. For several years Admiral Rickover assigned me an office close to his own. The proximity gave the opportunity for several conferences, conversations, and opportunities to observe the philosophy under which he and Naval Reactors lived. Visiting the Bettis Atomic Power Laboratory and the Knolls Atomic Power Laboratory, the Shippingport Atomic Power Station, the shipyards of the Electric Boat Division of the General Dynamics Corporation at Groton, Connecticut, the Newport News Shipbuilding and Dry Dock Company at Newport News, Virginia, and the Puget Sound Naval Shipyard at Bremerton, Washington, helped make these principles come alive. But the men and the ships themselves were the real measure of achievement. Nothing can match seeing superbly trained officers and men taking their ship out on her first sea trials.

Index

agenda, 62–63; reviews Portsmouth radiographs, 66; replaces silver-brazed joints, 67; place in Portsmouth organization, 70; meets Rickover for *Thresher* inquiry, 85

Hitch, Charles J., 131–32, 145–46

Holifield, Chet: on *Thresher* loss, 95; holds JCAE meeting on *Enterprise*, 126–27; praises *Enterprise*, 130; urges nuclear surface fleet, 148, 150; supports Rivers, 153; favors mandatory legislation, 162; favors Title VIII, 167; seeks larger civilian power program, 208; calls for seed-blanket study, 208–9; considers president's civilian power report, 211; favors California project, 214; hears California project canceled, 219

Hollingsworth, Robert E., 217

Holloway, James L., III, 164

Hosmer, Craig, 126, 167

Hubbard, Miles H., 106

Hubbard report, 106–7

Humphrey, William S., 235

Hushing, William C., 81

Ignatius, Paul H.: supports high-speed submarine, 36, 39; supports electric-drive submarine, 40; becomes secretary of the navy, 157; inquires about *South Carolina* and *Virginia* contracts, 159–60; negotiates on frigates, 162

Independence, CVA 62, 103, 128

Ingalls Shipbuilding Corp., 5, 60, 237

Intermediate power-breeder reactor, 195

Interview system, 92, 245–47

Iselin, Donald G., 202–3

Jackson, Henry M., 138, 140, 167, 233

James, Ralph K.: investigates HY-80 problems, 56; congratulates Rickover on *Thresher* trials, 63–64; faces piping problem, 65–66; at *Thresher* inquiry, 86; testimony on *Thresher* loss, 91; tries to cut nuclear propulsion costs, 104; plans for *Truxtun*, 119; forwards study of four-reactor plant, 130

James Madison, SSBN 627, 44

John F. Kennedy, CVA 67, 129, 142. *See also* CVA 67

Johnson, Lyndon B.: announces NR-1, 42;

associated with Connally, 116; receives appeal on *Kennedy* propulsion, 140; announces two-reactor plant, 143–44; hears McDonald on surface ships, 151; signs mandatory legislation, 153; Rivers challenges on mandatory language, 160–61, 162; opposes *South Carolina* and *Virginia*, 162; continues mixed-manning demonstration, 185–86; includes California project in budget, 216; holds hearing on Sputnik, 282–83

Johnson, U. Alexis, 269

Joint Committee on Atomic Energy (JCAE): holds hearings on *Thresher* loss, 89, 91–92, 95, 97; meets on *Enterprise*, 126–27; holds hearings on NATO, 173–74; holds hearing on Soviet threat, 38; publishes *Enterprise* hearing, 130; holds hearings on *Kennedy* issue, 136–40; Rickover discusses Russian visit, 177

Jones, Thomas D., II, 191

KAPL. *See* Knolls Atomic Power Laboratory

Katz, Saul, 81–82

Keach, Donald, 93

Kemeny, John, 273–74, 278

Kemeny Commission. *See* Three Mile Island

Kennedy, John F.: backs Polaris, 44, 116; campaigns for strong defense, 111, 112; signs *Truxtun* authorization, 119; reviews fleet, 128, 129; announces Cuban crisis, 128; supports McNamara on CVA 67, 139; cautions on multilateral force, 180–85; meets with Rickover, 182–84; proposes mixed-manning demonstration, 185; asks AEC to assess civilian power program, 208; receives civilian power report, 210; reappoints Rickover, 233–34

Kern, Donald, 90

Khrushchev, Nikita S., 175

Kintner, Edwin E., 6, 42

Kirby, Robert E., 191

Knoll, Denys W., 52, 55

Knolls Atomic Power Laboratory: General Electric operates, 5; studies organic reactor, 21; works on natural-circulation reactor, 24, 25; works on high-

Polaris missile submarines, 19, 43–44, 53, 56, 116

Portsmouth Naval Shipyard: in nuclear propulsion program, 5; builds *Thresher*, 54–58; has welding and piping problems, 57–58, 60–61, 66–67; organization, 69–71; overhauls *Thresher*, 69–71; tests *Thresher* silver-brazed joints, 74; prepares *Thresher* for overhaul trials, 74–77; role in *Thresher* loss, 88–89; faces allegation of radiation laxity, 269–71

Power-reactor demonstration program, 206

Pressurized-water reactor technology, 3–4, 15–16, 50–51, 196, 290

Price, Melvin, 118, 126, 143, 167

Prototypes: ownership, 4; use in training, 5, 247–48, 249. *See also* A1W; D1G; Mark I (S1W); S1C; S5G; S8G; Appendix four

Purcell, William C., 209

Pye, David B., 235

Quality control, 71–73, 91–93, 256

Quincy Yard: lays keel of *Long Beach*, 2, 102; in nuclear program, 5; lays keel of *Bainbridge*, 102; considered for speeding up *Long Beach*, 104–5; inspected for high costs, 105–6; Hubbard group investigates, 106–7; considered for *Truxtun*, 119

Raab, Harry F., Jr., 209, 226–27, 235, 240

Raborn, William F., 43–44

Radiation control, 257, 266–73

Radkowsky, Alvin, 6, 42, 198, 212, 214, 217

Ramage, Lawson P., 95, 97

Ramey, James T., 127, 131, 141, 214

Ranger, CVA 61, 125

Reactor, light-water breeder (LWBR): achieves full power, 190–91; origins, 207–13; in president's civilian power report, 210–11; Atomic Industrial Forum considers, 211; Bettis reports possibility, 211–12; Seaborg considers costs, 212–13; General Advisory Committee opposes, 213; Shippingport considered for, 213; California expresses interest, 214–17; Rickover cancels California project, 218–19; Rick-

over considers development options, 220; California project fuel-element trouble, 217; Bettis and Knolls work on fuel development, 219–23; Rickover gives personal attention, 222–23; environmental impact considered, 224–26; Pennsylvania approves operation, 226; achieves criticality and operation, 226–27; shut down, 227

Reactor design and development, philosophy of, 19–23, 24–25, 26, 274, Appendix One

Reactors, boiling-water approach, 21

Reactors, gas-cooled approach, 21, 289

Reactors, liquid-metal approach, 289–90

Reactors, natural-circulation: advantages, 23–24; Bettis develops, 24; Knolls helps develop, 24; assigned to Knolls, 25; construction of prototype, 25–27

Reactors, organic approach, 289–90

Reactors, small, light, cheap, 20, 108, 114, 125, 289–90

Reactors, sodium-cooled, 21, 196, 289–90

Reactor Safeguards Committee. *See* Advisory Committee on Reactor Safeguards

Reactor safety, design, development, and operation: responsiblity for, 4; design criteria, 20–21; Rickover considers for Shippingport, 198. *See also* Appendix One

Reagan, Ronald, 292

Redpath, John L., III, 120

Renegotiation board, 237

Rengel, Joseph C., 202

Rice, Paul D. 235, 273

Ricketts, Claude V., 131

Rickover, Hyman G.: at Shippingport criticality, 2–3; directs nuclear propulsion program, 3, 5–8; makes technology practical, 4; relations with field representatives, 5, 241–43; background, 8–13, 192, 195–96, 279–80, 290–91; establishes program principles, 13; fights for promotion, 13–14, 257; relations with Congress, 14, 16, 168–69, 287; on *Skipjack* trials, 18; begins S5W work, 18; design and development philosophy, 19–23, 24, 25–26, 111, 192, Appendix One; on fallacy of

The Naval Institute Press is the book-publishing arm of the U.S. Naval Institute, a private, nonprofit professional society for members of the sea services and civilians who share an interest in naval and maritime affairs. Established in 1873 at the U.S. Naval Academy in Annapolis, Maryland, where its offices remain today, the Naval Institute has more than 100,000 members worldwide.

Members of the Naval Institute receive the influential monthly naval magazine *Proceedings* and substantial discounts on fine nautical prints, ship and aircraft photos, and subscriptions to the Institute's recently inaugurated quarterly, *Naval History*. They also have access to the transcripts of the Institute's Oral History Program and may attend any of the Institute-sponsored seminars regularly offered around the country.

The book-publishing program, begun in 1898 with basic guides to naval practices, has broadened its scope in recent years to include books of more general interest. Now the Naval Institute Press publishes more than forty new titles each year, ranging from how-to books on boating and navigation to battle histories, biographies, ship guides, and novels. Institute members receive discounts on the Press's more than 300 books.

For a free catalog describing books currently available and for further information about U.S. Naval Institute membership, please write to:

Membership Department
U.S. Naval Institute
Annapolis, Maryland 21402

or call, toll-free, 800-233-USNI.